'When we chose a fearless leader for COSATU we wanted someone rooted in the grassroots movements. What really gives me fulfilment was seeing Jay growing wings and ensuring this great power did not go to his head. He remains a true son of the soil, a son of Africa and my much-loved son.'
EMMA MASHININI, 'Mother' of the trade union movement; founding General Secretary of the Commercial, Catering and Allied Workers Union of South Africa (CCAWUSA) and founding Land Claims Commissioner of the Commission on Restitution of Land Rights, South Africa

'Jay Naidoo was an inspiration to thousands of us, as activists, during one of the harshest periods of apartheid violence. This book will inspire thousands of people in Africa and globally to embrace the idea that principled progressive activism is a path that we can all follow if we want to bequeath to our children a world of justice, democracy and equality.'
KUMI NAIDOO, Executive Director of Green Peace International and founding Executive Director and Honorary President of CIVICUS: World Alliance for Citizen Participation

'As a major participant in the transformation from apartheid to democracy, Jay Naidoo writes with incredible clarity of the role of worker institutions and civil society in the ongoing struggle for social change. With fierce conviction, he speaks of the requirement of a global solidarity movement against hunger, poverty and social exclusion. We all need to respond to this urgent call to action.'
WILLIAM LUCY, International Secretary-Treasurer of the American Federation of State, County and Municipal Employees (AFSCME) and President of the Coalition of Black Trade Unionists

Fighting for Justice

Fighting for Justice

A Lifetime of Political and Social Activism

Jay Naidoo

Picador Africa

First published in 2010 by Picador Africa,
an imprint of Pan Macmillan South Africa
Private Bag X19, Northlands
Johannesburg, 2116

www.panmacmillan.co.za
www.picadorafrica.co.za

ISBN 978-1-77010-177-7

© Jay Naidoo 2010

While every effort has been made to ensure the accuracy of the details, facts, names and places mentioned, as an autobiography this book is based largely on memory. The publisher and author welcome feedback, comments and/or corrections that could further enrich the book. For further discussion with the author visit the blog site www.thejustcause.org.

thejustcause.org
BRIDGING VOICES

Editing by Andrea Nattrass and Sally Hines
Proofreading by Lisa Compton
Design and typesetting by Manoj Sookai
Indexing by Christopher Merrett
Cover design by K4
Front cover photograph courtesy of the *Sunday Independent*
Back cover photograph by Robert Etcheverry

Printed by Ultra Litho

Contents

For

*Bakkium, my mother, whose simplicity and humility
continue to inspire me;
Angamma, my great-grandmother, whose courage
changed my line of ancestry forever;
and Lucie, my lover, confidante and wife.*

Acknowledgements

As the isiZulu saying '*umuntu ngumuntu ngabantu*' reminds us, we are who we are through others. I am grateful to the long list of illustrious people who have shaped my life: from my great-grandmother to my mother and my siblings; from the iconic Madiba, to hostel dwellers in the various towns and cities that I worked in; from labour leaders such as Chris Dlamini and Elijah Barayi to the thousands of shop stewards, activists and community leaders whose stories are interwoven with my journey. I have had the singular honour of learning from their patience, humility and dedication to service.

This book was an ambitious attempt to reconcile a fascinating period in my life. I realise now the impossible nature of such a task, and owe a debt of gratitude to those who encouraged me to put pen to paper and who helped me chart a coherent course across a tumultuous era in South Africa's history.

In particular, I wish to thank Luli Callinicos, who worked tirelessly with me to create a workable manuscript. Similarly, to my publisher and editor, Andrea Nattrass, and her team at Pan Macmillan. A special word of thanks is extended to my wife, Lucie Pagé, who was always there to offer invaluable advice or a shoulder to rest on and remove my many doubts as to whether my life story deserved recounting.

There are countless others whom I wish to acknowledge (in alphabetical order): Omar Badsha, Nkosinathi Biko, Graeme Bloch, Céline-Marie Bouchard, Rachaad Cassim, Ashraf Coovadia, Susan de Villiers, Alec Erwin, Robert Etcheverry, Bernie Fanaroff, Howie Gabriels, Dhiren Ganasen, Stephen Gelb, Raj Govender, Isobel Gregory, Peter Harris, David Harrison, Sally Hines, Rob Lambert, Lesley Lawson, Andrea Leenan, William ('Bill') Lucy, Emma Mashinini, William Matlala, Moses Mayekiso, Asha Moodley, Sam Moodley, Omar Motani, James Motlatsi, A.C. Naicker, Dimes Naidoo, Inba Naidoo, Jayendra Naidoo, Kumi Naidoo, Logie Naidoo, Ravi Naidoo, Petros Ngcobo,

Joan Nowak, Chooks Padayachee, Geoff Schreiner, Hassim Seedat, Jabulani Sikhakhane, René Smith, Admassu Tadesse, Brian Tilley, UWC-Robben Island Museum Mayibuye Archives, Mark van Ameringen, Wouter van der Schaaf, Zwelinzima Vavi, Sahm Venter, Eddie Webster, Paul Weinberg, Kate Wild and those who gave willingly to this project over the past decade, from photos to interviews and words of support.

In telling my story I hope that in some small way I have done justice to the many people who – often at great risk to themselves and their families – laid the foundation of the democracy we now enjoy.

Prologue

All human beings are born free and equal in dignity and rights. They are endowed with reason and conscience and should act towards one another in a spirit of brotherhood.

— Universal Declaration of Human Rights

In 1975, I lay on a bed in Wentworth Hospital, Durban, suffering from a complicated auto-immune disease called sarcoidosis, which medical science knew little about. It was on the back of a year-long treatment that I had undergone for lymphatic tuberculosis. As the anaesthetic wore off after the biopsy to diagnose my debilitating illness, I looked up, drowsy and disoriented, the fan above my bed whirling sluggishly, and saw the furrows of anxiety in the faces of my mother and eldest sister.

They had come with an older woman, impeccably dressed in a sari and holding a rosary of meditation beads. Mrs Patel, a healer and sage, had come to do a prayer. She held my hand and as she clicked the rosary beads she slipped into a deep meditation chanting a mantra I did not understand. After a few minutes she stopped, turned to my mother and sister and said, 'He will be fine. He is touched by the spirit of service and has much to do in his life.' She gathered her things and left.

It would be many more years of struggle, surprises and promises of change before I fully understood what she meant.

* * *

I was fortunate to be born into an exhilarating period of our history. The chemistry of circumstances often provides wonderful opportunities. Mine was to play a role in our struggle for freedom, to interact with some of the greatest leaders of our time and to appreciate the magnificence of the collective experience, with few regrets. I sought the solidarity of our comradeship even in the many moments of great pain and suffering and sacrifice.

I was irresistibly drawn into the courageous struggles of our people across the political and class spectrum. I listened intently to their views and their wisdom stoked by the daily hardships at the coalface of apartheid. It was from the poorest of the poor, living in brutal conditions in single-sex hostels, torn from their families, from the township residents eking out a living in the poverty of our slums and from workers in the factories, mines and farms of our country that I learnt the most important lessons that shaped my life.

I learnt from this reservoir of humility, honesty, patience, tolerance and compassion as we sat down and shared a simple meal. It was here that I witnessed human dignity and a group solidarity and identity that would unite our people.

It was this tsunami of civic, youth, women, labour and religious organisations that became the unstoppable force that brought apartheid to its knees and compelled it into a negotiated political settlement. Our struggle was to give voice to the needs of our people and not for title or position for individuals or organisations.

History can influence events but human choices determine our current realities. We experienced a burst of optimism when South Africa joined the community of nations as a full member, proud of the democratic traditions and progressive Constitution that our new-found rainbow democracy brought in 1994. Our world was charged with hope for a better future, our sense of belonging achieved.

My foray into business, following my departure from government in 1999, ushered in a new phase in my life, one where I felt constantly challenged on a number of fronts. It remains a critical learning curve for me. Finding ways to get business, government and civil society to work together for our common goal of creating a better life for all is an opportunity to rethink the existing and outmoded paradigms of social change and development.

I believe it is possible to combine business acumen with a commitment to ending poverty and inequality. It *is* possible to build businesses that imbue the dynamism and innovation of the market but also serve the poor.

Writing this book has provided an opportunity to reflect on my journey and has enabled me to fine-tune my vision and the direction I have chosen. It has forced me to face some of the painful experiences, the betrayals and broken promises, but mostly it has allowed me to recount some of the many lessons that hold promise of a 'new' South Africa. My story is one of comradeship and is testimony to the many ordinary heroes and heroines of our struggle for freedom in South Africa, many of whom will not be written into our history books.

I have realised that the future of our destiny globally lies in our hands as citizens. The South African freedom struggle was one of the world's finest examples of global social solidarity. As we continue to fight for social justice in a world where insatiable greed continues to trample on human rights and our environment, let us not forget the lessons of our past.

The right to a 'better life for all' is a fundamental human right. That was the meaning in life that I found.

This is the story of my journey.

PART ONE

Meeting Mandela

We are not calling for his release on humanitarian grounds. We are doing so on political grounds. We are saying that he is our leader. This is the acknowledged leader of the group that most blacks support, but more than that we are saying he is symbolic because we want all leaders, all political prisoners, released not on humanitarian grounds but on the grounds that this is going to be part of how we build up a climate conducive to negotiation.

— Archbishop Desmond Tutu

Negotiated solutions can be found even to conflicts that have come to seem intractable and such solutions emerge when those who have been divided reach out to find the common ground.

— Nelson Mandela

1

I remember vividly that crisp morning on 11 February 1990. The mist shrouded the valley and mountains, hiding the enormity of the day. We were travelling to meet Nelson Mandela. Today our leader was leaving prison after 27 years and the whole world was holding its breath. I was with Valli Moosa from the United Democratic Front (UDF). I was the General Secretary of the Congress of South African Trade Unions (COSATU). Our anxiety about meeting the great man was palpable. We had fought hard and long to free the man who represented to me the epitome of our principled struggle against apartheid.

We turned into the entrance of the prison. The guards were cold and impassive. We were the enemy. 'We are here for an appointment with Mr Mandela,' we said as we parked alongside the heavily fortified guardhouse. They spoke in heavy Afrikaans on the intercom before turning to us: 'Wait here. Someone is coming to fetch you.' We were intruders in their fort.

We stared down the long road to the prison in the distance. Neatly trimmed hedges with symmetrical lines of flowers lined the driveway. Teams of prisoners shuffled up and down, pruning the hedges and sweeping the place until it was spotless.

We were taken by a security vehicle to where Mandela had been held for the past fourteen months. The isolated house was surrounded by a high fence with guards in sentinel towers. Victor Verster was a 'model prison-farm' near Paarl, a quiet town nestling in a valley in the heartland of the Cape's beautiful wine district.

After 27 years, Madiba[1] would continue his long walk to freedom alone. The apartheid government had removed him from all his closest companions – probably because they hoped to influence him – the age-old tactic of 'divide and rule'.

Yet the separation also freed Madiba to explore a strategy that he knew many of his comrades would find difficult. He wanted to push for a meeting with the 'arch-enemy', President P.W. Botha. He knew it was a high-risk venture, but he felt that, should he fall into a trap, the disaster would be his own and not that of the liberation movement.

Some in the Mass Democratic Movement (MDM) – the internal alliance of labour and community organisations formed to resist apartheid – were very concerned that this represented a dangerous engagement. But the unions, steeped in the tradition of negotiating with the apparent enemy, understood the broad strategy. While there were legitimate concerns about the bona fides of the enemy, it would be a gross exaggeration to label this as 'Mandela having sold out'.

Over the years I had come to realise that there are times when a leader has to step ahead of the collective. These occasions require careful judgement and often risk the leader's credibility and safety. I was inspired by Madiba's qualities as a leader and by his supremely logical yet courageous decision.

A tall, remarkably fit and energetic man, regal in stature, emerged from one of the rooms, his arms outstretched in a warm welcome. In a booming voice he said: 'Hello my comrades, welcome. Welcome to my home!'

What do you say? I was expecting a well-built boxer, as Mandela had appeared in one of the few photographs of him I had seen. Instead, here was an elegant man, slim in build and towering in height.

'Let me show you my home,' he said as he escorted us from room to room.

This cottage had once housed the head of the prison – a loyal servant to apartheid. Now the larger-than-life icon of our struggle filled it with his positive energy.

It was an overwhelming experience. His energy, warmth and humility were overpowering. The house, by contrast, was featureless and conservative – this was a prison after all. In the bedroom, lounge and even in the thatched hut next to the pool, Mandela in a hushed voice said: 'This is where they have placed microphones.'

'Now sit down and let me get you some tea,' he added. The security officer cum butler leapt to his command. He too was a prisoner of apartheid.

So, here we were: Valli was an activist whom I had worked with in our student days. This was the first time I was meeting Mandela. When COSATU had met with him in December the previous year, I had been travelling overseas. I had, however, corresponded with Mandela, had sent him information on the violence pertaining to our conflict with Inkatha, and he had replied – on green paper in the most beautiful handwriting, I remember – saying how much he appreciated and admired the courage and strength of organised workers under COSATU.

We received a message that Winnie Mandela was arriving at the airport. I went with a driver to fetch her. It was late morning and the expected time of Mandela's release was fast approaching.

Winnie was and is an exceptional and volatile person at the best of times. She radiates enormous charm and has a presence that dominates the landscape when one is with her. At that stage she was not only the wife of Nelson Mandela, but a political figure in her own right.

By the time we returned, a steady stream of visitors began arriving, and hundreds of journalists representing the world's media gathered outside the prison gates. Apartheid was now completely discredited internationally. Change was inevitable. The question, however, was at what cost? How much more blood would have to be spilled? Mandela's speech would need to reach out to whites, but it importantly also needed to connect to the mass campaigns of the 1950s, the Freedom Charter and the contemporary context. The present was built on the rich tradition of the past, but the speech also had to offer a view of what the future could hold.

Valli and I, along with other Mass Democratic Movement leaders, including Trevor Manuel, Dullah Omar and Cyril Ramaphosa (who by now had arrived from Johannesburg), were going over the speech that had been prepared with input from the African National Congress (ANC), the MDM and Mandela himself.

The whole world was waiting to hear what he would say.

Mandela's main concern was that his guests should be comfortable. It was like meeting your grandfather at a family gathering, rather than *the* Mandela. I was astounded and moved by the ability of this great man to transcend his iconic status and demonstrate humility in the most unpretentious way.

A renewed but heated debate transpired about where Mandela should speak first. Winnie was adamant that he should speak in Johannesburg – that was where the main struggles had been fought, where he was originally convicted, and the place that best represented the people's struggle. The debate continued literally for hours as people poured their hearts out and some tried to claim the mantle of Mandela.

Mandela listened carefully to all, before concluding that Cape Town had been his home for 27 years; this is where he had lived, and this is where he should give his first speech to the nation.

And that closed the debate. One single, softly spoken sentence ended a long discussion. His final word, after astutely listening to the opinions of all, was to become a distinguishing feature of Nelson Mandela's leadership style. He had made a decision based on their input; and people did not counteract that because he had listened to them. That was to be an enduring memory of Madiba in the years that followed – listening carefully, never raising his voice, simply stating the obvious.

*   *   *

Mandela finally emerged from Victor Verster, immaculately dressed. He was a calm, stately and noble presence, with a confident stride. The debate on where to proceed to had delayed us, and it was close to 4.00 p.m. when we all finally got into a motorcade and drove towards the exit.

Halfway along the driveway, Madiba got out of the car as arranged and walked hand-in-hand with Winnie to the entrance and out of the prison gates – into freedom. Mandela's and Winnie's fists were raised. Hundreds of the world's camera and news people were clicking away, making a noise 'like some great herd of metallic beasts' (as Mandela himself later wrote).[2] Reporters were shouting questions, supporters were singing and cheering and the television crews zoomed in.

Out of sight, you could hear the roar of more crowds, curious, joyful and impatient. We were extremely nervous about his safety as the state had abandoned the responsibility for Mandela's security and we had to act as his only bodyguards. Madiba and Winnie had been seated in a modest sedan, the best car we could organise, which belonged to someone Trevor Manuel knew and was driven by a Cape Town activist called Sonto. Cyril, Valli and I were piled into Trevor's beaten-up Toyota.

As we drove out, we were astounded at the sight of the people congregating on the highways, waving and cheering. It was a cross-section of people – African, white, coloured, Indian – jostling to get a glimpse of this mythical figure.

We arrived in Cape Town's city centre, the streets choked. Driving down towards the Grand Parade, where thousands had gathered, we realised that there was no way we could get through. We were surrounded, being physically crushed by a wave of excited humanity.

We retreated, organised that Sonto and some other comrades take Madiba back to the civic centre close by, and we set out to find the best route to the balcony at the city hall, from where Madiba would address the nation and the world. When we got back to the civic centre we found that Madiba had disappeared. The driver had panicked and, guided by a traffic officer, had sped out of the city centre. We were aghast. We had brought the apartheid government to its knees so many times and here we were bungling the biggest moment in our history.

At some point one of the traffic officers handed his walkie-talkie to Trevor, saying that there was someone high up in the security establishment who wanted to speak to him. The person on the other side said: 'Trevor, you must go and fetch Nelson Mandela and bring him here. The city is going to burn if you don't. This is the address where he is.' With the location in hand, we sped off to fetch Madiba and Winnie.

We raced out to Rondebosch and found Madiba and Winnie seated in the car talking to a white couple, Vanessa Watson and Desmond Woolf, and a crowd of people who had gathered. 'Well comrades, where have you been?' he remarked smilingly to us.

According to Vanessa Watson: 'Mandela and his convoy of cars had parked in the narrow road outside of my house, seemingly to escape the traffic. We were glued to the television, when a visiting friend told us that Mandela was sitting outside our house. We went into the street with our one-year-old twins and saw Mandela and Winnie in the first car. I raised a fist in salute and he beckoned us to the car. '"Can I hold your baby?" asked Mandela. I passed Simon through the open window and Mandela joyfully bounced him on his knee.'[3]

It was getting late now and we had to go. Mandela had walked out of the prison gates hours later than planned, and the tens of thousands assembled in the Grand Parade were growing restless. The mood was electric – excitement and anxiety were palpable.

Throughout this time, Mandela remained amazingly calm. How did he do it? With all this chaos around him, with the prospect of the nation's freedom finally at hand, with so much lost time to catch up, and all our hopes on his shoulders, he remained remarkably collected.

I wondered how I would have coped in a similar situation and, mostly, what was going through his mind; what was he thinking and feeling?

It was only later that I began to understand more clearly the iron will that he mastered during his years of incarceration – never to reveal one's feelings or vulnerabilities in any political environment. It was a characteristic I was to see often in my interactions with him. The rare moments when Mandela lets his emotions show are in the company of children and the comrades with whom he has shared his life.

Finally the traffic department agreed to clear the roads and our journey resumed.

* * *

As we neared the city hall the level of excitement rose. By the time we reached the now-famous balcony, using a back entrance, the skies were dark and the heaving crowds of men, women and children were restless. Mandela had to speak now.

We sat in the inner room during the speech to plan the next steps. This was bigger than anything we had anticipated. People were pressed against the city hall portals – desperate to get a glimpse of Mandela and hear him over the poor sound system we had installed. The joy and heady beat of the liberation chants were creating a powerful atmosphere. The audience swayed and sang, full throated, as one.

As Mandela appeared at the balcony there was wild cheering as the masses of people erupted in a dance of joy. Humanity, squashed in a familiar togetherness, awaiting the words of the most famous prisoner of modern times.

As he began to speak a hushed silence fell over the square. His first public words rang out quietly:

I stand here before you not as a prophet but as a humble servant of you, the people. Your tireless and heroic sacrifices have made it possible for me to be here today. I therefore place the remaining years of my life in your hands...

This theme has been repeated many more times in the years I have known him. Mandela represented the 'collective will', always striving to reach consensus even with those he fundamentally disagreed with. As with any human being, there would be the exceptions. But he always strove to keep his ego in check – a human frailty that many others struggle to contain.

Mandela's legacy shone through his vision of a South Africa freed from the shackles of human bondage, of a nation with its human dignity restored and a passionate commitment to human rights and social justice in the world.

In his speech, Mandela connected the past to the present and spoke about the honest and humble traditions of Oliver Tambo, who had led the ANC throughout the lonely years of exile. He saluted national organisations as well as the international community for their efforts against apartheid and expressed 'deep appreciation for the strength given to me during my long and lonely years in prison by my beloved wife and family. I am convinced that your pain and suffering was far greater than my own.'[4]

Mandela also used the occasion to affirm his loyalty to the ANC and to clarify the basis of his talks with the regime, which he argued aimed to normalise the political situation in the country. To counter any rumours that he was undermining the ANC through discussions with the F.W. de Klerk government, Mandela elucidated further:

> *We have not as yet begun discussing the basic demands of the struggle. I wish to stress that I myself have at no time entered into negotiations about the future of our country except to insist on a meeting between the ANC and the government ...*
>
> *There are further steps as outlined in the Harare Declaration[5] that have to be met before negotiations on the basic demands of our people can begin.*

He concluded his speech with the famous and unforgettable quote that had resonated around the world during his trial in 1964, when he was facing the real possibility of the death penalty:

> *I have fought against white domination and I have fought against black domination. I have cherished the ideal of a democratic and free society in which all persons live together in harmony and with equal opportunities. It is an ideal which I hope to live for and to achieve. But if needs be, it is an ideal for which I am prepared to die.*

As the thunderous cheering slowed, the patient crowds departed, taking their euphoria back to the trains, buses, taxis and to their homes. Madiba was cheerful, but clearly exhausted. He and Winnie departed for the leafy suburb of Bishopscourt at the foot of Table Mountain, to spend the night at Archbishop Desmond Tutu's official residence.

As they left I wondered what it meant to share a bed with another person after such a gulf of separation. It would take an extraordinary man to walk out of prison, face a country and world full of expectation, deal with the surging personal and emotional currents and then hold in his arms – uninhibited – his wife, who had fought for her husband's freedom for many years.

As one of the most important days in our historical calendar came to a close nothing could stop the rising tide of hope and expectation. De Klerk as the last President of apartheid South Africa had made a courageous move, far beyond what we expected. There was no turning back. With Mandela walking out of prison a free man we had reached a point of irreversible change.

I was optimistic and excited by the prospect that transformation was imminent. Little did I realise the extent to which we would continue to walk a difficult path before we could taste the fruits of our struggle.

PART TWO

Shaping Identity

The past was never beautiful
But through its knotted strings my ancestors
Speak to me with apocryphal gestures
And languages you will never understand
And dances that would strain your gait

— Ari Sitas

A driving thrust of Black Consciousness was to forge pride and unity amongst all
the oppressed, to foil the strategy of divide-and-rule, to engender pride amongst
the mass of our people and confidence in the ability to throw off their oppression.

— Nelson Mandela

2

In my youth, I was not really interested in exploring the faraway origins of my family – I was too involved in claiming, through struggle, my identity as a black South African. The apartheid government, in its insane desire to separate people on the basis of race, relocated millions of people into a patchwork quilt of ethnic districts that emphasised division and sought to use culture as a divide-and-rule tactic. As political activists we resisted this and insisted that we had little in common with our Indian ancestry and that we were part of the black oppressed in South Africa.

It was only later, after our democratic transformation in 1994, that I felt comfortable to trace my Indian heritage and began to realise that I owe my existence to the immense courage – and perhaps desperate determination – of those pioneers who left their motherland for the distant shores of Africa. These disparate trailblazers laid the foundations of my destiny.

One of the most powerful inspirations for my family and I was the discovery of the historic voyage of my great-grandmother on my mother's side, Angamma.

Angamma was born in 1852 in the rural village of Gollapalli, in the district of Chendragiri, North Arcot, in South India. I have often speculated about the reasons for her abandoning this small community, and daring to take a giant leap into the unknown. Did she have an understanding of how far away and how utterly different her destination would be?

All I know of Angamma, daughter of Maraina Pillay, is that she left home, aged thirty, with her seven-year-old little girl, Munyamma, whose father was Ramakisten Pillay. My family has come to learn that Angamma, who had a scar over her right eye, may have left India to escape an abusive marriage or in-laws.[1]

In India, life in general was hard for everyone at this time. People lived in the most basic conditions, and there was a constant battle for survival. The entire area of Tirunelveli in North Arcot was annexed by the British Raj in 1801, and had become impoverished under the burden of taxes and the need to plant crops that were required for the English marketplace.

This was probably why British colonial entrepreneurs were recruiting people from the poorer villages, vulnerable to their seductive promises of a new, prosperous life elsewhere. Many were also attracted to guarantees that there were opportunities for market gardening, in which numerous people in the rural areas in India were highly skilled.

As scholar Raj Govender later explained to me: 'Recruiters told them that there were lots of other opportunities: "It's very prosperous in South Africa; you will never survive in this village." And once they agreed, they were contracted to work as low-paid indentured labourers on British-owned sugar estates around the world – Mauritius, the Caribbean or South Africa.'[2]

* * *

More than a 100 years later, in 1999, I visited Gollapalli, which seemed to have changed very little over the years. At the time, I was Minister of Posts, Telecommunications and Broadcasting in President Nelson Mandela's cabinet. India had been a staunch ally of the anti-apartheid struggle, and that solidarity was cemented in strong relations with the post-apartheid government.

It was late at night when we arrived at the village, one of the hundreds of thousands that make up the heart of India. I remember a solitary light shining in the dark. I had been driven there with official escorts, so our arrival caused a bit of a stir. Apart from the installation of a telephone line, nothing much seemed to have happened in the village since the 1880s.

The people who ventured out of their homes were suspicious, as no one visits that late, especially in such 'grand style'. I was apprehensive. Would anyone remember Angamma, my great-grandmother? Was this the right village?

Officials and villagers chattered excitedly in Tamil, my great-grandmother's vernacular. Though I looked like one of them I realised how much of a foreigner I was. As I left the officials to talk I walked around. Most homes were not more than thatched huts. The road was unpaved and the verges were overgrown, not unlike rural villages in Africa. People eked out a living and life remained unchanged from one generation to the next.

We discovered very little and agreed to return the next day.

The following morning, the villagers were much friendlier when we arrived, thanks to a few officials who had gone ahead to break the ice. And once people realised that I was there in search of my roots rather than to lay a claim on my ancestral land, we won not only their sympathy, but also a deep interest. Was it possible that someone from their village had travelled across the world and that her descendant had returned like a prodigal son who was now a government Minister? Not just any government, but that of Nelson Mandela. For even in this remote village, people had heard of Mandela, who was often compared to Mahatma Gandhi, the Father of Modern India.

Nothing like this seemed to have happened before. The people were effusive, chattering amongst themselves excitedly in Tamil.

I remember, in particular, an old lady with ears almost identical to those of my mother, long and substantial, bursting with curiosity. She looked 90 years old and remembered that her mother had talked about someone who had travelled to a faraway country in Africa.

I learnt that my ancestors had owned a small piece of land that would have reverted to communal ownership. I was led to a hut that was falling apart and the old lady pointed out where the person had lived. Apparently there was someone who knew more, but who had left the village decades earlier.

I visited the local temple, which was awe-inspiring. It jutted confidently into the air, marking its rendezvous with the universe. Its towering edifice was an architectural wonder with its beautifully carved statues. The smell of incense hung in the air. Beautiful lamps burned brightly. A courtyard filled with light housed each deity, adorned with fresh flowers. All I heard was the soft tread of bare feet, the gentle sounds of spiritual intonation. I felt a warm energy flow over my body as I did my *pooja*, a prayer to the seven gods and goddesses in the temple, which a priest told me represented seven planets. I spoke to him about my great-grandmother and he confirmed that this was the main temple of the area and she would have most definitely come there before her departure; seeking the protection of the gods was a part of daily life.

As I walked around this thousand-year-old wonder I could feel the presence of my great-grandmother. I was tracing the steps she would have walked over 100 years ago. Whatever her circumstances, this young, single, courageous mother took a gigantic step alone, without a man or patron to protect her. She had to believe that better prospects awaited her if she undertook this perilous adventure. And so she agreed to go.

Today, Madras, now known as Chennai, is a few hours by car. A century ago there were no cars, so Angamma would have gone by cart, if she could afford the fare. But just as likely, she and her child began their journey on foot – the first steps on her long walk to freedom.

It was for me an incredibly humbling experience. Nothing I have done in my life could compare with the courage that my great-grandmother summoned to take that dramatic step into the new and unknown world. The line of my ancestry was irrevocably altered.

*   *   *

When Angamma and Munyamma finally reached Madras, they were housed in a crowded compound until the ship was ready to depart – a stark transition from the village to the world of the indentured. In the compound they were stripped and medically examined to ensure that they had no defects. No birthmarks were recorded and they were deemed fit enough to withstand the hard labour of agricultural work. She was given a shipping number: 28330. This was her new identity.

After waiting for weeks while the *arkatis* recruited enough people to fill the boat to capacity, they finally boarded the ship, *Coldstream 1 (EA)*, in February 1882.

We can assume that the vast majority of passengers were seeing the sea for the first time and had never been on a boat. The six-week journey was traumatic. Lodging in crowded and strange spaces robbed people of their security and control over their immediate surroundings. The constant rolling of the ship beneath their feet would have been terrifying; all evidence of land had completely disappeared. Instead there was endless sea. The constant lurching of the ship brought widespread, unbearable seasickness.

The shortage of food and water added to their misery. Many felt that the endless ocean would swallow them up. History tells us that some passengers, realising the enormity of the step they had taken, fell into utter despair and jumped overboard.

Besides their dreams to comfort and reassure themselves, the passengers only had each other. Now their point of reference was a colonial shipping number. During the long and difficult voyage, passengers formed lifelong friendships and others short- or long-term liaisons. Some romances broke up as soon as they landed. For many, the urge to create a family to replace the ones they had left behind, perhaps forever, was irresistible.

For Angamma, a single mother, cut off from family and home, Narainasami Pillay (a man she met aboard the ship) became a valued and loved protector.[3] In return, perhaps Narainasami was willing to begin married life with a ready-made family – coincidentally, much the same as when I married.

Having declared themselves a married couple, Angamma and Narainasami were assigned to the sugar estate of Thomas Cross Redcliffe, under the management of a Mr Milner, for a five-year period and a choice then of another five-year period or return to India with free passage. History has taught us that indentured labourers were forced to work seven days a week from dawn to dusk. The sugar cane barons were insensitive to the needs of their indentured labourers. They economised costs, issued the most meagre rations and provided the barest accommodation in crowded barracks. Labourers were confined to the plantation and any infringement dealt with by arbitrary justice in the form of fines and whippings. In brief, indentured labour was akin to slavery and was used as the legal recourse by plantation owners now that slavery had been abolished by the British parliament in 1833.[4]

And here the curtain drops over the experiences of my great-grandparents. But we know that close to 150 000 indentured labourers were brought to South Africa over the next few decades, fragmenting their family and social ties in India. Many believed they had broken a religious tradition of *kalapani* (literally, the fear of crossing the ocean), which meant being cut off from the regenerating waters of the Ganges and entailed the end of the reincarnation cycle. This justified the decision of many to stay in South Africa permanently.

In the meantime, both the indentured labourers and the free Indians contributed to the increased prosperity of the Colony of Natal and dominated local commerce and market gardening. They posed a big threat to white traders who insisted that free movement and trade restrictions and taxes be imposed on the community.

Years later I would join the Sweet, Food and Allied Workers Union (SFAWU) and my first major assignment was organising workers in the sugar industry. It was an ironic twist that I was to engage with the very sector that had treated my ancestors as nothing more than hard-working serfs in a feudal colony. My fight in the union for a living wage was inextricable from the struggle for the rights of sugar industry workers to be treated with human dignity rather than as commodities.

It was during their time as labourers that Angamma gave birth to a son and two more girls. One of them was Ammani, my grandmother. When she grew up, Ammani married into a Chetty family of Telegu-speaking traders, originally from Andhra Pradesh. They had come out as passenger Indians, who paid their own way, via Mauritius. Ammani relocated to Newcastle, a small coal-mining town and a bustling centre of commerce that attracted people from the rest of the former northern Natal region.

The couple had two daughters. Tragically, one died at the age of twelve, possibly in the flu epidemic of 1918. My mother, Bakkium (or Thyla as her father called her), the younger daughter, was born in 1913.

My mother grew up in a home that was comparatively well off. She was precious to her parents and they sent her to school in Newcastle, giving her the benefit of an education, which was very unusual for girls in those times. Even more remarkable was her driver's licence – the first for a woman in the Indian community of Newcastle.

Thyla grew up to be a smart and independent young woman. She helped her father in the business, drove her parents around in a car and elected not to marry until she was 28 (equally unusual in the Indian community, where teenage marriages were common).

A marriage was then arranged with a widower whose wife had died giving birth, leaving him with a son (who was an elder brother figure to me). My father, Valanthan Naidoo, was born in 1898, of a trading family in Colenso, a small town about 120 kilometres from Newcastle. They were horse dealers, but one of their clever young sons – my father – had gone to high school and had risen to the highest position (as an Indian) in the civil service of the judiciary, an interpreter of the court. He would never be able to hold a higher position than that of a white person, something that must have rankled deeply.

Thyla and Valanthan were married in 1940. The union was fruitful – within twelve years they had six children. Then, in 1954, Thyla became pregnant again and I was born on 20 December – my parents' youngest child.

3

The image of my mother loomed large in my life. She raised seven children largely single-handedly. My father was present but played less of a role in our upbringing. He was of a generation that interacted with children through their mothers, and he was 57 when I was born. His most important contributions were towards our dedication to study, an appreciation of the need to master the English language and a passion for reading.

My mother, by contrast, made us feel that there was a special place in her heart for each of us; and later, for our spouses, children, friends and family. Our house felt like a railway station because it was always full of people.

Mother would be the last to eat, especially when we brought friends home. Our pleasures were simple, yet we never felt deprived. Important visitors would be greeted with a chicken meal that Logie, my brother, and I (barely in school) had to catch and slaughter. No part of the chicken was wasted – the giblets, liver, feet, and even the head and the blood that were collected were delicacies for us. But our turn came after the visitors and family elders had chosen the tastiest morsels.

We lived frugally and used what was available in the garden, which was filled with avocado, guava, pawpaw and mango trees. Fruit was plentiful – the beautiful peach blossoms announced the coming of spring and decorated the pathways, banana trees were filled with bunches of succulent bananas and we collected wild figs in the bush. We planted beans of all sorts: the broad double beans that were a must for chicken curry; and the fresh green beans cooked in a sauce and wrapped in bread and dipped in hot tea that were an antidote for any hunger. The fierce electrical storms brought the wild 'thunder' mushrooms that we collected in the fields and which were a favourite dish for me.

The running of the home was all due to my mother's dedication and work. She was able to cope with any unforeseen occasion. I remember her sometimes only eating bread with tea, because unexpected guests had arrived and she had made sure that everyone else had eaten first.

Her relationship with people – even the beggars who arrived at the door – was based on equality and respect. She exuded strength, compassion and integrity. Yet she wasn't a very verbal person. It was her eyes that communicated as well as the powerful aura of her being and the kindness of her touch and intention.

I would learn so much from Mother. Although she had none of the flair for speaking that my father possessed, she was an avid reader, devouring my siblings' university set books and accurately summarising the content of each one.

Education was revered in our family and in our community, which set aside part of its meagre income to build schools. Before marrying, my mother had been a successful, independent and non-traditional young woman. She was relatively well-educated and, critically, had her own money, which she had inherited from her father. She lived for and through her children – the model that dictated the lives of millions of women who were trapped by the asymmetry of power within a male-dominated world.

My mother was deeply spiritual, but not religious in a ritualistic way. She prayed to Saraswati, who, in Indian mythology, represents Mother Nature. I used to love sitting with her in prayer. The ceremonies were accompanied by an abundance of flowers and water, milk and fresh food – sweetened rice, banana, coconut, apple, oranges – and things that cleanse – a burning lamp and incense. During important prayers she would offer a coconut to the gods, saying to me: 'Remember that the water inside this shell represents the purity of our spirit and peelings of the layers of husk are our desire to strip the arrogance of the ego in all of us.'

Mother would often say: 'All religions are but tributaries of the great river of humanity. Always treat other religions and cultures with respect and tolerance and learn from them. There are many avenues to God and no true believer professes only one path to spirituality. It is not so much the rituals, or how often you pray, or attending temple regularly that is important. What matters is what you actually do with your life, and how you serve your community and people without expectation of reward. You walk in the footsteps of your ancestors; remember to bless that heritage with kindness and compassion.'

She lived these words, which made a lasting impression and have remained with me throughout my life.

* * *

My father was a powerful man – physically well built and with deep intellectual insight. He was a voracious reader and there were always copies of *Time* magazine, *Readers Digest* and newspapers in the house. On many evenings I can remember us children being commanded around a radio to listen to the BBC. I developed a profound thirst for knowledge from him.

Father was always elegantly dressed and he wore a suit and tie every day. He shaved twice a day and scrubbed his scalp with the vigour of a man possessed. His magnetic charisma attracted a lot of attention from women.

He worked as a court interpreter in the nearby town of Dundee, a small mining town in northern Natal, where life was dominated by the 'coolie mentality',[5] and racism was the order of the day. At that time, court interpreters were the voice of the local Indian community, the highest level of authority – like doctors and lawyers. It was the pinnacle of achievement.

The court interpreter wielded enormous power for those he represented. Most magistrates could not even begin to understand the discourse – the language, the way of thinking or the culture – of the 'lower classes'. In most instances, manipulated by the verbal proficiency of my father, the magistrate was an unwitting rubber stamp. I remember as a child that there were always queues of people at the door to our home, pleading for justice from my father. He was the 'head chief in a tribal court'. I recall thinking he always had time for them but not for me.

Essentially an agnostic, Father had no romantic illusions about culture, language or custom. Life was to be lived in the harsh reality of apartheid. In fact, he dismissed the Indian caste system as an apartheid equivalent determined to keep the majority (in India) in subjugation. 'Never let anyone patronise you. Develop your mind. That is your advantage over racial oppression' was his motto in life.

I understand now why he was unconcerned when I arrived home after my first day as a child in a vernacular, Tamil school. I had been asked to leave the class because I was mischievous. He agreed. 'Let the boy concentrate on his

English.' I was, of course, overjoyed. More time to play, plus an opportunity to avoid the wrath of the disciplinarian headmaster who did not hesitate to use the cane.

I now regret not learning an Indian dialect, particularly since visiting India. I would have loved to have conversed directly with the people in my great-grandmother's village. I would have loved to have woven myself into that community and to have felt the pulse of life that she would have experienced. But I can understand my father's reasoning as well. Language was a means to achieve an end. Tamil was of no commercial value in apartheid South Africa and certainly no ferry out of poverty.

Even today as I travel the cities of the world I marvel at the mystique of multi-culturalism. I love to wander the 'Chinatowns', Italian quarters, Bombay centres and taste the uniqueness of the cuisine, smell the fragrances and the spices, and experience the people and the cultures. As some of these communities struggle with the questions of their identity I think back to my childhood. For my parents, South Africa was the only country that their children would know. They encouraged integration into that reality while maintaining our cultural identity. For us, South Africa was our country of birth; India was the home of our ancestors and the foundation of our culture.

My dislocation from my father (during my youth) had to do with our lack of communication and the fact that he was much older and, quite simply, could not understand me. His presence was like that of a grandfather, more interested in gambling on the horses and tending to his banana trees than playing with children. I disengaged from my father's influence and was raised by my mother and my elder sister, Dimes, while Pat, my eldest brother, became more of a paternal figure.

Many years later, with my own family, I returned to Dundee, where my father had worked. I retraced his steps from the office in the courts to the house he lived in. I talked to the descendants of the friends he had, and they recounted the stories of a man they had all respected. He was a towering figure in the community with access to levers of power that could help them through their difficulties with the law. They respected his integrity.

I recall sleeping restlessly that night. I rose early to climb a nearby mountain, making my way through the pathless bush to the summit. The sun was just beginning to break through its slumber and cast rays of filtered light, when I stumbled towards a rock and sat there. And there was the town that I had visited the day before, spread out before me. As I meditated I was drawn into a conversation. I felt his tangible presence. I talked about hurt, of emotions long suppressed.

My mind rewound. 'Why did you never hug me? Why was there never a sign of the physical love I yearned for? Why did you swim the Tugela River in flood because of a wager with a friend or swim to the shark nets in Durban's Indian Ocean with Dimes on your back and never teach me to swim? Why did you never teach me to ride a bicycle or play chess?' I felt the anger pour out of me.

After several hours I rose – a cloud had lifted. I felt freed of the burdens carried for such a long time. At the same time I had freed my father of any responsibility to me. We forgave each other and embraced.

I was left with the memory of the one time my father had held me tightly in his arms when I had burnt my foot running across a smouldering bush fire barefoot. He had rocked me to sleep after a nurse had dressed my wounds. I felt safe and comfortable.

* * *

In my earliest childhood memory I am four years old, playing with just a brick – imagining it to be a heavy-duty truck ploughing its way through piles of sand to forge a road. Suddenly real lorries appear. They seem to be making their way to our side of the street.

I remember running around the house to get a better view of them. There was a major arterial road that crossed the Umgeni River and travelled to the North Coast townships of Avoca, KwaMashu and Inanda in Durban. My parents had relocated from Dundee several years earlier and we lived in the close-knit community of Greenwood Park, a suburb of Durban. I loved our wooden house with its brightly painted green roof nestling in a valley at the end of a winding driveway. We had a dozen caves and secret hideouts.

The greengrocer at the corner of the street had been there forever. He knew every child and parent in the neighbourhood. He had to know them – he offered credit on the basis of trust and family history. We lived in an intimate community that shared homes and meals.

My idyllic childhood world was abruptly shattered when we were evicted from our house as a result of the Group Areas Act.[6] Greenwood Park was on the border of a white area. Our street was declared a 'coloured area' as part of apartheid's highly developed form of racism and social engineering that sought to divide all communities by the colours of their skin. It was another random apartheid demarcation – and we were on the wrong side of the street. One side of the road was white; the other side was largely Indian – a shocking arbitrariness executed by some unfeeling bureaucrat. In real life the two sides of the road never met.

I was four years old. I did not want to leave my home to go to some strange faraway place but I was forced to accept my fate, although it did leave me with an unformed sense of loss that lasted until I confronted it consciously, many decades later.

I have very little memory of the actual move, but it affected my older siblings and parents quite badly. The community mobilised against the eviction and took the government to court. A settlement allowed a significant part of the community to stay but our home was excluded, and we had to go.

When we moved we lost our community. Our new suburb, Reservoir Hills, was largely uninhabited at that stage – the Group Areas Act had relegated black communities to the periphery, away from accessible suburbs with shops, transport and amenities that were allocated for white residents only. While our house boasted magnificent views over the hills our memory was of being forcibly evicted because we had lived in a 'black spot'.[7]

In time, we rebuilt an intimacy and a community spirit. My playmates and I spent our time carving paths and caves in the virgin bush, always tempting fate. Riding carts constructed from wooden tomato boxes with precious ball-bearing wheels was a highlight. The terrain lent itself to this exciting adventure, and my scars bear testimony to the terror of careening carts screeching down the curving hills of Reservoir Hills.

More houses were built all the time. Roads were developed and electricity was installed. I was always conscious of workers labouring on roads. Etched in my mind is the image of workers digging trenches or working on roads with their picks and singing in melodious harmony, working together in flawless rhythm, most of them bare-chested in the hot summer, sweating profusely, a symbol of strength and fortitude.

There is also always the image of the white supervisor – ever-present, sitting in a deckchair under an umbrella, doing nothing. It completely offended me that people in the community would make tea for the white man and ignore the black workers who toiled in the blistering heat. It made a very deep impression on me.

A suburb was in the making, and it seemed after a while that affluent people were moving in. I had thought that we lived in a large rambling house but this was being rapidly dwarfed by the sprawling mansions of the rich. We formed little gangs, usually picking on our snobbish peers in the neighbourhood.

Sometimes John, the man who worked in our garden, took me to his home in a nearby rural area. I enjoyed spending time with him. We crossed the Umgeni River and caught shrimps, scooping the shallow waters with an old vest.

Then we would climb the steep mountains bordering the deeply sunk Umgeni River with its myriad of caves to reach his homestead. We would sit down to a delicious meal of *phutu*[8] and beans.

John taught me a lot: making slings out of branches and showing me how to aim; identifying the fruit we could eat in the wild and those that were poisonous; watching out for dangerous snakes and spotting the spitting cobra or the deadly green mamba. He would teach me to make my carts, play marbles and to create a playground with bricks and a spade, carving out little roads to traverse.

Our community celebrated and shared all the cultural and religious festivals. We would enjoy the delicacies and the feast that had been prepared, skipping in and out of each other's homes. We were Muslims in Eid ul-Fitr, which marks the end of the holy fasting period of Ramadan, and Hindus during Diwali, the festival of lights to signify victory of good over evil within an individual.

But it was Christmas, coinciding with the summer holidays, the year end and the country winding down to a standstill, that most excited us. It was the time to stop and take a breath from the pressures of the year. As a child a favourite activity was window-shopping down West Street, the bustling nerve centre of the Durban metropolis with its brightly coloured Christmas lights dazzling our spirits. Crowds of people came to celebrate the decorated store fronts. We had the chance to buy candy floss from street vendors as we skipped up and down the street.

It was on these occasions when we ventured into the wider world of the city and the seafront that we were confronted with the ugly face of petty racism. We could not afford much of what was advertised and when I did venture inside these stores the shop security was quick to make me feel unwelcome, with suspicious surveillance shortly followed by, 'Hey coolie, what do you want here? Be on your way!' Blacks were not encouraged to enter this high Mecca of 'The White' shopping paradise.

But our Christmas treat was not only a trip to the city. It also included a mandatory detour for ice-creams to 'Clover Leaf', the patch of the Indian Ocean that had been allocated to Indians by the apartheid city planners.

Obviously the beach alongside the glittering five-star hotels and the public facilities such as the carousels and merry-go-rounds were all reserved for whites. We watched and our unasked question was, 'Why am I not allowed to ride these galloping horses on the roundabout?'

The only black people we saw there were the shuffling African and Indian municipal workers, heads lowered to avoid the eyes of even the white children, picking up the garbage left by the revelling white crowds. These workers were invisible.

We were 'the hewers of wood and the carriers of water'. It left a bitter taste in my mouth and a smouldering resentment against the system that created it.

4

My childhood spanned South Africa's 'golden age' of a confident and boastful apartheid. At the beginning of the 1960s, political silence followed the banning of the liberation movements, the African National Congress (ANC) and Pan Africanist Congress (PAC), after the Sharpeville massacre in 1960.[9] The decade had been characterised by fear permeating the populace as apartheid repression stalked the land. The very mention of politics reared the demons of burly policemen breaking down doors and people disappearing, in many cases forever. Our parents and the community were petrified and preferred not to talk about the past resistance struggles.

This was the high noon of apartheid. H.F. Verwoerd was the Prime Minister of the independent white Republic of South Africa and he moved swiftly to tighten the noose around the throat of the black majority. The apartheid laws in place were being ruthlessly applied – the pass laws, which controlled the mobility of African men and women, and the Group Areas Act, which segregated the residential areas according to race. Race in turn was decided by the Population Registration Act,[10] which divided people into 'Bantu', several categories of 'Coloured', a couple of categories of 'Asiatic' and, of course, 'White', which was only one category – no divided population there.[11]

The 1960s had seen foreign investment flourish and spectacular growth in the economy at a rate much higher than in the industrialised world. An unholy alliance of dominant white capital and the apartheid state was united in its pursuit of white supremacy, made possible by the extreme exploitation of the labour of the black majority.

Boosted by the witch-hunt against communists and radical elements of the Left, particularly in the United States, the apartheid regime passed the Suppression of Communism Act in 1950, which allowed harsh security action against anyone suspected of undermining its rule. The government was confident that it had the full support of the major Western powers. Apartheid was seen as a bulwark against the danger of global communism in Africa.

Moreover, the regime had demonstrated that it could control its black subjects in the aftermath of Sharpeville. The state had no hesitation in banning individuals, detaining them, torturing them and even pronouncing their 'accidental deaths' while under interrogation.

At home my life was one of exploration, making new friends and raiding fruit trees that grew in the gardens of neighbours. And then a miracle happened. We celebrated the first car in the family when my brother Pat drove a spanking new Volkswagen Beetle into our yard. We were stunned. Only rich Indians and whites drove cars. I would wait for him to arrive on weekends and just sit in the car listening to the radio or take the greatest pleasure in polishing it lovingly. He was usually accompanied by some attractive woman who would always bring me presents as a way of endearing herself to the family. Of course I loved to play that game.

Then there were the times when Pat arrived with friends he was studying with at Durban's medical school for black students, which fell under the legal jurisdiction of, but was not integrated into, the 'whites only' University of Natal. They were dynamic, talkative and confident as well as intensely political. I would absorb every word and was fascinated by the African friends he brought home. It was a new world opening up for me that was different from the mainly working-class black people (Indian and African) I saw and interacted with.

Now we had begun a new decade – the 1970s – and were inspired by the Black Consciousness movement, which was the first stirring of radical opposition since the banning of the liberation movements. My friends and I had vague social memories of the struggles in the 1950s that the ANC had led in the period up to its banning on 8 April 1960. But the brazen display of firepower by the regime was designed to intimidate the populace. Open resistance became history, hidden from the generations that followed.

Black Consciousness gave confidence to a lost generation that was disconnected from the heady days of the 1952 Defiance Campaign, which had been led by the likes of Nelson Mandela and Walter Sisulu. To us, a generation later, they were important but distant memories.

* * *

The impact of the 1968 revolts in Paris had spread worldwide, culminating in massive demonstrations against the Vietnam War. The increasing turbulence of black American politics and the civil rights movement led by Martin Luther King Jr and the 'black power' defiance of Malcolm X reverberated across South African university campuses.

NUSAS, the white-led National Union of South African Students, was the organisation leading the protests against apartheid among students. Increasingly, however, black students felt alienated from NUSAS. They became aware of the need to organise and express their frustrations and aspirations in an undiluted way to the institutionalised racism of apartheid. Black students were united by their blackness and the injustice of oppression. There was no divide to bridge. In fact, there was no middle of the road or grey area – just black and white. As Steve Biko said: 'Blacks are tired of standing at the touchlines to witness a game that they should be playing. They want to do things for themselves and all by themselves.'[12]

The (black) South African Students Organisation (SASO), which was formed in December 1969 through a break-away from NUSAS with which it maintained amicable relations, was to be our platform and our voice.

The big strikes starting amongst Namibian workers encouraged political philosopher Rick Turner at the University of Natal in Durban to mobilise some of his students to publicise the exploitative conditions that African workers were living and working under, right there in Natal. Soon afterwards, radical Marxist white students set up the Wages Commission[13] on the major South African campuses. Research revealed that the value of the workers' low wages had deteriorated even further while the cost of living was rising.

The strikes in the early 1970s by workers in KwaZulu-Natal and in Namibia were the first stirrings of labour unrest.[14]

In 1972 the General Workers Benefit Fund was set up in Durban, benefiting from the strike wave. Over 60 000 striking workers rocked Durban to its foundations, starting at Coronation Brick and spreading to the textile and garment industry and eventually to the Durban municipality. There were no demands and no identified leaders, but employers hurriedly improved wages.

At the same time, the Western Province Workers Advice Bureau in the Western Cape and the Urban Training Project (UTP) in Johannesburg were formed as benefit societies and advisory bodies to black workers, whose rights to form trade unions were still denied.

With a strike wave sweeping Durban and the rest of the country a number of unregistered unions, representing African workers and with no legal rights to collective bargaining, were launched. Many of them eventually formed the foundation of the modern trade union movement.

During this time we were reminded by the screaming media that 'agitators and communists' were behind the strikes. I was in high school and found myself impressed and intimidated by the power and fury of workers who had exploded into action against an exploitative system of cheap labour. I was also struck by the graphic details of the growth and spectacular propaganda of black power organisations. We protested against the celebration of 'Republic Day', which the white government attempted to foist on us, and burnt the hated national flag.

Our DNA was being wired by a new generation of confrontational political activism. It was now up to us. But it would be several years before I reconnected to the pulsating energy of the workers in action.

* * *

On 17 May 1971, when I was seventeen, the bus driver knocked at our door. My father had had a heart attack on the bus, and died. The bus had retraced its route and with its load of passengers arrived at our home. I was not at school because I was studying for a major exam. I watched as people carried my father's body into our home. The house was quiet and my mother remained dignified. There was no screaming and crying; only the stillness of death and the haunting looks of neighbours who streamed in to offer their condolences and support.

By the evening the funeral arrangements were made and, as is traditional in Indian custom, the cremation was set for the next day.

The rituals of death always stir mixed feelings in me. I prefer not to dramatise mourning. Death is inevitable. Notwithstanding, I tended to the rituals as the youngest in the family. I felt the sadness but could not bring myself to tears. He was my father, but somehow the biological link was the only one I was conscious of at that moment. The eulogies at the funeral fell on my ears as an observer of death.

The next day we collected his ashes and as we stood along the banks of the Umgeni River we placed them on a piece of banana leaf, lit a camphor stick and watched his remains drift downstream. From then on, even though my father and I had not communicated much, my life changed.

After his death rebellion became my hallmark, an act of defiance, a trademark. Smoking and drinking were a way of life. It was as if any motive to prove myself had disappeared. I no longer needed to impress anyone. Life became one big party. I began to bunk school and was on the way to becoming a delinquent. My grades plummeted. We sold black-market tickets at the cinemas through an arrangement with the ticket sellers to buy block tickets and then sell them at a higher price. Cinemas were a main form of entertainment then – an escape to a world of fantasy.

The year tumbled on. There was no parents' association, no quarterly meetings with the teachers to review progress. Unlike today, the only contact with parents was when a student was suspended or expelled for a serious offence. Corporal punishment was the only remedial 'solution' offered. Many of our teachers were dedicated, but given the sizes of our classes (usually over 40 pupils) there was not enough time for individual attention. In particular, there was no way of helping students with social problems within the home or community.

For the last two years of high school I transferred to Sastri College, an old established institution with an outstanding reputation for results, but my rebellion against authority continued. I would go to school in the morning, sign the attendance register, leap over the wall a few periods later and then go into town, invariably to watch a movie, hang out on the city streets and in the arcades and then get back in the afternoon. On many other occasions I simply did not bother to show up for school.

Days went by slowly. The roads had improved but the dreary trips, in the heat of the afternoons, to and from home and the city were still in ancient, smoking buses cutting across the rich fields adjoining the Umgeni River before spluttering up the winding hills of Reservoir Hills.

One of the most interesting spectacles of the trip was passing by the patchy green fields of the Springfield sports grounds, where aspirant black golfers practised alongside soccer teams. The facilities adjoined the rubbish dump and the shanty settlement called Tin Town that sat on the river banks that housed the poorest of the poor.

The first time it dawned on me that black people played golf was in 1963, when there was an outcry over Papwa Sewgolum, a golfer of Indian descent, winning the Natal Open at the Durban Country Club, a bastion of white privilege. He beat Gary Player, the renowned international golfer and (white) South African champion. However, at the prize-giving Papwa was forced, because of the apartheid laws that reserved the clubhouse for whites, to receive his trophy outside in the pelting rain, while the white golfers sat in comfort inside.

Papwa had first won the Dutch Open Championship in 1959, and went on to win it several times, but was made to feel like an outsider in his own country. He was not the first or the last athlete who was recognised abroad but shunned at home in South Africa.

Notwithstanding, Papwa's triumph was seen as a political victory by the overwhelming black majority. During the height of apartheid, the black majority consistently backed the opponents of South African teams. Particularly in white-dominated sports, it gave us a flush of victory to see the white South African teams whipped. These were not our teams but those of a colonising oppressor; we would never be able to represent the country of our birth because of the colour of our skin.

Boxing, in particular, was a great sport to watch as many of the best international boxers were black, and when they floored South African competitors it resonated with us and was a devastating body blow to apartheid.

Muhammad Ali was a symbol of black pride for us, his defiance a rallying point. His conversion to Islam and his rejection of his Christian name was a slap in the face for those we saw as the arrogant purveyors of the world. It fed our anger and drew us to Black Consciousness. When, as the champion of the world, Ali captured American hypocrisy by his courageous refusal to fight in the Vietnam War it was a declaration of social solidarity. He was speaking on our behalf when he articulated those immortal words: 'I ain't got no quarrel with them Viet Cong...No Viet Cong ever called me a nigger.'[15] Ali had become a global political figure and his internationalism resonated with us when he said: 'Boxing is nothing, just satisfying to some bloodthirsty people. I am no longer Cassius Clay, a Negro from Kentucky. I belong to the world, the black world. I have a home in Pakistan, in Algeria, in Ethiopia. This is more than money.'

* * *

In these high school years my brother Logie, two years older than me and a charismatic leader both intellectually and on the sports field, became an important influence. He was at the Springfield Teachers Training College and had come into contact with the Black Consciousness movement.

Logie became active in SASO, which was led by the passionate and fiery Steve Biko, who was convinced that black students (African, Indian and coloured) needed an organisation of their own.

One hot summer's afternoon I went with Logie to a public meeting held in the Lutheran Church in Reservoir Hills. The hall was crammed with people. It was stuffy and humid but the air crackled with excitement. Two large cars had swept into the parking area and unloaded a bunch of burly men with barely concealed weapons under their ill-fitting jackets. They marched into the church and took up seats on the front benches.

I stood at the back watching this spectacle unfold. A young African man walked out to the front. Biko clenched his fist in the air and shouted 'Amandla!'

'Ngawethu!'[16] responded the audience.

The hall reverberated with the sound of the slogans. The apprehensive crowd became more confident. We outnumbered the security police who were there to intimidate us.

'Black man, you are on your own.[17] We have nothing to lose except our chains. There is only black and white in this country. There is no middle ground. We must take a stand. We are either for justice and freedom, or apartheid and servitude.'[18]

This was a leader – an inspiring leader. Steve Biko's words fed every cell in my body like a super boost of adrenalin. He was right! The man before me eloquently captured my frustrations and fearlessly articulated them. It was truly inspiring. My body quivered with emotion. By the end of that afternoon, the security policemen who had tried to intimidate us were retreating, speeding away dramatically, but defeated in their purpose.

Following his writings I was enthralled. 'Being black', said Steve Biko, 'is not a matter of pigmentation – being black is a reflection of a mental attitude':

Merely by describing yourself as black you have started on a road towards emancipation. You have committed yourself to fight against all forces that seek to use your blackness as a stamp that marks you out as a subservient being.

What we should at all times look at is the fact that:

We are all oppressed by the same system.

That we are oppressed to varying degrees is a deliberate design to stratify us not only socially but in terms of aspirations.[19]

I remember the countless times I had asked my parents: 'Why can't I go into that whites only cinema, sit wherever I want on that bus, play in whatever park I want? Why can't we swim in the nice part of the beach? Why can't we go and spend time in the toy shops without some rude security person asking us to move on? Why do we just accept the logic of a system that rejects my identity because of the colour of my skin?' Crushed by the weight of repression their response was to shrug their shoulders saying, 'That's the way it is.'

Over the next few months I experienced a shift in consciousness. Biko was the catalyst to my early political stirrings. There was more to follow.

5

After I matriculated in 1972 I had to write a supplementary exam for an exemption to attend university. At this stage I was pretty uninterested in furthering my studies.

Early one morning, in April 1973, I decided to leave home for the fabled Johannesburg, the 'City of Gold – Egoli'. It was as far away from Durban as my horizons could contemplate.

My mother tried to persuade me to stay in Durban and pursue a university career. But I wanted to discover a new world and said I would return in time for the next year. She was worried but also recognised that I needed to work out my own life.

It was a hot day. I got on my bicycle, inspired by the tale of a cousin, and started my journey to Johannesburg. I saw my mother standing at the door as I rode off. I did not turn back – as for millions of others, for me it was a life ambition to be drawn into the swirling epicentre where we believed that the streets were paved with gold.

I was really unfit. Eventually I reached Pietermaritzburg, some 80 kilometres away, in the late afternoon, helped by a sympathetic driver who had stopped and offered me a lift on the back of his truck. I stayed with my cousin Tilley, who was the daughter of my father's sister and lived in a small two-bedroom duplex in the centre of the city. We became very close friends. I sold my bicycle and lived there for a few months.

The house was full of books, which I devoured. I really liked the town, unaware then that some of my most important experiences as a trade union organiser would come to me there, less than a decade later.

After a few months I hitched a lift with my cousin Yeggie, who did a weekly trip to the fresh produce market in Pietermaritzburg to stock up for the weekend trade for the shop he and my other cousins, Vassie and Sunny, ran in a small town called Colenso, a few hours' drive away. This was where my father was born and his father had set up this trading store.

I was warmly welcomed by the family. The shop was the main store in the town, providing most of the fresh food and groceries. Behind the shop was the sprawling house. Life was slow. The shop opened at 6.00 a.m. and closed at 9.00 p.m. The early morning traffic was bustling with mainly black workers buying their daily meals. The town came alive on Saturday mornings. Everyone dressed up in their best clothes – bosses and workers ('madams' and 'maids'). The shop was the main focus of activity in the town, a fascinating microcosm of South Africa. But, white people ruled the town, and everyone knew their place. Black people walked with their heads bowed. Looking directly into the eyes of a white girl was being too familiar and could easily earn you a whipping.

It was here that I met the beautiful Sibongile. Slim and curvy, she turned heads. At night the (white) police captain, overweight and intimidating, would rendezvous with her. She would submit and we would see the police van carrying her speeding past us to a venue far from the prying eyes of a small town with prejudiced minds.

In the winter months, night fell swiftly. The curfew imposed its iron curtain at 10.00 p.m. No black person was to be seen in public. After we closed the shop we would often sit outside on the *stoep* (veranda or porch). We were tolerated because we owned the shop. The police captain swept through the town like clockwork to ensure obeisance to the law.

Back then, at nineteen years old, I decided that this was not what I wanted for the rest of my life. I packed my bag and hitchhiked to Pretoria, where I stayed with family in Marabastad, at that time an Indian ghetto on the outskirts of the town.[20] At least I had crossed the provincial line and ventured into the city adjacent to the fabled city of gold.

As I was making plans to get to Johannesburg I received a call from my mother. 'My son,' she said, 'I want you to come back home. I want you to enrol in university. Education is the one right that no one can take away from you. It would make me very happy if you returned now.'

I sat back and reflected. Two years had passed since I had left school. Although my physical health was already declining, I felt that my dream had been snatched from me. Johannesburg beckoned but I was torn emotionally. In disappointment, rationality won and I prepared for my trip home.

Back in Durban, I felt my life was in limbo. My siblings had all left home to start their new lives. Pat was training as a specialist physician at the 'coloured' Somerset Hospital in Cape Town that fell under Groote Schuur.[21] Ironically he was prevented by law from studying cardiology, his first love, as it was a profession reserved for whites, and he had to contend with watching the spectacular first heart transplant and associated advances in medicine from the sidelines. Now married, we had had little contact with him since he had left King Edward Hospital in Durban after a strike to fight wage discrimination against black doctors.

Dimes, my eldest sister, worked as a senior lecturer in the ML Sultan Technical College in Durban. My brother Iyaloo had settled into his life as a radiographer at King Edward Hospital; my other sister, Nisha, was a public sector nurse; and my brother Popeye had moved to Pietermaritzburg to work as a manager in a furniture factory. All of them had married and set up their own lives.

I returned to a house with only Logie and a boarder living with our mother. Logie was now a teacher. Dimes found me a temporary job at a telephone directory company. I spent the morning placing paper clips in plastic packets. At lunch time I went to my sister's flat. I realised the futility of packaging paper clips! I had lasted precisely five hours in the first formal job I had. I didn't return after lunch.

* * *

It was now 1974, and the government began to act strongly against Black Consciousness and other groups. On 8 March, eight leading members of SASO and the Black Peoples Convention (BPC), the political body of Black Consciousness, were placed under restriction orders.[22]

During that year, five prominent SASO members left the country, including Onkgopotse Abraham Tiro, who was killed by a parcel bomb in Botswana. The murder of Tiro made a lasting impression on me. I had followed his outspoken views when he was expelled in 1972 from Turfloop University where he had made a militant speech at the graduation ceremony as the Student Representative Council (SRC) President condemning apartheid.

As a result of SASO's mobilisation a national student strike swept through black universities. Proposing the boycott at the University of Durban-Westville

(UDW), a speaker said: 'We are not voting as Indians but as Blacks. We need solidarity to eradicate this repugnant system.'[23] Action against Black Consciousness had been swift and severe.[24]

An attempt in 1972 to form an SRC at UDW was stopped by students when the campus management tried to impose its own constitution on it. The Council's constitution barred affiliation to SASO or NUSAS and prohibited student publications and press statements.

In the same year, the collapse of the Portuguese dictatorship opened the way for independence in Mozambique and Angola and, with this, new possibilities for the liberation movement. To students in South Africa, the changes in Mozambique signalled that political change was possible in our lifetimes.[25] We were ecstatic. For us the heady days of revolution seemed imminent. Pro-FRELIMO rallies[26] were being planned and I was keen to attend.

In response, the Minister of Justice prohibited any meetings anywhere in the country to be held by or on behalf of SASO or BPC between 24 September and 20 October. Moreover, the Riotous Assemblies Act (No.17) of 1956 was amended, allowing government to act within a far broader definition of what constituted a 'gathering'.

Despite the ban, meetings were held at Curries Fountain in Durban and at Turfloop University (now the University of Limpopo). Listening on the radio I heard the pandemonium that followed. A police officer issued several orders through a loudhailer, calling on the crowd to disperse. It was reported that stones and bottles were thrown at police. Using dogs, the police broke up the meeting and made several arrests.[27] After the meetings, police searched the offices and homes of SASO and BPC members at various centres, arresting more people.

On 12 March 1975, thirteen members of SASO and BPC appeared in the Pretoria Supreme Court, charged with conspiring to transform the state by violent means; to foster feelings of racial hatred and antipathy by blacks towards whites and/or the state; to condition black population groups for violent revolution; to produce, publish or distribute subversive and anti-white utterances and publications; and to discourage foreign investment in the South African economy.

Those charged included people I knew, such as Saths Cooper and Strinivas ('Strini') Moodley. Strini, long haired with a bushy beard, who lived two streets away from me, looked the part of a revolutionary. I had been fascinated as a youngster, listening to them talk of struggle and revolution and Black Consciousness. I absorbed these discussions and they became part of my socialisation, an expression of my rebellion.

This was the climate in which I began my first year at UDW in 1975, the year that the SASO trial began. I decided to follow in the footsteps of my siblings and enrolled to study for a B.Sc. as a precursor to medicine.

* * *

UDW was a world of Indian students, Indian lecturers, Indian cleaning staff, Indian chefs in the canteen; Indian culture oozed from the concrete.

I was stuck in an Indian universe. I had attended an Indian primary school, an Indian high school, and now an Indian university. I lived in an Indian area. My head was exploding. We were in Africa. I knew no Indian language and felt I would probably be a foreigner in India if I ever visited there.

By now the student leadership was largely underground and the bulk of the student body supported the politics of boycott.[28] We had adopted the principle of complete non-collaboration. We did not form any student societies and refused to take part in sports or use the world-class facilities that existed on campus.

Pravin Gordhan, Bobby Marie and others had spearheaded the student leadership before I had arrived. Pravin was a savvy but intense student leader whom I was to encounter later in my community organising work in the townships around Durban. Bobby Marie was a more relaxed intellectual and married to Shamim Meer, a fellow activist. As I entered the labour movement, I would gravitate towards them, often using their car for my early morning factory visits. My first driving lessons were very much evidenced by the scratches and dents I left on their car but both Shamim and Bobby never said a word.

The political leadership had argued for no student activity until we had won our freedom on the basis that we were attending a racial university under duress. At its 1974 conference, the South African Non-Racial Olympic Committee (SANROC), the anti-apartheid sports lobby group, had declared its solidarity with organisations working for non-racialism in sport and resolved to discourage black teams from participating in multiracial and multinational sporting events or using facilities at the ethnically divided 'bush' universities.[29]

A meeting was called in 1975 by a group of well-meaning students to discuss a renewed attempt to form an SRC. Our group of left-wing students sat scattered amongst the 2 000 students in the hall, ready to enforce the policy of boycott. The organisers attempted to start the meeting, saying: 'We have convened this meeting to ...' We interrupted from different corners of the hall with a question. 'Who is *we* ... who is *we*?' Soon the whole hall was chanting 'Who's we, who's we?'

With chaos ensuing our group rushed on to the stage and grabbed the microphone, proclaiming loudly: 'These are collaborators; they want to sell us out. Who do they represent? Who have they been meeting with?' The meeting was closed. We were there under duress. We were not going to legitimise the apartheid state with setting up an SRC and beginning to use the sporting facilities.

I'll always remember that meeting and what I learnt from it. Meetings are held by people; they are about emotions. It takes very few people to disrupt a meeting. This was an important lesson for me, when I myself became a speaker in contested situations, on how to pre-empt disruptive elements. It taught me a lot about strategy and tactics.

The year wore on slowly. A group of activists began to coalesce. At first we were seen as a bunch of social delinquents hanging out under the cafeteria stairs. We were discontented, but leaderless. My health, however, was deteriorating; the intensive treatment I was receiving for a non-infectious form of lymphatic tuberculosis I had picked up somewhere on my trip to Pretoria was taking its toll. Then I was diagnosed with sarcoidosis and landed up in hospital. My eyesight deteriorated and I was having difficulty breathing. I could feel the coldness of death at the doorway.

Lying on my hospital bed I wondered what the future held for me.

6

I recovered from my illness but had to live on a potent combination of steroids (cortisone) for the treatment of my sarcoidosis. The perennial visits to doctors, the countless X-rays, the antiseptic smell of hospital, the crowds of sick people, the long queues and failing infrastructure were depressing. I turned to my studies but a restlessness of spirit persisted.

At the same time we followed the SASO trial, which dragged on. News reports noted that 'there are no physical acts of terrorism or recruitment alleged in the 82-page indictment apart from charges of writings allegedly composed or distributed by the nine accused'.[30] Instead, the charges related to the September 1975 'Viva FRELIMO' rallies called to celebrate the victory over Portuguese colonialism by FRELIMO, the people's movement that had waged a war of liberation against Portuguese colonial rule. Freedom in Mozambique, we considered, brought us one step closer to our own liberation in South Africa. The trial had become recognised as the 'Trial of Black Consciousness' rather than of the nine accused.[31]

Then out of the blue, 16 June 1976 hit us like a whirlwind. We had been in contact with student groupings across the different universities and understood the rumblings in the African townships about the forced introduction of Afrikaans as a medium of instruction in schools. But we were not prepared for the tumultuous events that were to change the political landscape of South Africa.

On 16 June thousands of students congregated along Vilakazi Street in Soweto, intent on marching to Orlando Stadium to demonstrate against (amongst other things) the imposition of Afrikaans . What ensued was nothing short of a massacre as tens of thousands of children and young adults were confronted by the police. Initially, tear gas and vicious dogs were set upon them before live ammunition was sprayed – without a warning.

Hector Pieterson, a twelve-year-old boy, was one of the first to be killed and the photograph of his lifeless body being carried by Mbuyisa Makhubo (accompanied by Pieterson's sister) is forever etched in all our memories.

When the news of the June 16th uprisings reached us we galvanised the student body into action, marching around the campus with placards and singing struggle songs. We sprayed slogans across the campus and around the town; the mood ignited a massive student boycott. The sense of solidarity gave us hope that we were on the brink of a revolution.

After a few weeks of tumultuous activity we realised that our actions were not sustainable. Students began to drift back to lectures. Mid-year exams were upon us. We had to call off the action. I was astounded at the apathy of our fellow students.

My alienation from student politics reached a peak after the death in detention of Mapetla Mohapi on 5 August 1976. Mapetla had been the Permanent Secretary of SASO, and was arrested without charge a month after the June 16th uprisings. The Minister of Police, the notorious Jimmy Kruger, claimed that Mapetla had died by falling against a chair while police were trying to prevent him from committing suicide. The post-mortem revealed various injuries that could not have been sustained in this way.

I had joined a busload of students who went to Mapetla's funeral in Matatiele in the Eastern Cape. It was a long and tricky journey – driving through the night, crossing roadblocks, avoiding livestock that loomed up in the headlights. We arrived very early in the morning in this remote rural village to find rows of buses from all over the country and crowds of people.

It was like a typical Bantustan village – very poor with mud huts, but exceptionally beautiful with the backdrop of the Maluti Mountains. I could feel the quiet anger in the rows of people who were lining up to see the body, then queuing to wash their hands, and share a meal. They were trying to find some sort of consolation.

It was my first real political experience of rural African life. In twenty years apartheid had entrenched deep divisions between races. I was captivated by the quietness, and by the strength in people's faces – worn down by decades of hardship and poverty.

I sensed a deep trust in these rural people, which one day would mould my affinity with migrant workers. The funeral had a big impact on me. After this profound experience, I found student life frustrating and I was very demoralised.

I tried to mobilise students but it was not an easy task. At a public meeting in the university cafeteria I rose to speak. My body quivering with emotion, I asked: 'How can we be bystanders when such social injustice is being perpetrated against our people? Mapetla was innocent – today he lies murdered because he stood up and fought for all of us!'

There was a lukewarm response.

I realised we were out of touch with the student body. Our heady notions of a revolutionary fervour that would bring the apartheid edifice crumbling down were replaced with the reality of students returning to classes and preparing for exams.

I retreated. I abandoned my studies for that year, became a recluse and voraciously read any historical and political books or texts I could lay my hands on. It was intense, sleeping during the day and reading the whole night. My mother was worried, always enquiring, 'Why don't you visit your friends or invite them here for a meal?' I replied in a quiet way, 'I will but now I am studying the history of the country and the world. Please don't worry about me.' But she did worry.

* * *

In the meantime, judgment on the SASO accused was finally delivered on 15 December 1976. I left home and travelled to Pretoria. I wanted to be present at the sentencing. I joined the crowds with clenched fists as the 'guilty' left in speeding police vans to a life on Robben Island for the next five years.

Returning to university to resume my studies in early 1977, I organised a group of fellow activists and we had a discussion with Terence Tryon, then the Secretary General of SASO. I wanted to go beyond the political discussions in our study circles. We agreed to revive the Durban-Westville branch of SASO. We formulated a plan that involved Valli Moosa, who was later to become a key leader of the UDF and then a minister in the first democratic government. We started to grow our circle of activists and then began to look at community-organising initiatives in some of the desperately poor squatter camps burgeoning around Durban.

It was at about this time that I met Jayendra Naidoo, who has been one of my closest friends and comrades ever since. Jayendra came from a political family. His uncle, 'MD', served time on Robben Island from 1977 to 1982. His father, M.J. Naidoo, fondly known as 'MJ', was a well-respected lawyer and acting president of the Natal Indian Congress (NIC), the political organisation that MJ was leading efforts to revive.

The NIC was originally formed by Mahatma Gandhi to fight discrimination against Indian traders in Natal in 1894, but later had been transformed into an organisation defending the rights of all Indian people in South Africa. It was in South Africa that Gandhi formulated the policy of *satyagraha* – resistance to tyranny through mass civil disobedience based on the principle of non-violence.

In the 1940s, the NIC came under the more radical leadership of Dr G.M. Naicker and Dr Yusuf Dadoo, who argued that the political rights of the Indian community could not be divorced from those of African and coloured people. They called for a multiracial front and a relationship with the ANC, which was evident in the 'Doctors Pact' (signed by Dr Naicker, Dr Dadoo and Dr A.B. Xuma).[32]

I had gone to MJ's office to meet with him. As leaders in SASO we were opposed to the revival of the NIC. We felt that we had moved the struggle beyond the ethnic question. We were a generation that shared a vision of black solidarity. In SASO we were not Indian. We were the black oppressed. We felt included. It gave me a sense of identity. I was a black South African first. The only boundary in my mind was the line between black and white. It was a line between justice and injustice. It was in this context that I met with Jayendra, MJ's son, who was working in his office.

MJ was opposed to Jayendra's attending the ethnic UDW and he also believed that Jayendra would become involved in frivolous activities and wanted him to study law through correspondence with the University of South Africa (UNISA) and continue working as a clerk in his office. Jayendra, always strong willed, wanted to study engineering and refused to concede. Eventually his father relented as the deadline for registration approached, and Jayendra went to UDW but agreed to study law. We quickly connected and I found Jayendra to be a serious comrade, intellectually sharp and determined to follow his own path in politics.

Jayendra, Valli Moosa and I became co-conspirators in the building of SASO at UDW. Black Consciousness was implacably opposed to the issues of ethnicity or minorities. For us there were no minorities – just people – and the only language that apartheid understood was protest and mass action.

In September 1977 Mangosuthu Buthelezi came to address the students and we organised a protest that disrupted the meeting. In the Black Consciousness movement, Buthelezi was seen as the enemy: a homeland leader, a collaborator, anti-progressive, and someone who had taken very conservative positions in relation to the mass popular struggle in South Africa.

Stopping his meeting at UDW was part of our denying a platform to anyone, especially a leader, who was associated with the apartheid state. The meeting was scheduled for the largest lecture theatre. We occupied it and when we were being evicted someone exploded stink bombs that rendered the room unusable for a few hours.

The organisers relocated the meeting to the Great Hall but we occupied the stage and refused to move. Eventually the lecture was cancelled and Buthelezi left the university.

The next morning the headlines were 'Buthelezi warns of a repeat of 1949' – an inflammatory statement referring to the notorious racial clash between Indians and Africans, which many speculate was instigated by the security forces but which cut a swathe of destruction and chaos across Durban. This was in response to an increasingly militant Non-European Front that had been mobilising mass defiance and passive resistance across the oppressed racial groups.

I thought that Buthelezi using this spectre of racial violence reflected on him as a symbol of the state. I did not have personal feelings against him. The meeting was a turning point for us because he became personal, abusive and racist.[33]

After this incident we mobilised students into community work. We identified Malagasy township as a good place to become involved. We visited with a group of students and engaged in discussion with the community on how we could become involved with them in dealing with pressing social issues. We held poetry and protest theatre shows to raise money.

Much time was spent producing inflammatory pamphlets. Our notions of an underground press were the hours we spent at the black medical school in Durban churning out propaganda on an ancient cyclostyling Gestetner machine that broke down constantly and made a mess. On one occasion we had spent many hours producing a special pamphlet for the 'winter school' run by a religious group. We had 'borrowed' my brother Logie's car for this important political task while he was on his first trip abroad on honeymoon with his wife, Corona. The car was his pride and joy.

Late that night we retired to a pub in Reservoir Hills. When we finally emerged, hours later, there was no sign of the car. 'My God,' we wondered, 'has it been stolen? We are surely in a lot of shit.' Then we spotted it. It had rolled down a hill and was lodged in a ditch. I had forgotten to pull up the handbrake. Years later we would laugh hilariously at the incident.

The pamphlets we had produced were taken to the 'winter school' by Jayendra and Saggie and Inba Naidoo, who were part of our political group, and left on the tables when the students went to lunch. Before they returned a priest found the pamphlets, read one, and all that was left of a hard night's work was a burning pile of our revolutionary rhetoric in an oil drum brazier used to keep the students warm.

At about the same time we began to explore Marxism-Leninism. We could see the clashes coming. The BPC embraced a traditional African communalism ideology and rejected Marxism-Leninism. In SASO, we were veering to the left, while the BPC remained virulently anti-communist. I could never understand why.

We started to prepare for a meeting with Steve Biko. Black Consciousness, while it laid a powerful foundation of our political education, could not explain the form of racial capitalism that had emerged in South Africa. I felt that it was unviable to return to a traditional communalism of the past. The African masses had been dispossessed of the land and forced into a cheap labour system that was a prerequisite for the mining industry and agriculture. I had many unanswered questions but I respected Steve and believed that he had an openness and a humility that we could engage with.

It was extremely sensitive how this was to be done, given the close watch the security police kept on him and the fact that the leadership of the BPC decided who would see him. Regretfully fate intervened and this meeting never materialised.

On 12 September, Steve Biko, by then the Honorary Life President of the BPC, was savagely murdered in police custody. He had been detained by the Security Branch in Port Elizabeth 24 days earlier. Brutally assaulted by the notorious security police and suffering serious brain injuries, he was shackled and bundled naked into the back of a police van and driven more than 1 000 kilometres to Pretoria. He suffered a painful, lonely and desperate death lying on the floor of his cell in Pretoria Central Prison.

At the inquest into his death, security police claimed that Biko had 'become violent' during interrogation and had to be 'subdued', in the course of which he hit his head against the wall. Harold Snyman, Gideon Nieuwoudt, Daniel Petrus Siebert and Ruben Beneke Marx, members of the security police in Port Elizabeth, applied for amnesty in the 1997 Truth and Reconciliation Commission (TRC) hearings for Biko's death, but stuck to the story they shared at the inquest.[34]

I went to the funeral in King William's Town on 25 September 1977. It was a mass event, with an estimated 15 000 attending. People travelled from all over the country to bid farewell. Tension was high and the air was thick with a simmering anger. We were outraged by the presence of representatives of Western embassies. These were countries we felt had collaborated with the apartheid regime and therefore with the murder of our leader. The funeral turned into a political rally as Biko's body was lowered into a muddy plot adjacent to the railway line in King William's Town. The cry reverberated in the stadium filled with clenched 'black power' salutes that echoed the demand for homeland leaders to resign and was a stern warning that the apartheid state was stoking the flames of a violent backlash from our ranks.

7

I returned to Durban and, like thousands of other activists, we began to discuss our options. A month later, on 18 October 1977, the state clamped down again, closing the progressive *World* and *Voice* newspapers, detaining the courageous editor Percy Qoboza and banning 22 organisations, including SASO and BPC.

In the early hours of that morning we were rudely awoken by a loud hammering on the door of our flat in Sydenham, Durban, where we had moved to. It was the jackboot security police. My mother tried to reason with them but was pushed aside. A group demanded to search the room I shared with Logie. They overturned the bookshelves and clothing cupboard searching for banned literature and suspicious documents. They refused to answer any questions and did not produce a search warrant. Their intention was to intimidate.

The raid was also designed to terrify my mother about the consequences of her son continuing to be politically active. The men's parting words to her were: 'You'd better control your son or he will disappear one day.' It was only when we turned on the radio that we heard about the nationwide swoop alleging that certain forces were planning violent action against the state.

Left with very few options, and with the key leadership in jail, we tried to regroup. But fear had gripped the land. Thousands abandoned their education and left the country to join the ranks of Umkhonto we Sizwe (MK), the armed wing of the ANC.[35]

In the 1960s the MK high command included Nelson Mandela, Govan Mbeki, Walter Sisulu, Dennis Goldberg, Ahmed Kathrada, Raymond Mhlaba, Andrew Mlangeni and Elias Motsoaledi. The leaders were hunted down, and the close to 200 acts of political sabotage formed the backbone of the apartheid state's case in the famous Rivonia Trial. Mandela and his comrades were found guilty and sentenced to life imprisonment.

For some time I toyed with the idea of leaving, as comrades I had worked with left the country. There was a certain appeal. This was an armed and brutal police state that knew no boundaries. We were innocent victims in this travesty of social justice. But in the end, I resolved that I would stay. We had much work to do and the police crackdown on remaining activists continued with thousands of detentions.

* * *

I decided to abandon my pursuit of a medical career and to spend my life dissecting society rather than bodies. Together with Jayendra Naidoo and others, I chose the path of becoming a permanent revolutionary. There was no space for a personal life. In fact I was aggrieved when Jayendra announced that he was getting romantically involved with fellow activist Pregs Govender. 'We don't have the time for relationships. They will distract us from our single-minded focus on the struggle,' I said.

As the police net was tightening I decided in discussion with our own circle that I should disappear from Durban for a while. Our amateurish flirtation with violent protest had resulted in wide-scale arrests and detentions. I would come to understand much later just how deeply our ranks were infiltrated. It was the lesson of a lifetime.

I spent several months dodging the police.

It was the loneliest period of my life. A strange car stopping outside the house, or any person looking at you more than once was enough to induce terror. My life became dependent on a few individuals for all my needs – from being able to eat, to go out and to have a home. I had to wear a variety of disguises. Once on a train from Port Elizabeth I heard the loud voices of railway police searching the train. Fearing that I would be arrested I disembarked at the next station, which happened to be Ladysmith in northern Natal.

It was a freezing cold night and rain was pouring down in torrents. As I picked up my bag on the platform I could see and hear the police chatting loudly in the railway office. I could not stay there. Black people were not allowed to loiter. I disappeared into the rain, walking through the ghost town and eventually reaching the highway that passed the town. As I waited in the rain

I felt the tears of loneliness pour down my face mingling with the freshness of the stinging rain. I longed for a warm bed and a hot meal prepared by my mother in my own home.

I decided I would return home. I phoned and told my mother. Two days after I had arrived there was a hammering at the door. The security police had arrived. I was taken in for questioning. The security apparatus seemed pervasive and all-powerful, confident that they had smashed the resistance. I was slapped about, threatened with indefinite detention and taunted with the fate of comrades killed mysteriously in jail.

After spending the night in a prison cell I was taken and dropped off in the city with a warning to stay out of politics.

I reconnected with Jayendra. He was leading the student protest at UDW. I needed to return and throw myself into the trenches. While I was in hiding the political networks were being revived and a systematic community-building campaign was under way, spearheaded by Pravin Gordhan.

* * *

A pharmacist by training, Pravin worked out of a crowded, busy pharmacy nestled under the flat that he lived in, in Prince Edward Street in Durban. It was a little India with traders and customers of all races scrambling over a chaotic marketplace. But it provided an ideal cover for secretive meetings of activists. Sitting at the centre of a spider's web of intrigue Pravin masterminded a new strategy of community organising. He was quietly spoken and a strategic thinker, articulate, but an unrelenting taskmaster who brooked no failures or bureaucratic inertia.

Theoretical study was a prerequisite. We reverted to reading the 'classics' of Marxism-Leninism. One book that was prescribed reading was John Cowley's *Community or Class Struggle* (1977), which argued that any socialist revolution was based on building strong community-based organisations.

It was a new approach to organising. Our first targets were Phoenix and Chatsworth, both large, sprawling working-class townships where many Indians had been relocated as a result of the Group Areas Act. Our preparations were painstaking. We spent weeks rehearsing scenarios and role-playing the bread-and-butter issues affecting local communities. The political regime allowed no room for error. Night after night, weekend after weekend of our preparation paid off.

We entered the homes confident: we knew how to address the wife, the husband, the child, depending on who answered the door; how to deal with hostility; and how to insert ourselves into the reality and hardship of the constituencies we wanted to organise. All this was done under the radar screen, concentrating on local issues, because we knew that preaching politics would scare off these communities. A Phoenix Working Community became the de facto credible community organisation mobilising public opinion against a move to an autonomous local authority populated by puppet councillors. As the campaign grew so did the political confidence of the community to defy the unilateral imposition of autonomy.

This organising style was to play an enormously important role in shaping my interaction with the poor. But at that moment, I felt the stirrings of something new. Life was about to change again for me.

At the same time, Jayendra and I continued to rebuild our political network but now we had learnt from our experiences. Our parents were terrified and the security police were keeping a close eye on our activities.

Once I went to meet Jayendra at his flat in town and his mother, Sanna, answered the door. She seldom stayed there, so I wasn't expecting her. She said to me:

'Who are you?'

I answered: 'I'm Clive, I'm looking for Jayendra.'

After entering, I spent what seemed like an hour talking to his mother. Sanna was very persistent, so I wove a story: 'I'm an art student and I'm doing some teaching. I met Jayendra on campus and we wanted to teach students in townships about art.'

To my horror, I discovered that she loved art and was an avid painter. Thankfully, Jayendra soon rejoined us and came to my rescue. The pretence continued for almost a year. We did not want to alert our parents to the details of our involvement in politics. Every time I met Sanna I had to have a conversation about art. She became like a second mother to me – and she still calls me Clive!

Over the year we had also graduated from Black Consciousness to socialism. Class analysis was able to provide answers to many of our questions. What we now understood to be the core of the system of racial apartheid was the need for a continual supply of cheap labour. We were attracted to the ANC and the South African Communist Party (SACP) because of this. At the same time, the ANC influence was becoming more pervasive and its principled non-racialism engaged us. The ANC in exile was overwhelmed by the mass exodus of thousands of young activists. It was not prepared for what had happened in 1976; no one had anticipated that.

We started listening to Radio Freedom, the ANC radio broadcasts from Lusaka. The annual 8 January statements of Oliver Tambo, President of the exiled ANC, were a call to action. Community struggles were flaring up countrywide.

Although we had moved on, Black Consciousness laid a very, very important foundation. In fact, it was essential to the development of most of the modern-day leadership. It gave us confidence, a feeling that we could create a uniquely South African identity that was inclusive of all the racially oppressed, that was empowering and insurgent – we could be proud of our blackness and find strength in that.

There was a line carved in the rock: black and white. There were no grey areas.

*   *   *

At the end of 1978 I discussed with Jayendra my need to get out of Durban for a while. I applied for a job as a temporary teacher and was sent to work at the Actonville Primary School in Benoni, near Johannesburg.

I shared a bachelor flat with Chooks Padayachee, a friend from Durban who I had grown up with, together with Amrith Manga, a comrade from university who lived in the area. We ended up teaching at the same school. Wearing borrowed ties and jackets the three of us presented ourselves for an interview with the principal the day before the school term began.

He took one look at us, a bedraggled bunch, and his jaw fell. He demanded to know what we were doing there. 'We are your temporary teachers sent by the Department,' we replied. We were reluctantly allocated our classes and so began our adventure in Benoni.

All three of us had read the writings of Paulo Freire, the revolutionary Brazilian educationalist, especially *The Pedagogy of the Oppressed*, which viewed the pupil as an active participant in the learning process. This theory of popular education was very influential in our work in SASO, and our approach was that we were there to learn as much as to teach.

But in a system dominated by Christian National Education, which enforced military-like discipline and left little space for independent and critical thinking, our experiment at self-motivated, independent learning initially died a miserable death. Fortunately, our relationship with our students was innovative and we found a way to reach them. We interacted with them as scholars whose opinions we respected and with whom we were prepared to debate. The local community, recognising our commitment, adopted us and we were treated to the most delicious foods sent to us on a regular basis. Life began to settle into a rhythm.

Some months later the ugly face of gangsterism raised its head. Local thugs walking past our flat decided to have a go at us. Apartheid bred a dynamic of brute power – white against black, men against women, urban versus rural. We were from Durban and people perceived us as taking their jobs and being the less well-off cousins who could be trampled on and bullied.

On this occasion the thugs insulted the memory of our mothers, who in my mind, whether living or dead, are sacred. I went downstairs with a cricket stump behind my back and asked them to repeat their insults. They duly did, drawing their knives confidently because they outnumbered us. Soon some lay injured on the floor and the rest beat a hasty retreat.

What I had not understood was that we had beaten the son of one of the big bosses of the underworld. They returned that evening, armed to the teeth. A running battle took place and we defended ourselves with the support of the local people.

Clearly this could have escalated into a full-scale war but we were fortunate to have a soccer star staying with us temporarily who mediated a truce. We never had any insults thrown at us again.

At school, however, my relationship with the principal was steadily deteriorating. The final blow came around the celebration of Republic Day. He gave strict instructions that the hated apartheid flag had to be raised and the detested national anthem sung. Knowing that the staff was divided, he made it mandatory for all to attend, but the three of us stayed behind in the staffroom while the rest of the school complied.

Later that day I was called to the office of a principal clearly fuming at our insubordination. 'Listen here, Mr Naidoo, there is only one principal and head of the school here. If you are not prepared to accept my authority then you need to leave.'

I listened to him quietly, did not say a word and then left his office. I will never respect blind loyalty and sycophancy. Personal commitment and service have to be earned.

Some months later the relationship had become intolerable and the political heat had died down in Durban. I announced my plans to leave. It was a sad parting with my students. I had really enjoyed my stint as a teacher and the lessons I had learnt would always remain a key feature of my organising style.

Years later, as the General Secretary of the Congress of South African Trade Unions (COSATU), when I was chairing the 'Teacher Unity Talks' that led to the formation of the South African Democratic Teachers Union (SADTU), I reconnected with my erstwhile principal as a participant. Now he was part of the founding leadership of a new teachers' union. It was a bittersweet moment as I welcomed him to the head office of COSATU.

PART THREE

Unity, Struggle and Power

Lessons from the Workers

Any attempt to divorce the link between the struggle for basic trade union rights on the factory floor from the broader struggle for human rights in society was not only undesirable but impossible in the South African context.

— COSATU statement

How many times has the liberation movement worked together with workers, and at the moment of victory betrayed the workers? There are many examples of that in the world . . . [prolonged applause]

You must support the African National Congress only so far as it delivers the goods, if the ANC government does not deliver the goods, you must do to it what you have done to the apartheid regime [prolonged applause, and shouts of 'Buwa! Buwa!'].

— Nelson Mandela

8

When I returned to Durban towards the end of 1979, I reconnected with Jayendra. 'Why don't we go down to Central Court and check what is going on in the unions?' I suggested one evening when Jayendra, myself and a few community and student activists were discussing the limitations of student and community politics.

'You must be mad! Why do you want us to get mixed up with a bunch of hard-line white workerists?' was the general response – except from Jayendra. Unbeknown to me, Jayendra had been drawn into an underground network and was key to the political organising tasks in Durban, including dealing with some of the old worker activists in the ANC.

He agreed to go with me – it would be a bit of an adventure. After my brief experience in education and my frustration with student politics, I was longing to put body and soul into something more challenging and fulfilling. This was the first time I articulated my interest in labour issues.

Students, as I had experienced repeatedly, could provide no continuity to the struggle. And while organising in the Indian community had taught me a lot about the skills and approach to organising poor people, which would prove invaluable in the future, the work was slow and painstaking. There was much prejudice amongst people who felt like the proverbial ham in the sandwich between white domination and black nationalistic aspirations.

The Indian community was buffered from the harshest aspects of racism that African communities experienced. Over the years, although hit by mass removals that created the dormitory Indian townships of Phoenix and Chatsworth, it proved to be a stable reservoir of semi-skilled labour for the manufacturing sector – in particular, the garment, leather and textile industries. Job reservation[1] still applied to these workers, but with the right to a better, but still unequal, education they occupied a higher position in the social hierarchy.

However, as a minority group South African Indians suffered the consequences of their own identity crisis. From the time of Mahatma Gandhi they resisted the oppression of colonisation, which gave birth to the philosophy of *satyagraha* (or non-violent mass protest), but equally, many feared the rule of the black majority.

While the educated class in the Indian community was almost unanimous in its opposition to apartheid, on the factory floor a deliberate tension was created between black and Indian workers by management. It was a prime example of apartheid's successful divide-and-rule policy.

I realised that the minority communities in which we worked were not going to be the engine for a revolution, no matter how important the work we were doing.

The union movement appealed to me. Perhaps it went back to my childhood, the frustration of those workers on the road, or to the impact of the 1972 strikes on me in high school when thousands of workers marched down the streets of Durban watched by heavily armed police and won their right to improved wages. The white racist regime had lost a fight and the defiance gave us hope that the government was not invincible.

I had read and reread Lenin's *What is to be Done?* My life up to then had reflected everything he had written about the naivety of student activism. I warmed to the student activist in *Anatomy of a Revolution* by Crane Brinton, who, like Lenin, concluded that workers, not students, were the vanguard of the revolution.

It was, nevertheless, an unusual step for a political activist to take. At this time, the union movement was very isolated from the political mainstream. Political activists considered unionism to be reformist and syndicalist in its approach and focus on narrow shop-floor issues.

The embryonic unions were led mainly by radical white intellectuals who were cautious about overt links with political movements given the history of repression that had decimated the South African Congress of Trade Unions (SACTU), which was aligned openly to the ANC. Determined to survive, the Federation of South African Trade Unions (FOSATU) had established itself as a tight federation with strongly centralised decision making and policies binding on affiliates. It focused on the battle with the bosses and the strengthening of the working class through unionisation and the power of their labour at the point of production.

The factory was the key. FOSATU pioneered the principle of direct worker control in South Africa, with worker delegates constituting the majority in all structures of the federation. It also developed a system of union branch executive committees composed of delegates from every factory. Other key principles included non-racialism, shop-floor structures, the training and development of shop stewards and the independence of unions from political organisations. It favoured intensive organising, based on the targeting of key plants.[2]

Although we had read up about the union movement, it was a completely new area for us. We also felt a bit uneasy because we were not sure of the reception we would get. Jayendra and I set off for Central Court, the head office of FOSATU, which was housed in a poky little apartment block in Gale Street in Durban.

There we met John Mawbey, who was the Regional Secretary of FOSATU in the former province of Natal. We spoke generally about who we were and that we were interested in volunteering, but said nothing about our political involvement.

Mawbey asked us to come back the following week. I returned, but Jayendra felt that he would not have the time and it would be too much of a compromise, given his high-profile leadership in the student movement.

Mawbey proposed that I help them revive the Sweet Workers Union – which was an old registered Indian union. It had been very prominent in the 1950s, but it collapsed in the aftermath of the banning of the liberation movements. By now, the union was barely lingering on. According to FOSATU we could use it to organise all workers in the sweet industry. It helped that it had a registered status so that we could demand the right to collective bargaining. I agreed to volunteer for the task but before I could begin, I had to be vetted by John Copelyn, one of the founding leaders of FOSATU who was banned at that time. John was an astute strategist and, as I got to know later, a gruelling taskmaster who would brook no opposition.

At this time I knew I was going to meet someone who was important, the mover and shaker behind the scenes. Copelyn and I had a friendly discussion but he would occasionally drop a penetrating question. 'So what are you politically involved in?' I was expecting the question so I looked him in the eye and casually replied, 'No, I'm not involved in any political organisation. I am keen to support the important work that FOSATU is doing.'

Our meeting ended after a few hours and when I went back to the offices two days later Mawbey's comment was: 'So are you ready for some real work?' My reply was instantaneous: 'Of course. What shall we do?' I was in, albeit as a volunteer.

After this I separated myself from community work and threw myself into this project. The factory we targeted was Beacon Sweets, where the union had been strong but had become dysfunctional. In the 1960s there had been a major strike and many Indian workers were victimised and replaced with Africans.

I would rise every morning and scramble into a Volksie (Volkswagen Beetle) borrowed from Bobby Marie and Shamim Meer, who were trusted political activists living close by, in order to connect with the shift change. I would do that three times a day. It would be years before I finally got a driver's licence. I stood at the side of the road, usually alone, and stopped people going to or from work, often making arrangements to meet them at their homes. I would choose older workers who might have been active in the union before.

It was lonely work. I would be there at 4.00 a.m. to catch workers changing shifts at 6.00 a.m. I learnt to be concise. I would have 200 metres from the bus stop to the factory gate to have a conversation. At first there was little reaction. 'You want to get me fired?' I would persist day after day. When someone took a pamphlet explaining the role of a trade union it was a start. My first lesson was 'don't talk politics'. I had spent weeks researching the factory, understanding the bread-and-butter issues, winning the confidence of those who stopped and listened. My opening line was: 'The union makes us strong; it unites us to win our rights to have our grievances heard, to stop unfair dismissals or arbitrary deductions from our low wages.'

Seeing me there week after week, workers began to engage with me. I started building a list of contacts. I began to offer workers whom I identified as potential leaders a lift into their communities, meeting with them in the safety of their homes, away from the prying eyes of management. An organiser's key job was spotting the 'leaders', the core cadres who, once won over, would begin organising inside the factory.

As the momentum grew, the conservative management reacted ferociously. They photographed workers talking to me, intimidated anyone who talked about the union inside the factory and at one stage tried to run me down as I stood outside the gate. The owner, Mr Zulman, was a friend of Chief Buthelezi, with whom I had already had one close encounter at the University of Durban-Westville (UDW).

* * *

I soon had my first lesson in the strategy and tactics of the trade unions. I knew nothing of the contemporary debates around registration of the new black unions, but Bobby and Shamim helped me to navigate the minefield that embraced the debate about whether to register our unions or not. I was a keen listener and I learnt fast.

The registration debate was boiling hot at the time. Professor Nic Wiehahn had issued his report – ironically on 1 May – recommending that trade unions with black members be allowed to participate in the collective bargaining system of the Industrial Conciliation Act, thus legalising the unionisation of a section of African workers.

The objective was to create a controlled environment within which these rights would be exercised to insulate the apartheid economic system from the increasing radicalisation and politicisation of the black working class. The apartheid planners were well aware that if unions remained unregulated, worker uprisings might result.

The initial proposal was that the reforms should only apply to workers with Section 10 rights. These were people who had been born in the urban areas and could be employed on a permanent basis, unlike the millions of migrant workers who worked under annual contracts and formed the bulk of the emerging unions. These migrant workers were to be excluded.

There were various other conditions for registration that we rejected as well. The debates around these conditions actually strengthened unionisation efforts, as thousands of workers could now legally contest the issues of collective bargaining and unionisation.

As an organiser, I was involved in explaining and discussing the issues. My sympathies, arising out of the non-collaborationist politics of my student and Black Consciousness days, were with those who opposed registration. But I learnt that we should not make a principle out of a tactic and I had to agree with the leadership of FOSATU that the reforms offered us the legal space to build democratic unions. I plunged into the debate to support the move towards registration on our terms. The critical question was whether it would advance or constrain our efforts at organising the working class.

The contestation of ideas around registration continued fiercely in the emerging independent unions as a whole. The General Workers Union (GWU) in Cape Town and the South African Allied Workers Union (SAAWU) took a principled position against registration. The standpoint for this bloc was not to register because this would lead to collaboration with the Industrial Conciliation system that aimed to co-opt certain sections of the black working class.

In hindsight not even P.W. Botha realised that the door was being opened to the growth of the most militant and organised workers movement in South Africa's history and that it would one day become one of the biggest challenges to his authoritarian rule.

*   *   *

At Beacon Sweets, years of inactivity and the memory of management victimisation made workers terrified to talk to me. However, we persevered, involving other FOSATU organisers and even the administration staff.

I used my experience of community organising; instead of standing outside the factory gate where people could be victimised and identified, we met with workers at their homes. It was a combination of community-based organising and factory organising.

On Saturdays the Gale Street offices of FOSATU were full of people. There was an amazing vibe, bringing scores of worker leaders together in earnest debates about growing the fledgling union organisation. The smell of sizzling meat and 'bunny chows'[3] filled the air. It was like a railway station bustling with all sorts of volunteers.

I became involved with a new circle of friends. It was the first time in my life that I had worked with white people. It was a remarkable experience and a shock to my system to meet white activists who were as committed and passionate as I was. There was a deliberate sense of egalitarianism and race played no role. I met Merle Favis, a labour activist from the same political background as me, who was working on the *South African Labour Bulletin* but fully involved with FOSATU. We were both being very careful not to blow our cover and expose our political affiliations. After a few months Merle and I became romantically involved and I moved in with her. She shared a house with a group of progressive white activists.

Merle had links with activists in the former Transvaal, such as Barbara Hogan, an ANC campaigner connected to the labour movement. Barbara was a disciplinarian who did not tolerate incompetence, and I often imagined that she would have made a great head of a boarding college. Through Barbara I connected with other activists such as Neil Aggett, Gavin Anderson and Sipho Kubheka, who were linked with SACTU and the ANC.

I stayed in touch with Jayendra, who continued to be active in student politics and the broader political project in Durban, and I would meet with Pravin Gordhan on a regular basis to learn more about the work of the ANC network. It was a time when the ANC underground movement was growing.[4] There was a certain pressure to participate but I felt that my energies would be better spent concentrating on my work in the fledgling union movement. I stayed in touch with my comrades and shared my experiences, but reacted negatively to a suggestion that I forward information about meetings.

By now the underground network was becoming increasingly conspiratorial and secretive. While it was an effective and coherent intelligence-gathering operation and provided sophisticated political analysis to our ANC comrades in exile, its weakness was an increasing tendency to centralise control over all strategic decisions inside the country. The majority of these comrades in Durban were Indian activists and this would later lead to an unfortunate racial typecasting of their participation. While I considered myself an ANC activist I believed very firmly that my primary loyalty was to the union movement.

9

I had been organising at Beacon Sweets for about six months when another opportunity presented itself. At the FOSATU offices I was introduced to Mfezeko 'Prof' Sineke, a young man who was an active leader in the textile union. He worked in a factory called South African Fabrics in Clairwood, Durban. He arranged for me to be employed there. I felt that it was an opportunity to gain real experience of workplace hardships and organisation. Prof was articulate, confident and full of energy. We became good friends.

My first twelve-hour night shift at the factory was a nightmare. I had not slept during the day. As I took a crowded bus from the central terminus in Durban and we wound our way past all the factories that lined Umbilo Road, I watched the shift change leaving long queues of tired workers waiting for their transport home. I was one of them now, I realised, as I disembarked at the bustling centre of Clairwood and made my way to work.

I arrived at the factory and was dispatched by security to a shift supervisor who stared at me and said: 'No loafing around here, sonny. You will be out of that gate as fast as you came in. Go and change into your overalls now. I will take you to your department.' I became an assistant operator. There were two rows of knitting machines, and there were hundreds of needles knitting the fabric together. My job was to watch and if I saw a needle had broken, I had to stop the machine and call the operator so that the needle could be replaced.

I had to walk up and down the factory floor to monitor the many machines on either side. Initially I thought, oh this is fine, it's an easy enough job. But when you are watching hundreds of needles you need to be very observant and alert if you are to see even one needle break and cause a fault line.

As the night went on I found I was beginning to sleepwalk. At midnight there was a half-hour break and I slept so soundly that they had to shake me to get me up afterwards. I went home that morning to sleep, and had to be shaken awake to go back to work in the late afternoon.

What I learnt at South African Fabrics over the next few months was not only the discipline and the harshness of work, which are not things to understand theoretically, but how deep-seated apartheid's rule was in the economy.

The factory was divided into Indian and African departments, each with its own change rooms. I spent time sitting here with other Indian workers, who were not aware that I had come in through the union. There was prejudice, in one sense, and they really wanted nothing to do with unions. Break times here revolved around playing cards – *thunni* specifically, a game that had been imported through indentured labourers from the south of India. I sat and listened. It was fascinating to find out the issues that affected them and to try to understand the psychology of working-class Indian life.

There was a great deal of insecurity and apathy. They worked very hard and were dedicated. I was also struck by the loyalty they felt for the company. They talked about their families, and a lot about women and events in their neighbourhoods. Politics did not seem to concern them. I felt isolated and I could not relate to the conversations. At the same time, I acknowledged that we would have to organise the Indian workers to build a union in the factory. It would be a hard task.

I threw my lot in with the black working class. Prof Sineke and I discussed how we could organise the Indian workers in the factory and I suggested that he visit the Indian dressing room. When he appeared, people said, 'Ah, we are not interested in your union; what do you want to do – get us dismissed or worse still thrown into jail?'

But he returned the following week and by this time I had started to sow some seeds in the minds of my fellow workers. My explanation of surplus value was now informed by practical experience – the number of steps and kilometres we had walked per night, the value of the cloth spawned by these giant machines and the profit margins that the bosses had earned.

Gradually people started to listen and understand the issues. And when I was given another job, to go to the dye house to test regularly the dye on pieces of cloth, this was a brilliant opportunity to connect with all sorts of people. We were organising, meeting and talking, and soon the union had a majority.

The factory became a base for the National Union of Textile Workers in the Clairwood/Mobeni industrial complex of Durban. Strong leaders, such as Andre Joyisa who became important in the textile union and COSATU, came from that factory. I had learnt so much from the workers and shop-floor activists that I felt ready for my next challenge.

* * *

Sometime in 1981, A.C. Naicker, a charismatic Indian leader of dissatisfied leather workers in Pietermaritzburg, approached FOSATU for help. Ironically, it was not the bosses he was unhappy with, but the union. As he explained:

> *The General Secretary of the union collaborated with the bosses. The bosses were given to understand that we weren't fighting for the rights of the workers but wanted to introduce a black union to take over control. So the General Secretary blacklisted me. He said that I'm the one trying to get the black people to take over.*[5]

Having demonstrated my commitment to the workers' movement, Alec Erwin, then the FOSATU General Secretary, asked me to relocate to Pietermaritzburg as a paid FOSATU organiser and help with their efforts. I discussed the possibility with Merle and we both felt that it was a great opportunity to develop my organising experience. This was to be my project and the goal of organising Indian and African workers in the leather industry, a major employer in Pietermaritzburg, was a tangible one.

A.C. Naicker was articulate and forthright. He attacked the union leadership for its complicity with the bosses. He would have risen to great heights in management if he had not taken a principled position against union corruption. Together with AC, we used the community as the entry point, organising workers at house meetings before going to the factory. Our objective was to build a leadership grouping as well. It was quite a small community, so with AC's help I was quickly able to identify the key leaders, factory by factory.

The old union was resistant to change, so workers were ripe to join a new formation. At that time FOSATU was growing quite rapidly in Pietermaritzburg in the metal industries and so we decided to put together a leather workers' project. Out of this we formed the Tanning and Allied Leather Workers Union.

The work was hard but I felt fulfilled. There was an innate wisdom in the workers living in the hostels and in the townships, with none of the intellectual meanderings of student politics. Here it was the grindstone of daily existence.

I learnt patience as a virtue. My instinct to snap back at management if I felt my rights had been infringed was tempered by the sure knowledge that slogans and rhetoric would never win us our freedom. It was a painstaking and arduous task to unite, organise and empower our selected constituencies to fight their own battles; and the place to start was the bread-and-butter issues that affected their daily lives.

It was during this time that I met Geoff Schreiner, who was the National Union of Metal Workers of South Africa (NUMSA) organiser in Pietermaritzburg. A white intellectual without any political affiliation, though deeply opposed to apartheid, he represented an important layer of the white community who translated their opposition into action. Geoff was one of many white comrades doing unpublicised work to strengthen the movement against apartheid.

We hit it off from the start. He shared a flat with his wife, Josephine, and I stayed with them for a few months while learning the ropes of being in Pietermaritzburg again. I enjoyed their company. Later I found a run-down flat in the centre of town through some friends.

The FOSATU offices were right across the road. This was unlike other cities in the country – not all black people had been relocated and Indian residential occupation was tolerated in certain streets. The offices were in a block with the downstairs area occupied by retail outlets. The upstairs was a large area haphazardly divided into untidy offices. There was a modern telex machine and at the entrance was a rickety desk at which the hauntingly beautiful and graceful Dorah Khambule sat. She was always elegantly dressed, often in black dresses, making her look so much like a schoolteacher.

She spoke with a lisp that took some time to understand but her friendly smile and warm disposition was perfect for the face of the office. I never heard Dorah utter a harsh word. She always listened patiently to the woes and travails of every person. She was our resident psychologist, caring for the emotional distress we all went through periodically. When my mother was ill she would hold my hand and say, 'Jay, don't worry. I will pray for her and for you. She will recover. Let us go back to our work. God will look after her.'

While I consider myself more spiritually inclined than religious, there was a deep-rooted belief system amongst ordinary people that I instantly trusted.

It was an embedded spirituality, an honesty that was tangible, and it connected Dorah and many others to my mother throughout my years.

Then there was John Makhatini, the wise *tata* (father) who was the elder of the office. Barely educated, he was the salt of the earth and bursting with life. He communicated with passion in meetings with workers, firing them up and giving them the confidence to overcome their fears of dismissal and arrest. He was a marvellous storyteller, like so many of the older leaders who had grown up during the political struggles fought decades before, and we would listen intently as he regaled us with stories of the struggle.

Each story carried a lesson: how to talk to workers terrified of losing their jobs; how to relate to families and the customs of traditional life when organising in rural communities; how to talk to the police when they confronted you. These were not the competencies you learnt in a university or a volunteer textbook. I found myself in an exciting laboratory of life, with ordinary people as the best teachers.

The most important lesson I learnt would last me a lifetime: that the bedrock of resistance to apartheid was the working people, whose remarkable fortitude broke the back of apartheid.

I often went with Makhatini to his home in Klaarwater, on the outskirts of Pietermaritzburg. He drove an ancient truck that broke down more times than I can remember. We would huddle around the engine trying to find and solve the problem – usually with success. We had very little money and transport was scarce. We made do with what we had.

Then there was Moses Ndlovu, who joined us later as we began to expand into organising paper workers. He was a driver at Browns Supermarket. Another great and intuitive leader, he had been banned for years. Moses's order had just expired and in spite of the danger he joined our small band of organisers. When Moses came to the office he radiated confidence, his face constantly wrinkled by infectious laughter. Moses was as solid as an elephant, as his name denoted,[6] always firm and unwavering in his commitment.

This was the initial 'gang of five' – the union office team that was set up to consolidate and expand the FOSATU base in Pietermaritzburg. We were a family, spending much time together – days, nights, weekends – in interminable meetings and seminars and training shop stewards. The union office was our home and this was very satisfying.

At the same time, I connected with established ANC activists in the Indian community, such as Dr Chota Motala, an eminent doctor in the community, whose surgery was a meeting place for community activists and whose daughter, Shireen Motala, worked in FOSATU as the education officer. Together with A.S. Chetty, these were the stalwarts who connected the struggles of the Indian and African communities. And they provided the welcome fragrance of home-cooked curries on a regular basis.

There was also a group of younger community activists whom I had recruited to help in our organising campaign at the factories: Faisel Ismail, later to become our World Trade Organization (WTO) representative in Geneva; and Ahmed Bawa, a brilliant international scientist. We had developed a mass-attack strategy. We would arrive in numbers for a massive blitz outside a factory.

At 5.00 a.m. during winter in Pietermaritzburg, the 'sleepy hollow' was often below freezing. But there was always activity: vendors selling *magwinyas* (fat cakes) and mealies (corn on the cob) grilled over a large drum of glowing coals; workers wrapped in blankets and worn-out overcoats streaming in and out of the factory gates. They were tired by the weary toil of eking out an existence in these old factories.

It was drudge work. The long haul from their homes for the long wait in queues for buses, then the tough grind at machines that churned out the goods that these workers themselves could not afford.

We started a campaign. Day after day, we would have five or six people standing outside the factory gates handing out pamphlets, talking to people, making contacts. The situation became vicious because the employers were determined not to have FOSATU in their factories.

Even though we had signed members, we couldn't get workers on stop order; we had to hand-collect our fees, and the bosses were still victimising workers who joined us. The only real income we would have in those days was what was collected from workers in subscriptions. We would live on a diet of what workers ate – *amasi*, a fermented milk, mixed with bread and sugar, a bunny chow or more often than not I would go to bed with a bowl of ProNutro breakfast cereal. But workers trusted us.

We struck on the idea of using the constitution of the Benefit Fund as an organising weapon. The strategy came from A.C. Naicker during one of our discussions. He explained that there were people who were entitled to benefits who never received them:

The Industrial Council had a sick fund. Now if you were sick the union was supposed to apply for that sick fund from the Industrial Council. So this lady went and gave all her benefits, all her certificates from the doctor to claim from that Fund. She made her claim but she never received any money. Every time she went to the office there was always a story given to her. It turned out that the cheque had been cashed by somebody else.[7]

We organised the majority of workers to sign a petition and demand a general meeting calling for us as the new leadership of the Benefit Fund. That became a major strategy and ended up with an independent arbitrator presiding over a mass meeting of all the workers who voted for the new leadership of this Benefit Fund, led by A.C. Naicker.

The employers, agitated by this victory and terrified of the uncompromising non-racial trade unionism of FOSATU, reacted. Victimisation became the norm. AC was fired; and because he was blacklisted by the union as it was in bed with the employers, it was impossible for him to get a job. It was a sacrifice he had to live with for the rest of his working life.

AC is a true working-class hero – one of many. This tough experience taught us important lessons: how do you organise workers in a conservative 'yellow' union; and how do you deal with established unions? We learnt that a full-frontal assault did not work. Our timing was also not right, because the Trade Union Council of South Africa (TUCSA) unions, the old, predominantly white-dominated trade unions, were strong and we were still struggling for the basic rights to represent workers and be recognised.

But this experience taught us, after TUCSA fell apart in 1987, how to integrate their unions into the progressive labour movement.

10

The FOSATU unions in Natal were expanding. The Springs-based union in the food sector – the Sweet, Food and Allied Workers Union (SFAWU) – under Chris Dlamini, was planning to open a branch in Pietermaritzburg.

My first impression of Chris was that of a 'township dude' very much in my mould. I was drawn to him. He was intellectually agile and clearly a survivor, like most activists. I suppose our commitment to the cause steered us away from a life of delinquency we could have easily followed. Chris had an effective way of handling people – remaining engaged but never threatening, with only the implied risk that life could get very serious if his leadership was undermined. I have seen that quiet sense of steely determination in many working-class activists.

Back in Pietermaritzburg, one of the NUMSA organisers, Willie Manthe, was deployed to set up the fledgling SFAWU. He was from Woodlands, a coloured township close to the city centre, and was active in the local coloured Labour Party. Its tactic was to exploit the legal space within the apartheid system. The Labour Party worked closely with Inkatha, which also pursued a similar strategy. Manthe was hard-working but my impression was that he was easily influenced.

Over Christmas in 1980, Geoff and I left Makhatini and Manthe in charge of the office and drove down to Cape Town in Geoff's old Volksie for a holiday. We were exhausted after months of slogging it out with the enemy in the trenches, and really looked forward to a few weeks of summer fun in the laid-back and carefree Mediterranean climate of Cape Town.

We encountered Howie Gabriels at a beach party. He was a union organiser with the GWU and was to become a close friend with whom I would share my union life in later years. He was not an ideologue and it was refreshing to have him as a confidant.

Howie was with Trevor Manuel, a comrade and leader in Cape Areas Housing Action Committee (CAHAC), which was launched in 1980 in Cape Town and involved in organising rent boycotts and community struggles on the Cape Flats. They had heard that some progressive trade unionists from Natal were in town and wanted to have a meeting with us. We were not really interested. December was vacation time; even the security police took a break.

It was strange for me to meet comrades who spoke Afrikaans as their home language. I had grown up in Natal, an outpost of the British Empire. Afrikaans was the language of the security establishment spoken with the harshness of apartheid rule. I was fourteen when I was given a choice between Latin and Afrikaans as a second language. It was not a choice. I associated everything that did not respect my being, my culture, my cuisine, with the Afrikaans language. But here was Howie and so many other comrades whose mother tongue was Afrikaans.

After a lazy few weeks in Cape Town, we returned to Pietermaritzburg and found Norman Middleton, the Natal leader of the coloured Labour Party, occupying the desk in the central foyer of our offices.

Our exchange of greetings was frosty. Battle lines seemed to have been drawn across the floor. We huddled together with Makhatini to find out what was happening. He told us that a meeting had taken place while we were away, and that there had been all sorts of allegations made against Geoff and me about being anti-Inkatha and critical of Chief Buthelezi.

Detailed information had been sent to Inkatha's headquarters in Ulundi about us and it had been discussed in the highest ranks of Inkatha. It transpired that Buthelezi and his key advisers were outraged that some 'fifth column' was developing in the union movement.

At this stage FOSATU was walking a very thin line in its relationship with Inkatha. An uneasy truce existed. FOSATU espoused a political philosophy that shunned popular politics and which was later to develop into a notion of an independent workers' party.

This was spelt out in FOSATU General Secretary Joe Foster's speech to the 1982 FOSATU Congress, in which he 'cautioned against "unprincipled" alliances with "non-worker groups"',[8] arguing:

Fosatu's task will be to build the effective organisational base for workers to play a major political role as workers. Our task will be to create an identity, confidence and political presence for worker organisation. The conditions are favourable for this task and its necessity is absolute.[9]

In the ranks of Black Consciousness, Inkatha was reviled as a collaborator; but amongst workers there was respect and admiration for Buthelezi. Here was a leader working within the system but often forceful in his comments.

Buthelezi had cleverly used the symbols and the traditions of the ANC and its much loved and distinguished President Chief Albert Luthuli of Groutville, Zululand, and Africa's first Nobel laureate.[10] In fact, the launch of Inkatha in 1975 was supported by the ANC, which had hoped that this would represent a mass base for the liberation movement within the country. But the relationship quickly unravelled as influence and power grew in the bureaucracy around Buthelezi.

In this period of the early 1980s, Inkatha was a powerful force and the bush telegraph had informed us that the Inkatha executive had taken a decision to bring Buthelezi and his entire cabinet to Pietermaritzburg. The intention was to convene a political rally to deal with us, 'these young radicals' who threatened the political hegemony of Inkatha in Natal.

This was the first crisis that reverberated throughout the organisation, threatening to split our ranks. How would we deal with this? FOSATU was barely out of the starting blocks. There had been a conscious decision to steer clear of politics. We had spent an inordinate amount of time in our education seminars and discussions on the challenges of overt political unionism. This, we felt, had been the weakness of SACTU. When the political leadership was detained or jailed or when it fled into exile, it meant that it also decimated the ranks of SACTU because many activists played a dual or triple role. In addition, the political reality was that the working class and the bulk of the population were loyal to Inkatha and Chief Buthelezi.

There were powerful leaders, Jeffrey Vilane, Dumisani Mbangwa and others, who would later play a leading role in the future consolidation of the progressive union movement and the ANC but were then closely linked to Ulundi and Inkatha. I had been particularly careful to avoid any political discussion. Our concern was how to organise workers and win our rights on the factory floor. Workers in places such as Isithebe, and Ezakheni in Ladysmith, which legally fell under the control of the Zulu homeland, were excluded from the provisions of labour law.

This was a boon to employers who wanted to avoid the clutches of unionism. They enjoyed the added protection of homeland henchmen to keep the unions out and avoid even cursory attention to the limited rights granted to black workers.

When the reports to Ulundi of Willie Manthe and Norman Middleton came to light, the FOSATU executive, now dominated by the growing base in Johannesburg, decided to act decisively. Chris Dlamini came down and convened a National Executive Committee of SFAWU. Manthe was dismissed and Middleton's employment not recognised because of the view that the branch was not duly constituted. A major crisis ensued.

Inkatha viewed this as a full-frontal assault and all hell broke loose. Camps were formed. Every meeting was seen as hostile. Attacks seemed imminent and battles broke out in the factories. Shop-steward committees were divided. Tensions rose in the region. Months of tenuous organising were thrown into jeopardy and the whole federation was rocked by the conflict. Workers were extremely conflicted. We were paralysed.

I was incensed. I felt abused by politicians who used workers as 'cannon fodder'. I detested the self-appointed arrogance, but I knew I had to bide my time. We would fight back another day. Now it was wise to retreat and collect our forces. Workers across the province were being mobilised by Inkatha. People were being press-ganged into making a decision not to belong to FOSATU. It was certainly not going to be the last time this happened.

The entire episode affected me profoundly. Although I had been careful, I understood that this was fragile political terrain, and my student populism had endangered our painstaking efforts at organising the working class. I would forever afterwards remain sceptical about populism. It is easy to bring down a house that has taken such a long time to build.

Strategically, we understood that we were too young as an organisation. There was a danger of the tide turning against us purely through the ferocity of the attacks. We had to negotiate.

* * *

Alec Erwin, the FOSATU General Secretary, was appointed to lead our team into discussions with Inkatha. It was a grave moment for us. He and the rest of the leadership of FOSATU had some tough words with us but they were loyal to us and threw their support behind us. It would have been an easy way out of the crisis to sacrifice Geoff and me. But we fought on principle, and this was to lay the foundations of a deep and lasting friendship, even in the times when we disagreed with each other.

FOSATU also realised that if it did not take a firm stand it would be forever subservient to the Inkatha demagogues. This was another lesson that I would revisit later in my life – to avoid the tendency for leadership to use workers' organisations as conveyor belts for their political aspirations. I would always insist that the democracy of the unions be respected.

The regional conference of FOSATU was held in Pinetown to discuss the conflict with Inkatha. Every union branch and local committee came to the meeting as this was an explosively emotive issue. The morning rang with the ominous sounds of the Zulu war dance; its slow rhythms, the stomping of the feet, the spring of muscular legs, the drum of the heartbeat pounding.

The two factions faced up to each other in a space that was too small for the throbbing crowd. We were in the old offices in Pinetown, just outside Durban. The meeting opened. The chairperson brought the rowdy house to order. He led with an impassioned prayer that called for the ancestors to guide the leaders that day.

Alec presented a report of what had happened. He appealed for calm and asked for the worker leaders to exercise caution in the decisions they were about to make.

After what seemed like an interminable debate in which very little movement was made by either side, Jeffrey Vilane, the dynamic leader from the heart of Zululand and a senior member in Inkatha, stood up and made a rousing address that set the tone of the meeting.

He said: 'Brothers, we are all Inkatha leaders here. We are not discussing that. Inkatha is our political home and that is the reality. No one here questions that. But here we are in a FOSATU meeting. Here we are to discuss FOSATU issues. And what has happened here in Pietermaritzburg is a breach of the FOSATU rules and policies that we as the workers have decided. You, Manthe and Middleton, by going behind our backs, have breached the democracy of our union, which we control and we have developed.'

This intervention saved the day and swung the conference, which endorsed the dismissal of Manthe and the cancellation of the illegal appointment of

Middleton. Worker leaders dealing with us day after day, week after week had more confidence in the union taking care of their worker issues. This was their union and they had respected our commitment and sacrifice as the intellectuals who had worked with them.

It was a major leap of faith. They had decided against the wishes of Inkatha that had their loyalty and political allegiance.

But now, in this period, the challenge was to undo the damage of the crisis. Factory by factory, we fought a battle to retain the loyalty of members. Meeting late at night in small towns, darkened villages on sugar cane farms and in townships, it was a fierce contest. In the end we still lost a minority of factories to an alternative Inkatha-aligned union that was started by Manthe and Middleton.

The contradictions became severe. Inkatha reacted to our being able to organise on the factory floor. Intimidation started against our leading activists and this forced them to make a choice.

Then we were hit by a spontaneous strike at Union Co-operative, a sugar mill we were organising in the small town of Dalton, close to Pietermaritzburg.

The factory was run largely by Germans in an area that reflected a bygone era, from the station commander at the local police station to the local farmers. The Dalton strike was a bitter one. All the workers were dismissed. When Alec and I arrived, management refused to talk to us. By the end, close to 400 workers had been arrested, herded into police vans and sent to jails around the area.

That first afternoon in Dalton, Alec and I stood at the top of a hill and looked down at the sugar cane fields and the smoke coming out of the factory's chimneys. The management had got in scab labour and the white workers were still running the mill. We watched as police took workers away. I looked at this huge expanse of sugar cane; with the wind blowing across this peaceful blanket of green I could sense the tension.

By now it was late afternoon and a few domestic workers came to us and reported what they had heard in their employers' homes.

'Leave immediately. When night falls they are going to kill you,' they warned.

There were a dozen places where we could have been ambushed. It made no sense to report this to the police because they could have been at the centre of the plot. We wasted no further time. We drove back in silence until we saw the twinkling lights of Pietermaritzburg.

But we went back the next day. Black people dared not speak to us openly. In the end, the workers were evicted from the hostels. We went to the police station and confronted the commander. Alec spoke about the actions of the police, which were so one-sided they were increasing the tension. This was later to be quoted in the drawn-out court case as an example of our violent strategy to attack the police station!

The legal action we took was around the armed dispossession of people's homes. A spoliation order was sought against the fact that 400 people were evicted from their hostels and had nowhere to go. It was one of the first times we used the law in defence of workers' rights.

Every morning during the trial, the workers marched in single file from the Edendale Lay Centre where they were staying, through the streets of Pietermaritzburg and to the court building. The whole event played an important role in building a spirit of defiant unionism in the Midlands region that would eventually see some of our fiercest battles against apartheid.

Our legal team fought a valiant battle in court, but we lost. The law clearly was intermeshed with apartheid in most cases. The daily sight of marching workers camped outside the Supreme Court building was also an intimidating sight for the all-white judiciary, whose mandate was the execution of apartheid laws. The fear of the 'swart gevaar' (black danger) with 'rooi gevaar' (red or communist danger) threatened their stable and civilised white preserve.

For months I had lived with these workers. I had got to know many of them personally and shared their hardships, hopes and frustrations. Now it was over and they could only contemplate being shipped out to the Bantustans, forever to be blacklisted by the labour recruiters and condemned to poverty.

I felt the loneliness of my life in my room that night. This was my first strike and it was a bitter experience that left me drained and empty. I analysed every step of the dispute. There were not many alternatives we could have pursued. The edifice of apartheid seemed invincible.

11

In 1981 Chris Dlamini, President of SFAWU, offered me a job as an organiser. My immediate challenge was to stop the loss of factories to the new Inkatha-affiliated union set up by Manthe and Middleton. They had offices a few streets from ours.

The battles were fierce. Huddled in the headlights of our car late at night we would meet with workers from the Noodsberg Sugar Mill. We had to fight, section by section, to keep the workers in the union. I was joined in this endeavour by Petros Ngcobo and the team from the office. The arguments were bitter. Were we anti-Inkatha?

It took months of painstaking work to convince workers that we represented their best interests. A big part of this victory was our principle of worker control. All our structures in the union were dominated by shop-floor workers. This was their home, almost akin to their church, and our commitment was never in doubt.

But we were fighting three battles simultaneously: against employers for recognition; defending ourselves against a hostile state; and now a third front had opened up with Inkatha keen to destroy our presence. Caution had to be our hallmark.

We plunged back into the slog of organising and saw a steady strengthening of our unions. The apartheid regime had introduced a new plan to freeze pensions and prevent workers from accessing their pensions until they were 65. It was aiming to transfer responsibility for providing old-age state pensions to individual workers. Coming on the back of other worker grievances, including company pensions and the struggle for union recognition, this was the spark that started a bush fire.

In 1981 a wave of pension-related strikes paralysed different sectors of industry. FOSATU convened a range of workshops aimed at analysing the grievances of workers and developing alternate proposals. Key to this was the right of workers to take their pensions in a lump sum at their retirement and to stretch the provisions of funeral and disability benefits to their extended families. The demand, in line with our campaign for the right to democratically elected shop-steward committees, was for joint control of these new schemes.

Using this as a competitive advantage SFAWU launched a campaign across the sugar industry making these issues part of our organising. The sugar industry had already introduced a 'sweetheart union', the National Union of Sugar Manufacturing and Refining Employees, headed by Mr S. Nsibande, who had been given full right of entry to all the factories. Local management supported the new union, which was endorsed by Chief Buthelezi. They hoped to stymie the growth of the independent unionism of FOSATU.

By 1983 we had made a breakthrough in several mills and achieved the right to negotiations separate from the bargaining council. Using the workers' grievances, we then formulated a new scheme that led to the first provident fund in the country. This was jointly controlled by the union and management in the CG Smith Group of companies, one of the two dominant companies in the sugar industry. The launch in 1984 was a major victory for workers and shook the foundations of the pension fund industry. The fund was to be managed by eight trustees, of which four were to be elected by us, allowing us equal say in the running of the benefit scheme. The new fund went a long way in addressing our problems with pension funds.

Soon SFAWU membership was growing at a tremendous rate in the food sector. We split the region into three primary nodes of operation: Pietermaritzburg, Durban and Empangeni. I left the social network that had provided me moral, political and social support and relocated to Durban to drive the efforts along the coast, leaving the experienced Petros Ngcobo heading the Midlands region of the union.

I spent time with Chris Dlamini. He and I shared a vision of the union and a common political cause. We were also both risk-takers. Chris was tenacious and a life of hardship, often in dangerous environments, had made him a savvy revolutionary. He knew when to avoid bloody confrontation, and when to mobilise for a bitter fight. He commanded respect, not just on the shop floor but in the community. We had endless discussions in his home in Springs into the early hours of the morning, or while trawling through shebeens,[11] and we founded a unique friendship based on trust and confidence.

Kellogg's, where Chris worked, was a hotbed of politics in Thembisa, on the East Rand, past the old mining towns of Benoni and Brakpan. An international company, it tolerated our activities and even tacitly allowed them. Sanctions were tightening and they were feeling the pressure. We were building a base insulated from the glare of security force attention.

In Durban I negotiated the use of a set of offices in Gale Street. I was now the Regional Secretary in Natal. The run-down office got a new coat of paint and I hired a secretary, Maud Dhlomo, who was highly efficient. She was young and dynamic and would later become a leading activist and the Deputy Director General in the Department of Foreign Affairs. Right now, in the ex-flat, we had to toss a coin for who would have the bigger office. She won and got the ex-kitchen and I was assigned to the ex-bathroom. We needed the bedroom space for our meetings.

The morning organising drive usually began at 4.00 a.m. and a momentum was building up. We began organising a number of large food factories along Umbilo Road – BB Bread, Clover Dairies, iJuba (a sorghum brewery). Strikes over recognition and wages exploded. A new strategy – 'siyalala' – emerged. This was a sleep-in strike where workers occupied the factory premises. It brought us into stark conflict with the employers and security forces but proved to be very effective in making our voices heard.

It was in one of the annual wage negotiations with the sugar conglomerate Tongaat Hulett Group in Empangeni that I first encountered Blade Nzimande, who was later to become a leading intellectual and then the Secretary General of the South African Communist Party (SACP), and later (in 2009) the Minister of Higher Education and Training.

He was in training, sponsored by the Tongaat Hulett Group, to study industrial psychology. When Blade Nzimande walked in with J.B. Magwaza, the head of corporate affairs, one of the first senior black executive appointments in the country at that time, I remarked: 'How now, Mr Magwaza, you have decided to bring another black face into your team. But power still remains in white hands.'

We had a good relationship and Magwaza was active in the Black Management Forum, a body representing black professionals and managers that I had spoken to and which was in many ways caught in the crossfire between the unions and management. We had an unforgiving view at that time of co-option and anyone who accepted appointment into any level of management was soon removed from a union leadership position.

Blade Nzimande was to become a confidant; he soon departed the ranks of management to join those of labour.

We had many pressing issues to handle. The unity talks were proceeding slowly. State repression was not going to accommodate the egos of working-class leaders – a time bomb was ticking.

* * *

On 5 February 1982 Neil Aggett was murdered in detention. Neil was a young doctor at Soweto's Baragwanath Hospital and an official of the Food and Canning Workers Union. He was found dead in his cell at John Vorster Square, the 51st person – and the first white – to die in police detention since 1963. Police said he had hanged himself.

The inquest, on 29 June 1982, revealed that he had endured severe inter-rogation and it was after a 60-hour session that he was found hanging in his cell. A Mr Lerumo testified that he had seen Aggett being escorted back to his cell only hours before his death, and that he had appeared to be in pain, had a spot of blood on his forehead and walked with enormous difficulty, like an extremely ill man.[12]

Neil had been a friend; the news left me drained of feeling, I guess because my grief and loss were overwhelmed by a sick fear. Death was stalking us. Who would be next? Life as an activist was dangerous. Life as a trade union organiser could be fatal. We were attacking the core of the apartheid state. The point of production was its Achilles heel.

Since 1978, Aggett had helped the union to set up a Johannesburg branch in his spare time. He was arrested in 1981 in a police crackdown on emerging unionists. Amongst those held without trial in that period were other union colleagues: Emma Mashinini, Thozamile Gqweta, Sisa Njikelana and Sam Kikine.

The shock of Aggett's death was to give new impetus to the halting movement towards unity between emerging unions. Two solid years of painstaking deliberations were marked by mistrust and conflict. They were stymied by differences of political outlook, organisational methods and personalities.

The roots of the inter-union conflict lay in the rapid growth and rising militancy of the union movement. The wave of industrial action in the Border region and in SAAWU was taking East London by storm.

FOSATU's growth had been steady. By 1982 it had about 54 000 members, the largest bloc among the emerging unions. Some of its affiliates had developed into national industrial unions. The Food and Canning Workers Union (FCWU) was beginning to break out of its Western Cape base, to which it had been confined since the repression of SACTU during the early 1960s.

At this time, we became aware of another phenomenon – 'community unions', which were strongly influencing the style of union organisation. In 1979 we had experienced the Fattis & Monis strike, organised by the FCWU in the Western Cape. Weak and vulnerable, unskilled workers turned to their communities and mobilised them to boycott employer products.

In the same year, workers at Ford's Cortina plant in Port Elizabeth went on strike after management dismissed Thozamile Botha, a Ford worker and leader of the Port Elizabeth Black Civic Organisation (PEBCO). The strike spread to other factories in the area and Botha was reinstated.

The rationale behind this kind of action was that workplace interests were inseparable from community interests. By the early 1980s unions like SAAWU were arguing that the shop-floor demands of the workers could not be separated from their daily lives and political problems. After the PEBCO strike, many township-based community organisations began organising working-class constituencies. Political scientist Tom Lodge says that this tactic was 'borrowed from the history books', or rather, from oral history, and had been employed by SACTU in the 1950s.[13]

Significantly, too, the new community unions advocated open identification with the liberation movement. Unions began to support the political perspectives of the banned ANC. After its formation in 1983 they affiliated to the UDF. I felt a sense of empathy, but our approach in FOSATU was far more cautious. I was still finding my feet in the unions but, more importantly, I felt that with such a vulnerable base, an open identification with politics could also endanger our attempts to build a powerful labour movement in the long term.

While FOSATU tried to guard its independence and keep its distance from the 'populists', it could not remain completely aloof. The spirit of the times demanded that it should begin to discuss the political role of the trade union movement. Already in SFAWU we were debating a more nuanced approach to politics.

Although there had been talk of unity as early as 1979, it was not until 8 August 1981 that a meeting was held at Langa in Cape Town. The meeting was convened by the GWU and was attended by over 100 representatives of all 29 of the major emerging unions, including the Cape-based FCWU and GWU, the newly formed SAAWU and affiliates of FOSATU, the Council of Unions of South Africa (CUSA) and the independent Cape Town Municipal Workers Union, representing mainly coloured workers.[14]

The immediate objective of the Langa summit was to develop a united response to the newly introduced labour laws that had emerged from the Wiehahn report. These laws aimed to divide the emerging unions, but they also extended some rights previously denied to black unions. This went to the heart of the division. Should unions refuse registration? Or should they use the space created by the law?

My view coincided with that of FOSATU. I felt we needed an opening, a legal space, and that if we could benefit from registration, we should go ahead. But, like most of the other FOSATU leadership, I believed we could not comply with the proposal for separate branches or the exclusion of migrant workers and that we should be allowed to join the Industrial Council.

I remember the SAAWU guys arriving for that meeting. The tension hung thickly in the air. It was like bringing together in one room people who would be prepared to confront each other physically. Later we would be united by the repression of the government, but at that time, before the brutality intensified, there was less urgency about unity.

The registration debate, of course, reflected a broader political debate, that of collaboration and non-collaboration. The talks took place against a background of political upheaval and change, which eventually culminated in the formation of the UDF. Although the differences were too sharp even to begin to lay the basis for unity, it was a start.

As Jeremy Baskin records: '[T]his meeting of unions was undoubtedly the beginning of the long process culminating in the launch of the Congress of South African Trade Unions, COSATU.'[15] The Langa conference put unity on the agenda, although it offered little in the way of practical progress beyond a promise of future cooperation through solidarity committees. We knew it would be a long and difficult process.

The Langa conference also agreed on several other issues, and unions concurred to cooperate with one another in resisting the state. It was five months after that conference that Neil Aggett's murder stunned the union movement and galvanised the first work stoppage in decades. Because it happened in the factories, where unions were strongest, there was little the police could do to stop the solidarity action.

The stoppage was a limited action by comparison with later events, involving 100 000 workers in the main industrial areas of the country. It was significant that the majority were from FOSATU affiliates as well as the FCWU. But it was momentous in that it was the first union initiative that attempted to mobilise workers nationally at their places of work over an issue that went beyond the factory floor.[16]

Two days after the stoppage, on 11 February, the emerging unions marched to the funeral behind union banners through a shocked white suburbia, singing their last tribute to Neil Aggett. I was in Durban and we held a memorial service at our offices to celebrate his life and rededicate ourselves to the selfless commitment he had made to the worker struggle.

But there was also an important, longer-term outcome. The stoppage gave FOSATU – two-thirds of whose members responded to the call – confidence in its mobilising ability to deliver in terms of mass action. Neil Aggett's death brutally marked the beginning of the repression of the trade union movement, and began to lay the basis for serious unity talks.

12

Two months after Aggett's death, FOSATU's Second National Congress was held in Hammanskraal. The spirit of the times demanded that it begin to discuss the political role of the trade union movement. Already there were differences between the affiliates on this issue.

SFAWU was on the left of FOSATU and new political influences began to emerge in the union that matched my own experiences as a student. In Springs on the East Rand the shop-steward movement was developing and making links with youth formations. Chris Dlamini had approached me to stand for election as the General Secretary of SFAWU against Maggie Magubane, a feisty woman who was one of the founders. It was a cheeky move, but given the emerging organisational strength of the Natal regions and Chris's political support it was a fait accompli.

In SFAWU we could relate to the community unions, although we felt that they were not particularly well organised on the shop floor. The politics of that type of union appealed to us, as did the sense of mobilisation of workers. Chris Dlamini and I concurred that we should fuse these two traditions to create a formidable organisation.

In April 1982 the Second Summit of Unions was held at Wilgespruit just outside Johannesburg. The explosive discussions focused on the formation of a new federation. The furore over registration raised its head sharply again. Several unions walked out but discussions continued, reaching an in-principle decision to form a new federation.

It was here that I connected with Cyril Ramaphosa, the charismatic leader of the National Union of Mineworkers (NUM) who would one day lead the negotiations over the country's first democratic Constitution. There was James Motlatsi, a wily leader, powerfully built and an incredible organiser from the shaft floor, hailing from Lesotho, who could move tens of thousands into action. He would be a pillar of strength for me in the future. And there was the irrepressible Elijah Barayi, an old ANC activist, originally from Cradock, who was to become the first President of COSATU. I also reconnected with Howie Gabriels, who had just joined the NUM. They were all serious trade unionists, already leading the country's biggest union. The combination of intellect and worker strength attracted me, and around this grouping we began to amalgamate the seeds of a leadership that would construct a new labour giant.

I used to travel quite often to Johannesburg and this became the way in which we could build a national network. I was living with Renée Roux at the time. We had rented an apartment in Overport in Durban.

I would pop in from time to time to see my mother. It was always a fleeting visit but she would bring out little containers of my favourite meals that she had stored in the freezer for me. I would sit holding her hand and feeling her positive energy. She was my recharge. We never discussed the danger of my work but I knew she approved of what I was doing. As I would leave, laden with food, she would whisper in my ear, 'Be careful, my son. I pray every day for your safety.' We would hug and I would be on my way. I believed deep in my heart that her pure spirit followed me everywhere.

I worked a lot with Thomas Dlamini, a strong Inkatha supporter. He was the chairperson of my branch. A very humble man, he lived in a hut in Mariannhill, where he was building his own house.

Thomas taught me a great deal about traditional Zulu culture – including the respect Zulu people pay to their elders. This is very similar in the Indian community: we respect our elders and we respect experience. I never tried to influence Thomas's politics; my job was to build an organisation and he was a very important person in my life and in the formation of a democratic union movement.

The union started growing rapidly. We were expanding at Bakers Bread, Clover Dairies and iJuba Breweries in Durban. A good friend, Gino Govender, who was an activist in Chatsworth, was working in a comfortable job at Caltex and I persuaded him to leave his job, take a lower, more erratic salary and work longer hours. In those days activism was driven by passion and volunteerism. People respected us for our commitment.

Even some criminals were beginning to have a grudging regard for us. When I was once surrounded by thugs wanting to strip me of my belongings, the mention that I was working for the unions was enough to get them to retreat apologetically.

In July 1982 the Third Summit was held in Port Elizabeth. The opposition to registration had reached a crescendo. Seven largely community-based unions set seven non-negotiable principles. The first was non-registration. The seven unions, later termed 'The Magnificent Seven', after the famous western movie at the time, walked out and the meeting collapsed.

The talks were effectively dead. The broader talks were to continue later amongst like-minded groupings, but I did not attend these because my team was involved in a bitter struggle to penetrate the sugar industry, already dominated by the sweetheart union of the employers.

We had discussed participating in Industrial Councils and had decided that it was too early to go in. But we were organising three sugar mills and we could not bargain individually. Some were stronger, some were weaker. How do you build up a collective strength? How would we negotiate more effectively than our rivals in the Industrial Councils?

I felt that the issue of building a base for SFAWU was more important than the ideological debates about registration. While I could empathise with my comrades in the community unions, I felt it was a fatal error to make registration a principle, especially when there was very little difference in other key principles. The only other substantive difference was industrial versus general unions.

By April 1983 a Fourth Summit was held in Athlone, Cape Town. It was well attended with large delegations of worker representatives from different unions. 'The Magnificent Seven' had retreated from their non-negotiable stance in the face of mounting state repression, and at the meeting agreed on practical steps on the way forward. Key in this agreement was the establishment of a Feasibility Committee to work towards the launch of the new federation and an agreement to build cooperation at a grassroots level.

In August 1983 the UDF was launched with huge enthusiasm in Cape Town. It captured the imagination of the moment with its wide-ranging cross-section of grassroots organisations and religious leaders. Thousands of civic movements, women's, youth and student organisations had pledged their support. Many community-based unions also joined. I was keen that we attend, although I did not favour affiliation to such a diverse umbrella of organisations.

We had discussed whether or not FOSATU would attend the launch of the UDF. The response was very negative. FOSATU even convened a series of seminars ostensibly to discuss the launch but designed to discourage any link with the UDF. Part of this was the experience of how repression had undermined SACTU as an organisation because the leadership had been so intertwined with the political movements of the time. To me it made sense to maintain an independent existence, but at the same time to forge strong campaigns together, based on a shared vision and programme of action.

Political affiliation remains a central question even today. A trade union federation represents the collective interests of its members and the broader organised working class. But to advance its interests most effectively, it is paramount that it fiercely defends its independence and avoids the pitfall of becoming a conveyor belt for any political party.

The launch of the UDF was an important milestone on our political journey, and it signalled a new phase of struggle. But right then, I felt overwhelmed by the challenges of building unity in the labour movement.

* * *

The optimism of the Athlone Summit was short-lived. Conflict broke out when the Steering Committee met to discuss demarcation, paid-up membership and a host of other issues. Within FOSATU we resolved to begin bilateral talks with like-minded unions.

I was also becoming fed up with the haggling over unity. In my mind it was obvious and imperative that we build strong shop-floor-based industrial unions with a capacity to take on the apartheid state and capital. There could be no compromise. Yet even within the food industry there was prevarication about this.

I committed myself to building a relationship based on trust with Jan Theron, the General Secretary of the FCWU, which had built a solid foundation in the Western Cape and was now expanding nationally. Jan was an austere comrade of complete integrity and with a resolute conviction in the values of the working class, but he was vigilant in protecting the independence of the union he led. In essence, I have rarely met a more committed socialist than him.

In March 1984 the Feasibility Committee met in Johannesburg. A deadline was given to those wanting to participate: they had to commit to joining a new, tightly knit federation in which non-racialism and industrial unions were basic principles. The community unions that were not prepared to be assigned observer status because they felt they were not ready for such commitments left the meeting, and the Feasibility Committee continued to meet over the next few months without them.

In the meantime, the political momentum was gathering pace. Protests were erupting across the country, sparked by an active students' organisation, the Congress of South African Students (COSAS). Community struggles were driven by a civic movement emboldened by the launch of the UDF. The country was seething with anger against apartheid.

The government had launched a new Tricameral Parliament[17] with an Indian, coloured and white chamber (the largest by far being the white chamber). This was an obvious attempt to co-opt the minority Indian and coloured communities into a conservative alliance with the white-dominated parliament. Elections were planned for September 1984. A massive campaign against these fake, racially based elections was mobilised by the UDF and supported by all democratic organisations, including FOSATU and the democratic trade union movement.

The union movement began to witness incredible growth as workers flooded to union offices wanting to become members. Our years of painstaking work were paying off. In September 1984 workers in the Simba chips factory on the East Rand went on strike and they were all dismissed. This was a particularly brutal strike. Workers were locked out and damage was caused to industrial equipment.

But Simba was also a classic product on which to launch a community-driven boycott campaign. We mobilised the community in a massive consumer boycott of Simba products. We had a range of student and consumer organisations behind us and I spent a great deal of time talking to them. The community-driven boycott was a first for a FOSATU affiliate and we had to argue for these alliances within the structures.

The Simba boycott was victorious and everyone was reinstated. I was enormously relieved. This had been another harrowing strike. I had spent time with the striking workers and their children. I was living in the face of their poverty, which highlighted the full measure of the burden of responsibility that lay on our shoulders. Strikes divert huge organisational energy and I would always be reluctant to use this weapon, except as a last resort.

It was also crucial to mobilise FOSATU into dropping its fear of community movements. Chris Dlamini and I were conscious of the need to mobilise the community behind workers' strikes in order to build a social solidarity and to discourage 'scab labour' in townships where poverty and unemployment were high.

The Simba strike around wages and working conditions was a turning point in FOSATU politics. It convinced many that we could succeed in a difficult balancing act: maintaining the integrity of our organisation and building the leadership at the point of production; but at the same time driving that organisation into alliances with like-minded bodies. For me it was not only impossible but undesirable to separate the struggle for rights on the factory floor from our broader struggle for freedom in the country.

After the strike students started to come to our shop-steward council on the East Rand to canvass workers' support for their demands for student representative councils in schools and to remove the South African Defence Force (SADF) which had been brought in to support the police in the townships. The townships had become battlefields with soldiers occupying schools and conducting house-to-house searches for 'revolutionary and criminal elements'.

There was a huge debate in the FOSATU executive, with the conclusion that we had to support the students. This was an assault by the state on the children of working people. We called on our members to support COSAS and participate in a call for the stay-away across the industrial heartland of South Africa. Chris Dlamini and Moses Mayekiso, then General Secretary of the Metal and Allied Workers Union, were the FOSATU representatives participating in the Transvaal Regional Stay-away Committee.

The committee met on 27 October 1984 with the representatives of 37 community and trade union organisations to organise a stay-away on 5 and 6 November in support of the students' demands. They called for democratically elected student representative councils; the withdrawal of SADF troops from the townships; the release of political prisoners such as Nelson Mandela; and the resignation of township councillors.

What distinguished the action taken by the Transvaal unions in support of the students and residents was that for the first time the union and community organisations came together as independent organisations and negotiated a plan of joint action. This meant the risks to the unions could be weighed up and minimised; they were not simply passive participants in a community-driven action.

This differed sharply from the political unionism typical of the regional general unions, who saw themselves both as unions and community organisations.[18] The strike's success was the result of the phenomenal increase in union membership among black workers whose militancy had not been dampened by recession and the threat of unemployment.[19]

The stay-away was monitored by a specially formed Labour Monitoring Group (LMG).[20] Unionised factories gave overwhelming support. All sectors where unions were present were uniformly affected, bar mining. Both migrant and township dwellers participated equally.

The Minister of Home Affairs, F.W. de Klerk, said the government would not allow 'destabilising actions' in any area, and told an employers union meeting in Cape Town: 'South Africa cannot afford to allow its labour and economic spheres to become a political battlefield . . . strong action will be taken against instigators, arsonists and radicals . . . order shall be maintained.'[21]

The state began its counter-attack. The state-owned enterprise Sasol dismissed 5 000 production workers at its Sasol Two and Three plants in Secunda – virtually the whole of its African workforce. Police with dogs and in hippos (armoured vehicles) patrolled the streets of the Secunda township, eMbalenhle, to supervise the removal of workers from their hostels. The stay-away was also followed by a wave of about 30 arrests and detentions.

Capital, by contrast, adopted a more cautious approach. No employers envisaged disciplinary action: most deducted wages; some treated it as paid leave; others paid wages in full. After the detention of the CUSA leader, Piroshaw Camay, three major employer associations (the Association of Chambers of Commerce, the Afrikaanse Handelsinstitut and the Federated Chamber of Industries) sent a joint telex to the Minister of Law and Order, Louis le Grange, warning that the wave of detentions was exacerbating a very delicate labour situation.

They feared that state action of this kind would curtail even the current limited reform programme and their working relationship with the state to implement these reforms. Minister Le Grange, however, was not persuaded, and responded aggressively to business. Fearing challenges to the free enterprise system, business called for further and accelerated structural reform, particularly of influx control. Its aim was to head off a challenge to the free enterprise system itself. A United States/South Africa Leadership Exchange Programme conference brought together representatives of capital and potentially sympathetic black leaders.[22]

International pressure was stepping up too. Earlier in 1984, the International Metalworkers Federation pledged support to the struggle of black workers for trade union and political rights.[23] Pressure was mounting internationally for sanctions against the apartheid regime. We were hugely encouraged by the people-driven sanctions movement demonstrated so admirably by the Dunne's Stores' workers in Ireland and their union, which refused to handle South African goods. Eventually the Irish government stepped in and agreed to ban South African products until apartheid was ended. This was a massive victory, particularly in relation to the appeasement policies of the Western countries led by the United Kingdom and the United States of America.

There is no doubt that the stay-away and the political realignments it produced did much to shift the ground, both in the unions and more broadly. Johan Maree has analysed a number of significant factors. Firstly, he says, the state's reaction to the stay-away crystallised the central contradictions in its attempts to 'liberalise' without political and social change. The result was further politicisation in the union movement, demonstrated by calls for a 'black Christmas' to highlight the torture and deaths in detention. Secondly, the stay-away brought together the major opposition forces in the Transvaal for the first time. This new alignment furthermore united extra-parliamentary political and community groupings.

Buthelezi's vocal opposition to a stay-away and his interference in the Sasol dispute distanced him still further from the mainstream, and weakened Inkatha influence amongst workers on the Rand. The failure of the authorities to undermine the solidarity strike increased the scale and geographic spread of the resistance, despite their continued vulnerability at the hands of state-run enterprises like Sasol. Levels of violence increased and the number of detentions continued to rise.[24]

From the SFAWU point of view, the significance of the stay-away was its influence on the direction of FOSATU and the unity talks. FOSATU's powerful Transvaal region, as well as the leadership of Chris Dlamini, now the federation's President, were beginning to influence FOSATU's political direction. FOSATU regional leaders had begun meeting with a number of representatives of UDF-affiliated unions. At a meeting of Transvaal shop stewards in early 1985, the re-inclusion of the UDF-affiliated unions in the unity talks towards a single federation was adopted.

The FOSATU executive simultaneously called for a resumption of the talks. Although some unions in the Feasibility Committee were unhappy about this, they agreed to the proposal, provided that the progress made since the walk-out was not reversed.

By now, SACTU, conscious of the powerful combination of joint labour and community actions, supported vigorously the formation of 'one democratic trade union federation', based on the principle 'One Industry, One Union'. After the November stay-away, it began to urge the Feasibility Committee to open talks to all unions, at the same time bringing its influence to bear on the UDF-affiliated unions in an effort to persuade them to resume participation in the talks.[25]

These events transformed the political discussion in FOSATU and put our grouping in the forefront of the debate. The FOSATU leadership realised that it would be counter-productive to form a new federation without the cooperation and support of the ANC and SACTU.

With the leadership of Chris Dlamini, Moses Mayekiso, Cyril Ramaphosa, James Motlatsi and Elijah Barayi, we were able to steer the talks, maintain the balance and use our influence in the union movement to persuade the leadership of the different camps to make the necessary compromises. I was in close contact with the old FOSATU grouping, such as Alec Erwin, Joe Foster and John Copelyn, as well as Jan Theron.

It was like navigating a minefield. Talks stopped and started all the time, but the central issue was the political direction of this new movement. We were being battered by the state. The repression was forcing us together, making our differences smaller than the need for unity. Soon we found that there was more that united us than divided us.

The unity talks staggered on through 1984 and 1985, absorbing much energy and time. For me, the breakthrough was the conference held at the Ipelegeng Centre in Soweto in June 1985. Unions were asked to bring their national executives and were to comment on a draft constitution for the new federation.

The representative from the Black-Consciousness-aligned unions stood up and gave an intellectual analysis about the need for black working-class leadership and the detrimental influence of white intellectuals in some unions. He went on and on.

Then Elijah Barayi, Deputy President of the NUM, stood up and spoke in Xhosa. He said: 'You know, I don't understand you people. We talk so much about how we have been colonised and taken over and how people don't understand, and yet all the people who are talking here are talking in English.'

He launched a blistering attack on the ideologues who prevented the unity of the working class at this historic moment when worker rights and, indeed, our political struggles were under direct attack by the apartheid state. The key question he posed was: 'Who are *you* representing? I am representing mineworkers who want this federation – and we want it now.'

No one had the temerity to challenge this fiery working-class leader. The new federation was on the brink of formation. Now we just had to settle the details.

PART FOUR

A Giant has Arisen

Workers on the Move

As a representative of our working class, COSATU is seized with the task of engaging the workers in the general democratic struggle, both as an independent organisation and as an essential component of the democratic forces of our country.

— ANC-SACTU-COSATU talks

Adriaan Johannes Vlok and Johannes Velde van der Merwe, respectively the then Minister of Law and Order and Police Commissioner, testified about the revolutionary climate of the day and the circumstances that led to the decision to damage, by means of explosives, COSATU House . . .

Having given the situation much thought, Vlok and Van der Merwe concluded that the only way to counter these activities at COSATU House was to render the building unusable for purposes that promote a revolutionary climate. The intention was to cause an interruption in the logistical support structure of the perpetrators, including members of COSATU, by damaging the building.

— Amnesty Commission Report of the
Truth and Reconciliation Commission

The first four months of 1987 have witnessed a rising militancy and resolve among the black workers unprecedented in the history of our struggle. There have been more workers' strikes during these four months than the whole of last year . . .

In a series of impressive general strikes we have demonstrated the united strength of our entire people, raised the issue of people's power and reduced Botha's election to a sideshow. The giant democratic trade union federation, COSATU, has grown and is making advances in many industries.

— O.R. Tambo

13

Summer in Durban is hot and humid. I remember, when I was young, how I used to hug the cement walls to cool down. Right now our extended and tense discussions needed a pillar of cement to hold up the organisation. It was the last weekend of November 1985. Unresolved differences had produced a day weighed down with difficulty and fraught with danger.

The venue was the Howard College campus of the University of Natal, a liberal university perched high on the ridge overlooking downtown Durban. It was one of the few places we could use that was secluded enough for us to escape the watchful eyes and intrusive presence of the security police.

A sense of euphoria filled the hall as the 760 delegates from the 33 unions representing 460 000 members massed around to register. But there was also anxiety and tension. There were a number of unresolved issues. The air was thick with political tension and suspicion. I was very nervous. If elected to a leadership position I was going to have to pull together disparate elements that seemed to be always at loggerheads with each other. At the same time, I shared the excitement of something great being born. We were writing a new chapter in the history of labour and politics in South Africa.

The night before, hundreds of delegates had arrived in buses, rickety cars and combi (passenger van) taxis. For many it was their first trip to Durban and included a compulsory visit to the beach – filling up empty cold-drink bottles with seawater which was to be used in an ancient tradition of cleaning the digestive system, and for which I had no heart.

Cyril Ramaphosa was the convenor of the launching Congress. We had canvassed late into the previous night how to contextualise this inaugural

Congress, given that there were many eyes, most positive and enquiring, but many hostile even to the idea of our existence. It was imperative that we held this fragile unity together.

Cyril was in pain and unwell that day, and I was aware of the stress he was under. He was our linchpin, and if he was sick we were in trouble. But he soldiered on. At 10.00 a.m. he convened the Congress.

We had planned that his address would be concise, spelling out a bold vision that situated the Congress, but balanced to give all attendees a feeling of belonging. This was even more urgent given the news that the debates had already led to a physical fracas involving some senior comrades. Cyril proclaimed:

> *The formation of this Congress represents an enormous victory for the working class of this country... In the next few years we will be putting our heads together, not only to make sure we reach Pretoria, but also to make a better life for workers in the country. What we have to make clear is that a Giant has risen and will confront all that stands in its way.*[1]

We were casting the federation in a mould of militant political unionism that would forever be our hallmark. But we also needed to send a clear message from COSATU that politics was the business of the constitutional structures: we should focus on building a powerful shop-floor base to give content to the constitution, rules and policies to guide the federation to take on the employers and the apartheid state. Trade union democracy and its right to independent political action were to be jealously guarded.

One key debate was on the role of women in the federation. In the process of unity talks the issue of gender was marginalised. At the inaugural Congress there was a determined push from female delegates for the new federation to embrace gender equality. But we faltered as the candidates' slate represented different groups who were still dominated by men, and although there was support the most we achieved was to redesign the COSATU logo so that it also reflected the role of women. However, the challenge of gender representivity was flagged on our agenda, but it would be eight long years before Connie September, a fiercely independent fighter for women's rights from the shop floor of the South African Clothing and Textile Workers Union, was elected as the first woman in the top leadership of COSATU. By this time the seeds of gender representivity were sown across the ranks of the democratic movement and a determined push was being fought for the sharing of leadership positions equally.

Some principles had been agreed on in laborious and painstaking negotiations prior to the Congress, but there was still heated debate about many clauses. My primary role as part of the group that were the midwives of the process was to keep the balance between the cautious unions in FOSATU and the politically based general unions that were part of the UDF.

To some, the debates were clearly not a matter of much importance – in one part of the hall some workers were listening to a Kaizer Chiefs game on the radio, instead of listening to the simultaneous translation on their headsets. Every now and again they would give themselves away by cheering out loud.

But for many in the audience, a sticking point was the clause proposing an Assistant General Secretary for COSATU. This was presented by the UDF-aligned unions who felt that because of their numbers they would be swamped by the larger industrial unions. Many from the FOSATU/independent union fold were deeply suspicious of this, and so was I. But in principle we had agreed to this addition for the sake of progress.

Sydney Mufamadi was the General Secretary of the General and Allied Workers Union (GAWU). He was the youngest in the team and I found him an affable and constructive person. We worked well together and for me this was an advantage in that we would have an avenue to the broader political leadership, which we could influence as much as they sought to influence us.

Elections were held on the last night. Elijah Barayi was elected President, and I the General Secretary. It was a supercharged environment. Barayi and I and other national office bearers were carried on to the stage on people's shoulders while the whole hall rang with celebration as the delegates chanted the inaugural COSATU song:

iCOSATU sonyuka nayo [COSATU is rising up]
masingen' enkululekweni [Let us go with it to freedom]

The relief from the tension and stress of the days before was visible. Barayi was a fiery speaker. Brought up in the political maelstrom of the Eastern Cape, he had been influenced by Reverend Calata, a former Secretary General of the ANC in 1936 who laid the basis for the leadership of Nelson Mandela and his comrades in the 1940s. Barayi had also participated in the 1952 Defiance Campaign, whose major success was on the rebellious shores of the Eastern Cape.

'You must all know that a lion has been born,' he told delegates after his election.

'To the South African government I say: your time is over ... We do not apologise for being black. We are proud of it. As from today Mandela and all political prisoners should be released.'[2]

On our way home that evening, Howie Gabriels and I promised each other that we were going to make this organisation work. I knew I could count on his support at all times. But I was anxious. A big task lay ahead. Would my shoulders be broad enough to carry this enormous challenge? We walked slowly beneath the bright stars that night, not knowing what the next day would bring. Both the quietness of the night and the meandering road through leafy white suburbs disguised the violence that lurked below. Would my life ever be the same again? How did I, a person of Indian ancestry, arrive at a point of leading an almost exclusively African organisation?

I was never to experience that doubt again in my work in the labour movement. There was a total embrace of my commitment. Non-racialism was the social fibre woven into the fabric of the movement we were building. Years later, after one of our mass rallies, Cyril jokingly recounted being in the audience when a drunken mineworker balancing precariously on a wooden box was screaming *'ikula ka rona'* – translated loosely as 'This is our "coolie"; he is our leader'. While ordinarily a derogatory term denigrating Indians, 'coolie' was now being used as proud acclaim. In all my years in the labour movement and our struggle against apartheid, I was never once made to feel my 'Indian-ness'.

We held our big rally at Kings Park Stadium on 1 December 1985. Although there were only about 10 000 workers there (fewer than we expected), the atmosphere was electric; people were singing and dancing and there was a sense that our organisation was coming together. There was also a heavy police presence.

In his opening speech, Cyril introduced the newly appointed office bearers. Barayi spoke. He simply rolled up the speech that had been written for him by Marcel Golding from the NUM, who had stayed up much of the night to write it. Barayi used the roll of paper like a baton, making a spontaneous, revolutionary speech: 'P.W. Botha, I am giving you six months to get rid of the pass laws or COSATU will call on the people to burn their passes.'[3]

On the back of an excited mass of our supporters, Barayi went on to attack the Bantustan system and singled out Chief Buthelezi, accusing him of being 'the running dog of the apartheid state'. Barayi's speech, while striking a chord with the crowd, had not reflected on the challenges we faced in building a sustainable organisation.

I felt this was a mistake. It was not my style. My political approach was more like Amilcar Cabral, the revolutionary leader opposed to Portuguese colonial occupation in Guinea-Bissau, who in 1964 wrote the brilliant essay *Revolutionary Thought in the Twentieth Century* – and the famous quote: 'Hide nothing from the masses of our people. Tell no lies. Mask no difficulties, mistakes, failures. Claim no easy victories.'[4]

As I took the stage as the first General Secretary of COSATU, I was conscious of how fragmented we were, with no viable structures – not even a bank account or a single employee. COSATU was born during a State of Emergency[5] – at a time when P.W. Botha argued that 'ordinary law and order was inadequate'. Otherwise known as the *Groot Krokodil* (Big Crocodile), Botha was breathing heavily down our backs.

* * *

Cyril and Howie had first raised the prospect of my standing as the General Secretary of COSATU. I had earned my credentials as a trade unionist in SFAWU, the food union. I was respected by the FOSATU unions and had built strong links with Jan Theron and Mandla Gxanyana from FCWU, Dave Lewis from GWU and the Cape Town Municipal Workers Union under John Erentzen. I could be the bridge between the contesting factions, and my own political background meant that I would have the support of the UDF because I came from the same political culture.

Cyril and I had a relationship that was built on trust. He handled the negotiations to distribute the key leadership positions across the political spectrum of the affiliating unions. I agreed with him. Our slate included Elijah Barayi, Chris Dlamini, Makhulu Ledwaba representing the Commercial, Catering and Allied Workers Union (CCAWUSA) and Maxwell Xulu from the Metal and Allied Workers Union (MAWU).

After I became General Secretary I had to move to Johannesburg to establish the COSATU offices. Before I left, I went to see my mother. She was now living with my brother Logie and his wife, Corona, in Reservoir Hills, the suburb I had spent my childhood in. She had watched the news and read the newspapers. She realised my mind was made up. This was to be my destiny. We had dinner with my brothers and sisters and laughed late into the night. I slept over that night.

By the time I rose, there was a hearty breakfast on the table. These were the times in which I could let my guard down. I was safe here. I could be exactly who I was – the youngest son of Bakkium Chetty, my mother. I saw the worry in her eyes but there was nothing I could say to allay that fear. There was the real peril of violence that hung over our heads. I did not speak and I held her hand, feeling her protective and positive energy.

I made my plans to leave for Johannesburg. It was complicated. Renée and I had a discussion about our future. We had shared a home for a few years but now I had a mission to accomplish. We talked of continuing our relationship but I knew that there would be little place for emotional attachments. The challenge of putting together a diverse organisation was daunting. It was a bittersweet moment.

The one person I knew I could rely on in Johannesburg was Howie Gabriels. I telephoned him. He was sharing a house with his family and Jeremy Baskin. There was no question; Howie offered me a room. His daughter Nina would sleep with him and Gertie, his wife. I had no money and no salary – nothing except the possessions packed in the boot of my Toyota Corolla.

14

Yeoville, where Howie and his family lived, was a colourful suburb heavily populated by the Jewish community and over the years it became a trendy and progressive mixed community. With its bars and cosmopolitan atmosphere it was a magnet for lefties and people yearning for a different South Africa. I really loved that place. Rockey Street was abuzz every night till late and the little cafés breathed an air of tolerance and co-existence.

But in COSATU, the early days were hard. There was a gulf between the expectations we raised and the reality of the situation. COSATU constituted a mixture of people, tendencies and ideologies. Every skill I had ever honed in the past was put to the test. Fortunately, Barayi and I quickly established a rapport and complemented each other in our pursuit of the common goal of building a responsive workers' movement.

We also had very divided affiliates with influential unions that did not agree with Barayi's speech. They saw it as premature – it threw us into battle on a terrain that we had not even surveyed. As a federation we had no resources, and the NUM agreed to accommodate us in its offices on the fifth floor of Lekton House, and even paid our salaries for the first year. I felt comfortable in the NUM offices. I had strong relations with all the key office bearers, who gave me the material, political and moral support to forge ahead with the main organisational tasks. After a few weeks I was able to employ Vivian Badela, a conscientious woman who was our receptionist cum secretary. She and Gertie Gabriels, whom I persuaded to leave a stable job, joined me to start the task of parenting a young organisation.

Almost at the same time I was invited to a meeting of the World Council of Churches (WCC) in Harare. I thought it was a good idea to go and canvass some support. It was our first public function after Barayi's speech and everyone was very interested in COSATU.

I also knew that I would meet with senior comrades from the ANC and I needed their support to implement the resolution on building strong national industrial unions and political unity. This was the biggest challenge we faced – the sensitive task of reorganising structures and leadership in the light of increasing state repression.

Underlying all of that, I also wanted a direct line to the ANC in exile unmediated by any internal structures. I wanted to connect to what I believed was the most serious liberation movement and to send a message to sectors and groups which felt they had a monopoly on contact with the ANC in exile. There were tough decisions to make and I needed to cover all bases. Contact with the senior ANC leadership was a critical priority.

Several people from the ANC attended that meeting – Mac Maharaj (a Robben Island 'graduate' and senior member of the ANC's Revolutionary Committee) and Joe Slovo (a senior member of MK's Special Operations and also on the Revolutionary Committee).

This was my first formal contact with the ANC in exile, and it took place at a very public meeting convened by religious leaders discussing the grave situation in South Africa.

After the meeting we agreed to a press statement that reported I had met for informal talks with the ANC and SACTU and that the talks were 'very fruitful and allowed frank and open exchange of views'.

There was considerable conflict about this in the federation and some people were asking: 'Are Naidoo and Barayi taking COSATU into the ANC camp?' But I had made sure that the office bearers, then in the major unions, were behind me. Cyril Ramaphosa, Moses Mayekiso, Chris Dlamini and I spent a lot of time talking to Alec Erwin, John Copelyn from the National Union of Textile Workers and others.

I reported on my Harare meeting with the ANC at COSATU's first Central Executive Committee (CEC) meeting in February 1986. The CEC passed a resolution about COSATU's political independence, although agreeing to further talks with the ANC.

But time was not waiting for us. Buthelezi launched an attack on COSATU,[6] calling it a front for the ANC, and stating his intention to set up an alternative to COSATU. Enormous pressure was piled on COSATU shop stewards to join the alternative trade union movement that Inkatha was going to launch. Violent attacks on union leaders became the norm and Inkatha moved its timetable forward to launch its union body. The political space had for some time been hotly contested in the community with the mobilisation of the UDF; now it moved to the shop floor.

In March 1986 a COSATU delegation including Cyril Ramaphosa, Sydney Mufamadi and I met with the ANC President, Oliver Tambo, John Nkadimeng (SACTU General Secretary), Kay Moonsamy, Thabo Mbeki, Chris Hani and Mac Maharaj in Lusaka. I found the leadership of Oliver Tambo warm and inclusive. He went out of his way to welcome the COSATU delegation and listen to our views on the way forward. I had the opportunity to sit with him after the formal discussions and I was able to plot the challenges that faced COSATU, particularly in relation to the principle of one union per industry. This, I argued, was a prerequisite to building a powerful federation capable of engaging the bosses on the factory floor in our fight for a living wage but also of engaging in the broader struggle for political freedom. I left that discussion assured of his fullest support for the democratic structures of COSATU.

It was here that I met Chris Hani and found him to be a charismatic leader who I connected with instantly. He was engaging and persuasive and there was unmistakably a working-class bias in everything he articulated. He would become a lifelong ally of labour and COSATU.

The meeting in Lusaka consolidated the direct relationship that COSATU had with the highest levels of the ANC and confirmed its unstinting support. Undoubtedly I would be able to drive the inaugural Congress decisions with the confidence that no other group inside of South Africa or in COSATU would be able to argue their position as the 'Lusaka line'. Also I felt that we needed a broader delegation of COSATU representatives to meet and debate the ANC delegation on the strategy and tactics of the way forward. Oliver Tambo, in his usual temperament, listened carefully to all our views, took the time to digest every word and then responded with great respect to each comment. It was a hallmark of a unifying leader who had given the ANC in exile a formidable presence and who displayed admiration for those who were in the trenches of struggle within South Africa. He won the support of the COSATU delegation.

After the meeting, we issued a joint communiqué, which focused on the crisis of the Botha regime, arguing for 'lasting solutions [that] can only emerge from the national liberation movement, headed by the ANC, and the entire democratic forces of our country, of which COSATU is an important and integral part'.[7]

COSATU's emergence was recognised as 'an historic event in the process of uniting our working class' and as an opportunity to 'immeasurably strengthen the democratic movement as a whole'. We also agreed on the unity of trade unions and on the independence of each organisation.

I went back to the challenge of building an organisation that had the capacity to deliver the liberation that would embrace the fundamental transformation we wanted. The path to unity was going to be as difficult as the process of the 'Unity Talks' that took almost four years.

My relationship with senior leaders, while at times heated, was respectful. I understood their dilemma, like those of the smaller industrial unions and the general unions. We had committed COSATU to building powerful national industrial unions like the NUM and NUMSA, the metal union, and FAWU, the food and allied workers union. The smaller unions would be swamped in these mergers based on paid-up membership since many were not registered and would have difficulty verifying their membership claims. This was also interpreted as weakening the political stance they had brought into the new federation. I spent many days with Sydney Mufamadi in discussions with key leaders, such as Sisa Njikelana and others from the ranks of the general unions.

In particular, I found Sisa's approach refreshing. We knew each other from our political past and moved in similar circles and trusted each other. I would call on him and my other contacts in the political movement, in particular the ANC and SACTU, as I pushed the merger process forward more aggressively.

In addition, many from the UDF unions still rejected the old guard of FOSATU, who were equally suspicious. For example, I had to fight hard to make Alec Erwin my education officer. Some comrades saw him as the person who had played a key role in the writing of Joe Foster's speech at the Congress in 1982; it had spoken of the need for 'an independent workers party'. I respected Alec's intellect and his commitment to the workers' struggle; he was also my line to a range of other people who carried important constituencies.

I was determined to win this battle to set the parameters of what I believed should happen. I also stubbornly believed in the right to have a diversity of opinions amongst the people on my team. I eventually won the battle. Slowly, day by day, I fought to ensure that COSATU's decisions were based on its own analysis, its mandates and its inputs.

* * *

One of my first major challenges was to build COSATU's financial sustainability. We could depend on a part of the revenue for running COSATU from our unions, but many were weak and had a small income base. We knew that we had to build our links with our traditional allies in Scandinavia, Holland, the rest of Europe and Canada.

In early 1986, a delegation comprising Cyril Ramaphosa, Sydney Mufamadi, Chris Dlamini and myself went to Brussels to meet the International Confederation of Trade Unions (ICFTU) as the dominant international federation with whose affiliates we had the closest links. We wanted to explain our resolutions of the inaugural Congress and our decision to remain non-aligned and non-affiliated to either the ICFTU, dominant in the Western world, or its 'alternative' body, the World Federation of Trade Unions (WFTU), which was allied to the socialist world.

The COSATU Congress had adopted an aggressive resolution that criticised the ICFTU as a front of imperialism, and clearly the ICFTU had received detailed reports on this resolution and was suspicious about our relationship with SACTU, which was affiliated to the WFTU.

My personal feeling was that we did not have time to indulge in political chess games. Our position on non-alignment was sufficient to insulate us from this fractious but peripheral issue to our battles at home. We needed to build our strongest links with like-minded unions fighting radical battles in the developing world and with progressive unions operating in countries with the strongest trading relations with South Africa in order to leverage their strengths at home with their governments.

The leadership at the ICFTU were suspicious of us but knew the members of the delegation who had proved their credentials as bona fide trade unionists over many years. COSATU was a force that could not be ignored.

Our next stop was Stockholm, where we met our colleagues in the Swedish LO/TCO (Trade Union Confederation/Confederation of Professional Employees). We were interrogated. 'Why would you want us to support you when you have attacked our mother body the ICFTU?' they asked at dinner on the first evening. As we explained our position late into the night they remained tight-lipped. They were clearly unhappy with our resolution but these were comrades who were committed to international solidarity and respected our trade union credentials. At the same time the social democratic political leadership in Sweden along with the rest of Scandinavia was historically close to the ANC, especially its President, Oliver Tambo, and supported our fight for liberation.

We returned to the formal meeting the next day but first we went to pay our respects to the memory of Olaf Palme, the Swedish Prime Minister who had been assassinated a few weeks prior to our visit. As a radical and progressive social democrat, with a strong identification with international causes, he was a stoic supporter of the ANC and had fought for sanctions against apartheid internationally.

We left Sweden on an inconclusive note and headed to Oslo, in Norway, to meet with our Norwegian LO comrades. None of us had seen such deep winter and the cold was unrelenting. As we participated in a vigil in the town square to commemorate the life of Olaf Palme with thousands of Norwegians we felt the cold bite through our flimsy shoes and clothing.

Returning to the hotel we quickly went to our rooms and dived into a hot bath. When we met for dinner we decided to go out to find some food and jazz. The taxi driver dropped us off at a restaurant where a jazz group was playing. We studied the menu and cover charge and realised we would not be able to afford more than one meal so we decided to search for a cheaper venue. While walking through the streets we bumped into a Rastafarian who became excited when he heard we were trade unionists from South Africa. He took us to a local night club and got us inside at no cost. Once again we counted our limited cash and realised that all we would be able to afford was a single beer and the cheapest sandwich.

Morosely we called a waiter. Then an announcement was made that changed our circumstances. 'Ladies and gentlemen, we have some special guests here tonight. They are trade unionists from South Africa. Let us welcome them.' As the music belted out 'Free Nelson Mandela' we were invited on to the dance floor and surrounded by new-found friends. That evening, with its endless supply of complimentary drinks and food, was just the boost we needed.

Our round trip took us on to Finland, Denmark and Holland and yielded a tentative agreement that these centres would review their support for the new

Congress and revert to us. But we felt confident that we had laid the basis for a long-standing partnership that was fundamental to the success of COSATU. These were comrades who put aside ideological issues and concentrated on international solidarity as a principle. Many were to become my lifelong friends.

As we continued on to London we were to face a more hostile reaction from the international department of the British Trades Union Congress (TUC). It was clear to us that there was little difference between their views and that of the Foreign Office of the British government, which, under Prime Minister Margaret Thatcher, was hostile to the ANC and saw us an appendage to the ANC.

That evening we had arranged to meet with a delegation from the ANC. It had to be done with some secrecy as I was sure we were under surveillance. We had supper with Joe Slovo and several high-ranking members. This was crucial as it consolidated my relationship with the senior leadership of the ANC in exile.

When I returned to my room that night I found that it had been broken into and ransacked. My clothes had been thrown out of my suitcase, the mattress was stripped of its covers and the drawers were all open. Someone had done a thorough search.

It was clear that this was a job executed by the South African security police. We reported the break-in but to avoid any further incident I slept at the home of Steven Faulkner, who worked for the Commonwealth Trade Union Council (CTUC), which would become an important ally as we fought for survival back home.

* * *

It was upon my return to South Africa from our international fundraising trip and during my early days in Lekton House that I had my first encounter with the harsh realities of union discipline. There had been several strikes in the mining sector that had resulted in dismissals, and the dismissed workers were unhappy with what the union was doing for them.

James Motlatsi was the President of the NUM. Like millions of others from southern Africa, he had been recruited into the hard life of a shaft worker. He was a natural leader and his ability to capture the imagination of tens of thousands of mineworkers in those mass meetings was an art and a science that I have seen in few others.

He always said to me: 'Jay, you know that we are elected as leaders and we must lead from the front. If you are faced with a difficult situation and have exhausted all avenues to find a solution, then make a decision – no matter how uncomfortable you or others are.'

It was an important lesson for me on the qualities of leadership and the attributes one should strive for. The ability to be inclusive but at the same time firm about the direction we were going in was a quality that James and I shared. As I reflect on those early days, I realise that I never got the sense that power had gone to people's heads. I suppose there were sufficient checks and balances.

One day, the dismissed workers occupied the offices. The NUM operated in a very strict way – if you broke the code it would be quite ruthless. I remember arriving at the office the next morning to find cleaners mopping up blood from the floors. The NUM had brought the marshals in and a bloody battle had ensued. No one said a word or did a thing about it; they didn't even report it to the newspapers.

James Motlatsi explains the context:

It was Christmas 1985 and there were miners who had been dismissed after a strike. We had a little money which had been donated from international supporters and Cyril, in a generous mood, felt we should give money to the strikers. Jay, who had a right to attend any of our meetings, supported Cyril in this. We had no strike funds and so we were able to contribute a little money, approximately R300 each.

Then, when the dismissed workers came back after Christmas there were more people. We had no records of who had been dismissed during the strike or for other reasons.

Then at Easter they demanded more money and when they came back after Easter there were even more strikers. There was disorder on all floors. They began to make impossible demands.

There were about 300 men and they were using our offices, refused to listen to us; they were all over, using the phones. It was disruptive, it was an untenable situation. I decided to remove them by force. It was either this, or no union.

I went to the NUM branch at Grootvlei mine and got them to remove the strikers.

When Jay came in the next morning he was unhappy but the problem had been solved.[8]

I didn't agree with the NUM's actions, but the question was, what alternative did we have? Without discipline there would not have been an organisation. Often these grievances against us were stoked by the 'dirty tricks' department of the security police – even when there was a legitimate basis for our actions.

James Motlatsi's attitude was: 'We were elected to lead, so don't ever ask us how we should lead. You must discuss and debate. Then you must act. There is no place for indecision in a war.'

Discipline became a hallmark of the organisation we wanted to build.

15

In 1985 COSATU had campaigned for May Day as a public holiday and we threatened that on 1 May 1986, we would make it a public holiday whether the state liked it or not. The state instead declared the first Monday of the month a public holiday but we refused to accept this and we mobilised around 1 May as a public holiday.

May Day represented a South Africa we were fighting for, in which workers' rights would be enshrined in our Constitution and the political and economic rights of the poor would be at the centre of a developmental state. It also connected us to an international solidarity movement that had fought for an eight-hour working day as early as the 1850s. This was International Workers' Day and solidarity with workers around the world would often be called upon when state violence sought to tear at our foundations.

When the day came, we mobilised countrywide. We were consciously forming our identity and brand. We had to build a national presence to stretch the resources of the state. Allowing it to target geographic areas would force the state to focus its limited security firepower area by area. I soon realised that our only real defence was the uniformity and strength of our union structures in every town, factory and mine. We had to be strong at the point of production, which the state could not target without economic consequences.

On May Day I addressed a rally in Durban at Curries Fountain. The stadium was full, with about 15 000 people, and the mood was sombre. Intimidation and the death toll from clashes with Inkatha were rising. I was fearful of the future. We would have to focus much more energy in order to build our organisation in this province.

May Day was also the day that Inkatha had chosen to launch the United Workers Union of South Africa (UWUSA), the party's in-house trade union. And Inkatha was holding a rally at Kings Park stadium where 60 000 people dwarfed our gathering. The state transport system had been harnessed and communities and villages were press-ganged into attending the gigantic launch.

It was a display of raw power with thousands of militant *impis* (Zulu warriors) chanting traditional war cries and brandishing spears and knobkerries. They did a war dance around the perimeter of the field and carried a coffin emblazoned with Barayi's and my name across its side. The message was clear – it held the menacing truth of what was to come: 'The instruction to bury COSATU and its leaders.' Buthelezi in addressing the rally made it clear that Zulu workers had to make a choice between Inkatha and UWUSA and membership in COSATU. To loud cheers he reiterated his opposition to sanctions.

Across the city we made a valiant effort to put up a brave front. Our rally was being videoed by a police crew and a heavily armed contingent formed an intimidating presence. A police helicopter hovering above the stadium drowned out our voices. I received the reports of the Inkatha rally with trepidation. 'We will not be intimidated by this!' I responded to our rally. 'We are the spirit of the militant, progressive trade union movement!' But deep inside I was afraid of the violence that could ensue. We had to be quick with our speeches. There would be bloodshed if our supporters clashed in the aftermath of the rallies on the trains and at the bus terminals.

For me, the critical issue was how much time, how much energy and how many people I had to build an organisation. If UWUSA had 60 000 people (despite the fact that a large number had been shepherded and brought in buses from rural areas), this meant that even if half of those people were 'rent-a-crowd' we had 30 000 people hostile to COSATU in areas where they weren't hostile before, and in reality knew nothing about us. While UWUSA could not match our organising capabilities on the shop floor, it had enormous potential with the support of the apartheid state and employers to stir violence against us.[9] The announcement that a businessman and KwaZulu member of parliament, Simon Conco, was the General Secretary of UWUSA and the presence of other employers at the launch confirmed this.

The launch of UWUSA was a declaration of war. This union was going to fight us, factory by factory, farm by farm, company by company, shop by shop.

I knew that we were going to start seeing conflict on an unprecedented scale.

During the imposition of the State of Emergency two months later, UWUSA remained unscathed. It was clear to me, as I declared at the time:

Uwusa was formed with the full sanction of the apartheid system and the fact that it has been taken advantage of by the state indicates their opportunism. We are convinced that their formation was a reactionary act taken by the state in collusion with some employers.[10]

COSATU openly identified with the demand for the release of Nelson Mandela and all political prisoners as well as the unbanning of the ANC and all political organisations.

All hell would break loose as the apartheid state mounted ferocious attacks against us in the coming months and years.

* * *

At midnight on 11 June 1986, there was a knock on the door of 46 Hunter Street in Yeoville. When Jeremy Baskin opened the door he was confronted by armed policemen. The house had been surrounded.

'Come with us, Naidoo,' they said. 'We are detaining you under the State of Emergency.'

Fortunately, Jeremy managed to persuade them that he was not Jay Naidoo and that I was not at home, and they left. Others were not so fortunate. This was the second declaration of a State of Emergency by the apartheid government and it gave extraordinary powers of detention to security forces. Thousands of activists were being arrested around the country as the government enforced a blanket ban on political activities. The press was gagged and prohibited from printing non-governmental accounts of civil strife, consumer boycotts or rallies. The 'police state' had arrived with all its brutality.

In the first few days of June, I was aware of over 170 unionists who were arrested and detained. COSATU officials were repeatedly arrested, harassed, physically attacked and even murdered.

We had known the clampdown was coming. There had been too much activity on the union front – and with the UDF paralysed as a result of mass detentions, the focus was on COSATU. After the arrests I rented a run-down little flat overlooking the highway in the centre of town and spent my nights there.

Angamma, my great-grandmother, who changed the line of my ancestry forever. *(Jay Naidoo library)*

The only photo of me as a young boy. *(Jay Naidoo library)*

With my mother and siblings. *(Jay Naidoo library)*

Strategising about building workers' power with Thomas Dlamini, the Chairperson of SFAWU in Natal, and Petros Ngcobo, the union organiser in the early 1980s. *(Omar Badsha)*

In a FOSATU Education Workshop in 1982 with Mama Lydia, Refiloe Nzuta, Jane Barrett and shop stewards. *(Jay Naidoo library)*

Thrill and trepidation on my election as the founding General Secretary of COSATU in 1985.
(Paul Weinberg)

The call to bury me and Elijah Barayi as UWUSA is launched by Inkatha in 1986.
(UWC-Robben Island Museum Mayibuye Archives, Billy Paddock)

The siege of COSATU headquarters in 1987. *(Eric Miller)*

A united front against the Labour Relations Act in 1989. With Piroshaw Camay of NACTU,
Ronald Mofokeng and Elijah Barayi. *(William Matlala)*

Mineworkers strike poster from 1987 – mobilising for the largest strike in South Africa's labour history. *(Cosatu archives)*

International solidarity with Namibia brought the scent of our freedom one step closer. *(Cosatu archives)*

Falling in love with Lucie in the frozen North Pole in 1990. *(Jay Naidoo library)*

March on Department of Labour Relations offices in 1990 to press our demands for worker rights and the restructuring of the labour relations system. *(William Matlala)*

Office bearers of COSATU and the NUM take comrades from Holland, Denmark, Sweden, Norway, Finland and Canada down a mine in Johannesburg in 1990. *(Wouter van der Schaaf)*

Mandela, dressed casually, at our first wedding in 1991, saying, 'I did not know trade unionists wore suits.' With Adelaide Tambo, O.R. Tambo, Louise Grondin, Lucie, Dimes Naidoo and Omar Motani. *(Jay Naidoo library)*

Our wedding in Joliette, Canada, in 1992 with Lucie's parents, Omar Motani, family and friends.
(Robert Etcheverry, Jay Naidoo library)

En route to court with Sydney Mufamadi in 1991.
(William Matlala)

Campaigning for the ANC in 1994. With Lionel
September, Elijah Barayi and Marcel Golding.
(Jay Naidoo library)

Solidarity with Gainers workers' strike, mid-winter Edmonton, Canada, in 1992.
(Paul Purritt, Jay Naidoo library)

Building international solidarity. Meeting between CUT (Brazil), CGIL (Italy) and COSATU at
the COSATU head office in 1993. *(William Matlala)*

Building peace through sport. Soccer match at Orlando Stadium, Soweto, including John Robbie, Themba
Khoza (IFP), Jayendra Naidoo (COSATU and ANC), Hennie Bekker (IFP), Brigadier Dirk Gous (SAP),
Meverett Koetz (National Peace Accord), Jay Naidoo (COSATU and ANC), Peter Harris (National Peace
Accord), Humphry Ndlovu (IFP), Tokyo Sexwale (ANC) and Sydney Mufamadi. *(Jay Naidoo library)*

It was a bare bachelor flat with a mattress, a few plates and cups and a small fridge. This was a hideout and the rest of the tenants looked as desperate as I did. It was an unspoken rule not to engage in any conversation; an imperceptible nod was the only sign of recognition between people living in the netherworld for a variety of reasons. I had a small suitcase of clothes that I kept in the car.

I would drop in for supper at various homes of friends and comrades. Some of them were just decent people with no political connections. In tough times these were the safest homes – friends of friends. Questions were never asked. I was given a key and came and went at my discretion. In this climate I learnt never to sit against a window – my back was always against the wall with my eye on the entrance of any venue.

I learnt never to make phone calls beyond those that were absolutely necessary. I worked on the suspicion that we were infiltrated. It meant that the apartheid state with all its resources probably knew what we were doing. I only needed to know what was necessary for the organisation. The less I knew about underground activity in terms of the armed struggle, the safer it was for me and the guerrillas involved.

The State of Emergency was disastrous timing for COSATU. Barely seven months since our launch, we were just beginning to establish ourselves, employ people and look for offices. The serious business of forming regions and merging unions was only starting.

In July we decided to mobilise people in demonstrations, culminating in a 'Day of Action' – to call for a stay-away was illegal. It was a failure as only a small percentage of COSATU members heeded the call. On May Day, only weeks earlier, the stoppage had been highly successful, with more than 1.5 million workers staying away. But now perhaps workers were exhausted by their earlier actions or perhaps they too were disheartened. The unions were crippled by state aggression. As we said in our COSATU call:

> Our leaders are detained, scores are in hiding, many offices are closed and our statements are censored. The industrial relations system which workers have painstakingly established over the years is being systematically assaulted.[11]

We recognised that a huge challenge awaited us in building the foundations of this new federation. Political rhetoric and slogans without substance was demagoguery and was not the path to building an organisation. Rather it involved painstaking work on workers' daily bread-and-butter issues.

We had to do some damage control. I spelled out the work that had to be done to recover from the state onslaught in the *South African Labour Bulletin*:

> [I]n the initial period our communications were disrupted, and structures were not able to operate normally – meetings were either disrupted or banned outright. In the Western Cape our publications have been banned, and on the [H]ighveld our meetings banned.
>
> In local areas, facilities for shop stewards have been denied to us. Scores of key leadership figures involved in sensitive negotiations have been forced into hiding ... In the second week of the State of Emergency meetings took place at various levels, where various steps were outlined.
>
> In cases where shop stewards had been detained, the unions should immediately elect a replacement. When officials had been detained, the shop stewards should take over. Shop stewards should demand time off to attend to trade union business. Moral and material support should be given to the families of the detained.[12]

We made demands that related to the continued operation on the shop floor – paid time off for shop stewards to attend to union business; guaranteed jobs and pay for detainees; the right to hold meetings on company property in company time.

The response of the employer organisations was mixed. Some openly welcomed the State of Emergency, saying that it would restore stability to the country. Other employers made statements of disassociation; but in our view these did not really resolve the attack on the trade unions. They needed to go much further and make fundamental demands on the government. Some employers conceded to our demands to enable us to regain our footing by holding meetings on company premises.

The failure of the July stay-away made me rethink my priorities. At this time there were more divisions in the federation than there were before we first formed COSATU. Politics could wait. I decided to focus all my energy on building strong, powerful national industrial unions. And I drove that policy.

'The guiding slogan of our organisation is that the union must be [strong] on the factory floor and not in the offices,' I insisted. 'That would mean that the labour movement in South Africa will survive any onslaught made on it. The political climate is also very different in that there is a high level of political awareness and confidence.'[13]

There was to be no retreat from this principle. I sought out the support of the key union leaders in the larger industrial unions and urged them to play a more decisive role in shaping the federation structures and implementing the Congress resolutions.

The mental and physical strain was taking its toll on me. I had to find an emotional escape. Howie Gabriels, Dirk Hartford, who became editor of *COSATU News*, and Frank Meintjies, who acted as my Information Officer, were all a key part of my social network. Howie and Gertie's daughter, Nina, and later their son, Paolo, became part of my family and provided the main social input I had. I enjoyed the suppers, the family picnics and the games we played. This was as close to a normal life as I thought I would ever experience.

Then there were the evenings of jazz at Kippies, Jameson's Bar, boisterous clubs in Hillbrow, the bustling no-rules multiracial high-rise flatland atop the Berea, where the police feared to tread. It was here that we binged on occasion, enjoying the throbbing music, wild dancing and even the terrible food. The crowd was progressive and on those rare occasions I found camaraderie and was able to let my guard down without the pressure of politics.

We lived life one day at a time.

16

A long with our internal efforts, international solidarity was also vital to COSATU's survival and growth. South Africa was well integrated into the Western world and many Western governments heavily involved in the Cold War saw the white-supremacist government as a bulwark against communism in southern Africa.

This was particularly so in the context where the MPLA (Popular Movement for the Liberation of Angola) and FRELIMO (Front for the Liberation of Mozambique) were Marxist movements supported in the armed struggle against Portuguese colonialism by the Soviet Union and Cuba.

Despite the fact that the ANC was being supported militarily by the Soviet Union and had a close alliance with the South African Communist Party (SACP), it was a nationalist organisation committed to a democratic multi-party state.

In South Africa we viewed the real content of apartheid as a cheap labour system benefiting a racial minority who sheltered behind an ideology of racism and white superiority. But the manufacturing sector continued to grow exponentially throughout the 1970s and 1980s. There was also the need for a more educated labour force. These factors, together with the solidarity from the millions of people across the world incensed by what the United Nations defined as a 'crime against humanity', proved to be a powerful combination.

From Norway to New Zealand, stevedores were refusing to load ships to South Africa. Even erstwhile supporters of the apartheid regime such as Ronald Reagan (President of the United States from 1981 to 1989) and Margaret Thatcher (Prime Minister of the United Kingdom from 1979 to 1990) were forced to make concessions to a universal demand for firmer action against apartheid.

At the Commonwealth Summit in the Bahamas in late 1985 a division in the Commonwealth between the United Kingdom and the developing world was only averted by the appointment of a credible team of eminent people who would intervene with the South African government to attempt to find a negotiated settlement with its black majority.

When the Eminent Persons Group (EPG) first came to South Africa, they asked to have a meeting with COSATU. We were not all that interested. We thought that as representatives of the Commonwealth, the group would be vetoed by Thatcher, who we saw as an unequivocal supporter of the apartheid regime. We wanted sanctions, not talks.

Building the broadest possible coalition to isolate the apartheid regime was paramount, and we had presented our case for sanctions. As a vibrant trade union movement, we were the legitimate representative and were a powerful voice in building the international sanctions movement. Our detractors argued that sanctions would hit the workers the hardest. My response was that while this was true, the apartheid regime was the greater evil that trapped the black majority in poverty and inequality, which was the biggest obstacle to a lasting solution to South Africa's intractable problems.

We found solid allies in the international anti-apartheid movements. By the mid-1980s the ANC had sharpened its diplomatic offensive and, backed by spontaneous demonstrations led by non-state groupings in the unions, churches and across campuses and workplaces, the campaign against apartheid reached its peak. This was the single biggest issue of the day and followed on the successes of global campaigns against slavery, colonialism and the Vietnam War. Now South Africa became the focal point of global mobilisation.

In the meantime, we agreed that General Olusegun Obasanjo of Nigeria from the EPG could come to our offices to discuss whether or not we could have a meeting. At the time, the COSATU head office was at Lekton House in downtown Johannesburg. The lifts weren't working and scores of mineworkers who had been fired in one of the many strikes of the time were sleeping on the floor.

General Obasanjo walked up to the fifth floor with us and stepped around the sleeping workers to get to my office. During that meeting he said to us: 'I don't mind if you want one man one vote, or one man two votes; at the end of the day we are here to help you. You decide that thing.'

So I gave him our views, saying that we had very serious reservations not about the members, who we greatly admired, but about the mandate and role of the government of the United Kingdom. But we agreed to meet with the EPG.

The gathering was at a venue in the Diocesan Centre in Soweto where we were having our CEC meeting. We had been trying to keep details of our venue fairly closed and under the radar of the security police, but the EPG delegation arrived in a fleet of cars with prominent security, which immediately offended us.

Speaking on behalf of COSATU I said: 'You can see what is happening in this country. This government is not going to listen to anyone. They are determined to use all means to cling to their racist power. We cannot see the purpose of you coming here. There is only one language the regime understands – mass resistance – and we want the government removed because it is the biggest obstacle to peace in our country. We ask that you impose tough sanctions against them.'

EPG member Malcolm Fraser was very offended. He said: 'It is outrageous that we would allow ourselves to be used. We are a delegation of the Commonwealth.'

It was a very tense meeting and ended inconclusively. We were not going to back down. We had every reason to doubt the sincerity of Margaret Thatcher and Ronald Reagan. The 'Iron Lady' was renowned as a union basher; her smashing of the United Kingdom's National Union of Mineworkers in the 1984 strike led by Arthur Scargill represented everything the apartheid state vowed to do to us in South Africa. And Ronald Reagan's policy of 'constructive engagement' was seen by us as nothing short of appeasement.

A week or two later, on 19 May 1986, the South African government bombed Lusaka. The Commonwealth Secretary General Sir Shridath Ramphal called the move 'a declaration of war' and demanded immediate economic sanctions against South Africa. The EPG mission ended abruptly, but the publication of its report in June 1986 and its call for increased and substantial economic sanctions did focus attention on apartheid and built a public momentum that the most important Western governments would find difficult to ignore.

For us, the government's actions in Lusaka were proof that this was not the time to trust the apartheid regime – a bitter battle awaited us.

*　*　*

The strike by over 10 000 OK Bazaars workers in December 1986 was a decisive test of worker militancy. Workers went on strike at 120 stores nationwide in support of our living-wage demands of R450 per month. The credibility of COSATU as an effective coordinating body for mobilising workers was on the line, as was our previous unheeded call for action. I knew we had to win this strike.

Everyone was watching the outcome: friends and enemies. This was the largest country strike with national demands – national collective bargaining had arrived, irrespective of the attitude of employers or their resistance to the phenomenon.

The OK management stood firm, understanding the implications and keen to hold the line against increasing worker militancy. The strike dragged on for 77 days. With very little resources in the union, no strike pay and with the logistical challenges of keeping information flowing and daily attendance by union members at pickets and report-back meetings, it proved to be a logistical challenge.

COSATU threw its weight behind the strike. OK was largely owned by Anglo American, South Africa's biggest conglomerate, and we convened Anglo shop-steward councils to build the pressure on them. We called on community support in favour of a boycott of the OK retail chain. We mobilised solidarity action and we connected to our international allies. The COSATU headquarters and the streets of Johannesburg shook with the militancy of the OK workers, mainly women, as they fiercely extended their strike.

My long-time friend Jayendra Naidoo was the national strike coordinator for the union and we spent much time discussing union strategy. In 1981 Jayendra had clashed with the key leadership in the Durban political under-ground on the micro-management of strategy and tactics on the student front and was increasingly marginalised. Then he volunteered in the Commercial, Catering and Allied Workers Union of South Africa (CCAWUSA) led by Emma Mashinini. Highly effective in building a Natal regional presence, he was quickly absorbed into its national structures.

The OK strike was important because it led to a chain reaction. Over a thousand workers were detained – 'most being released only after bail of R1 000 each had been posted. The arrests proved a burden on the union, which was forced to send a delegation abroad to seek financial assistance.'[14]

COSATU called a meeting of shop stewards from Anglo American companies on 8 February 1987, and over 300 shop stewards from all Anglo companies, representing every region and affiliate, met at COSATU House. The response: solidarity action, demonstrations and short work stoppages, which in turn sparked widespread public sympathy amongst black customers despite the fact that no boycott was formally called.

We were reeling from the impact of the second State of Emergency. There was deep anger at the army occupation of the townships, the harassment of students and attacks on the union and community organisations. Consumer boycotts were to become a potent weapon in the hands of communities barricaded by the security forces. Although the enforcers, mainly the youth, engaged in excesses that assaulted our decency, like forcing elderly people to drink the cooking oil they had purchased in towns and confiscating shopping bags, the campaign also provided a platform for action and solidarity.

In negotiations a mediated settlement was reached: a wage increase of R100 across the board; a minimum wage of R400 per month; improvements in staff discounts; and the return of all goods repossessed by the company during the strike. Of the 510 dismissed workers, 364 were reinstated.

The strike was a victory for the CCAWUSA, and more broadly for COSATU, and workers flooded into our ranks. The *South African Labour Bulletin* noted at the time: 'Within the community the strike provided a focus for mass mobilisation and practical involvement at a time when the state clamped down on other campaigns and there was a general lull in political activity.'[15]

Tapping into this spirit of defiance accelerated our growth in COSATU, and drove the membership up in its wake. I would use this momentum to drive ruthlessly the Congress policies on 'One Industry, One Union' and the consolidation of the COSATU regions.

I had found a flat in Yeoville and I tried to carve out a home for myself. It was an attempt to create a more meaningful life outside of COSATU. My work-days were long, fifteen hours, and frequently seven days a week. This was my obsession: I was accountable. The buck stopped with me. The awesome sense of responsibility weighed heavily. We were not an academic group debating strategy and theory in a classroom. This was the laboratory of life. Decisions we made could mean life or death to our leaders, the members and their families.

I learnt to survive on adrenalin and a few hours of light sleep. There was no place for a personal life beyond the casual relationships I had. That was the grim reality I realised as I hid behind a fatalistic denialism that death was nothing to fear. Somehow the image of my mother and her lessons of meditation always rescued me from the depths of the depressions that I sometimes experienced. That was the only emotional link I allowed myself.

17

Gradually COSATU began to emerge as a federation. By early 1987 people wanted to join COSATU – not the unions, but the federation. We were creating an image of COSATU that became a magnet. Membership was rocketing, especially as we began to build the national unions. In March 1987, amidst fierce opposition from the community and UDF-aligned unions, the CEC of COSATU resolved to give an ultimatum to unions: merge or get out of COSATU.

For me this was a crucial test of our discipline and commitment. There had been considerable opposition from certain leaders and I was determined to force the issue to a head. I had realised that only strong national unions with responsibilities and accountability to thousands of well-trained shop stewards and workers on the factory floors would behave responsibly given the challenges ahead. A war was in the air. We needed a well-disciplined army to defend our gains.

COSATU had moved from Lekton House to an eleven-storey building at the bottom end of Johannesburg. Doornfontein was a run-down, light industrial area close to the train station and taxi ranks and part of the decaying inner city. This was good. It would be the headquarters of our liberated zone. Cyril Ramaphosa and I went to see the building. It was dilapidated but it had potential, we thought. We proceeded to the landlord's office and were handed a thick legal document that we were asked to sign.

'You are the lawyer, Cyril,' I said. He had never signed a lease agreement before and neither had I. We perused the document, looked at each other, haggled about the rent and signed off. That was the last lease agreement that did not undergo the scrutiny of our legal firm Cheadle, Thomson and Haysom (CTH).

COSATU House, as we named it, became the hub of union activities in the industrial heartland of Johannesburg. My office was on the eleventh floor with a magnificent view of the central business district. We had graduated to a modern federation with centralised facilities for printing and documentation and mass meetings. It was a pleasure to arrive at the crack of dawn, missing the peak traffic, and to walk briskly up the stairs. It was the only real exercise I got but the practice remains a lifetime passion. Many of the major unions, including the NUM, NUMSA and others, occupied floors in the building and that gave us the confidence of critical mass and access to the resources of these well-established unions.

Before we had time to recover from the OK Bazaars strike the next one was upon us – the railway strike involving over 20 000 workers who walked off their jobs. The union, the newly revived South African Railways and Harbour Workers Union (SARHWU), was not strong enough to deal with the energy this strike unleashed and COSATU became closely involved.

It all began with the unfair dismissal of one of the worker leaders, Andrew Nedzamba, which led to a strike in the depot of City Deep, the major inland port for the import and export of manufactured goods through the main harbour of Durban. And then it spread like wildfire throughout the depots, astounding us.

The state-owned South African Transport Service (SATS) was part of the core of the apartheid state. The white workers enjoyed security of tenure, good salaries and government housing, and belonged to a sweetheart union set up by management to control the militancy of workers. Most of the black workers were migrant workers living in bleak, overcrowded single-sex hostels.

The hostels were designed to keep human costs to a minimum. No attention was paid to families or worker education or health needs. These were prisons of cheap labour. On the mines and in the state-run hostels, an internal jackboot security force was the law. In the SATS strike the major hostels around Johannesburg were barricaded by security forces as the strike took hold.

Yet we managed to infiltrate these controlled centres, and in the early days of modern unionism these hostel dwellers were our backbone. We won the trust of hostel inmates. We ate with them. We planned with them. We became one family; a bond of comradeship even in the face of hostility from the employers and the state.

When workers protested against the management allegation that Nedzamba, the dismissed worker, was suspected of financial irregularities, the company proposed that he pay a fine of R80. This was almost a quarter of a monthly salary and workers took a stand against this arbitrary deduction.

SARHWU at that stage was still small and weak. And COSATU was seen as a major threat to the system. The company was not going to give us one inch. The Minister of Transport, Eli Louw, enforcing the hard-line position against COSATU, issued a proclamation in the Government Gazette that gave the SATS management the right to fire the workers.

SATS rolled out its puppet union the Black Transport Union (BLATU) to undermine the strike by issuing thousands of pamphlets caricaturing the SARHWU union. This was the dirty-tricks department of the state security apparatus that would soon grind out its propaganda in a fierce tide as COSATU rose to top-of-the-list of public enemies of the state.

SATS started dismissing workers. The key leadership of the union was arrested and taken to jail. Quite quickly we had a crisis situation. We were sitting with new worker leaders – you could not even call them shop stewards. In our basement and meeting halls thousands of workers were milling around.

At that point, the headquarters of COSATU became the focal point. Every day thousands of workers gathered in our building and in the streets around our offices. They complained that 'attempts by strikers to speak to non-strikers were met with tear gas and assaults by police'.[16]

One striker remembered the malicious show of force of the police on the platforms of the railway stations when the strike first began: 'Before the train could leave . . . tear gas was sprayed into the coaches . . . When the train arrived at Mayfair station (a fellow passenger) was shot by a (white) person on the platform wearing private clothes.'[17]

Two factors made for an unpredictable situation. The new leadership was soon sitting in detention under the security laws; and a mass of workers, largely leaderless, was to provoke a series of violent incidents that would threaten the very core of COSATU in its battle with the apartheid state.

The police were constantly monitoring the situation and harassing workers. One day, looking over the balcony of my office, I saw that the police had drawn a swastika of the ultra-right-wing paramilitary group, the Afrikaner Weerstandsbeweging (AWB), on the bonnet of one of the many police vans parked just outside our entrance. It was clear to me that they were itching for a fight.

We had to intervene. I relied very heavily on leaders like NUMSA's Moses Mayekiso and Bernie Fanaroff and the NUM's James Motlatsi and Cyril Ramaphosa.

Bernie had studied physics at the University of the Witwatersrand and went on to complete a Ph.D. at the Cavendish Laboratory at Cambridge University. When he returned to South Africa he put his career on the back burner and joined the nascent trade union movement of African workers in South Africa. I found him to be a problem solver with a stubborn streak and a steely determination. He would spend nineteen years as a union organiser, negotiator and national secretary in the metal industry.

'Look, we've got to intervene and create the basis for a settlement,' I urged them. Thousands of workers had joined the union and we needed time to consolidate them and then, strengthened, resume the fight another day.

The situation looked hopeless. All attempts to communicate with the SATS management failed. They would only talk to BLATU, their sweetheart union. The state was communicating irrevocably that it would not deal with COSATU.

*   *   *

On the morning of 22 April, I received a message that there had been a battle with the police at our Germiston office. Three people had been shot dead by the police. Peter Harris, my lawyer and comrade of many years, Bernie Fanaroff and I rushed off to Germiston.

When we arrived at the Germiston office there was chaos. The police had thrown tear gas into a union meeting and as our members came running out, they had shot at them. In the ensuing panic to get out of the hall, men had thrown themselves through the plate-glass windows.

The whole place had been cordoned off and was patrolled by police with automatic weapons. Many of the windows were broken and there were pools and smears of blood and shards of glass everywhere. Another three people were dead. The body of a worker lay face down in the courtyard.

Others had been taken away by ambulance.

As we pushed through the cordon to the commanding officer, the fury rose in my throat.

'You bastards will pay for this,' I thought.

We got into a raging argument with the police who then wanted to charge us with obstruction of justice. We maintained that these were COSATU offices.

We had every right to be there. We had to demonstrate firm resolve while at the same time ensuring that the fully armed and edgy security force was not given the excuse they were looking for to take further action against us.

I turned to Peter. 'I have to talk to the COSATU officials and workers. Please continue the negotiations with the police to keep them off our backs.'

I wanted a chronology of exactly what had happened and a few witness reports. I spoke to the workers, reassuring them that I would make certain that we got to the bottom of this incident. COSATU would step in and support them. These workers had been brutalised.

Peter Harris in the meantime confronted the commanding captain of the security forces and was charged with obstruction of justice. Worse was to come.

*   *   *

Almost simultaneously with our altercation with the police in Germiston, COSATU House was being blockaded by the police. The workers in COSATU House, having heard about the death of workers in Germiston, performed a ritual with *muti* (traditional potions). They decided to march to the railway station, armed with sticks and knives, to catch a train to Germiston. Having taken their *muti*, they believed they were invincible. They met a street patrol of police and attacked them, injuring some of them quite badly. We heard on Radio 702 that three unionists had been shot dead and another five injured near Doornfontein station.

Peter Harris and I were still in Germiston, taking statements from the workers, when we heard that COSATU House was being attacked. We rushed back to find COSATU House under siege, completely sealed. It was like a military operation. The police had snipers on the roof and were armed with R4 rifles. We were effectively barred from our offices.

After mingling with the crowds, we went into an adjacent building and watched what was unfolding. A journalist showed us the way to the rooftop of the building behind us, where we get could get a much better view of the COSATU offices.

It was dusk. The lights were on in the COSATU offices, so we could see the police making their way up floor by floor, smashing down doors and breaking cupboards and desks. They were systematically destroying our offices. I could see the assaults taking place. Comrades were spreadeagled. Several hours later

COSATU employees and members in the building were let out in a single file. A number were herded into police vans and taken to police cells. CTH had a busy time late into the night, negotiating bail for those arrested.

'This is the beginning of the war,' I thought to myself.

We returned to the CTH office, and worked into the early hours of the morning preparing our Supreme Court application. We decided to seek the advice of the eminent and temperamental Ismail Mohamed, senior counsel. His verbal brilliance and incisive intellect, coupled with a healthy dose of arrogance, had made him legendary. I liked him and took pride in his lancet-like piercing of state arguments in the many treason trials around the country.

The following day the Supreme Court application resulted in a restraining order on the police, who were required to undertake that while on guard at COSATU House they would refrain from assaulting or intimidating COSATU members. Meanwhile, the railway strike continued. It was getting bloodier and workers were being evicted from hostels.

Even for a well-established union the strike would have been a daunting challenge. Here was a relatively new union, with much of its leadership detained, striking at the heart of the apartheid state. It would inevitably unleash, I sensed uneasily, a torrent of violence on all sides.

On 27 April, the bodies of four SATS workers were found near Kazerne hostel. They had been necklaced[18] – probably because they were perceived as scabs, or informers – *impimpis*.

For us this was an unmitigated catastrophe. The embryonic union with much of its leadership in jail or in hiding was leaderless. In this brutal and deadly contest some workers had taken the law into their own hands. Nothing could justify this meaningless loss of life. Again I felt a sense of impending doom.

The next day I phoned Peter.

'The building is being surrounded by the police again. Can you get down here now? I have told people to remain calm and not to panic, but if they come in again like they did last time, people will fight with whatever they have and a lot of people will die. That will be playing into their hands. People must understand that. The police are looking for the killers. We need to act before there is a bloody war on our hands.'

I went down to see if I could speak to the commanding officer and stall the police action. They alleged they had been assaulted in COSATU House, which provided a convenient opportunity for the state to mount this campaign and create the legal basis for action (both overt and covert) to begin against us.

I called Bernie Fanaroff and Cyril Ramaphosa. We agreed that the police were creating a climate under which individuals and extremist elements could take the law into their own hands. They had surrounded the building; it was like another military barricade.

We edged our way down the stairs. As we reached the fifth floor we ran into a heavily armed soldier coming up. Seeing his youth and nervous anxiety I shouted to him: 'Hold your fire. We want to talk to your officer in charge.'

We descended with an escort to the ground floor where thousands of workers were locked in the hall, with police lined up outside with automatic rifles. It was clear they were going to break the door down and get the workers to file out one at a time, so that their informer in a balaclava could identify the people responsible for killing the scabs.

Everything was being videotaped by a police team. We reached a tentative agreement – we would negotiate the opening of the door.

I said: 'Please guys, if they break down the door, a lot of people are going to die. These guys are trigger-happy and they are scared, so let's try and save lives. Open the door. We are here; if anyone is taken away we have got a team of lawyers that will act on it immediately.'

The striking workers replied: 'We don't have the keys.'

'Where are the keys?'

'We have thrown them away.'

After negotiation with the commander of the operation we agreed that we would break down the door. On principle we felt that we could not have the security forces breaking the door and we feared that the police would open fire.

First Cyril threw his shoulder against the door. It refused to budge. My attempts were equally futile as I tried to kick the door down. Bernie, despite having recently joined a gym, also found the door unyielding. Our deepening embarrassment was obvious and the workers continued to maintain that they did not have possession of the keys.

The line of heavily armed security police, their automatic weapons trained on the hall, rippled with amusement – we were supposed to be big tough union guys but we could not even break one door down.

The captain stared at us stonily and shouted loudly in Afrikaans: '*Rooi, kom breek hierdie deur*' ('Red [his nickname], come and break down this door').

'Rooi' swaggered down the corridor, his arms bulging with arrogant muscle and a smirk on his face. He grabbed the iron bars, raised his jackboot and smashed the door.

People filed out of the room. It was eerie and frightening with a hooded informer on one side and workers being frogmarched out on the other, a whirring video camera hovering and heavily armed security forces pointing guns at all of us. It was clear the footage would be used by the state broadcaster to paint COSATU as a terrorist organisation that had murdered innocent people.

We had to find a solution to this crisis quickly, before the state could use the situation to crush the strike *and* the entire movement – just as we were beginning to emerge and gain the confidence of the working class.

I sought advice from Peter Harris and Halton Cheadle from CTH on the legal remedy needed to create some space for ourselves. We agreed to meet with Ismail Mohamed. In the discussion the next day we managed to find a loophole in the law in which we could argue that SATS did not follow proper procedure in dismissing 16 000 workers. This would be the basis for a settlement and we applied to the Supreme Court for reinstatement.

The Court concurred in an agreement signed on 5 June 1987 that by 15 June the entire labour force of SATS workers would be reinstated. But the murder charges against eight workers remained, and served to coalesce the workplace struggles with a broader political struggle. After a lengthy trial they were convicted for the murder of four workers.

Despite this setback, the workers' reinstatement was a victory. A mass meeting was convened to celebrate the agreement. Hugely relieved, I found a comfortable bed and fell into a deep sleep.[19]

18

In the meantime, general elections had taken place on 6 May 1987. White voters had returned the National Party to power in even larger numbers – from 119 representatives to 178. It seemed clear that this racially exclusive electorate was increasing the mandate of the apartheid government.

The propaganda from the state-run South African Broadcasting Corporation (SABC) at this time was part of a coordinated military intelligence campaign against us. The SABC had broadcast images of COSATU House with the words 'Torture House' spray-painted on it.

(Looking back on it now, it seems poetic justice that, as Minister of Communications in the first democratic government, one of my initial challenges was the transformation of 'his master's voice' to an accountable public broadcaster.)

Winter had set in and the cold was biting. COSATU's leaders were taking extra precautions and sleeping in a different house every night to avoid the increasing attacks on our homes.

In the early morning of 7 May 1987 I phoned Peter Harris to inform him that I had received a call that COSATU House had been hit by massive bomb blasts. Peter fetched me from the 'safe house' where I had slept the night before. As we pulled up outside our offices we found the entrance cordoned off. We were refused admission to the building, so we decided to gain entry through the garage entrance to which I had a set of keys.

We slipped into the basement. It was devastated. Mountains of rubble were strewn across the floor, fused with twisted steel. Peter began to photograph the scene. The bombs had targeted the inner core pillars in an attempt to implode the building. The place seemed in imminent danger of collapse.

We were interrupted by a heavily armed SWAT forensics team who aggressively ordered us out. They were clearly there to sweep up any remaining evidence, rather than investigate the cause and origins of the blast. They were carrying duffle bags and scattered in different directions with the precision of a clean-up team. There was no room for negotiation.

It would be over a decade later before we would hear evidence from the mastermind behind the attacks. Eugene de Kock was a former police colonel and apartheid arch-assassin. As a shadowy figure from the apartheid era known as 'Prime Evil', he eventually appealed for amnesty for the attacks on (amongst others) COSATU House. In his application before the Truth and Reconciliation Commission (TRC), he detailed how he was acting under instruction of Brigadier Willem Schoon, the head of Unit C1, which, among other things, was responsible for covert operations by members of the group based at Vlakplaas. De Kock declared the order had come from the highest authority in government, presumably President P.W. Botha.

According to De Kock, COSATU House had been placed under observation leading up to the 1987 attack. The rooftop of a nearby building was used to spy on us and a camera concealed in a briefcase was used to video the inside of COSATU House.

The South African Police's explosives unit had a hand in the preparation of the explosives and, De Kock testified, he estimated that it took 'a team of sixteen operatives' and 'about 50 kilograms of explosives of Russian origin' to launch the 1987 attack on COSATU House. The implication in the state propaganda was that COSATU House was a 'terrorist nest of Umkhonto we Sizwe', the armed wing of the ANC whose weapons were supplied by the Soviet Union.

On the day of the blast, men armed with silenced AK47s and carrying cans of beer doctored with drugs to incapacitate our security guards set off from a safe house in Honeydew. They cut the bars to the building's basement and the explosives experts climbed down a rope to set the charges. The whole operation apparently took about four minutes. The 'bombing party' then 'watched the explosion from a highway east of Johannesburg'.[20]

The operation was clearly designed to weaken COSATU by disrupting our base of operations – the building was declared 'unsafe' by the local municipality – and our lines of communication. Houses and offices were being bombed and vandalised, activists were being arrested and the SABC continued to churn out endless propaganda against us. Many union leaders, including myself, went around in disguise.[21]

One day I passed Howie and Gertie Gabriels, my administrator at the time, in the street in Hillbrow. They were heading to a meeting venue with me. I followed them, and saw them sit down and order some coffee. I watched to see that no one had followed them and then went to sit with them. They looked surprised at first but then we made eye contact and laughed quietly.

Then, on 14 June 1987, the cars parked outside Howie's home, belonging to Dirk Hartford and Howie, were petrol-bombed. A Telkom van was seen speeding off into the night.

For weeks afterwards, I checked under the bonnet to see if there was a car bomb each time I returned to my car. But it became impossible to live in fear of death all the time. Our cars were always parked in the street. I sat in the car one day and resigned myself to not checking. Perhaps it was the fatalism in my genes – if it was my karma to go, then this would be the day. But fear had to be overcome daily as danger and death were constant companions.

*   *   *

Despite the tense climate, my focus on building COSATU continued in earnest. We engaged with Archbishop Desmond Tutu, the indomitable and charismatic leader of the South African Council of Churches (SACC), which was a progressive interdenominational forum of churches. Archbishop Tutu offered COSATU shelter at the SACC's headquarters in Khotso House.

My association with the churches had spanned many years. Several of the activists from the Young Christian Workers (YCW) were committed to the worker struggle and made strong organisers. The SACC and the Catholic Bishops Conference led by Archbishop Denis Hurley were close friends of COSATU and we could rely on their moral and financial support when we faced tough times as a result of state repression or protracted strikes. Often church halls were our last place of refuge.

In June the South African Commercial, Catering and Allied Workers Union (SACCAWU), the retail union, was created out of a merger of different unions, and the National Education, Health and Allied Workers Union (NEHAWU), our union for the public sector, was launched.

I was convinced that strong shop-floor organisation would be our key defence against state attack. We had to drive this point home relentlessly. The principle of organising robust national industrial unions into a tight federation was non-negotiable for me. Everything else followed from this.

My main ally in pursuing this goal was the very grassroots of the union movement. The shop-steward councils were a refreshing break from the tortuous debates we would sometimes have at a national level. The tension between these councils and national union structures was important to keep the organisation responsive.

My focus was to maintain the unity and strength of COSATU, which depended on our not enforcing a political line and allowing democratic debate to take place. Even if I disagreed with a point of view, it was imperative that we allow the space for people to articulate and advance their arguments and to fight for their views.

In this period I was resisting an increasing tendency to suppress debate and criticism, which I felt would be the end of COSATU. If we did not create an environment in which everyone felt they had a place and a stake in the ownership of the organisation, that could destroy us.

Our debates were intensified because the external repression required a political response, and the only viable political movement was COSATU. Labels of 'populism' and 'workerism' were flung around, which reflected a fierce battle for hegemony within the movement.

I had little time for those ideologues and their well-worn dogmas. They were usually the weakest organisers and invariably only kept their relevance by polarising debate and flinging 'counter-revolutionary' labels at others. This tendency, which is evident even today, is symptomatic of people who fear democracy and open debate and see others as pawns in a political game in which they position themselves as 'the representatives' of the poor.

Back in the late 1980s, these ideologues posed as the 'keepers of the Lusaka line', often determined in an arbitrary way by some self-appointed group. The consequence of this political practice was to threaten our ability to respond effectively. Our strategy had to build capacity and capability at a grassroots level. This meant the maximum delegation of authority so that local leaders felt confident to lead. The idea of the 'big chief' was inimical to our growth and exposed us when top leadership was detained. COSATU was the very essence of a modern trade union movement – thinking, debate and accountability were deeply rooted in our culture of struggle. The result was a Code of Conduct for Political Discussion in COSATU. The fight had to be public and the membership engaged.

'Leadership has to be earned daily' was my mantra. Organisation is not just a conveyor belt for anyone – inside or outside of COSATU. I considered myself to be an ANC activist, but my primary accountability was to the grassroots constituency that elected me in COSATU.

The debates rose to a crescendo at COSATU's National Congress in July 1987. This Congress was the supreme policy-making constitutional structure. Months before the Congress, I would circulate a secretariat discussion detailing the political and organisational review of the past and some of the policy challenges and future directions. Everyone understood that the key imperative was the stability and unity of the organisation.

But the leadership of the unions would use the Congress as a platform to contest their relative political standing in the organisation. Weeks of sifting through resolutions of the affiliates and negotiating compromises to frame the composite resolutions that would go to Congress were a nightmare for me. But, given the extent of state repression, it was important to manage the outcomes in a way that unified the organisation.

Politics always dominated the Congress discussions. In my mind it was not only undesirable but impossible to separate the fight for our rights on the factory floor from the broader struggle for our political freedom in society. What we needed was a disciplined alliance with other mass-based movements inside the country.

Undoubtedly the only political liberation movement whose leadership and policies on issues of non-racialism and the working class were tried and tested was the ANC. The key issue for me was to recognise that workers joined us, a trade union federation, irrespective of political membership; and that this had to entail a patient process to raise their political consciousness. I would not ram my views down the throats of our members.

In preparation for the Congress, I held a series of political consultations with comrades in the Mass Democratic Movement and we agreed to present a united front. The Congress was one of the few legal mass platforms operating at the time. Public debate, including mass protest meetings, activist workshops in the townships and street committee meetings were stifled by detentions and state repression.

Our key allies in the UDF were invited to address the congress – Peter Mokaba from the South African Youth Congress (SAYCO), Murphy Morobe from the UDF and Frank Chikane from the SACC. I had preparatory meetings with them to spell out the strategic objectives we had as an organisation and the need to preserve and consolidate the unity of COSATU.

Peter Mokaba's inflammatory and provocative speech at the Congress broke all the agreements and he had suddenly set himself up as the 'crown prince' of the ANC. I felt a cold fury rise in my guts as I listened to this self-appointed ideologue rave on about 'counter-revolutionaries' in our midst who were opposed to the adoption of the Freedom Charter. This was a classic example of demagoguery that I felt fitted the label that Lenin had termed 'an infantile disorder'.[22]

Everything Mokaba ranted about I had already discussed with the senior leadership of the ANC in exile, including Oliver Tambo, Chris Hani, Jacob Zuma and Joe Slovo, and they had been unconditional in their support for our strategy. COSATU was mounting a frontal attack on the apartheid regime and could ill afford internal divisions.

None of the other invited speakers that day did anything to relieve the tension. I felt it was a rehearsed show hatched in some back room; in a characteristic disregard for internal democracy, they had set themselves up as the decision makers of the Congress. A number of unions considered walking out – not because they disagreed with the fundamental principle of adopting the Freedom Charter, but because they took issue with the way in which it was being bulldozed through. I felt this was an undemocratic political practice that could undermine democracy, disempower the backbone of our organisation – the working-class leaders – and turn COSATU into the 'yellow unions' we had fought so hard against.

In spite of these differences the Congress resolved to intensify the Living Wage Campaign around a set of national goals that included our demands for a decent living wage and improved working conditions and job security; May Day as a paid public holiday; maternity leave; an end to the hostel system; and the right to education and training on the job. These were still the basis of our core demands in the collective bargaining strategy, in terms of which COSATU was the strongest representative of the working class.

But in 1987, we also faced our 'night of the long knives' internally. Certain comrades felt flushed with success that they had routed the 'counter-revolutionaries' because the political resolutions had gone their way. Many other more serious leaders realised how close we had come to splitting the organisation and agreed to work together to rebuild our unity. I criss-crossed the country, talking to our members and our supporters, and arguing for a respect for democratic political practice.

We needed a strong, vibrant organisation that reflected the unity of our purpose and a shared vision shaped by our people through democratic discussion. We needed a Code of Conduct that held our leaders accountable. As an open, transparent organisation, our mandate was derived from our internal democracy in which leaders from the shop floor carried mandates from our members. It might have been slow but this was how we operated. This was our most important defence against the brutality of the apartheid state.

My approach was to pose a set of questions for us to answer:

> We see COSATU as an active participant in the liberation struggle. We see ourselves as a political force at local, regional and national levels. And we are therefore forced to confront the following questions.
> What sort of politics?
> What sort of liberation are we seeking?
> Who are our friends and allies in the struggle?
> What are we fighting for?
> What are we fighting against?[23]

Our conclusion was that the union movement was not a conduit for political leaders to use as a conveyor belt because political organisation had been suppressed. We had to explore these questions for ourselves.

If we had had a schism it would have killed us. If unions had left because they couldn't maintain not a different political line, but a different *nuance* of that line, then we could have ended up with the whole federation being split. This was not textbook doctrine but democracy built in the laboratory of union struggle.

I was intrigued some months later to be invited to a secret meeting.

19

COSATU was like a locomotive that had taken a long time to stoke up but was now running at full steam. The destination etched in our minds was total liberation. There was no room for compromise.

It was in this context that the great Mineworkers' Strike of August 1987 broke out. Cyril Ramaphosa had come over to Howie's house, where I was staying, for a drink. In the deadlocked wage-bargaining talks at the Chamber of Mines he needed to canvass the consequences of a sector strike.

We discussed what had happened in the big strike of 1946 when the reaction was brutal and the strike smashed. Police using violence and live ammunition had forced striking workers down the mine shafts. In spite of the brutality 100 000 miners brought the mining sector to a standstill for a few days. Victimisation was rife and hundreds of workers were arrested, imprisoned or deported.

Later, as I read up more about this historic strike, I was amazed at the similarities between 1946 and 1987.[24] In the 1946 strike, before the decision was adopted, speaker after speaker mounted the platform and demanded immediate action. One worker said: 'When I think of how we left our homes in the reserves, our children naked and starving, we have nothing more to say. Every man must agree to strike on 12 August. It is better to die than go back with empty hands.'[25]

After the decision to strike was adopted, the union President, J.B. Marks, stressed the gravity of the strike decision and said that the workers must be prepared for repression by possible violence. 'You are challenging the very basis of the cheap labour system,' he told them, 'and must be ready to sacrifice in the struggle for the right to live as human beings.'

We finished a bottle of whisky and opened another, talking into the early hours of the morning. The mining industry was the core of the apartheid state. It was like a state within a state: it had its own army, its own rules, its own police force, its own system of recruitment, its own authority and vast resources at its disposal. We knew the industry would move very heavily, and considerable attention had to be paid to detail.

It was only five years since the NUM had been founded, but it had become the fastest-growing union in the country. This was not surprising given that the gross exploitation of the colonial past and the mining industry's ruthless pursuit in amassing capital had changed very little since the beginning of the twentieth century.

The migrant labour system was perfected by the mining industry – men were recruited from their villages, leaving their families behind, and came to work and live in the mines and their single-sex hostels in dormitories of 30 or more bunk beds. Housed along tribal lines, the men slept, cooked and ate there. It was a high-risk, unnatural life, without the company of women, children and the community. From time to time, unbearable tensions would erupt into what mine managers called 'faction fighting'.

Since I had first become an organiser in Pietermaritzburg, I had been acutely aware of the role of hostels in South Africa's political economy. The hostel dwellers were at the bottom of the ladder and extremely vulnerable. They were quick to grasp the value of labour organisation. If you lost your job, you got shipped back to your homeland – or, especially in the mining industry, to the neighbouring states. And losing your job was a very real loss of one's means of survival and it affected the many lives that depended on the breadwinner. It meant the difference between life and death.

Mineworkers had many grievances, ranging from the still-atrocious salary structure and retrenchments, to the living conditions and health hazards in the hostels, to racial discrimination, violence and safety issues underground.[26] These grievances were widespread and deeply felt, yet the workers' demands were not being met.

The NUM prepared very carefully. It would be as much a symbolic strike as a life-and-death struggle for recognition and mineworkers' control. The date of 9 August was chosen because it was the anniversary of the great strike of 1946. The bosses were caught by surprise by the organisation and discipline as a massive 360 000 workers walked off the mine shafts in major rallies across the country. It was phenomenal. Even our own leadership was surprised by the degree of support for the action.

The state and capital perceived this as a fundamental attack. We had to be crushed. The strikers were subjected to violence from police and mine security forces (dogs, shotguns, surveillance helicopters), tear gas was thrown into the hostels of striking workers and live ammunition was used in many instances. The security forces were brought in on the pretext that there was widespread intimidation.

After the violence of the railway strike there had been soul-searching discussion in COSATU and a Code of Conduct for strikes was adopted – albeit in a situation of war between us and the apartheid state.

Marshals, drawn from the ranks of the membership, were our military equivalent of the shop stewards keeping discipline and order in the battles that were now daily descending on us. Managing massive demonstrations and strikes galvanising tens of thousands of people required a more disciplined organisation.

The leadership of the NUM was under intense pressure. Workers were being brutalised by naked aggression and cruelty. We had to intervene to de-escalate it. COSATU decided to respond to the violence on all sides. While the state and bosses were in control above ground, we were in control underground. So we took a strategic initiative to deal with the ringleaders underground. Eventually we forced through negotiations that resulted in a truce. We knew we would not win against the state and capital in the short term.

To negotiate a truce, James Motlatsi, Cyril Ramaphosa, Chris Dlamini and I arrived at a police station in Welkom in the old Orange Free State. There we met with Adriaan Vlok, then the Minister of Police.

The white miners' union presented its side and we presented ours. But this was a negotiation in a public arena. We had to extract a commitment from Vlok as the Minister of Police to deal with the violence above ground before a solution to the violence underground was solved. We argued that the underground violence was a consequence of violence above ground. He had to take action against this. So, surrounded by the press, he was obliged to reach agreement – above ground.

The days dragged on, stretching into weeks. But support never wavered, even as the repression grew. The final weapon of this unholy alliance was mass dismissals. All pretences at a more liberal labour relations system were thrown out of the window: 20 000 workers were dismissed at Vaal Reefs by Anglo American, amongst them Zwelinzima Vavi. The next day 10 000 dismissals followed and by 21 August 50 000 mineworkers had been fired. By 27 August 9 mineworkers had been killed, 500 injured and approximately 400 arrested.

On the twenty-first day the NUM executive, fearing a total destruction of the union, and with COSATU's support, announced an end to this historic Mineworkers' Strike. Many were deeply angered by the decision, even within the union. Some also felt that COSATU had not mounted a sufficiently effective solidarity response to support the NUM strike. It would be many years before we were able to rebuild the NUM.

The images that remain in my mind are of the thousands of weary and defeated workers wrapped in their multicoloured blankets against the biting cold of the winter mornings being loaded on buses taking them to distant homelands and neighbouring countries. Life was a fight for survival for these workers.

The hard line had been driven by Anglo American, led by Peter Gush, who had been President of the Chamber of Mines just prior to the strike.[27] The mining sector establishment, under his guidance, felt that the NUM had to be tamed and the authority of the mine owners reasserted. The Chamber had based its actions on what had happened in the UK miners' strike in which Arthur Scargill and the British NUM had been brutally defeated, the coal mining industry scaled down and the British trade union movement weakened. It had been a major political and ideological victory for Margaret Thatcher and the Conservative Party. No doubt the mining sector had the full backing and collaboration of the apartheid state.

At the time, industrial unrest policing was overseen by the National Security Management System, which coordinated intelligence and state responses to strike action. According to Anthony Butler, at that point this position was a politically sensitive post, filled 'inevitably [by] an Afrikaner political insider who could be trusted by P.W. Botha. This hard-line minister was one of the few with direct access to the president at all times.'[28]

Ironically, the Deputy Minister at the time was Roelf Meyer, who would later become, with Cyril Ramaphosa, one of the two key architects of the constitutional negotiations.

* * *

Out of the experiences of 1987, COSATU steadily developed new strategies for a stronger, united front with our allies – internally, internationally and with comrades in exile. We knew that representatives of liberal capital itself were talking to the ANC in Lusaka and Europe. They could see that apartheid's contradictions were coming to the fore. The political balance was shifting.

In the southern African region, the implementation of the United Nations Resolution 435 towards independence in Namibia, originally adopted on 29 September 1978, was finally taking its first tentative steps forward although it was only finalised in December 1988. COSATU, determined to live up to the spirit of internationalism, had vowed to mobilise material and political support for our labour allies in the National Union of Namibian Workers and the South West African People's Organisation (SWAPO) led by Sam Nujoma. South Africa's illegal occupation of Namibia and its covert war in southern Angola in support of the right-wing UNITA (National Union for the Total Independence of Angola) forces turned into a full-scale invasion to repel an MPLA military push against the strongholds of UNITA.

Fidel Castro sent in his highest-trained troops in solidarity with the MPLA. His goal was not merely to defend Cuito Cuanavale; it was to force the South African Defence Force (SADF) out of Angola once and for all. He later described this strategy to South African Communist Party leader Joe Slovo: 'Cuba would halt the South African onslaught and then attack from another direction, "like a boxer who with his left hand blocks the blow and with his right – strikes".'[29]

The battle over control of Cuito Cuanavale in southern Angola pitted the might of the SADF and UNITA against a combined Cuban and Angolan government force in March 1988. It was to be a defining moment in our history. This was the largest land battle fought on the African continent since the Second World War and one of the flashpoints in the Cold War. With the SADF stalemated along with President Reagan's strategy of 'constructive engagement', a tentative agreement was reached that linked South African withdrawal from southern Angola, the realisation of Resolution 435 and the withdrawal of Cuban troops from Angola.

We were ecstatic and claimed victory against the invincible SADF. It reinforced our belief in regional solidarity and we eulogised the internationalism of the Cuban nation and its charismatic leader Fidel Castro.

While it strengthened our resolve and gave us the hope of justice in our fight for freedom, tragedy befell the workers of Pietermaritzburg.

20

September 1987 had seen the opening of a new battlefront in Natal, mainly in the district of Pietermaritzburg. In just one week 83 people were killed – the majority of them UDF or COSATU members. The psychological toll was enormous. I rarely ate and the constant worry gave me a duodenal ulcer while at the same time attacking my soul.

I would visit the homes of bereaved families and offer the little consolation I could. Many were innocent victims caught in the crossfire as the state continued its vindictive war to wear us down and dent our morale. Some of the victims were people I had met in my stint as an organiser in the Pietermaritzburg area a few years before. They trusted us as leaders and believed in the justness of our struggle. It made me more determined to build our defences. Ultimately we had to remove the root of the cancer in our society – the apartheid state. Nothing less would end the bloodshed.

The potential for violent conflict in Natal had been brewing for a long time. In May 1985, more than 900 workers were dismissed at the factory of BTR Sarmcol in Howick, a town some 20 kilometres north of Pietermaritzburg. BTR was owned by a British multinational that refused to recognise the union. As the workers' lawyer argued at the time:

This strike has been a tragedy for this community. It's destroyed people's lives here. There's incredible poverty here. Many of the workers, in fact, the majority of workers had an average of 25 years service with the company when they were dismissed. It was their whole livelihood and there's nothing for them at the end of the day.[30]

COSATU's plan had been to mobilise the entire Midlands region – to fan out from the economic hub of Pietermaritzburg, to Howick, Escourt, and then on to Ladysmith and Newcastle. We had identified Sarmcol as a base from which to start.

Within three days of the strike starting, the entire workforce was dismissed. The Metal and Allied Workers Union (MAWU) then responded with a wave of sympathy strikes as well as boycotts of white shops. We were mounting a campaign to fight for the workers' reinstatement when, on 8 December 1985, Inkatha held a rally there, bussing in hundreds of its supporters.

My long-standing friend Phineas Sibiya, chairperson of the Sarmcol shop stewards and the NUMSA regional worker leader, with whom I had spent much time, was a key labour leader. He was holding a strike committee meeting when armed Inkatha *impimpis* abducted and took the four committee members to the Mpophomeni community hall where they were tortured, then driven to a deserted stretch of road on the way to Lion's River. There three of them, Phineas, Simon Ngubane and Florence Mnikathi, were executed one by one and their bodies burnt together in a car on the scene. Only Phineas's brother, Micca, managed to escape. That same night, Alpheus Nkabinde, a youth activist in Mpophomeni, was killed in the township.[31]

These murders affected me deeply. I could not count the number of times I had driven a combi load of shop stewards around in the area. We were family. The battle had reached new heights; this was a state-condoned assassination strategy.

Tension with Inkatha went beyond politics. There were massive problems in the townships – high rents, overcrowding, high bus fares and not even the basic amenities of running water and sewerage, let alone electricity, shops or recreation grounds and centres. Communities were also mobilising against incorporation into the KwaZulu homeland system in which unions were banned and township civic and student movements were savagely repressed through an outsourced system of control in the hands of co-opted political machinery of Inkatha.

Inkatha was increasingly on the side of the employers. The contradictions sharpened. Workers were astonished that Inkatha was called in to support employers who refused to recognise unions and who were paying starvation wages. In KwaZulu, the so-called industrial free-trade zones – places like Isithebe and Mandeni – became flashpoints between workers and employers.

While Mangosuthu Buthelezi often said he was opposed to the government in his marathon speeches, the actions of Inkatha spelt the opposite. Gerhard Maré observed that the actions of Inkatha had done little to dispel its leader's words:

> [Inkatha] has a remarkably consistent record of verbal and physical conflict with other groups opposing apartheid, while its relationship with the state and parliamentary politics . . . has never broken down for long.[32]

Increasingly, the fight for the recognition of democratically elected shop-steward committees echoed with the demands of students for the right to elect their student representative councils and the rights of communities to negotiate on issues of rents, housing, water and electricity.

As Chris Dlamini, then the Vice President of COSATU, said:

> Workers are members of the community. Their kids also cannot go to school. Workers get no sleep because they are defending their community. They meet in factories. There they started talking, discussing these things. They are also part of the defence units. COSATU is now fully involved. Some workers were also attacked by Inkatha supporters because they are COSATU members.[33]

Then, during our battle against the Labour Relations Act, a war of attrition began that lasted for years. The rumour on the streets was: 'There will be no COSATU/UDF person left alive by nightfall.' The security forces watched as the two sides warred, only intervening when the situation worsened for the Inkatha *impis*.

The violence spread to Isithebe, Mandeni and Empangeni in northern Natal. It was heartbreaking to watch the senseless loss of life. Surely there had to be an alternative way to settle our differences with the Inkatha Freedom Party (IFP)?

* * *

Our working group on the violence in Natal undertook a frank assessment of the situation. It reported back to our CEC, noting that a cycle of revenge killing was increasing and that the level of discipline in the democratic forces (and this included the UDF/COSATU) was poor. The community was suffering, and becoming alienated from both sides.

Each time Inkatha was defeated in a round of attacks, the police force would begin its own cycle of killing and detentions of activists. The battle was 'unwinnable', we decided, unless we raised it strategically to another level.

We canvassed the legal options and brought in Peter Harris and Halton Cheadle, the founder of CTH, whose incisive mind was to be a regular source of thinking out of the box. They were joined at this stage by a bright but impetuous Matthew Donsin, an American lawyer working on secondment to CTH.

Could we use the courts as a buffer between ourselves and Inkatha/the apartheid state? We could apply in a civil action for the courts to order the South African Police Service (SAPS) and the state/Inkatha to act in a certain way towards us. Also we could begin to negotiate through the courts for a framework on peace as spelt out by the judicial process. In essence, we were negotiating with the state through the courts.

We realised that we could only achieve peace by isolating the warlords (often chiefs or *indunas*), who had developed tremendous power over ordinary members of Inkatha. They would extort money from the community through 'subscription fees' for Inkatha, and exercised control through violence and the force of arms.

Through our lawyers, we lodged about a dozen interdicts against Pieter-maritzburg warlords to prevent further attacks, but by December 1987 there had been another 113 deaths.

In January 1988 we succeeded in getting the Mthembu interdict. The traumatic experience of the Mthembu family in Imbali was typical of many families, and reflects a sense of the impunity with which these warlords exercised their violent methods.[34]

In his affidavit to the Supreme Court, Johannes Mthembu, a union member, described the day in August 1987 when his sons were attacked by Inkatha members linked to an Inkatha town councillor. In the ensuing fight, some Inkatha members, including the councillor's son, Dumisani, were injured. Johannes made a statement about the unprovoked attack at the police station.

Then, in January 1988, two of Johannes's sons, Elphas and Smallridge, were shot by Thulani Ngcobo, an Inkatha member and policeman. Johannes and another son, Simon, rushed home when they heard the news only to find

Inkatha town councillor named Mncwabe, Sichizo Zuma of the Inkatha Youth Brigade and Ngcobo waiting for them in the yard. Ngcobo pointed a gun at them and threatened to kill everyone in the house. Johannes and Simon fled inside and Ngcobo left.

This was when we decided to make an example of this bullying and murderous behaviour, but our charge did not restrain them. Sichizo Zuma had been informed of the interdict and in a rage he and some associates drove to the Mthembu house, using Ngcobo's car. Emboldened by police protection, he shot Smallridge Mthembu through the shoulder. His brother Ernest, seeing this, grabbed an axe head and smashed the back window of the car.

As Sichizo prepared to drive off, Simon Mthembu pursued them. Sichizo turned and shot Simon. He fell to the ground. Sichizo got out the car, took careful aim and shot Simon again. Simon remained unconscious until he died a month later.

The police never charged the perpetrators of these violent crimes. Instead, they arrested Ernest for public violence because he had smashed Ngcobo's car window.

The Mthembu family instructed our legal team to add an additional legal application order, restraining Sichizo Zuma from attacking them in any way. Despite the fact that Sichizo had violently broken his previous restraining order, the judge set a trial date eight months away.

In July, a couple of weeks before the hearing, the Mthembu house was attacked again. Ernest Mthembu went outside to investigate and was shot dead. Within a year, all of Johannes Mthembu's sons had been shot.

This story illustrates a pattern. Potential witnesses in interdicts were systematically eliminated, making it almost impossible to bring a case to a successful conclusion.

But there was hope. In September 1988, we reached an out-of-court settlement. It resulted in both parties, COSATU and Inkatha, agreeing formally to an accord. We both rejected violence and accepted the importance of freedom of association, and established a Complaints Adjudication Board (CAB) to handle individual complaints.

The UDF was not part of the accord. We had consulted with some Natal UDF leaders but were unable to reach the broader membership, who were very upset to see on television that COSATU and Inkatha had come to this agreement.

This was a lesson for us. We realised that the UDF did not have the structures, as we had with our factory base, to reach the membership to inform them of developments. We had to work hard to restore our relationship to its former level.

Meanwhile, the CAB initiative proved to be defective because it had no teeth. Only two cases were brought to the Board. Both judgments went against the Inkatha members. We knew that with the security forces, the hidden hand behind the violence, any real police investigation would lead to nothing; the justice system had failed our communities in its desperate hour of need.

This made no difference to the accused. They continued their activities as before. Soon after the judgment, Nicholas Duma was murdered. Ngcobo was charged but witnesses who had seen the murder were too afraid to testify. Ngcobo was released on R800 bail.[35]

Discouraged, we suspended COSATU's participation in the CAB. But we remained committed to peace. We had to be. A huge amount of our time was going into defending our members against attacks. We had virtually no time to fight for our union rights.

We proposed a peace conference to bring together a wide spectrum of organisations and people in Natal. After mediation by church leaders, a meeting was fixed at a neutral venue, the Imperial Hotel in Pietermaritzburg.

We agreed to hold 'five-a-side' (five representatives from each organisation) talks. This time we were well prepared. We were careful to inform the general public, including UDF members. Jointly with the UDF we distributed a newsletter, *Ubumbano*, throughout Natal. We held joint workshops and meetings explaining why we were undertaking peace initiatives.

We also worked out a step-by-step process: an immediate end to hostilities and verbal abuse on all sides; a joint peace conference of Inkatha, COSATU and the UDF; joint rallies for peace in all areas; and consultations on how to resettle tens of thousands of Natal refugees.

When our delegations met I was surprised that Buthelezi himself had refused to attend. Instead, he sent a deputy, Frank Mdlalose, to read out Buthelezi's twenty-page document in which he rejected the peace accord. Buthelezi accused Thabo Mbeki, still in exile, of having made an insulting remark about him in Copenhagen and cited a document which he said was written allegedly by the ANC calling for selective violence against Inkatha.

I had already made it clear that COSATU was not responsible for the ANC or UDF. I had written a letter to Inkatha, together with Murphy Morobe of the UDF, to explain that we were two distinct entities:

> We wish to clarify an important point ... COSATU and UDF are separate organisations. Each organisation must seek mandates and report back to their own structures. We co-operate closely, particularly in regard to the peace process in Natal ... However ... we are not affiliated to each other.[36]

This did not seem to matter to Buthelezi. He concluded his long, proxy response by calling for a moratorium on all talks 'until there is the prospect of success'. The end of the peace talks effectively condemned tens of thousands of Natal men, women and children to violence in the years to come.

In 1987, more than 400 people were killed in uMgungundlovu (the Pietermaritzburg area). In Durban, from 1987 to mid-1990, over 11 000 were killed. Edendale, where I had spent much time organising in the early 1980s, became a war zone. Visiting it in the aftermath of the so-called Seven Day War (which took place in March 1990), I climbed a hill with a panoramic view of the landscape. Homesteads in flames were still spread out across the valley and the surrounding hills. Marauding gangs had moved in, creating a swathe of destruction and death.

It was only many months after Mandela had been released that COSATU's extensive experience in bargaining, negotiations and laying down procedures for the way forward could be harnessed and eventually incorporated into the National Peace Accord, laying an invaluable foundation for our future democracy.

21

As the public debate on the issues of violence and peace talks and who was the legitimate internal leadership of the ANC was mushrooming in 1987 and 1988, an interesting and complex series of alliances was forming. I sought the views of key former political prisoners, especially Govan Mbeki and Harry Gwala.

Govan Mbeki was an independent thinker, firm if not rigid in his views. He had often in his political life differed with Nelson Mandela. In November 1987 Mbeki was released from Robben Island and based himself in Port Elizabeth. My brother Pat was his medical doctor and I arranged through Pat to meet with Mbeki. I shared my experiences with him and he became an ally. 'No one in the country has the right to claim the mantle of leadership,' he said quietly. 'We are part of the leadership of the ANC and you need to continue your role as the General Secretary of COSATU with the full understanding that you have my personal support and that of the ANC.'

I did the same with the fiery Harry Gwala, going to his home in the Edendale area in Pietermaritzburg to seek his advice. I drove there in silence, recounting my storyline in my head. I had to refocus on the main enemy aggressively undermining our very existence. These political intrigues were diverting important energies needed to shore up our defences. I knew that Gwala was being watched closely – the security police had taken occupation of a house directly adjacent to his home.

The young sentinels were waiting for me. I was flagged down at an agreed place, left my car to be guarded and travelled in a 'safe' car. I wore dark glasses and a jacket with an upturned collar. There was no need to alert the state watchers too soon. Gwala had suffered a rare motor neuron disease that left him paralysed in his arms, and led to his release from prison in November 1988. But he was very much a 'cult of the leader' character – and someone who was fearless in the face of the enemy. He had taken a strong view against any peace talks with the IFP; it was a popular view given the mounting casualties on our side.

I could not agree with Gwala's hard-line stance on peace talks with Inkatha, but I did appreciate it when he reiterated the view that no one inside South Africa had a monopoly on the ANC line. The internal democracy within COSATU was of paramount importance to the freedom struggle.

Emboldened by this, I became more publicly vociferous about our independence and I receive a coded message that I should meet with Billy Nair in Durban. He was another one of the senior ANC leaders who had been released and was an old stalwart of SACTU. We had dinner in Durban. After the discussion he intimated that there was someone important who would like to see me. I was intrigued, and agreed.

I anticipated that I would be meeting someone high up in the underground. But I had no idea who it would be. The trip there was made in silence. I recognised the area. It was the dense flatland of Overport, just below the Berea, a predominantly Indian and coloured area. I had previously lived there as a student. As we parked on the street and walked towards the building I rehearsed what my approach would be. Honesty and frankness had to be the basis of building trust, I thought.

We entered the nondescript building and my escort rapped on a door what I interpreted as a code. The door swung open and standing there was Mac Maharaj. He was in the country, sent by O.R. Tambo and Joe Slovo on a dangerous mission of consolidating the underground. There was absolute secrecy about the mission and the majority of ANC leaders, as well as Mac's children in London, were under the impression that he was receiving medical treatment in Moscow.

Mac is an operator, strategic with a razor-sharp intellect. But for the cause, he was highly secretive and manipulative. He explained his mission. I recognised the importance of what he was doing, but stressed that though I was prepared, as in the past, to work with the ANC, I would never take orders from him or anyone else. My accountability was to the constituency that I represented.

My view on the armed struggle had been influenced by the writings of Mao, who famously wrote of a 'guerrilla being a fish swimming in an ocean of people with a heightened political consciousness'.[37] There was a role for the armed struggle, but I felt that in the South African context we would be unable to defeat the apartheid state militarily. What we had to contend with was a strategy of 'armed propaganda' designed to drive fear into the hearts of the white minority, but our focus had to be to build a mass struggle. This meant that powerful, grassroots movements, including the unions, had to be built and defended as we waged our 'People's War' for freedom.

I stressed the complementarities to Mac and we both agreed that COSATU's internal democracy had to be respected. But for him and many underground leaders, given the high-risk nature of their work, their trademark had to be secrecy, conspiracy and intrigue. I understood that, given that in exile there was always the peril of infiltration.

But in South Africa I operated under the assumption that we were infiltrated anyway, and that we should believe that all our public discussions were being monitored – a fact borne out by Mac when he revealed that Maxwell Xulu, a national office bearer of COSATU at the time, was an enemy agent. Not only had the apartheid state infiltrated our ranks in the democratic movement, but we had infiltrated the security police and had a mole in their senior leadership.

We parted on a good note but I understood that Mac truly believed that he was the 'kingmaker'. His strategic intellect was considerable, but his sense of political self-importance ignored much of the home-grown strategic capability within COSATU.

For me the fact that we had not only survived one of the most brutal periods in our history but had built the largest movement capable of mobilising and galvanising millions in action against apartheid was a tribute to a grassroots-driven strategic insight and practice that made COSATU agile and dynamic, and distinguished our operation from our predecessors.

*   *   *

Along with my efforts to secure COSATU's internal links and structures, I focused on strengthening our external relationships and alliances. In September 1987 I took up the invitation by the Australian Council of Trade Unions (ACTU) to visit Australia at the time of the Commonwealth Heads of Government meeting. When we arrived at the airport in Johannesburg, Khetsi Lehoko, my Education Officer, and I checked in our baggage. The desk supervisor approached the agent and asked to see my passport. As my bag was disappearing down the conveyor belt he said, 'Excuse me, sir; I just have to check your passport.'

I turned to Khetsi and said, 'Let us part ways here. You proceed ahead and under no circumstances connect yourself to me. If I am taken from here do not attempt to intervene. You need to get to this meeting. It is important that the international community are informed of the wave of state repression against us. You also must meet with our trade union colleagues and ask them for concrete solidarity to strengthen sanctions and bring pressure on their governments to isolate the apartheid state.'

Khetsi reluctantly walked away as I stayed waiting for my passport. As I expected, the supervisor returned accompanied by two burly officers who smelt of the security police. I was escorted to a room and questioned on my itinerary. I refused to answer and they then informed me that my passport would be confiscated. I was taken to the plane's cargo section and asked to identify my bag. I refused and after some time they retrieved my bag and I was taken back to the terminal. I thought that it would be a long time before I tasted freedom again, but surprisingly I was allowed to go.

I understood what they had feared. It would have been an international incident of much greater proportions if I had been detained. I was scheduled to have a formal meeting with the Prime Minister of Australia and other heads of state.

I had been invited by Martin Fergusson, the President of ACTU, a fiery and charismatic labour leader determined to mobilise Australian workers against apartheid. The stevedores in particular were already militantly refusing to offload ships carrying South African goods. Prime Minister Malcolm Fraser registered a formal démarche to the South African government over that incident.

But our closest allies were in Scandinavia, the Netherlands and the Canadian Labour Congress (CLC). I struck up a close personal relationship with Bob White, who was the leader of the United Autoworkers of Canada and then went on to become President of the CLC. They were staunch allies without whom we would have suffered many more casualties. On his first trip to South Africa I had taken Bob White to meet with comrades in the Empangeni township of Esikaweni.

Accompanied by the Chairperson of the northern Natal region of COSATU we entered the township with armed guards. Bob never flinched, even when the sounds of gunfire could be heard and the weapons we carried were illegal and could have landed us all in jail if we had encountered a police roadblock. We met with Jeffrey Vilane and examined his home which had been raked with gunfire the previous evening. This was a demonstration of the kind of international solidarity that would build the bonds of friendship we would share for a lifetime.

COSATU also started to build relations with the other major players in Africa, such as the Nigerian Labour Congress (NLC). My first trip to Lagos was to visit my counterparts and to attend an Organisation of African Trade Union Unity (OATUU) conference. I had never been in such a crowded and chaotic city. It was alive 24 hours a day and the traffic seemed to be in permanent gridlock.

The NLC was suffering the same repression COSATU faced, but at the hands of a military dictatorship. Caught in a roadblock one night with John Odah, then an organiser but later to become the NLC's General Secretary, I recall him arguing violently with soldiers that he was with an international guest from South Africa. As we sat at the side of the road with automatic rifle barrels in our faces I remembered that the OATUU meeting was officially sanctioned by President Ibrahim Babangida. We were waved on after the soldiers had checked the authenticity of my invitation letter with their superiors.

On one of my trips to the United Nations (UN) to present evidence before the UN Committee Against Apartheid I encountered a dedicated group of activists who were key in our campaign to isolate the apartheid regime. There was the passionate Aracelly Santana, who ran the day-to-day activities of the UN Committee against Apartheid and who had roped in a broad coalition of trade unionists and political activists to work with us. The UN was a crucial arena of struggle that kept the spotlight on South Africa and compelled key Western countries, such as the United States of America and the United Kingdom, to account for their refusal to act decisively by implementing sanctions. Aracelly's office and home became the base of our mobilisation within the UN and, more importantly, the place from which to build a momentum amongst the American labour movement and civil society.

I connected with key activists such as John Hudson, Cleveland Robinson and Jim Bell, who, with Aracelly and many others from across the affiliates of the American Federation of Labor-Congress of Industrial Organizations (AFL-CIO), were in the dynamic New York Labour Committee Against Apartheid, which was mobilising thousands of labour leaders and members.

It was in this context that I met William ('Bill') Lucy, who was from the American Federation of State, County and Municipal Employees (AFSCME) and a key founder and President of the Coalition of Black Trade Unionists, launched to lobby the federation leadership in the AFL-CIO to change its views on COSATU. We became enduring friends. Bill is a towering man who is always impeccably dressed, with the personality of a gentle giant.

As an African American, apartheid reignited for him the lingering legacy of the slave trade. Here was a racist minority in a country in Africa in the late twentieth century, still treating black people no differently than slaves had been treated by their owners 200 years earlier in the plantations of the Deep South.

Our relations with the British TUC and the AFL-CIO in the United States were frosty. The AFL-CIO and particularly its international department, which was greatly influenced by Irving Brown, a prominent 'Cold War warrior', had already written us off as a 'bunch of communists' and we were still sensitive to their awarding Buthelezi the prestigious AFL-CIO George Meany Award in 1982.

But now we needed to convince the AFL-CIO national leadership under Lane Kirkland to work with COSATU as a legitimate representative of the South African workers. I knew they would always have their reservations about our politics, but they recognised our trade union leadership.

The work we were doing with these worker leaders, and especially the influence of Bill Lucy and the Coalition of Black Trade Unionists, together with Randall Robinson from the TransAfrica Institute and the American Committee on Apartheid, headed by the indomitable Jennifer Davis, was to have an impact on American Congress politics.

In 1986 the United States Congress passed the Comprehensive Anti-Apartheid Act (CAAA) proposed by Ron Dellums, a veteran anti-apartheid activist and a member of the Congressional Black Caucus. 'The CAAA delivered a crippling blow to a South African economy that was already reeling from the withdrawal of [United States] banks the year before.'[38]

As the state-sponsored attacks mounted, COSATU sent delegations around the world. On one such trip in 1987 I went to London with Peter Harris to meet with Labour Party activists and the British Anti-Apartheid Movement under the dedicated leadership of Mike Terry. The British Anti-Apartheid Movement, with the noble support of leading activists such as Archbishop

Trevor Huddleston and with the blessing of Oliver Tambo, had united a diverse and powerful range of forces which were all committed to a speedy end to apartheid through the imposition of comprehensive economic, academic, sporting and cultural sanctions since the Sharpeville massacre in 1960.

I also connected with Steve Faulkner of the Commonwealth Trade Union Council (CTUC), who I used as the coordinator of our trip amongst the union networks. We did our usual traipse to my favourite jazz bar, Ronnie Scott's. It was in the early hours of the morning, having consumed huge amounts of splendid London ale, that we stumbled home. Early the next morning I had to be shaken awake and, bleary-eyed, face a huge press contingent keen to understand what was happening in South Africa.

As we brought the press interviews to a close I overheard a journalist remarking: 'These guys look so harassed and exhausted.' I felt a tinge of guilt knowing that it was more than the struggle that had contributed to our poor condition that morning.

Another key alliance of unions we built was with the socialist-leaning union movement, the Italian General Confederation of Labour (CGIL) and the Brazilian Central Única dos Trabalhadores (CUT). Brazil fascinated us because of the militancy of the workers' movement, led by the fiery metal worker and President of the Steel Workers Union in São Paulo, Lula da Silva. As a metal worker he was at the centre of militant strikes in the sprawling industrial belt of San Barnado, and in 1983 was one of the leading founders of CUT.

Lula was at the heart of the campaign against the military dictatorship and a leader of the drive for direct democratic elections of a civilian President. We were intrigued by the Brazilian workers' experiences and the similarities we saw between the South African and Brazilian struggles. Our alliance with CUT fitted into COSATU's internal vision of South-to-South cooperation between progressive and independent unions which were determined to play a prominent role on the political stage.

Although language was a challenge, we built a solid basis for militant action and discussed how we would shape a global movement to challenge the dominance of the Northern unions in the international labour movement. We felt our brand of progressive unionism was fundamental to support the global struggle for worker and human rights and to challenge the growing power of transnational companies. Lula had by this time launched the Workers Party

(PT) to build an alliance of leftist forces to challenge for the presidency of Brazil and we had the opportunity to share our experiences together. He was a charismatic leader with a principled bias towards the working class and I found him open and frank about the challenges Brazil faced and why international solidarity was key to contesting the power of global capital.

Our firm friendship was illustrated a few years later when, in 1994, Lula was to visit South Africa after our first democratic elections and asked for a meeting with President Mandela. Although a tentative meeting had been pencilled into Mandela's diary, the Foreign Affairs bureaucracy baulked at the idea of Mandela meeting a contender it did not believe would win the election.

I got a call late at night from a close comrade, Sergio Xavier Ferreira, whom I had worked with in the CUT and who was now acting as the official translator and an adviser to Lula. He begged me to intervene to secure the meeting. After several robust conversations, the bureaucracy relented and permitted a closed meeting with Lula, Sergio and Mandela for thirty minutes.

As the meeting was about to finish, with Mandela's staff hovering in the background, Lula interjected and gave Mandela his view of the political challenges of Brazil and how similar the struggles were to those in South Africa. Mandela, ever passionate about freedom struggles and their international dimension, listened carefully, and in defiance of his staff went out with Lula to meet the rest of the delegation and to introduce Lula to the press.

This was an enormous coup for Lula at a time when it was being speculated that he had been rebuffed by an icon like Mandela. Later that night we celebrated with the delegation, which included a number of friends of ours from our COSATU days. Joe Slovo, Alec Erwin and other comrades and I had a wonderful dinner and our friendship with Lula and Brazil was sealed.

For us, in the heady days of our defeat of apartheid the foreign office bureaucracy was still subdued and the foreign policy ideologues who excelled in the art of political fencing had not entrenched themselves. Our foreign policy unabashedly reflected the content of our human rights struggle and culture and our solidarity with political movements of the South. When he eventually became the President of Brazil, Lula still retained all his links with labour, setting up a full-time secretariat within the presidency that gave the CUT direct contact to the seat of power. Lula always made it his duty to interact with labour leaders in the countries he visited, even meeting with a COSATU delegation led by Zwelinzima Vavi when he visited South Africa.

22

Nineteen eighty-seven was a decisive year. Two sides were pitted against each other. In September 1987, the state launched a new assault against the labour movement when it published proposed amendments to the Labour Relations Act. Adriaan Vlok, Minister of Law and Order, was quite upfront in clarifying his intentions.

'The security forces will continue to take out or remove revolutionary elements from society in order to establish security and normality,' he explained.[39] The new legislation had huge ramifications and aimed at devastating the workers movement. I saw this as a last-ditch effort by the apartheid government to subdue the mounting mass opposition to its rule.

The new labour law sought to restrict the right to strike – making it harder to stage a legal strike, providing heavy penalties for strike action, and making it easier for employers to dismiss and retrench workers. Under this Act, workers would be losing many of the hard-won rights we had struggled for over the years.

Significantly, the Act also protected the positions of minority trade unions (such as the Inkatha-based UWUSA) and the whites-only unions. The Minister of Manpower, Pietie du Plessis, promised employers that the law would bring the unions to heel. He told them that the legislation 'would hang like a sword over their heads'.[40] Clearly, the state wanted to cut us down to size.

COSATU's CEC made a statement declaring that this was an outright attack on us. In February 1988 restrictions were placed on COSATU, preventing us from engaging in a wide range of political activities. At the same time, the UDF and sixteen other anti-apartheid organisations were restricted – indeed, practically banned.

In a special congress in May 1988, COSATU resolved to defy the restrictions and increase action against the new labour legislation. Calling for a national stay-away was illegal, so instead we planned a three-day 'peaceful national protest'. We were delighted when, after initial opposition to the campaign, the National Council of Trade Unions (NACTU), our main rival, backed our call for a joint action plan. NACTU's forerunner was the Africanist-aligned federation, the Council of Unions of South Africa (CUSA).

Our three-day stay-away was a success – 3 million workers observed it, including public sector workers, although some industrial unions were not able to pull off huge participation. The NUM, for example, which had suggested the three-day action, was still reeling from the dismissals and blows of its 1987 strike, and only a small percentage managed to participate.

Newly merged unions also joined in – COSATU affiliates PPWAWU (Paper, Pulp, Wood and Allied Workers Union) and SAMWU (South African Municipal Workers Union) as well as unions not affiliated to us. We made history by pulling off the longest national stay-away in South Africa.[41] Furthermore, the strategy succeeded in cutting across the political divide. Opposition to the stay-away came only 'from small groups on the extremes of the political spectrum'.[42]

'The diverse range of groupings,' I commented afterwards, 'illustrates the point... that unity is forged in action, not around conference tables. The protest therefore laid the groundwork for the [anti-apartheid] conference.'[43]

Besides dealing with government aggression there was another factor that complicated our campaign, and that was our strategic but complex relationship with the bosses.

We agreed to meet the South African Consultative Committee on Labour Affairs (SACCOLA). This was an old organisation of employers formed in 1919. It had become discredited internationally when it was expelled by the International Labour Organization (ILO) in 1983. But the body revived its activities during this dispute over the proposed new labour law. Earlier, we had demanded to meet the employers. Our idea was not only to obtain their support against the Labour Bill but also to begin to isolate the apartheid regime. We knew that the sanctions lobbies overseas were pressuring the multinational companies in South Africa to disinvest.

Some of them, such as the American Chamber of Commerce and the German Chamber of Commerce, even made a cautious statement. In their opinion, they said, it was not necessary to introduce new labour laws. We hoped to be able to extend this attitude to local companies and corporations and prepare the path for a broad anti-apartheid front.

We also concurred with the Federated Chamber of Industries (FCI) Chairperson, Bokkie Botha (who was more progressive than the organisation he represented), when he complained to the *South African Labour Bulletin*:

> *I think it's most unfortunate that trade unionists persist in stereotyping all employers together. Do we go around stereotyping all trade unionists? Isn't it ridiculous to think of the 'white' Mineworkers Union and NUM in the same breath?*[44]

Unfortunately, many employers did exactly that, stereotyping the entire democratic labour movement. But it was in these toughest of times, as negotiators representing two opposing interests, that we shared a commitment to finding a solution. A full-scale war was disastrous for both sides and a 'scorched earth' policy brought no benefit to the constituencies we represented.

Even before the stay-away, COSATU had met nine SACCOLA affiliates in February 1988. We were looking at two items on the agenda: how employers should respond to COSATU's call to oppose the Bill; and whether they should meet with the unions to discuss common interests around it. The FCI and the Steel and Engineering Industries Federation of South Africa (SEIFSA) were willing to meet us, though the Association of Chambers of Commerce (ASSOCOM) said such a meeting would be 'premature'.[45]

The FCI tried to cover up the differences as best it could. 'We don't like rolling strikes,' admitted its spokesperson. 'To be honest, we don't like strikes. But we don't want to limit employees' ability to take action. We want to agree on procedure. But while we have a law we're going to operate in terms of it.'[46]

Eventually, in March, 25 delegates from COSATU and our affiliates met in the boardroom of the Anglo American Corporation. We were awestruck by its opulence: the oil paintings of the Oppenheimers, their portraits looking down on the meeting; the antique furniture and silver; the beautiful wooden boxes of Cuban cigars; the immense boardroom table around which we were uneasily seated.

The meeting itself did not yield fruitful results. But we did get something out of it. At one point, the employers retired to caucus. We were left in the boardroom and we wondered how much history this room had hatched that had dispossessed so many people of their birthrights. Almost as an act of defiance we lifted dozens of cigars from the boardroom table and then lit them on the steps of 44 Main Street – the headquarters of Anglo American, the symbol of South African capital.

After the three-day stay-away, SACCOLA asked us to reopen the talks to look for common ground. This time, we sent our lawyers to meet with SACCOLA and the Director General of Manpower. The Director General agreed to a postponement of the Bill until 1 September so that we could each submit our objections. A timetable to do this was worked out.

We handed in our objections on 7 July, as agreed. But SACCOLA, which was supposed to respond five days later, dragged its feet and submitted its document only on 1 August. Ten days later NACTU and COSATU met with SACCOLA and agreed that six of the most offensive clauses should be put on hold – SACCOLA had to persuade its less progressive members to accept a couple of COSATU's clauses and said it would get back to us.

Then, without warning or consultation, on the very next day the promulgation of the Act was declared in the Government Gazette. It was a bitter blow. We felt betrayed. Neither the government nor the employers could be trusted, and we had egg on our faces from sceptical members.

Yet, ironically, in the medium to long term, we emerged strengthened by this experience. We had firmed our friendship with the broader democratic alliance. We had obtained the warm and loud support of the international democratic and labour community. We had also been alerted to our weaknesses.

However, it was clear to us that schisms were opening up between the employers and a rampant apartheid state. The costs of maintaining apartheid was becoming too high. I realised that negotiations, while necessary, could not take the place of mass action. We had concentrated too much on the talks with SACCOLA and should now focus on isolating the apartheid state.

Scholars discussing the events twenty years later found that the anti-Labour Relations Act campaign laid the foundations of an important turning point in our transition to democracy. 'Central to South Africa's transition,' write Eddie Webster and Dinga Sikwebu, 'was the mobilising power of labour and the relationships it was to develop with employers.'[47]

* * *

Deep in the trenches as we were in 1988, we soon realised that we had to be forward-thinking on both the peace front and on the economic questions before us. Alec Erwin, COSATU's Education Secretary, and I agreed to assemble a group of progressive economists to work out the strategic options we would face in a post-apartheid South Africa. Erwin approached Stephen Gelb, who had already done work for COSATU in preparing the arguments we used in supporting sanctions, claiming that the removal of the apartheid state was the most important imperative in stopping the haemorrhaging of the economy and setting us on a new growth path that was inclusive and sustainable.

What we wanted was a detailed analysis of the different industrial sectors and the general economy so that COSATU would be able to evaluate its options. Stephen approached a number of the country's academic economists and we set up the Economic Trends Group. Khetsi Lehoko, who had now replaced Alec as the COSATU Education Secretary, was a quietly spoken and effective leader who then stewarded reports through the CEC.

According to Stephen:

We were actually well ahead of the government, of the game, in terms of putting [together] a comprehensive understanding of what the issues were that had to be addressed, like low competitiveness, overdependence on minerals, far too excessive a dependence in industry on imports, the automotive industry being a case in point, as well as issues around skills shortages and unemployment. The conclusion was that employment was a structural problem and addressing it required a complete transformation of the economy.[48]

On the peace front we had established a Joint Working Committee in Natal. By 1988 we were already deeply engaged with and got the full support for our peace strategy from Thabo Mbeki and Jacob Zuma in a conference in Lusaka. By the middle of 1989 we had met with a senior delegation from the ANC and SACP in Harare. I was still denied a passport and could not attend. We hired two small planes to take the COSATU executive delegates who had successful meetings which clarified our views on the peace strategy for Natal and the issue of negotiations.

By 1989 we were already engaged in a broader debate about the political transition. Madame Mitterrand, wife of French President François Mitterrand,

under the auspices of the French government, facilitated an engagement between the ANC in exile, us as representatives of the Mass Democratic Movement
and the ruling establishment for a frank exchange of views. Under pressure,
the South African government was compelled to grant me a limited-term
passport. Locked under tight police protection in a comfortable Paris villa, we
spent hours debating our various viewpoints. The ANC delegation was led by
Thabo Mbeki, whose sophisticated understanding of the obstacles in the path
of a smooth transition impressed the audience and won over sceptics who had
come expecting to meet ideologues.

We were chaperoned around Paris by police outriders to sample superb
French cuisine in bygone palaces. It was a glimpse of a different life and of
the political snare of privilege. At a dinner one evening I was seated next to
Madame Mitterrand and found her to be a very engaging personality. As a
typical trade unionist used to eating with my hands I was astounded by the
quantity of cutlery and wine glasses we were confronted with. Mischievously
I said to her: 'I guess the staff will have to spend quite a long part of the night
washing up the dishes after us.' She laughed in good humour, but I felt that the
lure of public life with all the frivolities of an affluent lifestyle often alienated
public figures from the grassroots.

In spite of the tough security, we felt we had to break out of the friendly
but pervasive embrace of the French police. At an event to commemorate the
assassination of our ANC representative in Paris, Dulcie September, I met
with the enigmatic and beautiful Maimuna Dialo. A Senegalese by origin and
hailing from a royal house, she volunteered to break me out of the team and
take me on what she described as 'a tour of the real Paris'. It turned out to be
a fascinating night of music, laughter, dancing and meeting comrades from
many of the West African countries who were as passionate as us about our
freedom struggle.

The meetings themselves were a breakthrough. They allowed us to debate
controversial issues as South Africans drawn from across the political spectrum. In this convivial environment we saw ourselves as compatriots rather
than adversaries. It was a series of these meetings, hosted by O.R. Tambo,
Thabo Mbeki and Jacob Zuma, that broke down the barriers of decades of
apartheid propaganda and unlocked the door to the ending of a deadly combat
that would have resulted in a full-scale civil war.

Another key moment for the Mass Democratic Movement was a meeting
that Pieter le Roux from the University of the Western Cape organised in

Switzerland in mid-1989. With the support of the Swiss government Le Roux managed to organise a gathering of about 50 economists from inside and outside South Africa. They met at a very luxurious hotel in scenic Lausanne. It was only then that ANC economists, such as Tito Mboweni, Max Sisulu and their advisers Ben Fine and Lawrence Harris from London, met us. It was also the first time that people from inside the country had met with business people and with government economists from the Treasury and the Reserve Bank. It was agreed that the conversation on these issues would continue in South Africa.

*   *   *

Despite all of these exciting developments and initiatives, the most momentous part of 1989 for me was on a deeply personal level. In November 1989 I was granted another two-week passport to travel to Copenhagen for a meeting with our international trade union colleagues.

As usual I phoned my mother a few days before leaving and discovered that she was unwell. 'Travel safely and you can see me when you return,' she said. Troubled but anxious to connect with my colleagues, I boarded the plane and arrived in Denmark. On the same day I phoned and found out that my mother had been admitted to hospital. We spoke, and she reiterated her message.

'You have important things to do. Finish your work. I know how much you love me and your spirit is with me.'

In the midst of the meeting some hours later an urgent call came through. It was Iyaloo, my elder brother. 'Mom has just passed away. You need to get back now.'

I froze. I asked for arrangements to be made for my travel. But I added, 'Let us finish the meeting. Many lives depend on our concluding the discussions on the support we need.'

That night I sat alone in my hotel room and wept. The tears dropped silently as I gazed through the window across the sparkling lights of Copenhagen shimmering in the waters of the North Sea. I felt my mother's presence. She was my guide, my conscience, my strength to overcome my fears and to share my triumphs.

She had always been there in our hours of need. Now she had left her mortal body and I would say my prayers at the funeral as we sent her spirit on its last voyage. I was convinced that this was the last of her cycle of lives. She had given selflessly of her life to us, the children and the broader community.

As I boarded a plane back to South Africa I felt a sense of trepidation. Coming back home was an unknown factor. There was a feeling of vulnerability as the plane landed and the gruff voice of the captain announced '*Welkom in Suid Afrika*' (Welcome to South Africa). I stared at the dryness of Johannesburg. The land was a geographically scarred reflection of apartheid: the clearly defined, overcrowded African townships enmeshed in teeming poverty and the gleaming, tree-filled luxury of the white suburbs with their glittering blue swimming pools buffered from the real South Africa where the majority of black people lived. 'How few of them have ever crossed the line to understand their fellow country men and women,' I thought. This was still not our country to claim.

A second plane trip brought me to Durban. My sister and brother were there to pick me up. My sister Dimes was sobbing uncontrollably. I held her in my arms and she continued to weep.

'What is it?' I asked, knowing that something was not right.

'The funeral was yesterday,' she said between her tears. There had been a misunderstanding on when I was arriving. The Indian custom is to cremate a body as soon as is possible.

I had wanted to say my final goodbye, but maybe this is what my mother wanted – the memory of her alive and well holding my hands and feeling her positive energy.

It would be years before I came to terms with my mother's death. It left a big gap in my life. Just months before the release of Mandela and the unfolding of a new era in South Africa, she had gone. The important connection to my emotional side had died. I felt abandoned and for a while my life crashed around me.

PART FIVE

Alliances and Commitments

In Moscow we did a lot of talking about class struggle. There was intense learning. We understood the weakness of unions which were not independent of the state. These were deep insights, dispensed with a lot of vodka.

— Alec Erwin

One night, the lights suddenly went out throughout the township. Residents in houses were woken by the sound of whistles and shouts coming from the direction of the hostel. A murderous attack took place. Houses, especially so-called 'Xhosa houses', were attacked and [the] occupants chased out or killed. The carnage went on for four hours. At the end of it all, more than thirty bodies – women, children, men – lay outside the police station.

— Luli Callinicos, *The Story of Sam Ntuli*

We started working on the forum of the Reconstruction and Development Programme. Because we wanted to have a union position that said that 'in any negotiation these are the kind of things that you've got to achieve'. And as that grew, the ANC started to become part of developing the RDP; so instead of being a union initiative – it became the programme for the Alliance.

— Bernie Fanaroff

23

The release of Nelson Mandela in February 1990 marked the start of a hectic year for the ANC and for South Africa. Mandela was being fêted around the world after years of isolation and South Africa was basking in the limelight.

But Mandela's release almost immediately unleashed greater levels of violence. Many of the reactionary forces armed themselves; the state's death squads continued their dirty business. In this context, Mandela's appeal to the South African nation and his calls for nation building, compassion and reconciliation were crucial for us to bridge many of the deep chasms that plagued the different races and groups.

An interesting and highly emotive debate around the suspension of the armed struggle began to take place within the broad democratic movement.

In a sense, we romanticised the armed struggle because it allowed us to summon the courage to challenge the tanks and the Casspirs,[1] and the might of the police state. We cast MK as the powerful organisation that was our shield which would protect us. It created uncertainly in investor markets, and when we were reeling in the onslaught its actions were an armed propaganda that rebuilt our spirits.

But now we had tough choices to make. We felt that we had to demonstrate our good faith in negotiations and seize the moral high ground. Given the escalating violence in the country and the emotive appeals of our people demanding arms to defend our communities, the decision to end the armed struggle was also one of the most courageous we made in our history of struggle. It was a vital element of Madiba's leadership.

The decision stirred anger in our communities and alienated our mass base. In township after township, leaders were shouted down and accused of betraying the revolution.

In this amphitheatre of violence our supporters in Natal were bearing the brunt of the brutality at the hands of Inkatha. On 25 February, fifteen days after Madiba's release, a massive peace rally was held at Kings Park Stadium in Durban. An angry crowd awaited Mandela. The mood was uncompromising. Our people were fuming. They were tired of burying the innocent dead. This was a recipe for serious revolt against Mandela's leadership. I shuddered, remembering the message that had been worked out the night before.

Mandela was adamant. 'Let us tell our people the truth. We have to end this cycle of violence. We have to negotiate peace. Let us not dilute the message. I want us to say to people, "This strife among ourselves wastes our energy and destroys our unity. My message to those of you involved in this battle of brother against brother is this: take your guns, your knives, and your pangas, and throw them into the sea. Close down the death factories. End this war now!"'[2]

I knew it would be a severe test of our leadership. Angry cries of protest pierced the air but Mandela continued in his own stubborn way. Young people singing derisive songs started leaving the stadium. But the majority of people stayed and listened. Mandela was determined to deliver his hard message of truth.

I marvelled at the man. It reminded me of the countless strikes we had lost, where leadership had to face the masses and tell people that we had lost and that we needed to admit defeat, go back and regroup and fight the battle again. It was not a loss of face or honour to retreat. It is a true test of leadership when leaders have to make tough and unpopular decisions.

The following weeks were taken up by us criss-crossing the country to explain to heated meetings of activists the decision to suspend the armed struggle. Mandela urged us all to lead from the front. This was our moment of truth where we had reached a point of irreversible change.

On 4 May 1990, the Groote Schuur Minute was issued, following negotiations between the apartheid government and the ANC. A working group was established 'towards the resolution of the existing climate of violence and intimidation from whatever quarter as well as a commitment to stability and to a peaceful process of negotiations'.[3]

That same month, COSATU held a consultative meeting with the South African Congress of Trade Unions (SACTU) and the South African Communist Party (SACP) to examine the challenges facing the working class. Inside COSATU, a discussion had taken place about developing a Workers Charter. We wanted to use it as a basis to support the ANC. The Workers Charter debate led to the proposal that a programme of action was needed.

But first we needed to define the Alliance. We concluded that the Alliance between the ANC, the SACP and COSATU had to be based on a programme. Up to now we had based it on defeating apartheid. Now that we were on the verge of defeating apartheid, the question was: what should be the programme for constructing a new South Africa?

Since the 1950s, the Freedom Charter had inspired the struggle against apartheid. In a sense, COSATU's programme was to reach the goals set out in the Freedom Charter, presented to, and unanimously accepted by, the Congress of the People in Kliptown in Johannesburg in 1955.[4] 'Freedom' was political freedom, but it had to mean more than the right to vote. It had to mean a better way of life for our people. We needed a concrete programme to take us forward to a South Africa that delivered what we promised to our people.

* * *

The role of COSATU was one of the key questions after the unbanning of the liberation movement. To begin with, we had to sort out our relationship with SACTU, which had been closely allied to the ANC since 1953. SACTU was hampered by the absence of legal rights for black workers and had participated in a number of high-profile stay-aways in the 1950s (so called because strikes were illegal for black workers).

There was pressure from some quarters for COSATU to merge into SACTU. In my view that was absolutely out of the question, and I argued very strongly against the idea, holding a series of meetings with John Nkadimeng, the General Secretary of SACTU.

John was deeply committed to the freedom struggle, an elder moulded in wisdom and with the same values as the generation of statesmen such as Walter Sisulu and Nelson Mandela. I found him refreshingly open and cognisant of the democracy within COSATU. He had been crucial in persuading the UDF unions to enter the COSATU fold. We had a trusting relationship and it eased the discussion on key issues. Always calm, he was a consensus builder. The following year, we met SACTU at its headquarters in Lusaka to celebrate the historic role it had played. We had agreed in the light of the new political developments that SACTU would dissolve and its personnel be absorbed into COSATU.

* * *

By 1990 a historic agreement had been reached by the South African Consultative Committee on Labour Affairs (SACCOLA), COSATU and the National Council of Trade Unions (NACTU) that acknowledged the basic rights of workers and established a subcommittee to discuss the future of the labour relations institutions, including the Industrial Court and the Labour Appeals Court.

The next stage was a meeting with the Minister of Manpower, Eli Louw, and an employer delegation in his offices in Pretoria. The meeting started in the afternoon and stretched late into the night. It was far-reaching in its commitment to restructure the labour relations system in the country.

At the conclusion of the negotiations we agreed to write up the document for the Minister to present to the cabinet the next day. Here we sat with the employer delegation, including André Lamprecht and Bobby Godsell and the Minister, when Halton Cheadle, our legal adviser, proposed that we drink a toast to the historic agreement. The Minister left and later returned with a bottle of whisky. He proposed a toast, saying: 'Well, tomorrow if what I agreed with you results in me being thrown out of the cabinet, I will be coming to you for a job.'

We laughed but it was a serious business. This was a radical departure and F.W. de Klerk's cabinet was split between the hardliners and the moderates. We could easily have been caught in that crossfire.

We had established the principle through the Laboria Minute that in future no changes could ever be made by the state to the labour market without agreement between business and labour.[5] By recognising our interdependence, write Webster and Sikwebu, we created a new labour regime. 'This tactical alliance laid the foundations for meaningful social dialogue in South Africa,' they conclude, 'and prefigured the negotiations that led to democracy a few years later.'[6]

This first tripartite agreement reached in 1990 was a forerunner to the restructuring of the National Manpower Commission and the establishment of the National Economic Forum and post-1994 led to the statutory National Economic Development and Labour Council (NEDLAC), the socio-economic council that was designed to enable the social partners to try to reach agreement in all social and labour policies before they were tabled in parliament. In this way the labour movement hoped to co-determine the way in which the legal framework gave substance to the safeguards we wanted written into the Constitution and the Bill of Rights.

We even made bold representations to the portfolio committee in parliament, explaining our objections to 27 clauses in the proposed Bill. It was quite a sight – militant trade unionists in the white-dominated parliament articulating positions on the labour dispensation in a more sophisticated way than they, the lawmakers, understood themselves. For us it was a tactic.

* * *

At the same time, we needed to think about our economic policy. The collapse of communism in Eastern Europe in 1989 saw ordinary people tearing down the Berlin Wall. It showed the fury of a people long suppressed and it took us by surprise. Why were people so outraged? Why did they topple the statues of those we had regarded as icons? Debates were raging in the Mass Democratic Movement about the future of socialism. We had to find out for ourselves.

I led a delegation to Moscow to meet with the trade unions and talk to political leadership in late 1990. It was a time of perestroika and glasnost. We were trying to understand what was happening in the Soviet Union because the Soviet Union had always been our ally. It had provided us with strong political and moral support and assisted our armed struggle. So it was a point of reference for us.

In Moscow we did ceremonial things and visited sites of significance. These included the Kremlin and Lenin's Mausoleum. For all of us this was a memorable moment, to view and acknowledge the perfectly preserved physical remains of the brilliant intellectual and strategist who had stimulated our imaginations and inspired our own activism in faraway South Africa. He seemed so real that I was tempted to interrupt his slumber and speak to him.

But we could see the discontent – we recognised the same in our own eyes. The dream of state-led socialism had been usurped by a minority masquerading as the advanced vanguard of the proletariat. Nationalisation of the means of production had just become a tool for a new economic elite who had now become used to the privileges enjoyed by their counterparts in the West.

I spent ten days with Alec Erwin, the National Organiser of the National Union of Metal Workers of South Africa (NUMSA), Bernikow Woolsdorf from the Southern African Clothing and Textile Workers Union (SACTWU) and Sam Tambani in a country going through its own massive turbulence as it sought to transform itself. We encountered a bureaucracy unsure of itself and unsure of its role as the Soviet state unravelled. I could see the similarities with the bureaucracy in South Africa – a lifetime of demonising one's opponent was over, and overnight the enemy had become legitimate.

I was most disconcerted by what we saw. I thought, 'My God, if I had been a trade union leader in the Soviet Union I would have probably landed up in Siberia!'

The unions were disappointingly apolitical. They were little more than a conveyor belt of the state and were reduced to running sports facilities and holiday camps. It was a sobering lesson and I was determined that this should never happen to COSATU.

Alec recalls some of the highlights of this trip:

We met Shubin, the Soviet scholar and expert on South Africa.[7] We met economists who explained the significance of Gorbachev's reforms. We were surprised to find out how far ahead the economists were in relation to trade unionists. We clarified many things, for example, the weakness of trade unions, and confirmed that we had been on the right track . . . This prepared us for when we met the SACP later.[8]

At the same time Joe Slovo wrote a courageous and brilliant essay, 'Has Socialism Failed?' It not only set out a realistic debate about socialism, capitalism and the restructuring of the world economy, but also clarified that socialism is not a blueprint cast in stone.

As Slovo wrote, the key questions we should ask ourselves are:

Firstly, have we the right to conclude that the enemies of a discredited party leadership are the same as the enemies of socialism? If the type of socialism which the people have experienced has been rubbished in their eyes and they begin to question it, are they necessarily questioning socialism or are they rejecting its perversion?

Secondly, what doctrine of pre-Stalinism and pre-Mao Marxism gives a communist party (or any other party for that matter) the moral or political right to impose its hegemony or to maintain it in the face of popular rejection?

Thirdly, who has appointed us to impose and defend at all costs our version of socialism even if the overwhelming majority has become disillusioned with it? [9]

These questions were the kernel of what I experienced in the founding country of socialism. I saw the heavy hand of Stalinism, the coercive powers of the organs of the state and a mass of people passive in their acceptance of this tyranny.

I had many discussions with Joe Slovo over the relationship of COSATU within the Alliance. I had already been exposed to some of the challenges of working with comrades who were returning from exile. I had the impression that there were many who considered themselves a victorious army marching in to claim the country that they had won as a government in exile.

I was glad that in Joe Slovo and Chris Hani I found kindred spirits who articulated a more profound understanding of the role of internal mass movements. As Joe expressed in his January 1990 essay:

We do not regard the trade unions or the national movement as mere conduits for our policies. Nor do we attempt to advance our policy positions through intrigue or manipulation. Our relationship with these organisations is based on complete respect for their independence, integrity and inner-democracy. [10]

The debate on socialism was fierce but I welcomed it. I saw it as a strengthening of our mass movement and key to the debate about the developmental state. It was clear that at home we were embarking on negotiations where there had to be compromises. We had not militarily defeated our enemy. With the dogmatic ideologues in retreat it meant that we could debate the programme that would underpin an Alliance for a new democratic, non-sexist and non-racial South Africa. In COSATU we had already started to discuss the idea of a reconstruction pact with the ANC and SACP. I felt confident that the failure of socialism had to do more with the tyranny of elite than with the science of Marxism-Leninism.

At the same time, Eastern Europe was fragmenting. The new world was becoming unipolar, moving towards the domination of an American culture and the Washington Consensus representing the market fundamentalism of a unipolar world. I returned to South Africa convinced more than ever before that our independence as a labour movement needed to be protected. The challenge was to define a programme of action that would see apartheid replaced by a people-centred developmental state.

Many of our leading union comrades were foremost in the negotiations process, bringing years of expertise and tactics of coalition building, collective bargaining and organisation building that had made COSATU a formidable force in South Africa.

And because of that crucial experience, comrades such as Cyril Ramaphosa were able to outmanoeuvre the National Party on the constitutional negotiations without jeopardising our need for a negotiated settlement.

But Cyril's commitment to the negotiations was also to be the undoing of his goal of succeeding Mandela. Cyril neglected the corridor politics of the ANC while others were busy building a base from which to seize political power within the ANC. Cyril was not alone in not understanding that lesson.

24

In the meantime, it was as if this historic opportunity for transformation also opened up new paths in my personal life. I was sharing a house with a close friend, Colette Tilley, who lived in Bezuidenhout Valley, a white working-class area at the forefront of change in character and milieu.

Relationships were always a challenge. What could you offer in these tumultuous times when attachments and routine might spell danger for those you love? I told Colette that one day I would meet a French woman who played the piano; and I was going to marry her. I have no idea why I said it, but that's what I felt.

On 27 October 1990 I took an international delegation of trade union colleagues to the re-launch of the ANC Youth League, which coincided with Oliver Tambo's birthday. Arriving at the rally in Orlando Stadium we joined tens of thousands who had come to celebrate. I was one of the speakers. Little did I realise how that fateful speech would impact on my life. That evening I took the visiting delegation to listen to jazz at Jameson's Bar in downtown Johannesburg. It had been an exhausting day and we were looking forward to an evening of good music.

As I descended the stairway down to the bar I was confronted by an attractive woman leaving the club who blurted out, 'Hey you, Jay Naidoo, I want to interview you.' I glanced at her and replied, 'Oh my God, not another journalist. I am not interested.' I heard her debating in French with her colleagues as I continued walking down the stairway.

Not long after she reappeared. 'Listen, my name is Lucie Pagé. I am a French Canadian journalist and I really want to talk to you,' she persisted.

'Well, if you want to stay that's okay with me. But we are not discussing politics' was my reply.

We spent the next few hours dancing and discussing our lives. At 2.00 a.m. I walked her back to her hotel. She had come to do a series of fascinating documentaries in the aftermath of the release of Mandela – on topics as diverse as health, jazz, women and politics – for a programme called *North-South*. I found her exciting and attractive. As I walked her through the streets to the Johannesburg Sun where she was staying, we were accosted by a gang of thugs who demanded money and her jewellery. I was furious. Fortunately they recognised me as the COSATU General Secretary and left us alone. I apologised and at the doorsteps of her hotel we kissed momentarily and took leave of each other.

One week later I invited Lucie to dinner at Colette's house. I cooked a meal and we spent the night together. She had a week left in the country. We had both broken off relationships and we found that we were physically and emotionally attracted to each other.

Lucie was incredibly beautiful and very intelligent and I immediately formed a bond with her. She began to awaken the half of me that was absent in the first part of my life, the more human side. It was an affair that had to be hidden from her crew. We would meet at night. She would put the 'Do not disturb' sign on her door. I would pick her up at night and drop her off in the early hours of the morning.

My affair with Lucie stirred some deep emotions within me. She made me laugh and dance with joy. She was Latin in temperament, French- speaking, and her moods mirrored how she felt. It was due to a mixture of fear, culture and tradition as a South African political activist, and a man, that I had closed down my emotional side. Yet with Lucie I shared my deepest fears and aspirations; I bared my soul to her.

Perhaps it was because she had none of the political baggage of South Africa or that we would never see each other again that made me comfortable to talk openly to her. She was an extraordinary listener, empathetic and independent.

A few years later, when she wrote a book about her first experience of South Africa, Lucie described how she was struck by my readiness to exchange my personal life for my long-term goal:

I listen to him carefully. I try to understand what it means to give up one's life for the cause. Finally I ask him where he finds the time for a personal life, a love life.

'I can't have any relationships,' he replies. 'My work takes up ninety-five percent of my time. And the five percent that remains is for sleeping.'[11]

I phoned Lucie in Canada on her birthday, 29 November, three weeks after she had left, to wish her well. It was a spontaneous gesture. She responded similarly. 'Do you want to come to the North Pole with me over Christmas and New Year?'

'What?' I said, surprised.

'Well,' she said, 'my mother teaches Inuit children in a little village in the Arctic Circle and if you can get to Montréal we can spend New Year there in a village called Umiujaq.'

I put the phone down and after a while thought, 'Why not?' It had been a tough year. I was exhausted emotionally. I had always taken time off over Christmas, even in the height of the anti-apartheid struggle. So why should this be any different? I borrowed the money to buy the cheapest ticket I could find, collected the warmest woollen clothing my closest friends had and headed off to Montréal.

As we arrived at Montréal airport, I gazed out of the windows and saw a blanket of white snow covering the land. It looked like a fairytale. The sky was deep blue, the sun's rays created fields of diamonds and smoke trailed out of the chimneys of farmhouses. Peace reigned below and my heart yearned for a piece of that serenity for my soul and my country.

I walked through the customs checkpoint feeling nervous, not knowing what to expect. Then I saw Lucie and made my way to her. All of a sudden a young child, Lucie's son Léandre, leapt into my arms and gave me the biggest hug I could imagine, saying in a really cute French accent, 'Bonjour, Jay.' It was a really nice feeling.

Not even the icy winds and a temperature of minus 20 degrees Celsius could dampen the joy and warmth in my heart as we hugged. Lucie led me to her car. That evening we had a marvellous dinner and she played the piano for me – she had grown up in a home with music. Her mother, Louise Grondin, had been a pianist, a music teacher and a singer.

The province of Québec is stuck in an English-speaking North American continent. Montréal has a different tempo and a free spirit that is refreshing.

The cars seemed more compact, the houses average, the people friendlier and the egos considerably smaller. I met Lucie's friends, all very animated and intrigued by this love affair but welcoming and warm. And her beloved son, Léandre, who was only three years old and could not speak a word of English, thawed my heart as he clung to my side.

Lucie took me to my first skiing experience, a children's ski run. All I remember is being the only 'darkie' on these white slopes, falling all over the place in a rather self-conscious way. By the end of the afternoon I was sweating profusely and in a foul mood and she was bursting at the seams with laughter. I promised myself that one day I would master this sport. (Indeed, I have since learnt to enjoy cross-country skiing tremendously but not downhill!)

At that time I was more anxious about meeting the mother of someone I was having a relationship with. I had never met the parents of anyone I had gone out with and here I was going to be trapped in my imaginary igloo with Lucie and her mother. The trip there was an adventure to start with. My clothing had by that time been exchanged for real winter clothing borrowed from Lucie's friends. 'Woollen clothes,' she laughingly told me, 'are quite useless for where we are going.'

It took two plane journeys to get there. The second plane, a flimsy ten-seater, was diving down to land and I could see no runway. And there seemed to be a herd of animals lying in our flight path! Surely we are going to crash into these animals, I thought, as the inside of my stomach climbed to the back of my mouth. It was only then that I realised that the first insane dive was designed to scare off the herd of caribou, which it did. Then we landed. There was a small crowd waiting.

The doors opened and an icy wind like nothing I had experienced before swept across my face as I descended the stairs. The temperature was minus 40. Lucie grabbed a very attractive woman and hugged her. She carried huge overcoats with which we immediately covered ourselves.

'This is my mother!' Lucie screamed as we bundled on to the back of a motorised sled and screamed through the snow to get to her little village. We entered the house and as we peeled off layers of clothing in this insulated and heated apartment it was as warm as if I were sitting in Johannesburg at 30 degrees.

Louise Grondin is an amazing woman, hip even today, at 72. She is friendly, warm and naughty. Divorced since she was 41, she was independent and had embraced a life she had always longed for. I admired her for that. Taking the plunge into the unknown is always terrifying. But here she was welcoming me. Later I was to learn that in response to Lucie's secret question as to what she thought of me, her jest was, 'Does he have a brother available?' That was the kind of mother-in-law I could live with.

That night, I woke in an absolute panic. Gunshots were going off around me. Was it a nightmare I was having? But this was the frozen North. It was close to midnight and the village was awake with the sounds of skidoos driving crazily and people with rifles and shotguns firing into the air to celebrate.

'Wow,' I said, 'this is a change!'

Gunshots in South Africa would mean innocent lives being lost and blood spilled at the hands of the security forces. Here, they were merely celebrating the arrival of the New Year – 1991.

It took at least half an hour to dress up and climb on to the skidoos. Then we careened about with no thought for rules of the road. In fact, there were no roads, just pathways for these mechanical sleds. It was a daunting introduction to the life of the Inuit.

The days wore on. The views were spectacular. We travelled out of the village. We made angels in the snow and felt the overwhelming silence. This was like no other place on earth I had been to. We dog-sleighed, walked on the sea with its frozen waves high in the air, encountered herds of beautiful caribou, and we fell in love.

Louise took us to her class. As we shed our large jackets and our caps, an elderly Inuit woman walked past and stared at me. She had clearly never seen anyone who looked even remotely like me. I wondered what was going through her mind – a dark, woolly-haired stranger holding hands with a beautiful white woman, the daughter of a much-loved teacher of their children. Coming from South Africa I was expecting the worst.

She moved closer, felt my hair between her fingers and then turned to Lucie and felt her hair. She then turned to me and gave me the thumbs up. My hair is thick and dense, very much like Inuit hair. I realised then that perception is sometimes our worst enemy. It is small incidents such as this one that have taught me the need first to check the facts and avoid making assumptions about the actions of people.

The children in the class had never heard of South Africa. But they had heard of Nelson Mandela. When Louise said that it wasn't Mandela but Jay coming, they answered, 'Jay Mandela is coming! Jay Mandela is coming!' And thus the rumour of the village was that the strange visitor was the son of Mandela. We talked for a long time as I tried to satisfy their insatiable curiosity. After I had spent at least two hours in the classroom a young child poked up her hand. Giggling, she asked, 'Are you a rich person? You have come so far, you must have lots of money.'

If only they had known I was wearing borrowed clothes, had bought a ticket on loan and lived hand to mouth back home. But I replied, 'Oh yes, I am enormously wealthy. I draw from the wisdom of my ancestors and that gives me much knowledge. I absorb the richness of wildlife and the mountains, rivers, forests and oceans. We are the meeting point of the North and the South and the East and the West and celebrate the wealth and diversity of our cultures. I work with the legendary Mandela and imbibe the nobleness and humility he carries in his soul. Yes, I am rich; richer than the person with a treasure trove of gold and diamonds. But my wealth is here,' I said, holding my hand to my heart.

The trip back to Montréal was tinged with sadness as our time together was drawing to a close. I was content like I had never been before – South Africa and politics were for the first time at the bottom of my priority list. As we said our goodbyes, I felt a deep awakening inside as I hugged the sobbing woman who had brought such light into my life. We promised to find a way of seeing one another again soon.

Two months after I left Canada I connected with Lucie in New York. It was a chilly St Valentine's Day, 14 February. I took her for a walk in Central Park and we sat next to the 'Strawberry Fields memorial', near the spot where John Lennon had been murdered. As a peace activist Lennon had inspired us as students. His famous lyrics in the song 'Imagine' were a lodestar for us.

It was here that I asked Lucie to marry me.

As Lucie recounts:

Jay takes out a book, a collection of poems by Pablo Neruda, the romantic Chilean poet – as passionate and gentle as the man who starts reading to me. He reads two, three, four poems, some passionately, some gently, always with expressive hand movements. I am seduced, but perplexed. 'Lucie, will you marry me?'[12]

Lucie stared at me intently and then said: 'I need to think about it. I have a son in shared custody and it would destroy me emotionally to be torn from him. I love you but I really need to think about the consequences.'

We agreed to meet again in Geneva a few months later when I would be attending the International Labour Organization annual meeting urging the maintenance of sanctions until real progress was made in the negotiations.

In the midst of frantic times and when we met in Geneva I found my refuge with Lucie. We enjoyed the few hours of intimacy we had each day and my heart ached for permanence in our relationship. Despite all the challenges, we both felt passionately about each other, a deep love we believed would allow us to bridge all the differences. Eventually, with tears pouring from her eyes, Lucie agreed to come to South Africa.

That decision was to cause us great pain and conflict but would one day bring us the blessings of love and passion.[13]

25

These were troubled times in South Africa. I was deeply occupied with a multitude of rapid and ongoing developments that were unfolding.

We had agreed to house the SACP in COSATU's building and Geraldine Fraser-Moleketi, who had recently returned from exile, was working there as a personal assistant to Joe Slovo and Chris Hani. This meant that the level of state surveillance of our activities increased dramatically. One August morning in 1990, Moses Mayekiso, General Secretary of NUMSA, saw a man standing suspiciously outside the building, talking through a walkie-talkie to someone sitting in a car round the corner.

We were legitimately paranoid at this time. Many of us were on death lists. Our colleagues had been assassinated by covert right-wing cells inside and outside of the state security system. We observed the man for some time and then went out and accosted him. We found him with a walkie-talkie, and when we emptied out his pockets we discovered a photograph of Geraldine. So we made a citizen's arrest and took him into the building and questioned him.

At this point there was a link between the ANC and the De Klerk government – a special line. If there were any problems with security, we had to phone the ANC, which we did and informed them that we thought we had captured a hit man.

I left the man in the care of some of my colleagues while I tried to get through to the special line on behalf of the ANC.

Many trade unionists had been killed, so my colleagues were understandably disturbed and angry. In my absence they stripped the man to see what else he was hiding, and then began to whack him around a bit.

When I came back in, I was horrified and I exploded: 'Get him dressed right now. How can you be so stupid to do this? And on top of it all, this is the COSATU head office!' It was this type of incident that hostile state forces were using to label the ANC and COSATU as a bunch of 'bloodthirsty terrorists'.

I decided we needed to pre-empt the potential adverse publicity. We called a press conference, at which I revealed the man and declared: 'This is what we found on him. We think he is a member of the death squad. We have phoned the ANC; they are coming across now and they have contacted the other side in government.'

On 6 August 1990 the Pretoria Minute had been signed, which included, amongst others, the matter of the suspension of the armed struggle by the ANC and its military wing Umkhonto we Sizwe.

We had also agreed on a line of contact between the two protagonists. Jacob Zuma, the head of ANC Intelligence, was the contact person and worked with a small group of operatives serving as a hotline between us for such incidents.

The ANC dispatched a person to our offices. He walked into the meeting room where we were presenting the suspected assassin to the media and gave him a mighty slap. I took him into the next room to brief him.

Suddenly a COSATU official burst into the room shouting: 'The whole building is surrounded by police and snipers. The police have broken past the security downstairs. They are threatening to break down the doors of the head office immediately if we do not open. They have a warrant to search and seize any property and want to arrest you.'

'Let me talk to them,' I replied, asking my assistant to bring Peter Harris immediately to the head office. I ended up arguing with the police. They had already detained and handcuffed Sydney Mufamadi, Moses Mayekiso and Lawrence Mawela. After some debate I agreed to accompany the police but refused to be handcuffed. A belligerent cop was preparing to strong-arm me when the senior officer agreed to the request. The four of us were taken downstairs by heavily armed men, loaded into the back of a police vehicle and taken to police headquarters at John Vorster Square.

Peter Harris arrived simultaneously and after a few hours of haggling while we were locked up in a holding cell, he negotiated bail while charges were formalised. We were charged with assault, battery and kidnapping.

The state felt confident that with these charges against us, an important mass organisation linked to the ANC would be neutralised by having its leadership tied into a lengthy and controversial trial. The trial would eventually get under way in 1991.

*   *   *

Out on bail, I wryly reflected on the turn of events that had resulted in us getting into trouble with the state over our friends, rather than the major and ongoing labour issues that were continuing to bedevil us. This was because right from its inception in 1985, COSATU had explicitly occupied the same space as political organisations such as the underground ANC and the UDF, which explained some of the tensions that existed between COSATU and the UDF.

There were those within COSATU who shared a view that the organisation should subordinate itself to the leadership of the ANC, but the majority had opted for a strategic alliance based on a shared vision of the Freedom Charter and elaborated in a concrete programme that would become our reconstruction pact.

South Africa had developed a range of civil society movements, in particular, local organisations called the Civics in virtually every township. The Civics opposed the Bantu Local Authorities Act and demanded delivery of services; they also comprised a powerful component of the UDF.

COSATU was the biggest organisation in civil society, and we felt very strongly that the ANC, the political movement that was marching in victoriously, should be accountable and should sign a reconstruction pact. COSATU was always clear that it could never be a 'rubber stamp' for any political party. No matter how much we supported the leadership and political party, COSATU could not allow decisions to be made elsewhere on its behalf. This was completely unacceptable to the culture of COSATU and we communicated this very clearly, to the UDF in particular.

In fact, there was a vigorous debate around a Code of Conduct and the way in which we were answerable to the structure of our organisation rather than to the structure of any other organisation. This culture of accountability went right back to the days in which we had the split in SFAWU (Sweet, Food and Allied Workers Union) and our big clash with Inkatha. The battle was won, not on the question of politics, but around the issue of democracy. These were the democratic workings of our structures.

A popular uprising – the 'Leipzig option' – was a last resort. If the right wing in alliance with the security forces staged a military coup we had to be prepared for a long, bitter and bloody fight. Given the increasing and orchestrated violence against the democratic forces, that thought did not seem too far-fetched at times. But we had to be cautious and I had no time for foolhardy leadership that put innocent lives at risk.

The struggle against the apartheid regime continued in a number of guises. Despite the heady political atmosphere, COSATU continued its core business of defending workers.

One of the labour movement's most significant clashes with the government was when the government wanted to introduce a Value Added Tax (VAT) to replace a General Sales Tax (GST). VAT would now have to be paid on things such as water, electricity, union subscriptions, medical services at private and public hospitals, rentals and all basic foodstuffs. This was a huge burden on the poor and another indirect tax that was also more complicated to administer, especially for small entrepreneurs.

In July 1991 the COSATU Congress took a resolution calling on the federation to take action. Initially COSATU's call was for the postponement of the implementation of VAT to allow for further consultations. The arrogance of the Department of Finance and Minister Barend du Plessis, in particular, inflamed grassroots organisations and the coalition soon represented over a hundred groups. Our central demands became: no VAT on basic foods, water and electricity; no VAT on medicines and medical services; and an easier way of administering VAT for small businesses.

COSATU, backed by NACTU and our broad-based coalition – including the Housewives' League, consumer organisations, religious groups, unions, civil society, NGOs and even small business – called for a general strike in November 1991. The list of demands grew to include an end to unilateral restructuring by the government and the establishment of a national negotiating forum between business, labour and government to deal with macroeconomic issues.

This was a very important moment of mobilisation and a turning point for COSATU too. We needed to demonstrate the vulnerability of the National Party. We needed to rock the boat in spite of some colleagues in the negotiations who felt that we were at a very sensitive stage of consultation.

Even the government mouthpiece, the SABC, was compelled to give us airtime. Lucie confronted me after I had undergone a particularly gruelling interview with a hostile journalist on the SABC.

'You were terrible. You were dressed inappropriately, your body language was aggressive and you ended up fighting and not getting your message across. The media is the Fourth Estate. It is a powerful tool but you need to understand how to communicate to people sitting in their lounges at home.'

Lucie had studied journalism and excelled in television work, so I had to agree with her. In the past it had suited the cause well that the white establishment media had portrayed me as 'maniacal and terrifying' – the 'Nemesis with Devil's Eyes' – who was the General Secretary of COSATU, known only for his calls for national strikes and leading mass demonstrations.

Our people recognised me for representing the fighting spirit of the working class. The white minority and conservatives saw me as their worst nightmare. It was an image I had cultivated as I had wanted to strike terror into the hearts of the racist establishment.

I realised now that I was going to have to address the fears and aspirations of all South Africans, and help to build the bridges to the new South Africa.

Sheepishly, I agreed to do some training with Lucie, who now had a full-time job working with the reputable Allister Sparks at the Institute for the Advancement of Journalism (IAJ), whose role was to begin training a new generation of independent journalists.

Soon the entire ANC and allied social movements, including Mandela himself, were put through rigorous media training courses at the IAJ. It was to pay off later as our role both here and internationally became more sophisticated and complex.

Now it was I who was able to provoke the Minister of Finance, Barend du Plessis, into a rage with my provocative remarks. They were designed to cause this reaction. It was always a spectacle to put a self-important government Minister on the spot in spite of him having the support of some self-serving, limp, embedded journalist.

At that point, the government was forced into a negotiation with COSATU leading the opposition. Professor Michael Katz, a brilliant and incisive lawyer who played a major role in the design of our post-apartheid tax system, was the facilitator. Cyril and I had various meetings with him to try to find common ground. We agreed to a meeting. The terms of engagement were clear. We rejected the imposition of VAT without consultation. The government had to make substantial concessions. In addition, we required a stand-off – that there should be no more unilateral economic restructuring of the state.

At the same time, we needed to demonstrate our ability to stop the country if the National Party insisted, as part of its negotiations stance, that it had minority protections, which inevitably gave it a veto right over our goal of transformation.

The stage was set and the country's attention was focused on this high-profile meeting held at the eminent Carlton Hotel, one of central Johannesburg's most famous landmarks. The government felt confident and had already prepared the media for what it believed was an open and shut case. We lined up on either side of the large conference table. Our side looked like a stereotypical bunch of revolutionaries and the government side was dominated by grey suits, all in obedience to the Minister.

Du Plessis began with a view from government, laying out an agenda of implementation that we immediately challenged. This was not what he had expected. Then he made the cardinal mistake of becoming belligerent and patronising. 'We have heard you talk about these issues and we are responding sympathetically. I'm prepared to make certain concessions, I'm prepared to exempt certain foodstuffs – and you, Mr Naidoo, if you really want, you can even include lentils in this – also intestines and offal.'

The meeting ended very abruptly. He had handed to us on a silver platter the *raison d'être* for a general strike. We stormed out to report: 'This illegitimate state not only is determined to ram an unpopular tax down our throat, but the only concessions are to zero-rate lentils and entrails. What do you think of this?'

The strike that followed was the biggest the country had ever seen. More than 3.5 million workers downed tools on 5 and 6 November 1991. The country came to a standstill as we demonstrated our power. The negotiations terrain had been levelled.

The government made some concessions but the big victory was the resignation of the Minister. The VAT campaign had a significant impact on COSATU, putting it on the map as a voice of all the poor and exploited people. The following year COSATU was taking up issues such as high food prices and it became active in forums dealing with drought relief, housing and electricity.

Derek Keys, the eminent and respected head of GenCor, was phoned while on a trip to China by President De Klerk to become the new Finance Minister. It was an interesting and intelligent choice. Keys accepted the appointment on the basis that he was not to be a National Party Minister but an independent, appointed in consultation with the ANC.

Derek Keys was an experienced businessman who was firmly committed to South Africa. He had an open and engaging personality and none of the ego of achievement. Within weeks of taking office, and in our first meeting, he presented his famous 'golden triangle', a partnership between government, labour and business. It converged with our thinking that we should have a binding reconstruction pact within the Tripartite Alliance that would form a new democratic government. Our discussions led to an agreement to set up the National Economic Forum (NEF) to begin negotiating the economic transition.

As the preamble to the NEF on 29 October 1992 stated:

> In recognition of the economic challenges facing South Africa, we believe that major economic stakeholders need to develop co-operative mechanisms for addressing South Africa's economic challenges... Organised labour, organised business and the governing authority have a central role in developing strategies geared toward the generation of sustained economic growth, the addressing of distortions in the economy, stability and the addressing of social needs. These areas need to be addressed as a matter of urgency if the political transition is to succeed.
>
> It is for this reason that we acknowledge the need to establish a National Economic Forum. We are mindful of the clause contained in the Laboria Minute of 14 September 1990, which reads: 'all of the parties record their willingness to discuss in an appropriate forum, the impact of labour relations issues on the economy.' Taken together with other developments, it is now necessary to expand the debate to ensure that broad economic and social issues are adequately addressed. The National Economic Forum will seek to support the transition to democracy.[14]

Jayendra Naidoo would lead the labour delegation and André Lamprecht and Bobby Godsell would head the business delegation. We would use the Development Bank of Southern Africa (DBSA) as the venue. The areas under discussion would be wide-ranging – from skills development to a strategy to deal with drought and job creation. Two working groups were set up – one looking at the macroeconomic and fiscal issues and the other a short-term working group looking at job creation.

The stage was set for us to deepen the process of national negotiations on the economic content of the transition we wanted. Alongside the NEF a plethora of negotiating forums had mushroomed. The National Housing Forum had brought together key stakeholders in the sector; and the National Manpower Commission dealing with labour market legislation was being restructured and COSATU had agreed to participate. The democratisation of policy making had taken root. COSATU was keenly aware of its societal role in fighting poverty and inequality, and as such it wanted to avoid the narrow corporatist model.

26

Omar Motani is my closest friend. We have been (unlikely) soulmates since first meeting in the late 1980s. I was the fiery and militant trade unionist – the nemesis of capital – and he was a businessman; there was a whole generation's age difference between us; and there was also a cultural difference – he is Muslim and I, Hindu.

We had met at a friend's home over a dinner attended by Chris Ball, then the Managing Director of Barclays Bank. Ball had provided the finance to pay for an anti-apartheid advertisement placed in several South African newspapers, calling for the legalisation of the ANC and urging government to negotiate with the nationalist guerrillas. A furious P.W. Botha, then President, decided to make an example of Ball and appointed a commission of enquiry into his activities to prove that he had broken security laws that made it illegal to advance the cause of an illegal organisation. Eventually Ball was forced to leave South Africa because of threats against him and his family. But it had been an important intervention that prompted many of his colleagues in the business sector to question whether the government under P.W. Botha was capable of steering the country away from the approaching storm.

Following an animated discussion at the dinner, I received a message that the reserved guest called Omar who had been there would like to meet me again. The next time we met, at the Three Ships Restaurant in the Carlton Hotel, I found myself unexpectedly opening up to a stranger. We talked about the country, about our families and also our mothers. We laughed. We were serious. It was as if we had known each other our entire lives. After several hours we realised that it was late afternoon. We left and Omar volunteered to give me a lift. We went down the escalator into the hotel parking garage.

As we searched for his car I realised how little I had spoken to anyone of my personal issues, yet I had opened up to Omar instantly. After fifteen minutes of traipsing the different floors we had still not found his car. By this time the security guards, all members of the union, had approached us.

'Comrade General Secretary. Are you looking for your car?'

'No,' I replied, 'it's my friend's car.' I turned to Omar to ask the make and colour of the car. He was a bit embarrassed: 'Well, it's a gold Rolls-Royce.'

Oh my God, I thought. Here was the General Secretary of the fiercely militant trade union federation hitching a lift in a Rolls-Royce, albeit an aging one, but a gold one at that! We never found the car in that parking garage. As we crossed the street to hitch a lift with a friend, Omar suggested that he might have parked it in another garage. Laughing uproariously we eventually tracked it down.

Omar is a self-styled entrepreneur who built his business from scratch, having to use a white nominee for his first venture to rent an ex-stable for his first factory because of the Group Areas Act. Today he owns five factories, employing over 1 000 workers, and is one of the most successful leather lounge manufacturers in the sector – a true tribute to a man who struggled against all odds.

As I came to understand Omar, my respect and admiration for his passion and determination increased. It is unbelievable to recall how many of the general strikes I planned in his home, yet he never once asked any favours of me. Even when his factories were hit by a protracted strike he refused to discuss the matter. His view accorded with my sentiment that our friendship was too precious to be diluted by work, business, politics and union matters.

Omar represented the nurturing father, the elder brother who understood my vision and in a hostile world I could openly share my emotional troubles with him. There was never judgement in our relationship; simply an acceptance that we had a deep respect and love for each other. There were also times when we reversed our roles and I was the elder brother in his times of distress.

As a black entrepreneur, Omar had made his mark – perhaps it was that shared history as black South Africans of Indian ancestry that led him in turn to admire my commitment to the labour struggle as much as I admired his role in building a significant business in spite of apartheid.

So, it was to Omar that I turned for help to lay the foundations of my personal life. Being in love and having jointly agreed that Lucie would relocate to South Africa meant a dramatic change in my life. In these dangerous times I had invited a foreigner from Canada, one of the most peaceful countries in the world, to share my chaotic life, which for so long had been gripped by the explosive adrenalin of revolution.

I felt that I had to make an effort to create some sort of normality for Lucie, and so I borrowed money from Omar in order to make a down payment on a house in Bezuidenhout Valley. I saw it once and although it looked pretty run-down, it had the most magnificent view and a majestic chestnut tree at one end of the garden. It also had 'potential' – a pool filled with junk and a large piece of ground parading as a long-expired tennis court. But the house was locked, so I did not really see the inside and only later discovered that it did not have a kitchen, just an old sink in a corner. It had to be completely rebuilt.

Lucie arrived at the airport. We went to have lunch and spend some time with Nisha, my sister, who had cooked a feast to welcome Lucie into the family. Lucie was clearly exhausted, her spirits reeling from being torn apart from Léandre, but she mechanically agreed to visit the place that I had bought in preparation for her coming.

We walked up the long stairway past the dilapidated outbuildings, past the junk-filled pool, the garden hidden under neglected overgrowth and into the house that I was also entering for the first time.

I was shocked by its state of disrepair. 'My God!' a tiny voice echoed within me as Lucie burst into tears.

I was at a loss. All I could offer was an inadequate: 'Look at the chestnut tree in the garden; it's a beautiful tree. Everything else can be built. You won't find a tree like this anywhere.'

I knew then that I had made a grave mistake. My sister gently enquired whether the deal was finalised. It was indeed done, but a few weeks later I discovered that there were still legal challenges to be overcome.

The Group Areas Act was still in force. Legally I was not allowed to buy a property in a white area unless all my neighbours agreed to my staying there. Fortunately, by this time most of Bezuidenhout Valley was populated by activists and new immigrants.

We secured the requisite permissions, signed all the documents and started the long journey of renovation. Lucie, unable to work as a journalist, threw herself into restoring the pool to its former glory, so much so that she ended up sick in bed for two weeks, having caught a bug from cleaning the infested pool. But later the pool became a blessing. For her, swimming almost a kilometre a day was a reflective meditation.

We sanded the wooden floors and windows, painted walls in bright colours and worked on the garden. One day, I asked Lucie if she would like any colours on the outside of the house, and she jokingly answered, 'Yes, I would like the chimney pink.' The next day, I climbed on the roof and painted her a pink chimney. Months later we could call this place home.

But then the reality of a tenuous transition in my country splintered the oasis of peace we had created for ourselves. I was away on a trip to deepen our fraternal solidarity with the Nigerian Labour Congress. It was a progressive federation of unions operating in the most populous state in Africa and under attack from the military junta. In COSATU we were keen to build links with a new form of independent unionism that would play an overtly political role without detracting from the shop-floor issues on which the organisation built its power.

Midway through my trip I received a frantic phone call from Lucie. She had spotted armed men carrying guns (which she later recognised as AK47s) on the hilltop heading towards our home. She had grabbed Léandre (who was staying with us for six months) and ran inside and locked the door, shouting that Jay was not at home.

'Phone Peter Harris if anything goes wrong and I am not here,' I had always said.

Peter had responded immediately, placing armed guards at the house. Lucie had taken down the number plate of the car the armed guys rushed off in. Peter later tracked the plates down and found that it was a car registered to the police.

This was not the life Lucie had expected and I felt an intense rush of guilt at what I had dragged her and Léandre into.

As the violence escalated, the jury was still out on whether our transition would be peaceful or end in a bloody civil war. At that moment, to many commentators, the general direction indicated the latter. Death lists were circulating in many covert quarters and as a leader in the most formidable organisation in South Africa my name naturally would be high on the lists.

Security had to be improved. COSATU discussed the issue with its international trade union comrades and a decision was made to install a security fence with barbed wire. Beyers Naudé arrived at our home with some money and said, 'Your friends want you to upgrade the security. We are worried about you and your family.'

We installed burglar bars and an alarm. 'Why are we putting iron bars on the windows?' Lucie innocently asked. Already under great psychological stress, she was not coping.

The situation forced me to question my own emotions; something I had shelved for a long time. I felt helpless and afraid for Lucie. We agreed to go for counselling, which meant that I had to deal with my own emotions. Until this point, I had always taken the easy way out.

As I had related to Lucie: 'My emotions are all clinically excised. I have no time to deal with them because they are like machine gunfire. So the easy way out is to cork them. It's like this fascinating fruit cocktail stall in the markets and beaches of Rio. All those brightly coloured bottles, each one with a suppressed emotion that I don't have the time to deal with. One day I will take them down and uncork them one at a time. Not now, because I don't have the luxury of time. My only hope is that they don't all explode in a fantastic firework display, because that will be the end of me.'

My relationship with Lucie provided a non-judgemental space in which I could deal with my emotions. Lucie is temperamental; she gives it to you on the chin. So I am forced to confront issues, whereas in my previous relationships, when they got too difficult, I would cut and run.

This time I couldn't run away. Lucie was here, she had given up her job, she had left her son behind, she had come to a foreign land, a foreign culture, a foreign language, and this in the difficult 1990s, one of the worst periods of violence and insecurity.

I was madly in love with her. This was the person I had scoured the world for and I was not going to give up without a fight. We both started going for counselling at the Family Life Centre in Parkview, Johannesburg. We made these times compulsory and it helped to have a professional distilling the issues for us. Many of my comrades, especially men but also women, might have felt that this was a waste of valuable time. But these sessions helped us to create a framework in which we could deal with the legitimate emotional issues that underpin any relationship.

*   *   *

Soon after Lucie's arrival in 1991 the trial against us – for the alleged kidnapping and assault of a police officer following on from our citizen's arrest of what we believed was a death squad member outside our headquarters – got under way. I had not had the opportunity to brief Lucie on the matter and a few days before I casually mentioned that I had to go to court.

'What do you mean, court?'

'Well, I'm being charged.'

'What are you being charged with?'

'I've been charged with kidnapping a policeman and assaulting him.'

She was devastated.

'Could you go to prison?' she demanded.

'Well, it's a possibility,' I replied.

I felt the full fury of her anger and realised that this was not someone I could take for granted.

The state proposed to drop the case if I disclosed who had been responsible for the assault of their agent at COSATU House, but I rejected this suggestion.

'We will play no part in our subordinates taking the rap. The buck stops with me. Let them proceed with the prosecution.'

The court date was set and the case dragged on for months. Lucie attended all the hearings, listening intently. To be difficult, we demanded translation but then we abandoned it because it took too much time. I was the key witness and my testimony was the only one offered. The chief prosecutor sought to distort every statement I made. Together with the magistrate he reminded me of the people my father had laboured under – evincing a self-righteous, undisguised and arrogant racism.

As was expected, at the conclusion, the magistrate pronounced the verdict of guilty. Two key witnesses arguing for the mitigation of sentence were Bobby Godsell and André Lamprecht, both senior private sector executives with whom I had spent many years in negotiations.

Lucie was devastated and crying. I took her home and we drank a bottle of wine.

'Don't worry. We can appeal,' I said, more concerned that COSATU could not afford the absence of three key officials. The next day sentencing took place. The courtroom was overflowing with COSATU leaders and a large, tense crowd had congregated outside under the watchful eye of the police. Would the apartheid state send senior COSATU leaders to jail in these sensitive times? In the 1980s they would have relished the opportunity. Now we were a country under the spotlight.

The dour magistrate began speaking in his monotone. His words dripped with the heavy hand of racism as he pronounced: 'Accused No.1 Jayaseelan Naidoo and others, I sentence you to three years...'

A hushed silence descended on the courtroom, and then he added: 'Suspended for five years.' The crowd erupted into clenched fists and rousing slogans as they ignored the rest of his speech. I was happy. The struggle would continue – *aluta continua*!

Lucie was silent. 'What's happening?' she questioned me. 'Why are you all celebrating? They have just found you guilty and sentenced you to three years in jail!'

I hugged her and said, 'Well, at least I don't have to go to prison. Come, let's go to dinner.'

On appeal the High Court set aside the conviction of assault laid down by the regional court. The Amnesty Committee of the Truth and Reconciliation Commission (TRC), on 30 June 2000, granted amnesty to three leaders of COSATU for kidnapping a policeman, Mongezi Joubert Maleka, on 28 August 1990. The Committee found that the three applicants made full disclosure of all relevant facts and that it was satisfied that the kidnapping was an act associated with a political objective.

*   *   *

Cheadle, Thomson and Haysom (CTH) was an incredible firm of talented lawyers who were deeply committed to the anti-apartheid struggle and who stretched the frontiers of legal thinking. They were often the thin line that separated us from the brutality of the apartheid regime.

Located on the sixth floor of an office building in Braamfontein, CTH played the all-important role as my back office in the 1980s. There was the combination of the razor-sharp brain of the flamboyant Halton Cheadle, later to be the architect of our labour market legislation; Fink Haysom, with his quiet but determined brilliance, who was later to become Mandela's chief legal adviser and now the head of the political office in the UN Secretary General's office; Peter Harris, whose calm belied an enormous will to pursue with steely determination the defence of his clients; and Norman Manoim, who worked tirelessly behind the scenes and is currently the Chairperson of the Competitions Tribunal. While I was close to all at CTH, it was Peter Harris who became my confidant and close friend.

We often sat late into the night planning our legal and political strategy, sustained by our comradeship, raw adrenalin and whisky. We had to think imaginatively. How could we shackle the renegade elements in the security establishment who were intent on wrecking our path to peace and stability? As the levels of violence continued to escalate and spread from Natal to the Witwatersrand, we often discussed if we could build on past attempts to negotiate peace with Inkatha. Jayendra had written a fascinating paper after our first failed peace talks with Inkatha arguing for a new broad-based approach by the COSATU/UDF alliance to the negotiations.

With strategic input from discussions with Peter and CTH I tested an approach with André Lamprecht, a senior executive at Barlow Rand, a major South African industrial group. Lamprecht had worked with me previously to settle a bitter and protracted strike at Nampak, a packaging company and subsidiary of Barlow Rand. We met in downtown Johannesburg at the Tony Factor Centre in Harrison Street. Given COSATU's alliance with the ANC we were clearly seen as a protagonist in the conflict. By contrast, the business community and the religious sector under the South African Council of Churches (SACC) were ideally placed to convene a peace conference.

We discussed what would be the outcome of such a conference and began to explore whether it was possible to regulate the relationships on the political stage by drawing lessons from the collective bargaining and recognition agreements governing relations between unions and employers. There were many procedures and rules regulating adversarial relationships on the shop floor. The issue was whether this could be replicated. André undertook to test this with employers and I would do likewise with our democratic forces.

We concurred that violence was reaching a tipping point and urgency was imperative. As the discussion took root it became clear that certain principles had to be spelt out. What were the rights and responsibilities of political parties? What was the Code of Conduct that would regulate political activity? What was the process of adjudicating complaints? What were the legal remedies and consequences to unsocial behaviour? A key challenge was the role of the state, given our deep suspicion that certain elements in the security establishment were involved in stoking the actions of warlords.

On the employer side it fell to the Consultative Business Movement (CBM) to steer the process. Dr Theuns Eloff, its Executive Director, was a versatile facilitator with leverage amongst the business community and had played a key role in taking a group of Afrikaner intelligentsia to meet the ANC in exile in Dakar, Senegal, in 1987.

A key issue was who would be the chief negotiator for the Alliance. My choice was Jayendra Naidoo. He had recently relocated to Cape Town to be close to his children and to work on an industrial strategy project that was sponsored by COSATU and headed by David Lewis, an experienced trade unionist who was now based at the University of Cape Town.

Jayendra, an old hand at handling complex multi-party groups, excelled in the task and, with strong support from the ANC and COSATU and working closely with employers, was able to navigate a minefield of political egos and achieve a consensus. After months of painstaking negotiations the stage was set and a commitment extracted that all the key political actors would attend the launch of the National Peace Accord on 14 September 1991. The historic Carlton Centre was the venue.

That day was also important for me personally. Lucie had been struggling with her life in South Africa. Her professional career was in jeopardy. She was seen as Jay Naidoo's lover, an extension of my political identity, and as a foreigner. The toll of shared custody weighed heavily on her shoulders. She had resolved that there was no place in South Africa or my life for her. Her bags were packed and flights booked. My emotions were shattered and I was overcome by helplessness. There seemed no way forward for a shared future.

But on 14 September she received an all-important call from Gilles Le Bigot, the producer of the French morning radio news, asking her to report as a freelance journalist for Radio Canada as the previous French correspondent had just left. The position was now open and Radio Canada preferred to have one of their own to report for them.

'It was a call from heaven,' I would say to Gilles years later. 'You do not know the role you played in keeping our relationship intact.' When we arrived home that evening, Lucie unpacked her bags. She had a life of her own now, and I understood with renewed force how important it was for her to have her independence, to work and keep her mind busy.

That night we celebrated. The day had gone according to plan. Every leader signed the historic accord. The sight of the key protagonists – Mandela, De Klerk, Buthelezi, John Gomomo and Joe Slovo – all seated in one room and committing their organisations to peaceful co-existence was a much-needed boost for a weary population exhausted by the sweeping violence.

To entrench the spirit of the National Peace Accord required a national commitment. Discussions with André Lamprecht and his colleagues in SACCOLA floated the idea of a national peace campaign. It was agreed that the religious constituency would lead a call for South Africans to commemorate a National Prayer Day, with the country coming to a standstill for five minutes at midday.

The outcome was overwhelming. At exactly 12 o'clock on 5 June 1992 the traffic rolled to a standstill, the church bells tolled, the machines went quiet across South Africa as the whole country – in the streets, the townships and suburbs, in the factories, shops and offices – prayed for peace. It captured the imagination of the country and our people.

The National Peace Secretariat established in terms of the Peace Accord would become a critical plank for stabilising the transition. It was well resourced by the Department of Justice and brought all political party representatives together at a national level and created regional structures with their own secretariats. In the Witwatersrand, a flashpoint for violence, André Lamprecht was the Chairperson and Peter Harris and David Storey were the team leaders. We achieved more success here than in any other region. The building of a corps of thousands of Peace Monitors drawn from across the political spectrum and branded with bright yellow flak jackets was a critical intervention to separate warring factions on the ground and implement the spirit of the Peace Accord. Through this network we were often able to use the intelligence garnered to pre-empt incidents of violence.

We tried to build a consensus using sport as a way to bring together the warring parties. The first experiment was a soccer match at Orlando Stadium in Soweto with key decision makers from the security forces, the IFP, ANC and COSATU. It was building the base of these interactions within the peace committees and in the community that we were convinced would bring an environment of political co-existence.

At the same time, there was a second priority: to rein in the renegade elements of the South African Defence Force (SADF) and the police. Subsequently, the Goldstone Commission, headed by the eminent judge Richard Goldstone, was formed to investigate complaints on political violence. This was a critical component of independent investigation capacity we wanted in place to apply pressure on De Klerk to act against his key Generals involved in the fomenting of violence.

The net result was that the Peace Accord created the momentum for us to move towards the Convention for a Democratic South Africa (CODESA) talks. It captured the imagination of the people. Even General Viljoen, influenced by his interactions with Mandela, threw his weight behind the peace campaign and contributed significantly to neutralise the threat of violence from the white right-wing extremists. Viljoen would go on to found the Freedom Front which would participate in the new democratic parliament in 1994, representing a powerful section of Afrikaners who felt alienated from majority rule but who would now commit to the democratic process.

27

Omar was the first person I talked to about Lucie coming to stay in South Africa, and now, in November 1991, we shared another big decision in our lives with him. Lucie and I had finally decided to get married. Léandre and Lucie's mother, Louise, were arriving in three weeks. When we mentioned the time frame to Omar he freaked out.

'Do you know that most weddings take a year to plan? It's not like making a reservation at the restaurant! Do you have a wedding list, have you thought about where you will get a hall, what food will you serve, and are you going to have a religious wedding and, if so, have you got a priest?'

Our answer was a NO on all counts. In fact, we barely had money to get Lucie a wedding dress and we had intended a small and intimate ceremony. By the time Omar and I had discussed who should attend, the list had reached 500. We decided that the best place to take our oaths of marriage would be on Omar's tennis court. It was a frantic rush to get ready for the big day.

On 14 December 1991 more than 600 guests congregated on Omar's tennis court to bear witness to our marriage vows. Almost the entire future leadership of government was in attendance, including Madiba, Albertina and Walter Sisulu, Oliver and Adelaide Tambo and many comrades of the labour movement.

Madiba, dressed casually, said to me: 'Well, Jay, I thought that as a trade unionist you would like me to come dressed without a suit. I do apologise. I have never seen you in a suit,' he said, to the laughter of the many people surrounding him. It is an instinct that he has never lost: the ability to disarm people around him even when he errs.

Lucie's list had only two people, her mother and Léandre, with Omar acting as her father and giving Lucie away. In addition, there was Léandre's father Serge, uninvited, who had decided he wanted to come to South Africa. We had the bizarre situation of him attending our wedding, staying at our home and even coming on honeymoon with us – along with my mother-in-law – because he knew no one in South Africa.

Given our multi-cultural relationship there were two priests. One was a French Catholic priest, Father Emmanuel Lafont, whose congregation was in Soweto and who is still a close family friend. He had lived in Soweto for many years, knew the local language and worked closely with the community and youth organisations. Father Lafont's church services were more like political gatherings at a time when the apartheid state was closing down many activist meetings.

The other priest was a Hindu priest popularly known as Guru Nadaraj, who was very closely associated with my family. Lucie and I have since been blessed by him on the birth of our children, when we moved into a new home and even when we bought a new car. He was originally from Sri Lanka and is a very humble person who cares deeply about people.

During the speech she gave at the dinner, my mother-in-law, Louise, handed Mandela a set of mittens she had knitted, emblazoned with the insignia of the fleur-de-lis – the national emblem of the Québec province. The contentious issue of English and French relations in Canada and the strong movement for independence in Québec were not at the top of our agenda. Mandela, ever generous, embraced her and displayed the fleur-de-lis proudly. The Canadian ambassador, one of the invited guests, was deeply upset. I was subsequently to learn more about the intricacies of English and French relations in Canada.

The biggest surprise for Lucie came during the speech of Albertina Sisulu. Turning to Lucie, she said: 'You know, Lucie, that Jay is already married.'

Lucie's mouth dropped in amazement and horror. Her mother's eyebrows rose in confusion.

Albertina clarified: 'Well, he is married first to the country and the nation. You are the second wife.'

Lucie still carries the burden of this lesson.

As the marriage ceremony concluded, we exchanged garlands. I realised that I had not bought any rings. Lucie had been too embarrassed to raise the issue with me earlier. The next day she asked curiously, 'Why did we not sign any documents?'

'I don't know,' I said. 'Anyway, we are married in the eyes of God, our friends and families.'

It was a short while later that I discovered that the Hindu rituals of marriage had not yet been recognised and that our Catholic priest had the right to marry people only in Soweto. Many years later I would be a keen supporter, in the new democratic South Africa, of the recognition of traditional and cultural rights of marriage.

While we were on honeymoon, the CODESA talks, under the chairing of the judges Michael Corbett, Petrus Shabort and Ismail Mohamed, began with a plenary session on 20 December 1991 – approximately 22 months after the unbanning of political parties and the release of Nelson Mandela.

I felt a tinge of pride as I listened to Mandela's speech at the opening of the talks:

> Today will be indelibly imprinted in the history of our country. If we, who are gathered here, respond to the challenge before us, today will mark the commencement of the transition from apartheid to democracy. Our people, from every corner of our country, have expressed their yearning for democracy and peace. CODESA represents the historical opportunity to translate that yearning into reality.[15]

I felt so optimistic. I was certain now that the end of oppression would come quickly. Lying in each other's arms that night I said to Lucie, as she shared her anguish about the joint custody of Léandre between two continents and her deep loneliness in Johannesburg, 'Don't worry, we shall settle things soon and we can even spend some time in Québec.'

* * *

I spoke too soon as our relationship was volatile and under constant strain. We had no time together and I was still the umbilical cord for Lucie's entire existence in South Africa. She felt strongly that the issues of women in South Africa had to be placed on the same standing as the political rights we were fighting. I was in complete agreement with the principle of this, but my years of activism had shown me that this was often easier said than done.

Lucie was determined to do something about it. Her research produced a statistic that even I was unaware of – that in South Africa a woman was raped every 83 seconds.[16] She threw herself into preparing a proposal and budget for what she knew best – making a documentary.

Once she had secured the funding, the hard work started. Where do you find victims and perpetrators prepared to be interviewed on camera? Lucie suggested the idea of putting an advert in the newspapers. I thought that this was sheer lunacy but did suggest that she use a pseudonym and make no mention of our address. For weeks we were inundated with obscene callers who warned her to steer clear of the subject unless she too wanted to be raped.

But this made her even more determined to do the documentary. Weeks went by and Lucie made no progress, until one day a call came in from Mary Mabaso, a large, generous woman and activist who had been working in Soweto. Lucie had her first lead.

Soon her days were tumbling forward as the story unfolded and the script was ready for filming. For weeks Lucie left early and came back late flushed with the intensity and problems that flooded her daily. But she had purpose and took this in her stride and actually relished the challenge. It was so good to feel her enthusiasm.

Then one night she told me that she had been feeling faint for a few days. Out of desperation she took a pregnancy test and the result was positive. Our natural method of avoiding pregnancy was not foolproof and that night we celebrated the impending new arrival with Léandre. We were all excited.

The launch of the documentary was a grand success. Lucie, who is always nervous about public addresses, prepared meticulously. I often marvel at the days she spends preparing a radio report that averages 70 seconds. Every word counts. By contrast, I frequently have to get a sense of an audience before I connect with the message that I want to share with them. It is our passion for what we do that unites both of us in speaking, in our relationship and in life.

There are many non-governmental organisations that still use the documentaries she has prepared on rape and women abuse for their campaigns and education work. Lucie's passion was to find its way into my work in government later as the Minister for Reconstruction and Development.

Summer in Canada arrived quickly. Lucie and I wanted to share our marriage vows with her family and friends, many of whom could not afford to come to South Africa.

In a civil ceremony in Joliette, a quaint town in Québec, with a grand total of 42 guests, our marriage was legalised. Omar Motani was my best man and we enjoyed an idyllic honeymoon together with Omar and family. It was such a relief not to worry about political intrigue or violence for a few weeks.

28

In 1992 the National Peace Accord was working unevenly across the country. In some areas the structures were too weak to manage the escalation of tension. One such region was the Vaal Triangle and the massacre on 17 June of 46 residents in Boipatong, near Sharpeville, was a lightning rod to the escalation of violence. Witnesses reported that the killers came from an IFP-controlled hostel.

Investigative reporters claimed that police vehicles accompanied the killers under cover of darkness. We were convinced that the security forces had connived with Inkatha vigilantes and orchestrated the attack.

I went to address a rally at Evaton. I shared the stage that day with Archbishop Tutu and Joe Slovo. As I walked through I could feel the anger of the crowd. I feared that unless it was channelled the whole thing could become very ugly and the leadership itself could become discredited.

One thing I like is reading audiences, and so I started off with a slogan.

'We have asked for our human rights,' I declared, 'and De Klerk has told us to go to hell; let me tell you, De Klerk must go to hell. And if we have to go to hell we will take him with us.'

'De Klerk must go; De Klerk must go!' I chanted.

The ground erupted with a rhythmic stamping of feet and soon the cry was taken up by the entire crowd screaming out their anger. I wanted the angry bile of hatred to pour out – it needed an outlet. Otherwise it was a potent mixture waiting to be ignited. I recognised the signs and I could read the eyes of anger as I carved my way through the milling youth armed with machetes, sticks and petrol bombs.

Indeed, I felt at one with them. I felt the treachery of the regime; I gasped and breathed the anguish and the hopelessness. I felt the blood pouring from gaping wounds; I smelt the deep fear. I heard the cries of the innocent; and I felt the mourning.

We needed to channel people's pain and militancy, and particularly bring the youth back into the organisation to restore their confidence in their local leaders. Reason and rational action would follow.

* * *

The news of the violence in South Africa had reached Canadian shores. Léandre was in shared custody across two continents – spending six months in each country.

His father, using information garnered from news stories about South Africa, was opposed to sending him back to us as we had agreed. Heavily pregnant, Lucie was particularly vulnerable and became deeply depressed. Her crying was continuous and uncontrollable. I was concerned.

Three weeks before the baby's due date, on the evening of 21 November 1992, Lucie experienced severe contractions minutes after receiving a letter from Léandre's father saying she would not have her son again. We alerted the midwives who had worked closely with us over the months of the pregnancy and rushed to Johannesburg General Hospital to meet them.

Along the way, I asked Lucie, 'Do you have any change? We need to phone family and friends using the public telephone.' She didn't, so we stopped outside a corner café in Rockey Street, Yeoville, and I rushed in to collect some change. (Mobiles or cellphones were not a reality then; and ironically, I would one day become the Minister of Telecommunications.)

Johannesburg General is a public hospital. Previously I was not allowed there because it was reserved for whites. The black staff were excited to see the General Secretary of COSATU and his wife delivering their child here.

After several hours Lucie delivered our son, whom we named Kami (meaning the 'black Hindu God of Love'). At just over 2 kilograms he burst into our world with a determined cry.

Within a few days I set off to Vancouver to speak at a Canadian Labour Congress meeting and hoping to pick up Léandre afterwards. Nothing was confirmed and we were all on tenterhooks. I had wanted to cancel my trip because of Kami's birth and Lucie's emotional state, but she wanted Léandre back and I got on to the plane reluctantly.

In Montréal I met with the lawyer referred to us. He had already dispatched a letter to Léandre's father. Confronted with a violation of the joint custody agreement he had signed and a letter from the Canadian Embassy saying that South Africa was 'still not a travel risk', he finally conceded to let Léandre come with me.

We arrived back to find that Kami, only ten days old, had dropped half a kilo in weight and had been rushed to hospital to undergo a series of tests. He was critically ill and unable to keep his milk down. The problem was eventually tracked down to an undeveloped oesophageal opening but there was no treatment for this; only two years later would he recover and sleep through the night without crying in pain.

Time does bring into perspective some comic relief. In the following weeks we went together to the Department of Home Affairs to register Kami.

The first debate we had was about his race.

'Our son is South African,' Lucie said. I was not with her at that particular moment. She refused to give the race of the father to be able to classify him. The lady ticked the 'White' box.

The next battle was to register Kami with both our surnames. Lucie carries her own name, both as an affirmation that she is an individual with her own identity, but also by Québec law, since 1979, which states that a woman keeps her name when she marries.

I was completely in favour of this because I believe that a marriage solemnises an equal partnership between two individuals. But for the officials of Home Affairs this was too complex.

'This is not possible in terms of the rules,' they replied.

After a lengthy debate we found the solution: first we registered him with my surname. Then we applied for a change of name and ended up with the double barrel of Naidoo-Pagé.

Lucie was emotionally and physically exhausted, her general depression now compounded by post-partum blues and the news of the death of her beloved grandmother. Kami was in constant pain and crying interminably because of his condition.

Lucie ended up with painful mastitis but she was determined that Kami would be exclusively breastfed. At night she would feed and then I would take Kami into my arms as he cried in pain for a few hours. Lucie needed the sleep. Her commitment to breastfeeding made a deep impression on me, and I robustly defended her breastfeeding, even in public.

Years later, as the Chairperson of the Global Alliance for Improved Nutrition, I understood the scientific reasons why breast milk was the best product for babies with the worst advertising. It would be a long struggle to build a campaign for six months of exclusive breastfeeding, which lays the foundation for the good health of children throughout their lives.

At the same time, Léandre, who was now with us for six months, found himself in an unfamiliar environment and unable to speak English. He became very introverted. He went to a nearby nursery school and every day he came home crying.

Two months passed and one day when I picked him up at school, he was dirty and laughing. We communicated through a mixture of English, French, hand signs and hugs. He had finally broken the ice and had started speaking English.

'I will teach you English and you are going to teach me French' was my commitment. Well, a few months later, his English was fluent and my garbled French remained at: *'Brosse tes dents'*; *'Fais dodo'*; and *'Ne fais pas ça'* ('Brush your teeth'; 'Go to sleep'; and 'Don't do that').

I had promised Lucie and myself that one day I would master the French language. Today all my children are perfectly bilingual. Their mother tongue is French – Lucie never spoke a word of English to them – but because they have lived interchangeably between Canada and South Africa they have developed two languages, two countries and two cultures.

Sometimes the clash of cultures was hard to handle. On one trip to Durban to visit my family when Kami was two months old, Lucie went to have an afternoon nap, which she rarely did. It was a family gathering with alcohol flowing quite liberally. The conversation turned to the ritual of shaving a child's head of hair. After much discussion we all agreed that the customary ritual needed to be performed. A razor materialised and volunteers made haste until we had a bouncing young boy whose head was completely shaven.

We were all celebrating this achievement when Lucie, bleary eyed, walked into the room and screamed: 'What have you done to my child? What have you done to my child?' Sobbing, she tore Kami from my arms and rushed into the bedroom, slamming the door. It was a sobering moment for all of us as we realised how sensitive the issues of culture could be – and I became aware of how short-sighted I had been.

* * *

Chris Hani was a revolutionary. He would always be the conscience of the country, I realised, when Chris, bowing to the wishes of the grassroots, decided against entering government, arguing that we needed strong voices in civil society. 'If you want peace then you must struggle for social justice,' he would say.

Chris and I struck up a rapport from the first time we met. I had offered to host the SACP in the building we were renting, together with NUMSA and the NUM, in Rissik Street. Later I would reach an understanding that COSATU would always host the Party. I was convinced that the Party would be a valuable counterweight to the concentration of power.

For me the SACP was an important guardian of our principle of non-racialism and of the aspirations of the poor and the working class. Obviously its close association with the Soviet Union had led to some blind obedience to a failed policy. But the SACP had never been in power in South Africa, had never abused power, had consistently fought for the human rights of the black majority and had contributed many heroes to the rich tapestry of the freedom struggle.

More importantly at the time, Chris was very supportive of the discussions around the Workers Charter and how to institutionalise these discussions into legislation and even the Constitution.

We discussed many issues, but one of them would be a deciding factor later in our democracy. Reflecting on the abuse of power by revolutionary leaders elsewhere in Africa and the developing world, we floated the idea of a two-term limitation to anyone holding the public office of the President. We jokingly suggested that one day we may be called on to stand against the very comrades we had fought with in the trenches. This issue would become hotly contested later in our history but I am forever grateful that in spite of the concern about such a provision, the position put forward by COSATU prevailed. We also agreed that we needed a scenario in which we retained a vibrant and powerfully organised civil society, so that free debate would remain the lifeblood of the liberation movement.

Chris never asked me to join the Communist Party. Both he and Joe Slovo respected my decision not to wear too many hats. I was the General Secretary of a federation that carried members of various formations and in which the issue of social unity was important. Both of them were of the opinion that carrying a card didn't make you a better socialist.

Chris's view was very strong that we should encourage the private sector to get involved and be patriotic about South Africa. It had resources, it had expertise, it had great influence in society, and it was important to make the private sector a partner and thereby keep it honest.

Ultimately, Chris was a pragmatist. At the end of the day, he believed that he could find good people that he could work with in every sector of society. We canvassed what to do in the face of the high levels of violence against us and what would be the worst-case scenario – the unleashing of a wave of violence against us that would put everything at risk.

There was a threat that we would see the return of the military, the National Security Management System, the securocrats and their worst excesses.[18] Already there were conservative elements in the police, army and in business supported by Inkatha and the other Bantustan leadership who were looking for a different political home. General Constand Viljoen, the former head of the SADF, was emerging as the likely leader of the white right wing. He carried huge sway over the security forces and presented a more rational political face than the buffoonery of Eugene Terreblanche, the head of the Afrikaner Weerstandsbeweging (AWB), the neo-Nazi ragtag 'army'.

There was the real potential for a right-wing coalition to mobilise tens of thousands of well-armed and trained former military operatives. While it would have been impossible for them to impose their will, it would have resulted in a protracted and devastating civil war. Mandela's overtures to Constand Viljoen were a prerequisite for a successful political transition. In addition both Chris and I believed that a strong vigilant civil society prepared to go back to the trenches was our only insurance policy.

Chris, like me, reluctantly backed the call for the suspension of the armed struggle but once the decision was made we threw ourselves into the heated debate, defending the position, often against angry youth and shop stewards accusing us of betraying the revolution.

This was not to ignore the need for a counterbalance should negotiations fail. We had to be prepared for that contingency and not only accept a Plan B (Operation Vula),[18] but anticipate what COSATU would do to pre-empt that. We had to be able to muster everything we had to prevent a *coup d'état*.

A bullying violence hovered like a dark cloud over the country. These were perilous times.

29

Easter 1993 promised a much-needed retreat from the turbulent world of politics and a long weekend with Lucie and the kids on safari in the Kruger National Park. It was my first safari and I was looking forward as much as Lucie to seeing the Big Five up close. Lucie was feeling much better now and slowly settling into South African life.

I couldn't have gone to Kruger before, even if I had wanted to, given that I was black. We joked about Lucie as a foreigner inviting me to see my own country's world-renowned safari park.

We took our first drive and came to within metres of a pride of lionesses in all their majesty, staring with disdain at us. We spent an hour quietly admiring these magnificent beasts.

The next morning, Saturday 10 April 1993, Lucie rushed into the room. 'Jay, I have just heard on the radio that Chris Hani has been assassinated!' Disbelievingly I rushed to turn on the radio and it was confirmed. A cold shiver darted up my spine. Lucie tried to console me but my body was shaking. I needed to be alone.

I crashed on to the bed and for the first time since my mother died my body convulsed with the pain of the loss. Chris was a friend, a comrade and someone I trusted implicitly. I knew that all hell was about to break loose.

I called Lucie and said quietly: 'Let us pack up and go back immediately.' The journey back to Johannesburg was overwhelmed by the silence of my grief. We arrived late at night and I dropped off the family and rushed to Chris's home.

I arrived at a house in mourning and embraced Limpho Hani, Chris's wife, holding her while she sobbed uncontrollably. I joined the comrades there who were planning the next steps. Outside the home in this previously white suburb, black youths were manning roadblocks. The police thankfully were not in sight as their presence would only have served to inflame emotions that were already on tenterhooks.

Chris, ever considerate, had told his bodyguards to take the Easter weekend off to spend time with their families. He had gone to the local shop to buy some bread and newspapers and on his return fell in a hail of bullets at the hand of Janusz Waluz, a Polish immigrant to South Africa and a member of the AWB, whose accomplice was South Africa's Conservative Party politician Clive Derby-Lewis.

This incident was a powder keg and it only needed another spark to explode into a bloody civil war. As we strategised, it was clear that only Madiba could calm down the nation. De Klerk, unable to intervene, had agreed to our proposal that Madiba address the nation on SABC.

Meanwhile, the preparations for Chris's funeral swung into frantic action. We traversed the country putting out fires. Angry youth and communities were in no mood to listen to reason. The country's whites lived in fear of revenge attacks. But for now we had to bury a friend and one of our great patriots.

The day of the funeral saw hundreds of thousands gathering at Soccer City near Soweto. The roads were blocked by burning tyres sending black smoke billowing into the air. I was travelling with Joe Slovo and the salutes of fully armed youngsters with eyes burning with fury revealed what was waiting for us. Thankfully hundreds of our Peace Monitors in their bright yellow jackets were marshalling the crowds and keeping tempers from flaring into violence. For now there was a sense of calm before the storm driven by the great respect Chris commanded. We had to have a solution – a demand that would satisfy our people that Chris Hani's death had not been in vain.

Mandela's speech on television communicated that we had a right to be feeling deep anger, but that this was the democracy Chris had died for, the democracy we were now giving birth to. And the fact that it was an Afrikaner woman who reported the crime meant that it could not be 'the whites' who were the perpetrators – extreme, right-wing vigilantes had committed this terrible sin. Mandela said:

Tonight I am reaching out to every single South African, black and white, from the very depths of my being. A white man, full of prejudice and hate, came to our country and committed a deed so foul that our whole nation now teeters on the brink of disaster. A white woman, of Afrikaner origin, risked her life so that we may know, and bring to justice, this assassin. The cold-blooded murder of Chris Hani has sent shock waves throughout the country and the world ... Now is the time for all South Africans to stand together against those who, from any quarter, wish to destroy what Chris Hani gave his life for – the freedom of all of us ...

This government is illegitimate, unrepresentative, corrupt and unfit to govern. We want the immediate installation of a Transitional Executive Council with one purpose: to ensure that free and fair elections are held in the shortest possible time. This TEC must put in place multi-party control of such areas as the security forces, the budget, foreign relations, and local government. An Independent Electoral Commission must be established. Above all, we want an agreed election date to be announced.[19]

The rest is history. From that day the de facto President of South Africa was the People's President, Nelson Mandela. Madiba's message allowed us to go back to our cadres and mobilise around the country. We worked very hard to make sure that we kept calm. Almost a year to the day later, Mandela would become our first democratically elected President.

*   *   *

Within COSATU, our focus over the past few months had been around the idea of a reconstruction pact based on a social compact between the key democratic partners and on a focused agenda of economic and social transformation. This would be the basis of our contract with our people. We had studied the lessons of the transition from a liberation struggle to government in other parts of the world in which a leadership group going into government becomes alienated from its mass base. We were not the victorious army marching in behind a People's Army to claim the mantle of leadership. In fact, the central pillar that compelled the apartheid regime into a negotiated settlement was the rolling mass action and struggles of ordinary people that had become an unstoppable force for transformation.

There was an anxiety in COSATU that the ANC would move quickly to sideline the internal movement. In fact, COSATU's Central Executive Committee (CEC) discussed the possibility of being represented independently in the talks around a political settlement. We felt keenly that certain rights should be enshrined in the Constitution and the Bill of Rights. I felt that we should agree to accept the two seats at CODESA offered to us by the ANC but the CEC delegates – upset that non-existent parties had a seat at the table and yet a major political player like COSATU was declined a role – felt that we should not accept that. It was a mistake and would reduce COSATU to being a bystander in the political talks.

However, we lobbied hard for key provisions, such as the right to strike and a limitation of two terms of office for the President of the country.

In an environment where various social forces were positing their own agendas we felt in COSATU that a reconstruction pact would commit a new government to a joint agenda. However, in the 1993 COSATU Congress it was broadened into an overarching programme that would be incorporated into the election manifesto of the ANC.

While the drawing up of the Reconstruction and Development Programme (RDP) was a vigorous and empowering process, and it was a bold document, it became a wish list of policy choices rather than an agenda of negotiated transformation. It was felt that the new democratic government would be the engine for the detailed planning.

It did, however, represent a courageous vision, drawing on the Freedom Charter and the aspirations of our people. Its legitimacy was unassailable and the challenge was taking it into the planning processes of our first democratic government.

At the same time global business agendas were piling on the pressure to manage our expectations into the narrow context of the Washington Consensus in a world where triumphant capitalism was on the march. The key contention was that foreign direct investment would flee South Africa if we 'rocked the boat'. Our vision was that addressing poverty, inequality and the creation of decent jobs was a prerequisite for long-term political stability. The constant refrain, increasingly strident, was that the RDP, even as a policy framework for going forward into the new democracy, was akin to the Greek mythological flight of Icarus from exile on the island of Crete. Icarus, in escaping, fashioned a set of wings constructed of wax and feathers and in his excitement flew too close to the sun which melted his wings and in the end he fell into the sea.

For me, the RDP reflected the opposite. It was visionary and idealistic. It was the cement that bonded our people and the fragile social fabric. Most importantly, it represented the hope and the aspirations of our people.

In my mind the RDP placed people at the centre of delivery, and that was why people overwhelmingly said: 'The ANC is the organisation for us. And Nelson Mandela is the People's President.'

The trade union movement could be very unforgiving, even brutal, toward leadership that it didn't respect. In a strike situation, if an organiser lost a strike because of rash actions and then told workers, 'We lost and therefore we've got to go back to work now, otherwise you will get dismissed', he (or even she) could find themselves in serious trouble.

Poor leadership had consequences in the union movement. You had to be an efficient trade unionist; you knew your mandate and made sure that people were properly informed.

COSATU was not simply made up of a bunch of clever leaders at the top. We had to build an army of development cadres prepared in many cases to give their lives for the cause. Our dynamism and enthusiasm were driven by this very basic reality and not by the cult of the big leader who knew what was best for the organisation.

The RDP discussions also broadened into a rigorous debate about ensuring COSATU views were represented in parliament. This resulted in COSATU nominating twenty of its leaders at the 1993 Congress to go on to the ANC list for automatic election to parliament.

Cyril Ramaphosa had left the NUM and had been elected as the General Secretary of the ANC. He and other senior leaders of the ANC reacted negatively to COSATU's list of leaders but we stuck to our guns. Mandela was favourable towards the idea when I discussed it with him.

Given that the issue was discussed in all COSATU structures, Cyril's position angered the COSATU cadres because he came from our ranks and was expected to be supportive. It was to cause a rift that would impact on him later when he contended for the Deputy Presidency. Constituency politics are always the deciding factor in the hard battles on a political terrain.

Our list included Alec Erwin, John Copelyn and Marcel Golding, who were not popular in the ANC camp. But the ANC needed the organisational strength of COSATU to go to the polls and that was not a debate. In fact, many of the branches in both the ANC and the SACP were led by shop-steward leaders from COSATU. We reached an agreement that there would be an ANC process and that the COSATU list would be tabled as part of the selection process.

For me this was an emotional Congress. Kami was a year old and Lucie attended the Congress with him. I was leaving COSATU, leading twenty union leaders on to the ANC list for parliament. This had been my home for three successive terms over eight years but I relished the thought of a new challenge – of translating our concrete struggles of the past into viable programmes for the future. We had fought for freedom in our lifetime. Now we had the levers of power to change our reality. I was infected with the enthusiasm of the moment.

PART SIX

Freedom, Power and Responsibility

Never, never and never again shall it be that this beautiful land will again experience the oppression of one by another and suffer the indignity of being the skunk of the world.

Let freedom reign. The sun shall never set on so glorious a human achievement!

God bless Africa.

— Nelson Mandela, Inauguration Address

I have just spent two months in Québec. Two months of strained relations with Jay, who did not come over. Not even for a week, not even two days... 'I have too much work. I am a minister, Lucie.' Too much work. Married to another woman – South Africa! Since we moved to Cape Town, we hardly ever see Jay any more. He is always away. At a meeting, in Cape Town, in Pretoria or somewhere else in the world, but absent. I am 'a happily married single mother', I say. But 'happily' doesn't ring true anymore... Love is not the problem. It's there. Strong. Powerful.

— Lucie Pagé, *Conflict of the Heart*

30

The mid-morning quiet of 24 April 1994 was shattered by the resounding thud of a bomb explosion. It was at the corner of Bree and Von Wielligh streets around the corner from the ANC headquarters where I was based. We rushed on to the streets but the area was cordoned off. Nine people were killed and many injured. The irony was that one of those killed was Susan Keane, a candidate on the ANC regional list for the province. At 37 years she made the ultimate sacrifice. She happened to be white.

I phoned Lucie, realising she would be panicking. My name had been circulating on a number of death lists and she was living in fear of a dreaded phone call.

The following day more explosions went off. The country was on edge. Would this election give birth to a peaceful democratic transition or to a bloody civil war?

I hardly slept, tossing and turning as I thought of the dawn of the new day. Would it yield the goal we had spent our lives fighting for? For so long we had teetered on the brink of the precipice. Now we were seeing the dream of uniting South Africans into a non-racial and harmonious society beginning to materialise. The election stretched over two days. The first, 26 April, was for the elderly, the ill and the security forces and emergency personnel who would be on full alert the next day.

On 27 April, I was up before the sun rose. There were many polling stations to visit and to keep the spirit of our people strong. Lucie was preparing for a long day, doing radio reports one after the other. The world was watching and this was the final countdown. We embraced and I said goodbye to her and Kami.

As I travelled through the townships I saw a quiet determination. This was our moment of truth and for the majority of people the first time they had voted. In the suburbs black and white, the 'madams' and their 'maids', were now all equal before the new interim Constitution. I saw patient and excited citizenry: young and old, rich and poor, men and women voters in the long queues snaking around corners having colour-blind conversations, reaching out as never before.

Some stations had not received the stickers that reflected the involvement of the Inkatha Freedom Party (IFP). The IFP had at the last minute, after the printing of the ballot forms, agreed, to our national relief, to participate in the election.

Towards midday I arrived at my polling station in Alexandra, the overcrowded teeming township outside the richest real estate on the continent of Africa, Sandton – a classic manifestation of the inequality in our past.

Veterans of the struggle, men and women, shed tears of joy. An old man coming out of the polling station jumped for joy and shouted: 'I have waited all my life for freedom – now I have voted, I can die happy.' I refused to head to the front of the queue and stood in line chatting to excited people. This had been a hotbed of political struggle and many union activists had passed through the streets and lived in Alexandra.

This was a proud moment for this stubborn and courageous community. Suddenly the very ground we were standing on trembled with the distant sound of a powerful bomb blast. We found out later that it had exploded near the Johannesburg international airport.

But our discussion turned to resistance. Unanimously we all voiced our conviction that we would never surrender our democracy. These were the dying kicks of apartheid.

The long day was over and the polling stations all closed. South Africans retreated to their homes to wait anxiously for the counting to begin.

The days went by and the results were still outstanding. There had been irregularities in KwaZulu-Natal that saw many ballot boxes in mainly rural areas stuffed with ballot papers. The ANC had a choice to make an issue of this given that it was predominantly in Inkatha-controlled areas, but the outcome was clear to everyone. The ANC was heading for a landslide victory.

Our celebration party was at the Carlton Hotel. We were drunk with the smell of freedom and thousands poured into the ballroom to hear the victory speech by Mandela. I searched for Lucie and Omar who had navigated the tremendous crowds in the street and we sang and danced as Mandela came on stage to make his speech. His opening words had us doubled up in laughter. Madiba had a touch of flu and his punishing schedule had not helped. But he could not miss this moment and with his usual humour he said in front of the world's cameras: 'Please don't tell my doctor I am here. He has confined me to bed.' He went on:

> *The calm and tolerant atmosphere that prevailed during the elections depicts the type of South Africa we can build. It sets the tone for the future. We might have our differences, but we are one people with a common destiny in our rich variety of culture, race and tradition.*[1]

We spent until the early hours of the next morning welcoming the dawn of a new democracy. At some point in the evening Lucie excitedly dragged me to see Danny Glover, the celebrated doyen of Hollywood films whom she admired. She was startled when he embraced me enthusiastically. Danny, I told her later, was an active supporter of COSATU and was keenly involved in solidarity work linked to the labour movement both in the United States and internationally.

As we drove out of the Carlton Hotel and entered Commissioner Street, my thoughts streamed back to the days when mass demonstrations rocked Johannesburg. We always feared the worst consequences of brutal action from the security forces or the reckless bullets of organised or individual renegade right-wingers who believed we were 'open game' and they were protecting the last enclave of Western civilisation in Africa. 'Watch the buildings alongside the marches for snipers,' I would caution our marshals.

But today the change was irreversible. Our new interim Constitution and Bill of Rights were in force in an undivided South Africa – free from racial bigotry of the past three centuries. Most importantly, De Klerk had phoned Mandela to congratulate him on an impending ANC victory.

I embraced Lucie and we loved each other tenderly that night.

* * *

And then we were in power! 'Freedom in our lifetime', almost unbelievably, had come at last.

The parliamentary swearing-in ceremony was a historic moment. Many of the comrades I had fought with in the trenches were there now representing the people of South Africa. I was elated by my role as a newly inaugurated MP, one of 400, in South Africa's first democratic parliament. It was hard to believe that this hated institution that had legalised the profound violation of human rights was now ours. We were consciously walking through the same corridors as the architects of apartheid.

'They are probably turning in their graves', I joked with Lucie as we passed the huge portraits of ex-Presidents, now relics of our shameful past. The parliamentary stewards, confused by the chaos of this multicoloured diversity, screamed: 'MPs here, wives above in the balcony.' Today marked another silent revolution. Not only had we defeated our racist past but we had broken the back of male hegemony in the highest decision-making institution in the land. Of the 400 MPs baptising the new democracy a quarter were women. This was a revolution on its own.

The diversity was astonishing. Former prisoners and 'terrorists', trade unionists and community activists, learned professors, rural women representatives, business people and professionals, urban and rural, rich and poor, the hues of the rainbow – we were here to deliver on a promise of 'a better life for all'. The air was heady with excitement and charged with hope.

Omar earlier had said: 'You cannot go to parliament dressed like a union organiser. You are a representative of the people to the first democratically elected parliament. You are going to wear a suit.' He brooked no opposition as he took me to a clothing store.

Right now in parliament the excited chatter of the newly elected parliamentarians held the hopes of our people. There was a sense of camaraderie across the benches and the roar of our singing and dancing captured our happiness. Never before had this parliament experienced the sounds of Africa, the swaying and chanting, the ululations and slogans as our excitement rang in the halls of this imposing institution.

We were giving birth to a new democracy expectant with the hope of a better future. Irrespective of our own political rivalries and past animosities and even deadly combat, there was a sense of history in the making. We would have to bear individual and collective responsibility if we permitted a deviation from what our contract was with the people of our beautiful South Africa.

In fact, the entire world was witness to our new-found victory over the reprehensible past.

The House quietened. The parliamentary steward announced the entry of the Speaker of Parliament in a loud voice. She entered and took her seat and the hushed environment broke out into tumultuous sounds of joy – with liberation songs and the hall reverberating to the stomp of the toyi-toyi for the first time in its rigid history. This was Frene Ginwala, a seasoned activist, known for her fiercely independent views and now chosen as the first Speaker of the new parliament. As she sat quietly in her throne, the first woman to do so in the history of our country, dressed in a beautiful Indian sari, it completed the picture of the transformation project we had fought for at a political level.

We had deracialised the highest decision-making institution in the land but we were soon to discover that building a non-racial and more inclusive economy was to be a momentous struggle.

We went up group by group to take our oath of allegiance to uphold our Constitution. It was a solemn moment. My mind flashed back to the generations that preceded me – the image cast strongly in my mind: 'This is my tribute to you, Angamma, whose courage, hopes and aspirations I hold dearly in my heart.'

After we concluded the ceremonies that ushered in our new-found freedom, we rushed to the Grand Parade to bear witness and to hear our President-designate speak to the people. The streets were chaotic as whites and blacks sang and danced with delight. We had liberated both the oppressors and the oppressed from the cloud of the past.

As Mandela ascended to the platform from which he had spoken at the time of his release the crowd went wild with its ululating elation. His words rang in our ears: 'Today we are entering a new era for our country and its people. Today we celebrate not the victory of a party, but a victory for all the people of South Africa.'

* * *

The next day, 10 May 1994, we were up at the crack of dawn. The world's leaders had made their way to South Africa for Nelson Mandela's landmark presidential inauguration.

As Mandela mounted the podium to take his oath of office, the crowd quietened. The roars of joy were still for a moment that would change 350 years of our shameful history:

In the presence of those assembled here and in full realisation of the high calling I assume as Executive President in the service of the Republic of South Africa I, Nelson Rolihlahla Mandela, do hereby swear to be faithful to the Republic of South Africa, and do solemnly and sincerely promise at all times to promote that which will advance and to oppose all that may harm the Republic; to obey, observe, uphold and maintain the Constitution and all other Laws of the Republic; to discharge my duties with all my strength and talents to the best of my knowledge and ability and true to the dictates of my conscience; to do justice to all; and to devote myself to the well-being of the Republic and all its people.

So help me God.

I was choked with the emotion of the day. I felt that our struggles and sacrifices had not been in vain. The skies opened with the thunder of a South African Air Force fly-past, a symbol of loyalty to the new Commander-in-Chief, Nelson Mandela. The army helicopters hoisting several new South African flags saluted the new democracy. I felt a shiver down my spine as I realised that these were now the armed forces of the new democratic state. They were swearing allegiance to our new interim Constitution.

We retired to lunch with the guests of the President and spent a colourful afternoon in celebration. It was fantastic to mingle with the icons we had only read about. We chatted excitedly to the legendary Fidel Castro. For many of us, Cuba symbolised more than any other nation solidarity with our anti-colonial struggle.

As the sun set on our celebrations we boarded the buses to the car park, arriving home exhausted. It had been a long day and I slept peacefully that night.

The next day my phone rang early. It was Mandela's secretary. 'President Mandela would like to see you in his offices at 9.00 a.m.' When I arrived there I found a number of comrades milling around, waiting to be called in one at a time to meet the President. This was to be the new cabinet. Soon it was my turn.

Madiba looked the part of the President. He was unusually dressed in a formal dark suit and conservative tie. He was sitting at his desk but rose to settle me on a couch. Mandela had in our earlier discussions on the composition of the cabinet suggested that I take the position of Minister of Labour, which I declined.

I felt that having been the General Secretary of COSATU, the post would have created too many contradictions. I had been central in many of the discussions on the new labour market dispensation.

I had raised the possibility of playing a role in implementing the RDP as a cross-cutting programme in an integrated government.

'How are you, Jay? We have a big task ahead. You have been driving the Reconstruction and Development Programme from my ANC office. We went to our people with that as our Manifesto and now I want it to be the centre of all our government programmes. That means we have to make it the policy framework for the new democratic Government of National Unity. That is a difficult task and I want you as the Minister without Portfolio in the Presidency to be responsible for the RDP.'

We hugged each other and I said, 'That's what I want. I know with your support we can succeed.' We would have to engage our own ranks and our previous enemies and learn to work together. I was confident but the responsibility weighed heavily on my shoulders.

Although I wished my mother could have been part of that day, as I walked out of Madiba's office I felt her lightness. She was there with me – and she was smiling and proud of her youngest child. The Chief Justice arrived and we were individually sworn in. The cabinet assembled in the President's boardroom and the first photograph of the newly installed cabinet was taken.

Mandela opened our first meeting by welcoming us. He announced the cabinet line-up and in particular the opposition parties, the IFP led by Chief Buthelezi and the National Party led by F.W. de Klerk, in this the Government of National Unity (GNU). It was a brief meeting.

Mandela's election victory speech and his inaugural address to parliament on 24 May 1994 set the tone of the new democracy:

> *Tomorrow, the entire ANC leadership and I will be back at our desks. We are rolling up our sleeves to begin tackling the problems our country faces. We ask you all to join us – go back to your jobs in the morning. Let's get South Africa working.*
>
> *For we must, together and without delay, begin to build a better life for all South Africans. This means creating jobs, building houses, providing education and bringing peace and security for all.[2]*

Our road to that glorious future lies through collective hard work to accomplish the objective of creating a people-centred society through the implementation of the vision contained in our reconstruction and development plan.

Let us all get down to work![3]

31

The RDP was the broad strategic policy framework that set a number of specific objectives and clearly had to be driven from the highest level of government. Its goal was to transform the state and bring about economic growth through an infrastructure strategy that aimed at addressing the massive backlogs in the provision of basic infrastructure to areas where the black majority lived. It was also the platform to drive the modernisation of the economy that would be the basis for efficiency and business development through a comprehensive reform of industrial strategy to create jobs, meet domestic demand and build a competitive export sector. And lastly it identified our Achilles heel – a human resourses constraint that could sabotage our transformation agenda because of the low skill base and institutional weaknesses. But it still had to be translated into an integrated programme of delivery with government.

The solution, I felt, had to be a planning capacity in the office of the Presidency. In retrospect, we should have negotiated this role within the Alliance and clarified our role, functions and powers as a cross-cutting Ministry. But time was running out and we had to hit the ground running without the necessary physical or human infrastructure in place.

There we were, President Mandela's first cabinet, composed of representatives of such divergent political strains of the GNU. Learning to work together and trust one another was the first of the daunting but exciting challenges that confronted us.

I brought Omar and Lucie to my new offices. It was a far cry from my first run-down union office, an ex-bathroom in a converted flat. We arrived at the gate of the Union Buildings. The guards, white Afrikaners armed to the teeth, stamped their feet and saluted me. Yesterday, the apartheid state had wanted me dead. Today, these men were saluting me. Omar couldn't believe it. In all seriousness he said to the driver: 'Will you stop the car and just reverse past the security. I want to see them salute again.' Laughing, I told the driver, 'Don't. He was just joking.'

As we walked up the stairs to my second-floor offices we admired Sir Herbert Baker's beautiful architecture and exclaimed, 'My God, here we are: everything that we have fought for!'

The offices themselves were bare. I didn't have any staff. I didn't have a budget. I didn't even have a kettle! The first step was building a team to develop our business plan. And time was of the essence.

I recruited a new cadre of leadership in government: Dr Bernie Fanaroff, who had a wealth of organisational experience and an outstanding intellect; Dr Tanya Abrahamse, an expert on rural development; Dr Chippy Olver and Pascal Moloi, both specialists in urban planning and development; Namane Magau, a human resources expert; and many others. All were seasoned activists.

I had to grapple with the tasks of being part of the Executive as well as accountable to a parliament that sat 2 000 kilometres away in Cape Town. I had inherited a beautiful office adjoining Tuynhuys – the official seat of the President.

As I sat behind my desk in Cape Town I saw a row of little buttons. Curious, I pressed one and a few seconds later, my secretary, on deployment from the Department of Foreign Affairs, came running into my office.

'You rang. Do you need something?' she asked.

I replied in the negative, realising that these were a series of buttons that were used to summon the secretaries in the previous administration for some task or the other. Embarrassed, I wondered what my mother would have thought of me. I immediately terminated this practice and spoke to my secretary on the phone or personally if I needed anything.

The President in the meantime had established rigorous targets. In the first hundred days we had to demonstrate that we were transforming the lives of our people. Day and night we slaved at producing a slate of programmes that would allow Mandela to signal that the new democratic government was committed to transformation and delivery of the 'better life' we had promised our people.

Two weeks later Mandela gave his State of the Nation Address. In slow, measured, almost pedestrian tones, he spelt out the values which we had fought and sacrificed so much for, and which were to inform the core of our first democratically elected government:

Today, I am happy to announce that the Cabinet of the Government of National Unity has reached consensus not only on the broad objective of the creation of the people-centred society of which I have spoken, but also on many elements of a plan broadly based on that Programme for Reconstruction and Development.[4]

Education and health for the poor were in a crisis and had to top the list. Our schools and hospitals were dysfunctional and required major infrastructure upgrades as well as a focus on preparing teachers with the appropriate skills and subject knowledge for the challenge of building a new democracy. Our townships were in darkness with only the huge spotlights erected along key transport corridors to allow the security forces rapid transit in cases of civil uprisings. Huge palls of smoke from coal-fired cooking hung gloomily over our townships, the pollution exacerbating existing health problems, and students studied in candlelight. These were deep structural problems that needed a unity of purpose and a powerful social contract between government and civil society, including the private sector, to deliver on our promises.

Derek Keys, continuing as the Minister of Finance, was a pivotal ally and had a huge body of wisdom on the delivery of projects. His advice to me and the team is as instructive today as it was then when he said:

I have never met a Chief Executive in the public or the private sector who will voluntarily reprioritise; they'll always ask for more money so if you want them to reprioritise, which, remember, we assumed we were going to do with the post-apartheid dividend – you've got to skim it off the top. I'm taking it off the top and giving it to Jay Naidoo. If you as a Minister want it back you must satisfy the criteria laid down by the RDP office.[5]

That was the context. We had inherited a civil service with an untransformed leadership, and there were no existing policies and laws to democratise our society. We were aware of the immense expectations of the people. The vision for the RDP was to give people hope by achieving the essence of the development state even if it meant it would take a long time. This was how we had built a powerful labour movement. There was ownership of the organisation by our members, mechanisms to hold us to account through the ballot box or recall and a trust that leadership had integrity.

At the same time we faced real difficulties. South Africa was in the throes of a crippling economic and social crisis. Gross fixed investment had dropped spectacularly and foreign investment dried up. With a bankrupt state already committed to a spending programme that ignored the needs of the majority we had very little room to manoeuvre.

In our policy debates we drew on the intellectual expertise of the policy experts and economists who were working for the World Bank, but we resisted the temptation to draw funds from the World Bank and International Monetary Fund (IMF). We felt in particular that the IMF had compromised itself in the support it had given to the apartheid state, strengthening it fiscally when it faced financial crises during the struggle for freedom. I fully realised that our imperatives of equitable growth had to be balanced with a responsibility and attention to the need for fiscal prudency.

We were convinced of the need for us to depend on our own resources. But our independence had to be guaranteed by our vigilance against corruption. We had to achieve a better return in development outcomes by increasing the efficiency of our state expenditure and investment.

This was only possible by reprioritising existing expenditure and moving money and people in the civil service into new programmes and jobs. This was not easy and required tough negotiations with the increasingly powerful trade unions in the public sector. Though this was bound to be controversial, I believed that a strong Alliance, acting as the engine of transformation and mobilising our people and mass organisations around the national priorities of the RDP, could achieve this agenda. But this was the time for us to make tough choices as a country.

At the same time we had to reform the policies, procedures, planning criteria and the business models of delivery. Performance and service delivery had to be at the heart of our strategy. Government could not do this on its own. We could not adopt the 'Asian Tiger' model. In those countries the state was in many cases a dictatorship and the political party hegemonic, characterised by the syndrome of the 'strong leader' and a civil society that was compliant.

South Africa was fundamentally different. Our democracy was won by the actions of mass struggles in which people occupied the centre stage.

Most importantly, given our history of apartheid, we lacked the technocratic capacity to impose the grandiose ideas of an all-powerful state. In fact, the economy was still controlled by a white elite, many of whom had to be won over, and the skills level of the black majority had been systematically undermined by an inferior Bantu Education system.

The central strategic thrust of the RDP was the establishment of a developmental state. Our key strength was our legitimacy and the enormous political capital combined with Mandela's iconic status in the world.

Within government, the parliament and civil society there was an air of excitement and optimism as we grappled with the huge financial and infrastructural deficits we had inherited and the social and education crisis that we faced.

Many Ministers had walked into institutions that were already there, established over many decades, and had developed structures, personnel and a culture of how they operated. Their key challenge was developing the new policy frameworks, the appropriate legislation and transforming their delivery departments to serve the *entire* population, irrespective of race or colour.

The RDP office was bursting at the seams with the amount of work to be done. We focused our attention on the process of awarding grants and the criteria we wanted to follow. We began to look for a project office from which we could coordinate the implementation.

On one of our early days in the Presidency, the extent of the damage the apartheid government had wrought on our region and particularly the Frontline States became starkly apparent. Bernie Fanaroff and I were searching for space where we could meet with our project team. We were guided by some of the long-serving staffers through winding corridors to the depths of the Union Buildings.

We entered a room that met our needs perfectly. But the menacing odour of death hung over us. On the walls were maps of the southern Africa region. Some of them still had bold arrows across the borders. We realised that this was where the State Security Council had met and where, under the militaristic leadership of former President P.W. Botha, numerous cross-border raids resulting in the bloody deaths and assassinations of many of our colleagues would have been discussed and planned. The room needed to be cleansed, and using it for the reconstruction and development of our country and region seemed a fitting tribute.

The RDP worked to link growth, human resource development, reconstruction, redistribution and reconciliation into a 'unified programme', held together by a broad infrastructure programme that would focus on creating and enhancing existing services in the electricity, water, telecommunications, transport, health, and education and training sectors. In particular, we realised that we had to tackle youth unemployment. From my union days I had realised that the structure of work and its discipline and organisational training gives us purpose. Now that we had won our political freedom we needed the glue of work to hold our society together. We engaged with the South African National Defence Force to use their countrywide infrastructure, camps and workshops to assemble a Youth Corps that would build a disciplined, skilled cadreship engaged in reconstruction. Every state institution, including the private sector and non-governmental organisations (NGOs), had to ask the questions: 'How do we deliver the RDP? How do we make the RDP part of our core business agenda?'

Drawing from study tours and meetings with government, agencies and civil society movements that we met as we criss-crossed the developing world from Mumbai to Kuala Lumpur to São Paulo and Buenos Aires, we drafted the first policy documents on urban planning and densification, rural development, people living with disabilities, the role of women and gender, and human resource development. The policy space was alive with vibrant and dynamic debates.

As the months wore on our team realised that human capacity and management were systemic weaknesses that impacted on delivery. The RDP Ministry formed an Implementation Committee staffed by project managers seconded from state corporations and business, which would receive applications from the local governments, community-based organisations and provincial governments. The Implementation Committee would then evaluate these applications before passing them on to the Urban Development Task Team to monitor and review the progress of the projects.

One of our most important conditions was to ensure that accountability was established across all spheres of government – the executive level at the national, provincial and local government levels, in parliament, and in their different state institutions.

Mandela echoed this in his address to parliament:

The RDP should, therefore, be understood as an all-encompassing process of transforming society in its totality to ensure a better life for all. It addresses both the principal goals of transformation and ways of managing it. The RDP is not a sum-total of projects, no matter how important each project may be.[6]

But back at the drawing boards things were more challenging. There was no 'silver bullet' in building an effective state. Part of what was needed was greater transparency in the way that government made decisions on projects, meaning that local communities had to be consulted and full disclosure made to pre-empt corruption.

That led us to putting up big, illustrated boards around the country, especially in the townships and informal settlements, to indicate the progress we were making. They detailed what we were delivering, how much it cost and who was responsible. It was part of building a real partnership with local communities as well as a way of ensuring accountability to public goals that the state had committed itself to.

The Masakhane campaign was a bold move to change a culture of boycotting rental payments and service charges that justifiably permeated our townships under apartheid. The campaign aimed to get those who could afford to pay to do so, while targeting the indigent and the poorest for free services.

This was a very sensitive matter and the top leadership of national, provincial and local government and community leaders were in the audience. Lucie had come with me and Kami in his 'terrible twos' was also there. Mandela, talking of the need for a social compact with civil society to improve delivery, was interrupted by Kami, who insisted on climbing the podium. Lucie and I were deeply embarrassed and took turns to fetch him and keep him quiet.

But he wanted none of these restraints and returned to the podium, staring at Mandela, who eventually said, 'Well, this young man wants to make my speech.'

He took Kami in his arms, placed him on the lectern and continued with his speech. Kami remained quiet, seemingly attentive to every word that Mandela uttered. It was a unique picture that was in all the newspapers the next day. It revealed the gentle and human side of our President.

32

In my first months in office, I felt quite overwhelmed. I was faced with the daunting task of being dependent on interdepartmental cooperation to deliver on the ambitious and very explicit milestones we had set ourselves in the election manifesto.

Above all, the global context had changed dramatically over the last decade, especially since the fall of the Berlin Wall. The ideological challenges were enormous. Endless streams of international bankers were battering down our doors. Their advice was usually the same rehashed diet of the need to maintain market fundamentals and create the conditions for attracting international investment. Many acted as the representatives of the South African conglomerates who preached that premature interference with the economy would create instability. Quite obviously ours was a 'negotiated revolution', the outcome of which was a mixed economy which I believed was the right choice.

But these were exciting times and I looked forward to carrying out the mandate of the people. The RDP was a transformation agent. The biggest challenge was the deracialisation of the economy and the creation of decent jobs.

The programmes that we supported were meant to leverage changes within the departments and not be a set of isolated ad hoc projects. The way these departments implemented their line-functions and aligned those line-functions towards the goals of the RDP would in themselves transform the old administration into a people-driven government.

It also meant that the right to additional money for rolling out projects largely came from the RDP Fund, because up to now a large part of the existing budgets went into recurrent expenditure and paying off the debt inherited from the apartheid regime. This created a contradiction. Certain colleagues would say, 'Well, why should I come to the RDP Committee and have to negotiate this with you?'

There were also issues around how to bring the IFP, the National Party and the ANC to the same table in relation to the RDP. After all, the RDP was the election manifesto of the ANC. Madiba himself explicitly gave it his blessing at his inaugural address to parliament:

> *My government's commitment to create a people-centred society of liberty binds us to the pursuit of the goals of freedom from want, freedom from hunger, freedom from deprivation, freedom from ignorance, freedom from suppression and freedom from fear. These freedoms are fundamental to the guarantee of human dignity. They ... constitute the true meaning, the justification and the purpose of the Reconstruction and Development Programme, without which it would lose all legitimacy.*[7]

We had to take an ANC programme and then make it a national government programme, and thereby begin to drive the decision-making process. I had no problem with the other political parties of the GNU. I found very ready acceptance in people who came out of the National Party, like Roelf Meyer, Leon Wessels and Dawie de Villiers, and even in the IFP with Ministers such as Ben Ngubane, to support the type of changes that we wanted to effect. Ultimately the beneficiaries were going to be the people, who belonged to all political parties.

The biggest constraint we faced was the capacity of departments in government to develop programmes that were based on clear business plans. I was reluctant to throw money at the problems I saw. My experience in building unions revolved around knowing what the impact of our work was. I knew where every rand came from and where every rand was spent and what outcomes I wanted to achieve. Suddenly I was responsible for billions of rands and subject to demands from Ministers that would have reduced the RDP to an accounting exercise. We had to think rigorously about the planning process.

With our international donors we negotiated an alignment between their funding and the key social deliverables of the RDP Fund, which became the conduit of development aid boosting the existing programmes that we had already kick-started from the RDP Fund. But there was a gulf between the promises made to Mandela and the money that flowed into South Africa.

I was also surprised when some international donors demanded conditionalities such as using companies and consultants from their countries and requiring a multiplicity of reporting requirements. Unlike many other developing countries we were not dependent on donor aid to balance our national budget and were able to dismiss these and drive a development trajectory of our own.

In my mind opening up their markets to our products and investment in our economy would bring a bigger peace dividend and result in job creation that would put income into the pockets of the poor. Nevertheless many of our international partners did play an important role in sharing intellectual experience and gaining access to leading thinkers and practitioners and finance.

Meanwhile in our socio-economic council, the National Economic Development and Labour Council (NEDLAC), we had set up a development chamber to harness the non-governmental sector towards delivery on the objectives of the RDP. We struggled to find common ground. The NGOs felt under siege and we felt arrogantly confident that this was the role of the democratic state. In hindsight this was a mistake. We should have worked for a new partnership, understanding the weaknesses of the state institutions to deliver to the poor.

Funding dried up for many of the NGOs, and a proper engagement with them did not take place. In the White Paper policy process we pledged: 'Organisations within civil society will be encouraged by the Government of National Unity to be active in and responsible for the effective implementation of the RDP.' We released the document to parliament in September 1994.

The Ministry started discussions in the sector aimed at establishing an integrated programme and led the launch of a National Development Aid Agency whose primary objective was the granting of funds to NGOs to strengthen our fight against poverty and to build a participatory democracy. But in reality we acted in a way that did marginalise the role of a vibrant civil society which also needed to transform and adapt to the new democracy.

The union movement, led by COSATU, was in the meantime involved in a big tussle, especially with the Ministries of Labour and Trade and Industry, around the movement's critical issues – labour legislation, tariff reductions, the right to strike and the Constitution, the Labour Relations Act Agreement, and the Health and Safety Agreement. These were the biggest issues that dominated the NEDLAC agenda.

As we struggled with capacity constraints within the RDP and across the government, it resulted in a time lag between what we announced, what we were going to do and when it got done.

A second problem across government was departments rolling over from year to year funds set aside for capital projects, due to a lack of project management expertise. Those constraints continue even today. This was complicated by the fact that local government elections had not yet occurred – and the hands and feet of the RDP, where many basic needs were delivered, was faced with a legitimacy challenge. It would only be six years later that those elections would take place. A related problem was the political accommodation that led to the establishment of nine provinces, many creating a new layer of political bureaucracy and cost to the country. There was no rational economic argument why we went from four to nine provinces.

Ironically, the greatest challenges were within our own ranks, inside the ANC. One sticking point was the extent to which the RDP Ministry would be allowed to assert its role. Effectively this meant tramping on the toes of other Ministers. The other Ministries had to submit business plans that met a set of criteria we considered to fit RDP programmes. Literally, then, the RDP Ministry had to wait for the new Ministers to understand their portfolios, understand the goals, and work out how to re-engineer the existing programmes, the expenditure and the human resources, towards delivering the RDP.

When we came into government in 1994, we had a civil service that did not have the background to understand what we were trying to deliver. In addition, it had to be transformed from delivering largely to a minority to now delivering to the whole citizenry. Indeed, we had a constitutional obligation to deliver the same services to all our people. Deracialising the civil service while aligning it to new roles with the requirement of new skills was an intricate challenge and was later to be deeply politicised as appointments were centralised in the Presidency.

To champion the integration was a complex process. We had inherited a government with existing portfolios; each had its own bureaucracy, and its own silo mentality, and was not geared to interacting or cooperating with other departments, which was what the RDP required.[8]

Madiba also had an imperious streak in his make-up. He would be deeply upset by a media story of a community in dire need and think, 'I need to do something about this', and twist the arm of some senior business executive to build a school or a clinic in some village without answering the questions of who would pay the teachers or nurses or the recurrent expenses of the school or clinic. But that was his human side which demonstrated his compassion and made him loved by the people who deeply believed he represented their best hopes. It was also this deep concern and empathy that he radiated which made us all strive to achieve a higher purpose and to experience our shared humanity.

*   *   *

I gradually began to realise that a change in our political culture was taking place. It was almost imperceptible at first. Criticism of government, even from progressive activists, began to be labelled as counter-productive. There was a 'don't rock the boat' ethos in the air. Many organisations were in limbo, uncertain how to interact with a now legitimate and democratic state, and the people's voice in the body politic began to wane.

Government gave us authority. We had our hands on the levers of power, money in a budget, staff, resources, and the conviction that this government by virtue of its democratic election was the only legitimate representative of the aspirations of our people. In the process of tackling so many challenges, we robbed the country of an enormous contribution that all other sections of society could make. Government would give people jobs, houses, social security, schools and clinics and knew what was right for the citizenry. People who had participated in the fight for change now became passive bystanders. At the same time any criticism of government was a criticism of the revolution.

There were also those people who felt that as exiles their contributions to the struggle had amounted to more than the efforts of those of us who were inside the country. In fact, one person openly said to me, 'Guys like you and Cyril Ramaphosa have not being brought up in the ANC tradition. You have only recently joined the movement. You have not been schooled in the revolutionary theory of our liberation struggle.'

I wondered about the audacity of these people. In my opinion, the real struggle for our freedom was fought inside the country. This tension between the 'inziles' and exiles contributed to complaints about RDP procedures. Very soon a set of personal conflicts arose and the political noise in the corridor began to rise. I was experienced enough to see that whispers and strategic leaks to the media preceded a more sinister action. This fed into a view of some Ministers who saw the RDP Fund as an unnecessary step where they had to submit proposals and business plans and justify to a colleague why their programmes met the criteria of the RDP.

Others, particularly the conservative business press and economists, were sceptical of the RDP from its inception, describing it as wishful thinking and doubtful because it had been initiated and driven by the labour movement, even though it had been through an extensive consultation process and was popularly seen to be 'owned' by the people.

The business lobby, backed by powerful international forces of capital, was determined that there would be no major changes to the economic trajectory of the past and that the priority should be the maintenance of market fundamentals.

In the absence of a strong endorsement from Thabo Mbeki, who was in essence the executive head of government, the chatter began to rise even as we soldiered on.

Acknowledging the need for a solid baseline of development information, we started to redesign the approach for the 1996 Census. In 1995 I appointed Dr Mark Orkin as the head of Statistics South Africa (Stats SA). Mark was a dedicated professional who had run the Community Agency for Social Enquiry, which had worked with COSATU and community organisations researching social issues in the 1980s. As Mark commented at the launch of the 1996 Census results:

> This was a decisive improvement over recent censuses in several crucial respects. All the residents in our new democracy were treated equally by the census for the first time... The nine million households were visited in the same way in all parts of the country, including rural areas and informal settlements. In the previous census, many of these areas were estimated from aerial photographs, or omitted altogether and estimated afterwards.[9]

The RDP did stimulate some outstanding examples of innovative thinking. One such proposal came from Professor Kader Asmal, who as a globally recognised human rights thinker had hoped to have stepped into the Justice portfolio but ended up being the Minister of Water Affairs and Forestry. While this was seen as the 'ugly duckling' of the cabinet, he quickly transformed the department into a robust organisation attracting some of the best experts in the sector. One day over lunch during a cabinet break he commented: 'Jay, I want to come and talk to you about an interesting RDP project on the removal of alien vegetation and improving the supply of water to poor communities.' I laughed and we joked about which aliens he was referring to but agreed to chat later.

When we did meet I was struck by the amount of profound thinking that had gone into the planning of the programme. Dr Guy Preston, the programme leader, was impressive. He spelt out the context that South Africa as a water-scarce country would face chronic shortages of water if something was not done immediately. Already close to 12 million South Africans lacked access to clean water and this issue was an RDP priority. But it was estimated that 'invading alien plant species cover 10 million hectares of land and, each year, use 3.3 billion cubic metres more water than native vegetation'.[10]

The programme that Kader elaborated proposed a variety of labour-intensive projects to eradicate invasive alien plants, which involved mechanical methods (felling, removing or burning), chemical methods (such as environmentally safe herbicides) and biological control (using species-specific insects and diseases from the alien plant's country of origin).

While the main goal of this initiative was (and still is) to recover scarce water, other components included the conservation of biological diversity, and the building and empowerment of local communities through job creation.

The programme turned out to be immensely successful in improving the availability of clean water in poorer, especially rural, communities, creating tens of thousands of jobs, training small entrepreneurs in management skills as well as environmental awareness, community organisation and education on a range of social issues from sports to nutrition.

This programme was passed with flying colours at the RDP Committee. Similarly, we started to receive some outstanding proposals from other government departments. The wheels of the RDP were beginning to turn.

'I remember Madiba saying to Jay,' recalls Bernie Fanaroff, at that time the head of the RDP office, '"I want to implement some visible deliverables in 100 days."'

Thinking back I should have said to Madiba, 'Give us a year to think about the programmes that will drill down to the level of delivery you want at a societal level. Let us orientate ourselves. Let's see what the delivery capacity of the state is. Then we'll give you a sustainable programme.' But we were in power and government works on the basis of popular vote in elections held every five years. That countdown starts the moment victory is declared. Politicians worldwide, I realise now, think very much in the short term, tending to measure success often in terms of media coverage and reviews.

While we were getting bogged down by the number of moving parts that had to be choreographed, I think we should have allowed a dynamic flexibility that would shape our implementation in the trenches. There were sectors and regions where the RDP *was* working and which had strong champions including the Working for Water programmes, the school feeding projects, the clinic-building programme, the integrated infrastructure projects in the key urban areas and a longer-term municipal infrastructure strategy around the basic needs of our people.

But it was the legitimacy of the RDP which, like the Freedom Charter, represented the will of the people and gave the poor, our constituency, hope for the future. I recall a meeting in Gugulethu that I attended with Joe Slovo, then Minister of Housing and the Chairperson of the SACP. We were subjected to a robust interrogation by the community on our promises. I clearly recollect Joe saying: 'You know, Jay, it's important that the masses bang on our door so that we can be on our toes.' It was a seed of wisdom.

But within government I needed executive support over and above the political endorsement of Mandela. Although not explicit, I knew that I did not share that relationship with Mbeki. The Tripartite Alliance was weakened. It was no longer the driving force of change. The ANC was deeply involved in constitutional negotiations at CODESA and COSATU was involved in the labour laws negotiations in NEDLAC. The political centre was not holding together the different forces and palace politics would begin to take hold.

33

A few months after I had been appointed Minister in the President's office, Lucie became pregnant. This was a planned pregnancy. We wanted to have another child and Lucie was very happy. She desperately wanted a girl. In fact, in poking fun at me she quoted the saying: 'Any man can make a boy, but it takes a real man to make a girl!'

This time, with the help of Sue Lees and Liz Harding, the same excellent midwives who attended the birth of Kami, we decided we wanted a home delivery During the course of the pregnancy Lucie went to Canada and had a medical examination. We did not want to know the sex of the child – we loved the idea of a big surprise. During the course of the examination, the doctor let slip, 'Oh, I see a little thing wagging in between the legs on the ultrasound.' Lucie was disappointed. Now we were expecting another boy and I knew that we would have to try again.

At the same time, the tide of media opinion was turning against the RDP Ministry. The key issue was implementation. We faced a barrage of criticism – people were expecting miracles.

Pieter-Dirk Uys, a well-known comedian, had created the fictitious Evita Bezuidenhout, a flamboyant alter ego in drag, as a social commentator on South Africa. Evita is well loved across the political spectrum for her outrageous tongue-in-cheek comments. Pieter had created the series *A Day in the Life of a Minister* that Lucie persuaded me to participate in.

'Bring out the human side of your personality. Show people that you are a husband and a father and not the wild-eyed revolutionary that the media have painted you as in the pre-democracy days. They need to know you are human and loving and caring,' she said.

The day arrived and I found that Evita had done her research well. She had uncovered my secret passion – to learn the tango. I was driven to a studio and presented with a tuxedo. I out-waltzed Evita, who was dressed to kill in an outrageous pink dress. We rehearsed the tango steps with professional dancers, and I had to concentrate on the steps, the graceful movements and the masterful shepherding of my swirling 'dame'. It took some time to get the dance sequence just right. By the end of the shoot my arms were weary as a result of holding Pieter-Dirk Uys's heavy weight for two hours and I sighed with relief when the producer shouted, 'That's a cut!'

We went on to do yoga in the park, an activity that has kept me sane over the years. Then home with Lucie and the kids tumbling in the grass and having fun. Evita had conducted an interview with Lucie, which I only saw at the premiere.

Lucie asked Evita during the interview: 'Do you know why Jay is the Minister without Portfolio in President Mandela's office?'

'No,' Evita replied, to which Lucie retorted: 'You know that Jay loses everything that he has – keys, glasses, cellphones, wallets. Well, if Mandela had given him a portfolio he would have lost it anyway.'

There was a great roar of delight from Evita and his crew and I laughed so hard I almost cried. I knew that this was going to be a national joke when it was aired.

On 16 June 1995, I was invited to participate in a live discussion on television, commemorating the 1976 Soweto uprisings and interacting with the youth. I left home, saying to Lucie that I would be away for two hours. Expecting the baby in only three weeks, she was content to stay at home and watch me on television with Omar, three of his daughters, our friend and family doctor, 'Foxy' Asvat, and my mother-in-law, Louise, who had flown from Canada for the birth of her third grandson.

The discussion started at 8.00 p.m. At 8.15 the studio was phoned to inform me that Lucie was having contractions. The producers, assuming that there was still a long time to go, decided not to tell me. Twenty minutes later her waters broke and the contractions started coming very quickly.

The studio was phoned again. They were left in no doubt that I was needed at home immediately. Halfway through a live appearance, I was yanked out of a robust discussion and the nation was told that I had to rush home to help with the delivery of our baby.

When I arrived home at 9.10 p.m., the place was like a madhouse. Lucie was busy trying to keep the baby in. My mother-in-law was running up and down the house talking to everyone in French and trying to manage the situation. No one understood what she was saying.

I herded everyone including the kids out of the bedroom.

'Roll up your sleeves,' shouted Lucie, 'and run a bath for me. The baby's coming out!' Lucie had decided long ago she wanted to have a water birth. The midwives had not arrived. They lived a fair distance from where we stayed. I prepared myself to deliver the baby but at 9.20 I heaved a huge sigh of relief when the midwives rushed in.

At exactly 9.28 a bundle of joy popped out. As I grabbed our latest arrival, I shouted hysterically at the top of my voice: 'Wow, it's a girl. It's a girl!' And so Shanti arrived to bless our family on 16 June. The day would later be commemorated as Youth Day to celebrate the Soweto uprisings of 1976. Shanti was our gift of peace.

* * *

Madiba's priority, rightfully so, in this phase of transition was on reconciliation and nation building, both critical to neutralise powerful elements, particularly in the state security machinery, that had the potential to destabilise our fledgling democracy. His overtures to the Afrikaner community, often criticised in our own ranks, were crucial in creating the space for us to tackle the difficult issues of transformation. His brilliance sparkled: tea with Mrs Verwoerd, the widow of the architect of apartheid; addressing white farmers, trade unions and communities across the country. Understanding the fanaticism of rugby among rank-and-file Afrikaners, he used the symbolism of the Rugby World Cup in 1995 to capture the hearts and minds of both black and white South Africans to weld a common identity, focused on passionately supporting a predominantly white South African team.

I was in the crowds in the final. It was the first time I had attended a rugby match. I would have been lynched if I had dared walk into this lion's den of Afrikanerdom in the past. And I certainly would have been backing the opposition team. Here, almost 60 000 fans, predominantly Afrikaners, stood chanting 'Nelson, Nelson, Nelson' as Madiba walked on to the field dressed in a Springbok rugby jersey sporting the number 6, Springbok Captain François Pienaar's jersey. He was the master of symbolism and had succeeded in uniting a divided nation around the powerful unifying energy of sport.

As the gripping finish came to a close with our victory, I felt such pride that tears came to my eyes. Mandela had conquered Afrikaner fears and brought them into the *laager* of the new South Africa. They trusted him, and his integrity and compassion allayed their worst nightmare of racial revenge. That was the political miracle that kept the new South Africa on its rails and allowed us to pursue the tasks of transformation.

* * *

My life continued to be a whirlwind of meetings, travel and missed opportunities with my children. Our country was like a live laboratory experiment. There was no blueprint. The heightened and legitimate aspirations of our people were spilling over into the streets. I remember feeling that the fight for power seemed easier than the exercise of power.

But I realised that the challenges we faced as a society were not unique. With representatives from different tiers of government I undertook international study tours to look at the experiences of other developing countries. We met the Brazilians and looked at their models of development that integrated the shanty towns, densified the housing settlements along transport corridors and dealt with access to health and education.

We had important side discussions with groups of doctors and teachers, all of whom were activists like us, fighting in the trenches for a better life. One of our discussions was on the impact of HIV/AIDS, which was just beginning to break into the public discourse. We spent time examining the approaches of South Africa and Brazil to the epidemic.

Both countries faced high levels of poverty and inequality and, in 1994, had the same levels of infection. The Brazilians were really concerned because of what they perceived as a laissez-faire social attitude in Brazil to sexuality, which was openly discussed. Their focus was on education to demystify and destigmatise the disease and the prevention of its transmission by people affected with sexually transmitted diseases (STDs), including HIV, and working with groups representing prostitutes, drug addicts and vulnerable communities.

Unlike South Africa, Brazil was able to contain the epidemic through a powerful partnership between the government and civil society, often in the face of stiff opposition from the global pharmaceutical sector and the conservative political approaches of certain religious groups. As a country they were the first to break the anachronistic patent law that puts treatment out of the reach of the poor. The government, declaring the impending AIDS epidemic a 'national emergency', licensed the production of generics that broke the monopoly of the multinationals.

Continuing my international travels I first visited India in early 1996 and was shocked at the level of poverty. On that trip I had asked Lucie to accompany me because we rarely spent time together. Shanti was barely eight months old and still being breastfed. Beyond the development experiences we hoped to learn about, I wanted Lucie to be with me on my first trip to the land of my ancestors, where she had already been before.

As we approached the arrivals hall in Mumbai airport, escorted by Indian state officials, I said to Connie Molusi, my communications adviser: 'Hey Connie, I have never been in a country before where the majority of people look like me. I feel swamped but also relieved that I don't stick out like a sore thumb.' We all laughed hilariously.

I was struck by how stark the inequalities were. It was almost midnight and as we emerged from the airport we experienced the teeming millions of the city. It was bustling, a collision of bicycles, ox wagons, tankers, motorised rickshaws and people. At our first traffic light we were surrounded by street children begging for money. Suddenly a woman, her youth ravaged by hardship and starvation, shoved an emaciated baby that looked almost dead in my face.

'Don't look at her eyes,' Lucie warned as my heart missed a few beats.

How can I not look? I thought as my chest heaved with heaviness and I caught the woman's pleading eyes, empty of hope and life.

That was my introduction to India and it has remained etched in my mind. On one visit to a local government road-building project I saw groups of women breaking rocks into smaller stones that were taken by other workmen to be set in the ground before the asphalt was poured in. I thought back to my line of ancestry. What made me different from these people? It was the fact that Angamma had decided to abandon her life in her village and travel across an ocean to a new land.

The state visit was a whirlwind of meetings with government Ministers and the representatives of business-seeking projects, visiting with NGOs and meeting some of the union leaders. Our delegation absorbed every detail and our spirits soared and on occasion sank when we experienced the realities of people. It was an inspiring journey in this huge continent of such diverse cultures, colours and cuisine.

I had, before the trip, shared with Lucie my need to explore more fully my culture and ancestry. In the new democracy Mandela encouraged a celebration of diversity and I felt the urge to search for my roots. My first step was to understand the spirituality of India. One group that I had encountered a few months earlier was the Brahma Kumaris, who were from a university of spiritual values in the state of Rajastan. We landed at the airport in Ahmedabad and made the long, winding and hazardous journey up to Mount Abu where the spiritual retreat was based. Lucie sat quietly in the back seat, her eyes closed most of the time, clutching Shanti close to her chest because there were no seat belts and the driver careened from left to right like a Formula One racer on a single lane that more resembled a bazaar than a highway.

When we finally arrived in the late afternoon we were ushered into a room where I met a wizened old lady who was introduced to me as Dadi Janki, one of the founders of the organisation. She was dressed in a white sari, her hair combed tightly into a tress that fell down her back. Her face was warm and wise. She reminded me instantly of my mother. I did not know what to do. She beckoned me to sit on a cushion in front of her, with Lucie and the others alongside me. She held my hand and stared deeply into my eyes without saying a word. At first I found her penetrating gaze invasive and intimidating. Then I felt a warm tide of positive energy flowing through my body and my mind found a serenity and stillness in which I felt the tangible presence of my mother. I broke from my deep reverie to see Dadi's smiling face. I learnt later that this was '*drishdi*', a sharing of profound spiritual energy.

My spiritual retreat at Mount Abu came at a painful time in my life. The political rumour mill had created huge self-doubt in me. The challenges seemed colossal and I sensed the undercurrents of resistance that were coalescing around Deputy President Mbeki. I plunged into the essence of meditation surrounded by hundreds of pure souls who had spent their lives in selfless service to others. I sought out the luminaries of the seminary named Shantivan and soaked up the peace. I learnt:

[T]he most important journey you can take is the journey within. This is a journey to the truth of who you really are. This is the place, just beyond everyday consciousness, where spiritual empowerment begins and…a

*grasp of this spiritual power gives you the power to choose creative thinking
rather than automated thinking, response rather than reaction, peace, love
and harmony rather than stress, conflict and chaos.*[11]

I learnt a lot from that visit and over the years constantly reconnected to Dadi
Janki. It helped to clear my mind and renew my passion for the development
of and service to my country. It readied me for the battles that lay ahead.

* * *

On 28 March 1996, barely a month after returning from India, the office of
the RDP was officially shut down. As Minister, I was not informed before the
decision was made, nor were satisfactory reasons given to me for closing the
Ministry – barely 23 months after the RDP programme was set up with the
enthusiastic blessing of President Mandela and all the Alliance partners.

I was called into Madiba's office and informed: 'The Government of
National Unity is coming to an end. We've made a decision. We are closing
down the RDP offices because we need to make certain changes in the cabinet.
De Klerk is leaving the government. I am appointing you as the Minister of
Posts, Telecommunications and Broadcasting.'

I sat there, stunned. But it is hard to say anything when the President
calls you in and presents you with an irreversible decision. I was the first to
acknowledge that the challenges and the structure of implementing the RDP
required more debate. The institutional and market failures in accelerating
delivery were an issue confronting all stakeholders and not only government.

Our social partners, especially within the Alliance, were critical players in
the shared vision of the RDP. This was a major political shift.

And it was uncharacteristic of Mandela. He had always pursued robust
debate, even in the face of the most contentious issues, whether about the armed
struggle or negotiations, or peace talks with Inkatha. It was a forewarning of
things to come.

In fact, years later someone who had been a senior official in Deputy
President Mbeki's office confirmed to Bernie Fanaroff: 'When we were together
at the Kennedy School of Government in Boston in a workshop on building
integrated government, I already knew of the decision to close the RDP office.
I felt awkward because I could not share this with you.'

Madiba was increasingly handing executive power to Mbeki and I began
to experience, along with many other activists, a steady reduction in the room

for democratic debate and difference. At the time I seriously considered the option of resigning as a matter of principle. But I decided to stay. I was pleased that the position as Minister of Posts, Telecommunications and Broadcasting was a single portfolio that I could manage with relatively little interference, or so I thought. But the decision to close the RDP reconfirmed my previous thoughts to serve only one term. Later I was to learn that Madiba had insisted that I remain in the cabinet because of my track record and relationship with COSATU.

By now we operated in silos – losing the heady space of frank and open discussions that had characterised the early Mandela period. Now each Minister was responsible for her or his portfolio; there was very little reference to others and the cabinet began to revolve around powerful personalities who were close to the heir apparent Deputy President Mbeki. We were falling back on the old construct of an all-knowing and powerful executive government in which people were passive and uniformity of opinion would be the norm.

It was also becoming a ruthless battle between power blocks of elites to drive the political direction of not only government but also the mass movement. I realised we were not unique in the world.

Thabo Mbeki had been steeped in the liberation movement, trained in the school of liberation politics, and sat sitting in the trenches with other liberation movements. There was a natural suspicion of anything that resembled a civil society organisation, particularly a trade union movement entering the terrain of liberation political movements. I could not be considered as one of his inner circle. I was seen as too closely aligned with COSATU.

As I sought to understand these dynamics and wondered why we were encountering such resistance from some quarters, I realised that I was caught in a web of conspiracy theories. The ANC in exile was a movement fighting a liberation struggle, with the underground operating in a hostile environment. The threat of infiltration had been very real. The movement had to operate in a secretive way. It had to be hierarchical.

The movement decided most things an individual could do: where you stayed, who would be allocated to which camp, who would get military training, who would be sent for what additional education. The ANC was the centre of life in exile.

Of course, under the collective and skilful leadership of Oliver Tambo, a form of consensus decision making had developed, where the leader genuinely listened and learnt, and tried to accommodate at least a part of everyone's opinion in the final resolution. But even this benign form of consensus was limited because the membership was scattered around the world, and many cadres were of necessity subjected to military discipline in the camps.

Internally, our circumstances were different. There was a lot more openness, even in our fiercest discussions and debates. Our structures were more horizontal and we could challenge tendencies such as the cult of the individual. Our view in COSATU was always that we would build a range of different leaders who had divergent influences. And that diversity was strength rather than a weakness.

I always operated on the assumption that everything I said or did was known – either to my detractors or supporters. During apartheid I knew we were infiltrated or bugged – we were a major political player. There was very little the government did not know and my strongest defence was ensuring that our cadreship and people were fully informed and involved.

Three months after the closure of the RDP office the substance of our ideological shift became apparent with the launch of the Growth, Employment and Redistribution strategy, otherwise known as GEAR, which politically buried the RDP.

34

In March 1996 NEDLAC formally tabled a process of discussing a shared economic vision that it fully expected to go through a consultative process. Both labour and business had tabled documents that called for negotiations around the most appropriate growth path. There was recognition that job creation and macroeconomic stability were imperative. Unknown to most of the political leadership in the country, another process exploring how the economy could be stabilised was being written up in the back rooms by a think tank. This was later to morph into GEAR.

This fact was accidentally stumbled on in May 1996 at a representative meeting of the ANC's Economic Transformation Committee (ETC) convened by Tito Mboweni and Max Sisulu and attended by MPs, unions, the Alliance and economists associated with the democratic movement. Stephen Gelb, a long-term ally of the labour movement who had played a key role in COSATU's economic policy-making process in the 1980s, was in attendance. Neither the newly appointed Finance Minister Trevor Manuel nor Alec Erwin, now the Minister of Trade and Industry, were present. In the course of the meeting Stephen was asked to talk about the Treasury-driven economic policy process.

At the time, Stephen was party to a highly secret series of meetings at the DBSA that had been occurring since late 1995 and were being convened by Alec Erwin when he was the Deputy Finance Minister. Key people in the group to examine a new economic policy included a number of business-orientated economists, many of whom had not been involved in the Alliance economic policy-making process. Not even the ANC's Department of Economic Policy was aware of the process.

Although Stephen had been 'sworn to silence', as a democrat he felt compelled to give a detailed report to this formal structure of the ANC.

There was absolute outrage that such a process excluded all the relevant structures of the ANC and the broader Mass Democratic Movement. The next day *Business Day* screamed a headline of a dramatic shift in government policy.

Gelb was crucified. In his words: 'I had to eat humble pie.' A few days later a meeting was convened at Mandela's residence. Those present included Zwelinzima Vavi and Ebrahim Patel from COSATU and Charles Nqakula and Jeremy Cronin from the SACP. The meeting was briefed by Alec Erwin. According to Vavi, Alec said: 'We are introducing a radical new economic plan. Big capital will react to this and it is imperative that we close ranks.' He was not specific on the details and the meeting became extremely tense. Mandela, having been briefed by the economic team leading the GEAR process, talked about 'our home-grown structural adjustment policy'. The leaders of the Alliance were aghast that there was no room for consultation. Eventually Mandela relented and asked Alec to convene another Alliance meeting and provide some details.

A few days later a second meeting was convened at Shell House, the headquarters of the ANC, and was attended by Trevor and Alec this time. They hurriedly presented their report and there was very little time for discussion as they were in a rush to catch a plane to Cape Town.

The Alliance partners were incensed. Coming on the back of the closure of the RDP office this was seen in many quarters as a replacement of the RDP. The greatest setback was that there had been no real attempt to canvass such a major policy shift in our ranks.

The following day the cabinet had its first sight of the GEAR strategy. Again there was no room for any discussion or changes. That afternoon Trevor Manuel presented GEAR, as the government's new economic strategy, to parliament as a fait accompli. The argument, said the Department of Finance, was to achieve 'a fast-growing economy which creates sufficient jobs for all work seekers'. It undertook to redistribute income, provide sound services to all, achieve a 6 per cent growth of the gross domestic product (GDP) and in the process create 400 000 jobs by the year 2000.

In fact, the language became exclusive. Phrases like 'Take it or leave it' and 'This policy is non-negotiable' were bandied about. Key activists across the country concluded, with justification, that the GEAR policy was being rammed down their throats.

To achieve these targets, GEAR was prioritising the elimination of South Africa's deficit, which had been accumulated during the last decade of apartheid. In this way, GEAR hoped to impress international financiers and open up the South African economy to foreign investors. It would relax exchange controls with other countries and encourage private sector investment in the productive sectors of the economy by reducing taxes.

It was promised that GEAR's more business-friendly approach would reassure potential international investors that the new South Africa was taking responsibility for its debts, deregulating and privatising, and this would stabilise the wobbly rand. (In the month of February 1996, the rand had taken a 20 per cent tumble against the dollar.)

With more international investment, GEAR's economists argued, growth would be stimulated and ultimately this would lead to job creation. It was, in short, a 'trickle-down' economic programme. Although most of the team denied that it succumbed to World Bank pressure, Stephen Gelb maintains: 'Close affinity with the Washington Consensus characterised not only the substantive policy recommendations of GEAR, but also the process through which it was formulated and presented to the public.'[12]

The financial crisis was indeed worrying. The markets were turbulent; our current account deficit was rising. But all of these were issues that we could have very realistically and rationally discussed in the cabinet, in the ANC NEC, in the Alliance Secretariat and in a summit; we could have reached a consensus about them. The failure to develop a consultative process laid the foundations for the turmoil and divisions that were to follow in the post-1996 period as the grassroots revolted.

Government withdrew into a cocoon of self-defensive denial and the theme in the corridors was that 'these comrades, especially in COSATU, don't understand the global realities we face. We know as the state what is best for South Africa.'

This was the new face of the democracy. The cement that held our fragile democracy together had been blown away, with irreparable consequences for our social transformation project going forward.

* * *

Despite these severe disappointments and challenges, the period from 1996 to 1999 was an exciting one for me. Having a line ministry meant that I had complete authority on what was happening there. I could make decisions and fundamentally shape the environment.

My vision, influenced by the RDP, was to deal with the challenge of universal service – a commitment that we had made to deliver a telephone line to every school, clinic, post office and village. I was part of a generation caught between a childhood with no television and a time when we started to communicate electronically with telex machines and beepers; now the world was rocketing into a digital age where the Internet and technology platforms connected our planet as one global village.

It was at this time that I met up with the legendary Sam Pitroda, who was closely associated with the phenomenal success of India as an information technology (IT) giant in the world. Sam was of humble stock, born in a little village in Gujarat. When he graduated from university, with just US$100 in his pocket, he set off to Chicago to build a successful IT company.

When he met with then Indian Prime Minister Rajiv Gandhi at a diaspora meeting in Chicago, he was told: 'Sam, you know about technology. Why don't you come back to India and help us put a telephone in every village?' Sam sold his business and returned to India. He offered his services at the princely sum of one rupee a year and was appointed as an adviser to the government of India at the rank of a Cabinet Minister.

He played a leading role in transforming the IT field, often working against bureaucratic resistance. At one point I asked him to what he would attribute India's success, especially given the overwhelming poverty I had seen first-hand in that country, which made our challenges seem small in comparison.

His words remained implanted in my head. 'It's hunger for knowledge,' he said. 'In every village across India, the poorest parents collect their meagre rupees to send one of their children to one of the many computer training schools to learn basic data processing. They usually end up in information factories in Bangalore and other cities, processing handwritten notes downloaded by satellite from the developed world into computer-based records. Many spend their lives in these factories and secondary call centre agencies that became a booming industry and spilled into software development. Thousands migrate to the famed Silicon Valley in California.'

However, instead of seeing this as a 'brain drain', the government of India recognised an opportunity to build a knowledge sector exporting IT as its competitive edge. China was fast becoming the 'workshop of the world', and Brazil the 'agricultural heartland'; India saw its advantage in becoming the IT bank of the world.

This vision was close to my heart. I believed deeply that we had the same capacity. Poverty was not an excuse. In fact, the exclusion of the majority of people as a result of apartheid presented a huge advantage. We could install the latest technology without the challenge of legacy systems. We happened to be hosting Africa Telecoms '98 and that was an opportunity to build an integrated African regional strategy. After all, telecommunications, like IT, knew no physical boundaries.

My mantra: 'Africa south of the Sahara has fewer telephones than the city of New York or Tokyo, but this does not make us a basket case.' It was a huge investment opportunity if we could build the economy of scale and develop powerful regional players. And telecommunication, unlike many other infrastructure sectors, was attracting huge private sector investment capital. This meant that we could finance development off the balance sheet of government, which faced huge competing social challenges in areas such as education, health and rural development.

Mandela had addressed the UN agency the International Telecommunications Union (ITU), and invited it to host its next major event in South Africa. This was a platform for building consensus and I worked with many other African Ministers, underpinned by a belief that African problems of connectivity could only be solved by African leaders, with African solutions that we invited the world to partner us in.

The world was bursting with the radical innovation of IT; the United Nations system was talking about closing the digital divide; technology was seen as the magic bullet. And here in South Africa we could transform telecommunication to address a range of economic and developmental priorities.

Of course there was a range of opinions, with some arguing for complete deregulation and others for greater state investment. With my background in COSATU, it was not top of my agenda to view deregulation and liberalisation as the magic wand. There was vibrancy around the debates on the Green Paper and the White Paper, and then with the unions around restructuring Telkom. This was a process in which I could be intellectually stimulated. I felt renewed.

* * *

One of the first things that I had to deal with as Minister of Posts, Telecom-munications and Broadcasting was the SABC and the privatisation of certain stations. We needed to create some diversity. In my mind the SABC still had the mentality of a state broadcaster and competition would be good for creating a diversity of views.

We could not concentrate the entire media into one institution. What would happen if that institution went wrong? I realised there was a role for the private sector. We created a process whereby we allowed the sale of five SABC radio stations. So that was the first privatisation, in 1996.

But for me the real possibility for diversity was presented by community radio, which would bring new voices into local and national debate. After all, radio was still the main source of information for the majority of people. In fact, some argued that 'more Africans own radio receivers than bed mattresses'.[13]

I recall some clashes with the religious sector, because each group wanted its own radio station. I was quite clear on the fact that we are a secular state and that community radio should reflect the diversity of interests in a community.

But it was Telkom that loomed large on my radar screen. This was a company that was highly bureaucratic and only recently separated from a debt-ridden and infamously inefficient department that knew very little about delivery to the majority living in poverty in the townships and rural areas. For me this was the priority – to deliver to our constituency. The mobile sector, while growing, was not really interested in going beyond the community obligation written into their licences.

The cost of modernising Telkom and delivering to the masses of people was astronomical, running into billions of US dollars in investment. Given the parlous state of finances in the country and the tightening of belts under GEAR and the other competing needs within the state, there were few choices.

Through an intense negotiation with particularly the unions and other social partners, we focused on what the targets would be for the telecommunications sector. We agreed that the priority was to connect the rural areas and underserviced townships to the network; to ensure that intensive training gave career path opportunities for Telkom workers; to digitise the network; and that investment should have a multiplier effect in creating jobs across the sector.

At the end of the process we had the choice of borrowing more money, dismantling the company and introducing free competition, or choosing a strategic equity partner that would inject capital and expertise and integrate us into the world.

It was a tough negotiation marred by insults thrown at me about 'selling out and betraying the workers' cause'. Even the union leadership in the Communications Workers Union was thrown out by its congress because it was felt that they were too close to government. The battle against GEAR had now become strident on both sides.

I worked with my team and continued our interactions one small step at a time. The unions were genuinely concerned about job security, improving training and transformation within the company and delivery of services to the poor. After exhausting all possibilities, consensus was reached that the only viable financing option was a partial privatisation under well-regulated conditions. It was agreed that we would allow the labour unions representation on the board, as well as joint participation in a well-funded training scheme to improve career paths.

It was also decided that the unions would be part of a roadshow that allowed us to meet potential partners across the world as we put out feelers. I felt that this decision, while it was an executive government decision, should follow a path of genuine consultation.

One meeting that remained etched in my mind was arranged by Franklin Sonn, a long-standing colleague and friend, and at the time the South African Ambassador to Washington. During my visit there he told us that a request had been made by Vice President Al Gore to meet with a delegation from our side. I had worked closely with the talented and incisive Telkom Chairperson Dikgang Moseneke, and together with Franklin Sonn we wound our way through the maze of security of the White House, intrigued by the interest shown.

The Vice President was very engaging. I had encountered him in other meetings when he had visited South Africa. But here he was playing the role of the champion of a United States corporate, arguing in surprising detail the case for Southwestern Bell Corporation (SBC), one of the most admired telecommunications operators in the United States.

I realised that even though this was a Democratic Party Vice President he was backing a company whose senior leadership in Texas was probably

Republican. This was the type of new economic diplomacy that had begun to characterise globalisation. Governments acted in concert with key national economic interests as multinational companies sought to increase their global reach and influence. The core of politics was now unabashedly business.

It made me think about the gulf of mistrust between business and government in South Africa. Meeting businesses internationally, we invariably encountered patriotism to their country of origin and a similar view from the government of those countries. It would be some time before we would build such a bond of trust in South Africa. A prerequisite was the representative ownership and management of the South African economy, which was no small challenge.

Despite the very competitive process, as it turned out, in the light of the first signs of a global downturn, of the final shortlist of two only a consortium that brought together SBC in the United States and Malaysia Telecom submitted a bid. The transaction, the first and largest privatisation investment in the new South Africa at $US1.25 billion, was a breakthrough.

We agreed that US$1 billion would be reinvested in the company to kick-start the roll-out plan estimated at about US$10 billion and to promote a multiplier effect across the information and communication technology sector. While there was unhappiness in the cabinet about this, the Deputy President had agreed with me that this was the correct decision – job creation and modernisation commanded a higher priority than the reduction of debt.

The transaction also created the obligation in the licence agreement to deliver 3 million new lines to previously disadvantaged areas, including every village, school and clinic, and connecting 2 000 schools to the Internet, with penalties for non-compliance with these milestones.

* * *

As time passed I felt that I was operating in a political environment that made me feel uncomfortable. Decisions that clearly were commercial were being subjected to political scrutiny. This was the type of political interference I had known well in my COSATU days and had fought against.

The first clash was in relation to the sale of shares held by Cable and Wireless and SBC in MTN. This was a major test for government. Johnnic, a major conglomerate, had been acquired from Anglo American by a broad-based black consortium and was being punished by the market for being unfocused.

As with many of the black empowerment transactions of the time, they were susceptible to market volatility with little room to manoeuvre because they were constrained by the special-purposes vehicle in which the shares were held and the repayment of the debt was through dividend flow. The real value would only be possible if it was unbundled and restructured under a new business strategy and management.

Irene Charnley, a Johnnic executive who had previously worked with the National Union of Mineworkers, approached me as Minister to inform me that they were trying to reorganise Johnnic as a multi-media company that would focus on communication and broadcasting. They wanted to consolidate their existing shares in MTN and to take control of the company.

There was a view from my department that government should insist that it had a pre-emptive on these shares, which I disagreed with. There was no clear legal basis for this and I detected the disagreement had more to do with a prevailing political view about Cyril Ramaphosa who, as the Chairperson of Johnnic, was seen as the erstwhile rival of Deputy President Mbeki.

I had no commercial or social relationship with Cyril beyond my respect for his political contribution. I disagreed with my Director General (DG) Andile Ngcaba, and the Johnnic Group and Transnet (the state-owned transport conglomerate and another existing shareholder of MTN) ended up acquiring the shareholding. A seed of dissension was sown.

*   *   *

I was enthusiastic about the potential of an African Renaissance articulated by Mbeki. Africa was the forgotten continent and any news of Africa was mediated through the prism of a Western view. The idea that we could build an image of Africa using our own infrastructure was hugely appealing.

Zwelakhe Sisulu had been appointed with acclaim across the political spectrum as the new Group CEO of the SABC. The son of Walter and Albertina Sisulu, both icons of the freedom struggle, Zwelakhe was a committed journalist who had spent much of his life in the media and had run a vibrant progressive newspaper, *The New Nation,* in the 1980s. I had great confidence in his ability to turn the SABC into an independent public broadcaster.

There had been much talk of the negative coverage we received on other international channels, such as CNN and the BBC, and I was attracted to the idea that we could be part of launching the first African news channel.

Zwelakhe had brought in Allister Sparks, a dynamic and internationally renowned journalist as his acting Editor in Chief for a year and to build a vibrant newsroom. They approached me with the proposal supported by the board that allowed the SABC to get out of a disastrous ten-year lease on a satellite that they were never going to use and which DStv, a digital platform for satellite subscription TV owned by Naspers, would take over. In addition they had negotiated that DStv would host an SABC Africa channel for African news that would reach Africa, the Middle East and even southern Europe. In the situation of conflicting demands on the fiscus leaving very little for broadcasting, the savings of close to R1.5 billion and the capacity as the largest news organisation on the continent to beam across Africa was an excellent idea.

After several presentations, the department opposed the idea. All I could fathom was that there was a political objection to working with Allister Sparks and Naspers. I felt differently. The SABC was an independent entity governed by a board selected by parliament. While we had oversight, my strong view was that this did not warrant us getting operationally involved in the company's decisions. I supported the SABC Board.

By now the relations between the DG and I had reached an all-time low and I raised the issue with Deputy President Mbeki. He suggested that we have a joint discussion with Kgalema Motlanthe, then the Secretary General of the ANC. The meetings were inconclusive and I pushed for a joint meeting with Mbeki. This meeting failed to resolve the issues we had and it was clear to me that I was the outsider in the conversation.

As the close of the first democratic term of office approached and Thabo Mbeki was anointed the successor, I was more convinced than ever that I would not be able to serve in the new administration.

Moreover, my relationship with Lucie was reaching breaking point. We had already decided that at the end of this political term she was packing up for Québec, taking the children with her. The choice was stark: my political life or my family?

35

The lead-up to the Telecom '98 event that South Africa was hosting was fraught. The UN agency the International Telecommunications Union (ITU), like many multilateral agencies dominated by the developed world, tried to act like an imperial agent ordering the colonial subordinates to organise the transport and the logistics while the content was shaped in Geneva.

But South Africa had a proud and independent history and I found it offensive that international bureaucrats felt they could preside over us. As the negotiations for the event dragged on, we extracted one small concession after the other. But I was determined that I would not be bullied.

Leading up to the event, we had built a broad consensus on how we should cooperate as a continent. We convened a series of conferences and workshops with African Ministers of Communications across the continent and produced a policy framework that we eventually called the 'African Connection' document which captured the essence of the challenges that faced Africa at policy level. It looked at the key issues of human resource development, financing, developing rural telecommunication, the harmonisation of policies, regulations and the spectrum. We realised that the way forward was building regional markets and attracting private sector operators. Telecommunications knew no boundaries, and if we were looking for the economy of scale of investment that was required then we had to talk about regional economies of scale.

The subject we were confronted with in many of the conferences was the associated dangers. How do we go into a country where there is civil war, where there is no proper governance? We are used to operating in developed countries where there is predictability and certainty of policies, a legal framework that creates a level playing field and where the political and business risks are mitigated.

One afternoon, while sitting in an international satellite conference, I was tiring of this refrain and turned my attention to Navin Kapila, an IT executive who was sitting next to me. In our conversation he spoke about the fact that he had completed an around-the-world rally and was a record holder in the *Guinness Book of Records*.

I replied: 'Well, I wish I could do a rally across the African continent through all the countries that these Afro-pessimists are talking about and mobilise Ministers, regulators and communities as to the potential of telecommunications to close the digital divide and leapfrog us into the modern economy.' It wouldn't be the imperial dream of that infamous coloniser Cecil John Rhodes who wished to subjugate the African continent, but more a revolutionary dream of great African Presidents of the past, such as Nkrumah, Nyerere, Nasser, Ben Bella and now Mandela, to liberate our continent from the vestiges of colonialism, tribalism and ignorance.

Some weeks later a fax arrived at home. Intrigued, Lucie asked me: 'Why does someone send you a map of Africa with a route delineated from Tunisia to Cape Agulhas?' Embarrassed, I related the story and she said: 'You're absolutely mad – it's too dangerous.' To which I replied: 'Well, exactly – how do you think we will be able to change people's perceptions if we do not do the bold and dangerous thing?'

The discussion ended but I was now hooked. Would this be possible?

The months passed and I met Navin again. He had done more research on a possible trip across Africa and had already raised the idea with senior telecommunications leaders in Africa. He reported an enthusiastic response.

By February 1998 plans had been crystallised, sponsorship raised and the date was set for the launch from Bizerte, the northernmost tip of Tunisia, and of Africa. The trip had morphed into a major international undertaking with scores of journalists and support crew. Country by country, negotiations were held to facilitate access and ensure that the logistics were in place.

In April I had breakfast with the Minister of Communications of Tunisia. I was anxious as logistical nightmares abounded. The most serious was that no arrangements had been finalised for the journalists to enter Libya, which was still under UN sanctions and closed to international travel.

With great fanfare we launched on schedule. This was the first cross-continental rally by a Minister of government. Lucie, who had understood my determination and did everything to support me in this trip, was present and I had my emotional strength reinforced for the journey home. She was anxious and so was I. A massed choir of Tunisian singers was there for the send-off. We visited a telecentre set up to celebrate the journey and, after speeches from the Mayor and ourselves, the Tunisian Minister of Telecommunications and I jumped into the first car. As I turned the key I was struck by the sheer impossibility of the trip. We had to travel treacherous roads, navigate the bureaucracy of different countries, face civil wars and deal with the ever-present danger of banditry. The South African Foreign Office had not been very supportive because of these challenges. But I was determined that it could happen and that we would demonstrate that cooperation across diverse cultures and political differences could be achieved.

As we left the launch I abandoned myself to the adventure, content to live in the present, experience every exhilarating minute and resolved to tackle the obstacles as we met them.

We arrived at the border with Libya late that evening. As we checked through the Tunisian side we heard the roar of people and stumbled into a celebration of singing, dancing and a gathering of thousands to welcome us into Libya. Though exhausted we joined in the shouting of revolutionary slogans and dancing before we departed for Tripoli.

So warm was the reception that the SABC secured the first satellite broadcast from Libya in years. The country was fascinating, from its preserved Roman ruins to the forests of green olive trees to the towns of adobe structures, its glistening deserts and brilliant sunsets.

Crossing into Egypt we landed in the bedlam and exciting chaos of Alexandria. Here was the city famed as an ancient site of learning, boasting the first library in the world, where we stopped off to see the amazing work being done to digitise these ancient records of our civilisation; then on to Cairo teeming with millions of people, who never seemed to go to sleep, watching the skyline of the fabulous history of the Pharaohs as I saw the pyramids for the first time. These awe-inspiring structures jutting proudly into the air were as magnificent as they must have been thousands of years previously. I could not but imagine immortality as a reality of the life and times of these imperial leaders.

We were hosted by a close friend, Hisham El Sherif, who was an adviser to President Mubarak on building the capacity of the Egyptian government to implement its radical strategy to transform government delivery using IT. Egypt had made great progress in this respect.

We left Cairo and seemed to enter a different country barely a few hundred kilometres away. The landscape changed fundamentally. Travelling along the Nile was the most intriguing experience; it was a forest of green agriculture and then the desert as far as the eye could see. We travelled in convoy accompanied by army carriers bearing machine guns. It was scary. At regular intervals we encountered well-fortified army posts. It reminded me of our own past – except for the dry barrenness of the countryside. We had been warned that travelling here at night was dangerous.

Deep in the south of the country we stopped for a short break. We were surrounded by armed soldiers and they freaked out when we tried to mingle with people and take some photographs. The people we saw were quiet, almost sullen, as they watched us and continued with the tilling of their fields. While the towns were vibrant and friendly we were left with the uneasy feeling that a substantial divide existed between the city and the countryside.

We arrived at Aswan. The Egyption border to Sudan was closed. They would not allow us to cross it – this was the consequence of an attempt that had been made on Mubarak's life when he attended an African Union Conference in Addis Ababa in Ethiopia. The claim was that the attempt was by militants from Sudan and so the border was closed. There was no room for discussion.

We piled our 4 x 4s into the huge transporter plane carrying the journalists and support staff and took off. A few hours later we landed in the middle of the desert in an abandoned airfield near the town of Dongola. An hour later the Minister of Communications of Sudan arrived. The Minister was a General. He welcomed us warmly and got into the car with me. We passed a small town and then the road vanished and I asked: 'What road should I take?'

He replied: 'My dear brother, you travel in this direction but you can choose the road. The desert is your friend.'

I turned the vehicle in the direction he had indicated. It was an adrenalin rush as I felt the boyhood thrill that every man should experience – the open desert and a 4 x 4 crashing up and down the towering sand dunes. Everything looked the same – dunes, dunes and more dunes, with no end in sight. Thankfully our guide knew the exact direction we were headed. At one point we stopped because we had to change a punctured tyre. A crowded bus came along, with people sitting on the roof with their goats and their chickens. Everyone was dressed in white reflecting the blistering heat of the desert.

Along the way we stopped at each village where people congregated to hear our message. At one village a terrifying display of horseback fighting was put on for us and I was presented with a sword by the local chief. As I held it in my hand and drew out the trusty steel to salute the assembled warriors I wondered how many people had suffered its sharp blade.

We arrived at the border with Ethiopia. This border was also closed. It took many negotiations to open it and as I crossed the dry riverbed alongside a destroyed bridge with the Sudanese Minister, we saw a delegation led by the Ethiopian Communications Minister coming towards us. For the first time in many years, the two Ministers met.

I was spellbound by Ethiopia – the people, the culture, the cuisine; it's a fascinating melting pot. We arrived at Gondar, the birthplace of the great Abyssinian Empire with the glittering remnants of its palaces. My latest gout attack was fierce – we had eaten nothing but meat since we left Tunisia. Here in Ethiopia the food was gentler and the spices spectacular. It was Lent and we were welcomed with a magnificent feast to celebrate our arrival.

This was a proud nation; a beautiful and graceful people who had never been colonised but were ravaged by decades of civil strife. We crossed rivers with bridges torn from their ramparts; tanks like burnt-out corpses littered the roads. It was a living insight into development in Africa, into the patience of people and the way in which they endure hardship. Inevitably we asked ourselves the question, 'Why can't we use these resources to build a better life for people?'

Addis Ababa was a thriving metropolis emerging from a civil war. The Mercado is Africa's largest market; we were told we could buy anything there, from bananas to machine guns.

We arrived in Addis Ababa in time for the Easter Festival. We attended the colourful ceremony, with Afro-Asian cadences in the music and chanting, rich textiles and incense, as well as glowing icons of the saints with their lustrous black eyes.

Many of the rituals struck a chord with me. The singing and dancing was entrancing. Jesus here, staring down from walls and ceilings, is no blue-eyed European but a brown-skinned Ethiopian. The Patriarch of the Ethiopian Orthodox Church took the time to bless the delegation and wish it well.

As we set off on our journey towards the border with Kenya we paused for an overnight stay. Our vehicles had been filled with contaminated fuel and the mechanics worked overnight to drain and clean the engines. We shared a traditional coffee ceremony with the crew and community leaders. Coffee is reputed to have been discovered in Ethiopia by a herdsman who had smelt the rich aromas after a runaway fire.

Here the coffee ceremony takes on a whole new dimension of community participation. And the ritual itself was a beautiful one – the way in which the aroma of coffee, even while the beans were being roasted, was wafted into each person's face so that you got the intoxicating smell. Drinking the coffee is more than simply getting your caffeine boost; it's about a community spirit, about conjuring up something esoteric, about creating an environment in which you can talk about difficult issues and settle family and community disputes.

Then we crossed into Kenya. The Deputy Minister of Communications arrived in a helicopter. His view was that the northern parts of Kenya were quite dangerous. There was a lot of rebel activity. As we sat down to dinner that night the Ethiopian and Kenyan Ministers met for the first time and discovered they were from the same tribe. They talked excitedly about the future work they should do to bring the two countries together.

The Kenyan Deputy Minister wanted me to fly to Nairobi but I insisted on driving. I was committed to being at the front of this expedition. It was quite late in the afternoon when the cars were ready and we were able to leave. We were accompanied by the army, which normally would not have travelled at night, and which, in this northern part of Kenya, only travelled in convoy.

The Great North Road was not a highway at all – it was a rut; bridges had been blown up and much of its surface was derelict. Our army escort was opposed to driving at night but I insisted as we had been delayed by the fuel problem and people were expecting us all along the way. One of my lasting memories is the image of the sky so close to the land I felt I could touch it. That evening, I experienced the surreal effect of the moon rising.

I met Lucie in Nairobi and the twelve hours we spent together gave me a much-needed boost.

We crossed into Tanzania. I took leave of the Kenyan Minister and was met by my Tanzanian counterpart. I learnt of the country's history and its cultures and people. I could feel the sense of stability. The people were friendly, the society open and the scenery with its rolling tea plantations reminded me of growing up in Natal with its hills of undulating sugar cane plantations.

I wanted to stop off at the Solomon Mahlangu Freedom College in Morogoro. It was a historic site of our struggle for freedom named after the scholar who left South Africa in 1976 to join MK. I felt a sense of déjà vu. We were of the same generation and my life could have so closely mirrored his. Solomon, together with Mondi Motloung, had infiltrated back into the country as guerrillas/freedom fighters. But they were caught after an attack on a warehouse in Johannesburg in which a man was killed. Motloung, suffering brain damage from being tortured, was institutionalised.

Mahlangu was sentenced to death and executed on 6 April 1979. His last words are inscribed on the walls of the college: 'The Tree of Freedom is watered by the blood of martyrs.'

For us as young activists, these words were immortalised and had reflected our determination to sacrifice even our lives for the pursuit of liberation. Mahlangu's execution had made us more determined to defeat the brutal apartheid regime.

We walked through the graveyard where so many South Africans are buried. It was quite eerie to imagine this site of enormous significance, the Solomon Mahlangu College, now unused and empty, as a centre that had nourished the minds of thousands of South African exiles. The place evoked deep memories and profound feelings about the sacrifices and hardships that people endured in exile, and how they battled to retain a sense of community spirit and comradeship.

From there, we travelled to Zambia. It is a beautiful country, with its winding hills and arable land. I contemplated the enormous richness of the land, the sight of women in the blazing African sun breaking the soil or harvesting their crops as they engaged in subsistence agriculture; these women were the backbone of economic activity, many still nurturing their babies. Yet by 2009 women, who are the soul of Africa and who contribute over 80 per cent of agricultural labour, own 1 per cent of the land, access 10 per cent of the credit in the market and are given only 7 per cent of the agricultural extension services.[14]

How we have failed them. Armed with grand ideas, the multilateral organisations forced Africa to abandon its dream of a 'green revolution' and embark on large-scale infrastructure projects like dam building, insisted on the planting of cash crops designed to meet the needs of the developed world and destroyed the capacity of Africa to feed itself in that process. All around me I could see the evidence of our failed experiment. But the elites who brought us these 'miracles' had long disappeared into comfortable retirement.

Nevertheless I was struck by people's patience and fortitude and their humility in the countless meetings and rallies we held along the way. I saw the inextricable link between eliminating poverty; promoting sustainable livelihoods, rural development and women's rights; and closing the urban–rural divide. It made me reflect critically on my own ideas and the development trajectory we had chosen at home.

As we continued our journey in collaboration with the various national governments we opened a number of telecentres to promote access to the information revolution for local communities.

Finally we crossed Beit Bridge, separating Zimbabwe and South Africa. While the gulf that divides us from the rest of Africa in terms of infrastructure was apparent, our challenges were the same. How do we deal with inequality and poverty? What is the appropriate economic development trajectory that will build a more caring, inclusive society that has suffered the ravages of centuries of colonial oppression and racial exploitation? In Cape Agulhas these were the questions that crossed my mind.

In 21 days we had completed this enormous journey of 15 000 kilometres, crossing the length of Africa. I knew then that my contribution to development would be outside of formal government.

Many of the hardships I saw were caused by a leadership vacuum, the way in which the wealth of Africa, the richest continent in the world, has been plundered by vested interests globally, and by our own domestic political elites.

My African odyssey had given me a sense of optimism that one day the aspirations and the resourcefulness and the hopes of the ordinary people would be achieved. What we needed was a vibrant civil society to hold our leadership accountable; a class of ethical and successful entrepreneurs able to add value to our commodities that power the global economy and who are independent from political patronage; and a state bureaucracy insulated from the corrupt influence of factions of political office bearers who see their title as a licence to sell favours and contracts and buy political votes.

36

In 1998 on a family visit to India Lucie and I decided to have a quiet renewal of our marriage vows at an ancient temple in Bangalore. This idea had been planted by Lucie on our second date, in November 1990. We were having dinner together in bustling Yeoville. The quiet Indian restaurant coincidentally was playing French music that night. We settled down to order and Lucie, who had spent a year travelling through India and China, said, 'You are so Indian in the way you act.'

I reacted sharply.

'Don't say that – I am South African. I would be a foreigner in India. I don't even speak an Indian language.'

I explained how throughout my life apartheid had reinforced a notion that South Africa was a land of minorities. 'You are not African but Indian' was the constant refrain as we fought to create a South African identity amongst the oppressed.

As I travel the world and see the ghettoisation of ethnic communities I can reflect on our South African experience. We have succeeded in building a respect for cultural diversity in South Africa. Official state functions embrace the range of cultures and religions but we have a long way to go before we can build a national identity and racial solidarity.

This third wedding ceremony, on 21 December 1998, had been arranged by old friends of ours, Lakshmi Chand Jain, the dedicated High Commissioner to South Africa from India, and his dynamic wife, Devaki, a social scientist. We dressed traditionally – Lucie in a sari and me in a *dhothi*. For hours we sat in a thousand-year-old temple in Bangalore through a fabulous ritual of the marriage of the gods, and then the priests performed our Hindu marriage rites. Our three children, Shanti, Kami and Léandre, three, six and twelve years old, Louise, my mother-in-law, and my sister Nisha and her husband, Sagaren, were present. In fact, Louise is the only person to have been present at all three weddings: in Africa, where I was born; Québec, Lucie's home; and India, land of my ancestry. With French, Irish and Mohawk genes being Lucie's ancestry, our children have the blood of four continents flowing in their veins; they are 'globalised' children.

As the ceremony started, the temple filled with devotees and curious crowds from the local community. This was India at its most festive. The multi-cultural shades and colours of humanity reminded me of my mother. Although I felt her spiritual presence I wished she was present physically. It certainly would have warmed her heart that I had finally embraced the cultural roots that had shaped my destiny.

Travelling south to Pondicherry, the French enclave, we stayed at the Aurobindo Ashram and built lifelong friendships with its Director, Vijay. We never got to know his surname because as he said: 'It's not important. What is important is what you carry in your heart and the values and the contribution you make to society.'

Those words were an echo of my mother's. Vijay, ever patient, serene and wise, was to become a mentor to Lucie, who turned to him whenever life seemed overwhelming. I was intrigued by Aurobindo, the one-time revolutionary nationalist who had taken on armed struggle against the British occupation of India, who had been on trial for sedition and treason and who had to flee to the enclave controlled by the French in 1910. It was here that he fully developed his spiritual teachings and met the 'Mother' – a French citizen, Mirra Richard, who would become a confidante and close spiritual collaborator.

I warmed to their teachings, especially the views on religion and science:

> *Though religion has provided a moral foundation, it has lost touch with its spiritual roots. In the coming age each individual can experience the spirit directly, not merely worship the founder. Also, each religion has but one ray of spiritual truth. We need to experience the vast multiplicity of truths of spirit. Science likewise is failing us, despite the great benefits it has brought. Like religion, it sees one truth – the material – and misses the vast multiplicity of vital, mental, and spiritual existence that are also the great determinants of life. Thus for every benefit it creates, it creates an equal harm.*[15]

These words struck a chord within me.

The Aurobindo Ashram, based on the universal teachings and values of its founders Sri Aurobindo and the 'Mother', was to become a permanent feature in our lives. But India also raised the contradictions of my own thinking. While the Indian Constitution was based on secular, democratic and even socialist principles, what I saw in the rural areas of India based on the caste system astounded me. The Dalits, or 'untouchables' as Gandhi described them, were the lowest strata of society who did the manual jobs and served the interests of the higher classes. The rigidity of the system reminded me of apartheid. They were not allowed to worship in the temples, nor access water or stay in the same areas as the Brahmins or higher classes. Intermarriage between classes is still forbidden. This social discrimination affected tens of millions of people and physical contact with them was considered to be impure.

I was offended. Why was such social injustice accepted? I went back to the iconic statesmen who were the founding fathers of India to understand their views. How could a religion like Hinduism, which was a way of life for the majority of people, embrace a caste system?

I discovered Dr Bhimrao Ramji Ambedkar, born in 1891, who was an Indian nationalist, jurist, Dalit, political leader, philosopher, anthropologist, historian, orator, prolific writer, economist, revolutionary and the revivalist of Buddhism in India. He was also the chief architect of the Indian Constitution. In 1933, Ambedkar said: 'There will be outcastes as long as there are castes, and nothing can emancipate the outcaste except the destruction of the caste system.'

Ambedkar was influential in shifting Gandhi's views on caste, and in 1946 Gandhi reiterated this view saying: 'You should become like Ambedkar. You should work for the removal of untouchability and caste. Untouchability must go at any cost.'

Almost 50 years later I encountered caste as a still-pervasive anachronism in India. I wondered what I would have done if I had been subjected to the same violence and social discrimination. I realised that I would have done the same thing that I did in South Africa – unite, organise and revolt against the social injustice.

* * *

At this point mere months remained of our term of office under President Mandela. It had been an eventful journey full of triumphs of the human spirit and the bitter blows of political infighting.

I had a conversation with Deputy President Mbeki to inform him that I intended to step down at the time of the elections. 'We should meet, chief, to discuss this,' he said. Time passed and I was still unable to organise the meeting. Eventually I wrote a letter to Mbeki explaining my position and a meeting was finally forthcoming. In the letter I outlined my feelings. I stated my intention to resign from government at the forthcoming elections.

'Now, why would you want to do that?' Mbeki asked.

We had quite an amicable conversation. I explained to him that given my family circumstances, and Lucie wanting to go back to Canada, I felt it was appropriate.

I was firm in my mind. Eventually we agreed that I would step down but that I would announce it after the election. I was number sixteen on the ANC election list. There would be many questions now if I took my name off the list. We agreed that it was not wise to send a signal that I was leaving before the election.

I had not discussed my resignation with Madiba but had a long conversation with Graça Machel at their house, in which I explained my decision. She listened carefully and said: 'Jay, I understand your position exactly – because I too have been there. I had to make similar choices in my life. At the end of it the family is important to keep intact.'

I left feeling that she would convey my reasons to the President and comrade I had respected and served.

After the 1999 elections everyday life was dramatically transformed. I had time to reflect on the historic, rollercoaster, frustrating, thrilling and creative experience of being in South Africa's first democratically elected government, enveloped by Madiba's magic. I had time to work out why my intellect concurred with my instinct that I needed to get out of government.

On the face of it, four episodes were emblematic of the reasons for my decision to leave government and formal politics. The first and most obvious was when the RDP office was shut down without forewarning. Not only had I not been consulted, but neither was COSATU nor the Alliance partners, including the constitutional structures of the ANC.

The second setback was the surprise unveiling of GEAR. I felt that the challenges we faced with the financial turmoil in the country could be handled in a mature and rational way within the democratic structures of the Alliance. It would have been contentious but it would have been settled with tough negotiations and compromises on all sides.

Chris Hani, SACP Secretary General and labour stalwart, joins a COSATU march against unfair dismissals in the early 1990s. *(Jay Naidoo library)*

With Madiba in November 1993. *(William Matlala)*

Campaigning for ANC victory. Mandela for President as part of the election campaign in 1994. *(Jay Naidoo library)*

COSATU Congress in 1993 elects twenty worker leaders to go to parliament on an ANC list. *(Jay Naidoo library)*

Historic first Cabinet in the democratic South Africa in 1994.
(Jay Naidoo library)

My first visit to India in 1995. With a BK leader, Lucie, Shanti (eight months) and Connie Molusi at Maduben in Mount Abu, the site of the University of Spiritual Values, run by the Brahma Kumaris. *(Jay Naidoo library)*

Meeting Fidel Castro, with my kids, on his first state visit to South Africa. *(Jay Naidoo library)*

Spiritual meeting with the Dalai Lama with Omar at the Carlton Hotel in 1996. *(Jay Naidoo library)*

Renewing our wedding vows in Bangalore, India, in 1999. *(Jay Naidoo library)*

President Lula, true to his background in labour, meets his trade union comrades. With Vincente da Silva and Zwelinzima Vavi. *(William Matlala)*

The three COSATU General Secretaries, Mbhazima (Sam) Shilowa (1993–99), Zwelinzima Vavi (1999–to date) and Jay Naidoo (1985–1993), celebrate the twentieth anniversary of CTH, the legal firm that defended the labour movement from its inception. *(CTH photo library)*

Receiving the Chevalier de la Légion d`Honneur award, with Emma Mashinini, Bill Lucy and Jayendra Naidoo, in 2006. *(Jay Naidoo library)*

With City Year volunteers and Rick Menell. Volunteerism has to be reinvented to ensure the deepening of democracy and accountability. *(City Year)*

Madiba with Shanti and Kami in October 2008. *(Jay Naidoo library)*

My sister, Dimes, her husband, Vasan, Rosie Tsebe and others attend the wedding of Léandre and Élise Anne Basque in August 2009. *(Jay Naidoo library)*

Meeting with the Archbishop of the Anglican Church of Southern Africa, Thabo Cecil Makgoba, to discuss citizen participation in deepening democracy and accountability as key to fighting poverty and inequality. *(Jay Naidoo library)*

With former Presidents and statesmen, Olusegun Obasanjo of Nigeria and Festus Mogae of Botswana discussing governance and leadership in Africa in Berlin in May 2010. *(Jay Naidoo library)*

With Emmanuel Faber (COO Danone), Muhammed Yunus (Grameen Bank) and
Franck Riboud (CEO Danone) in a public rally in Paris on building social businesses.
(General Community Meeting 2009, danone.communities)

My family is the anchor in my life. *(Jay Naidoo library)*

My third reason had to do with my flagging relationship with my DG in the Department of Telecommunications. He was raised in a different political culture. I have always declared a loyalty to the cause and the ideal and never to an individual, but loyalty to an individual seemed to be the new hallmark of the incoming administration.

Then to my deep disappointment I learnt that our trusted and capable childminder and housekeeper had been systematically stealing money, clothes and household goods. This in itself was a cliché in the still deeply unequal society of South Africa. Needless to say, we were shocked and hurt when the evidence came to light.

But linked to that incident was something more sinister. As the housekeeper was about to leave, her bags packed, she agreed to a search of her luggage. Hidden inside the housekeeper's suitcases was a file titled 'Secret Service military training', which explained, amongst other things, electronic bugging, spying techniques and how to make bombs. Attached to it was a certificate confirming that the housekeeper had 'successfully' completed a course on how to handle firearms. Another document was attached to it with a paper clip. It was a certificate of ownership and a licence to carry a firearm.[16]

Then I discovered through an investigation by someone I trusted within the security establishment that my house and phones were bugged. Someone high up in our ranks had authorised the planting of bugs in my house, and corrupted our housekeeper in the process. The incident made me recognise that paranoia had taken hold; state institutions were being used not against the enemies of the state, but within us as comrades.

Lucie was overcome with grief. The children in their innocence were deeply attached to the housekeeper as part of the family and could not understand the betrayal that was unfolding. As she was led away, it was painful to see the confusion and hurt in their faces.

And finally, on a personal level, there were renewed strains in my relationship with Lucie. The demands of government took me away from home for weeks on end. Lucie would ironically say that she would turn on the television to catch a glimpse of me. I was deeply involved with the challenging and revolutionary tasks facing me. In the pursuit of building a better life for millions of South African families I hardly saw my own family. I knew that at the end of my term, I would need to do something drastic to hold on to my family. It was not the absence of love that was tearing us apart but my physical absence from all things to do with an equal relationship with Lucie and my children.

On the political front, with the privilege of hindsight I realise that I could have done things differently. No one, myself included, comprehended the massive growth of mobile technology that would revolutionise business and communications and make it a tool of the poor.

At a policy level I had recognised that while the first five years was a trade-off on the regulatory side to drive universal service in communications, the future had to be to drive down the costs with an aggressive approach to competition. This was already a key part of the next five years. We needed to break the monopoly of Telkom decisively to achieve this. I should have done that before I left. The Internet was the future and would be the revolutionary technology to leapfrog Africa into the twenty-first century. The advantage was that it could be financed by the private sector and the drive for financial return would result in innovation that brought more of the poor people at the bottom of the pyramid into the new digital age.

Today the mobile phone is the most pervasive technological platform in the world. Of the 7 billion people on Earth, nearly 2 billion have Internet connections and close to 5 billion have cellphones. As the applications have developed, it brings services such as banking, monitoring of treatment in infectious diseases, accessing market prices for emerging farmers and a host of other uses within reach of the poor at the bottom of the pyramid.

In the late 1990s, as I walked around our townships and rural areas looking at the thriving phone shops that had been set up by local entrepreneurs, I saw the excitement and realised that we should be investing heavily in supporting this sector. The Universal Services Agency at that time, which was funded by an annual fee from all operators, was bureaucratic and slow to respond to the needs and energy of these new entrepreneurs. But this would have to remain a dream deferred. There was so much to do and I felt emptiness as I was leaving government.

I had made my choice.

37

My relationship with Lucie was passionate and loving, but not easy. I was keenly aware of how much my family missed and needed me during my hectic five years in the service of government.

In dealing with the political challenges my emotional energy was depleted and there was little time for me to spend with Lucie and the children. Sometimes I could snatch a precious few hours alone with Lucie and share with her my 'other life'. This was not unique. Most political activists faced the same dilemma.

I missed the first step that Shanti took, the first word she spoke. I had lost touch with my daughter and she could not even speak English because all her interactions with Lucie were in her mother tongue. I was an absent father. The crunch came when she was three years old and she was asked at her nursery school what her father did. She responded in French: 'Mon papa travaille dans le ciel' ('My father works in the sky') – because all she knew was that I was always going to and from airports.

At the same time, our son Léandre felt that he wanted to complete his high school in Canada and stay with his biological father. Lucie's feelings of guilt about leaving Léandre in Québec combined with her depression were too much for her to handle. It was not very long before she was hospitalised.

It was a shock to me. I asked her mother, Louise, to come to Cape Town and to take care of the kids. As much as I cared about and loved Lucie, politics left so little space for personal challenges.

One day, Lucie said to me during one of our rare pillow talks, 'Albertina was right; I am the second wife. The country is your first wife.'

'No,' I replied. 'That's not true. You are my only wife.' But inside I realised that Albertina was right, even though I did not want to admit it, even to myself. I was just beginning to understand this and its effect on my personal life. How could I marry the two?

I couldn't give up either, even though I knew the toll South Africa was taking on Lucie, with its guns and continuing racism and poverty. She lived in constant fear.

But I shared a synchronicity with Lucie. I could talk to her about my difficult and inchoate feelings. I valued her intuitive insights into who I was and the way she helped me to connect to my deepest suppressed emotions.

But was this reciprocal? No! Lucie was alone in a foreign country with none of the family, cultural and professional networks that could sustain her. She was locked up in the beautiful barracks of Groote Schuur Estate and very much a prisoner of the times.

In a country where women still had to assert their constitutional rights to equality, she was still 'Mrs Jay Naidoo'; a non-person in spite of the fact that in Québec law she had her own name and her own identity. No matter how much I tried to assert that she was Mrs Lucie Pagé, the grinding traditions of culture resisted change.

I was fascinated by this and eventually tracked the fight for a woman's right to maintain her maiden name to Lucy Stone, an American abolitionist and suffragette, vocal against slavery and a champion of women's rights.

Beyond the obvious issue of women's rights, I have always wondered what it must cost the state to have to deal with the administrative complexity of changing passports, identity documents and social insurance that today constitute modern life. It must take an army of bureaucrats, a huge budget and valuable time that could be more usefully deployed to serve the urgent social needs of our people.

At the same time, Lucie's professional life suffered, even though she worked non-stop feeding radio reports to Radio-Canada – the French Canadian Broadcasting Corporation. There was always the unspoken expectation that she should be content with being a Minister's wife.

In banquets or official gatherings I was careful to forewarn the bureaucrats: 'Please ensure that my wife's name card records her name as Lucie Pagé.' On occasion I would see the anger rising in her eyes, particularly when asked, 'So what do you do when your husband is working?' The implication was that she should be content as a Minister's wife to host tea parties and be the gracious hostess.

When she replied that she was a freelance journalist and a writer, their faces reflected surprise and the unasked question, 'But why?'

Sexism was so deeply rooted in our patriarchal society that it would be another struggle for the majority of women to achieve their equal role under the Constitution.

Yet it was so different with Mandela. He would stride up to her, taking her hand, and ask: 'So Lucie, how are you today? How is your mother? How are the little ones? Is your work as a journalist going well? You must come and have tea with me!'

But Lucie never used her personal relationship to seek an interview. Many of her colleagues could not understand why she always followed the proper procedures, waiting months before she would get a response. She would not even ask me to talk to Mandela, whom I met nearly every day. She was vigilant in protecting her professional integrity.

Lucie's professional life was fundamental to her self-esteem and sense of achievement. In time, certain individuals back at Radio-Canada in Montréal tried to impugn that being married to a South African political activist and Minister meant that she could not be independent and therefore should not be employed by the broadcaster as a freelance journalist. That was a stab in the back.

Lucie, who prized her professional independence above everything, was devastated and thankfully her producer, Gilles Le Bigot, fought valiantly to defend her integrity. He even smacked a stack of her reports on the big boss's desk and told him: 'Tell me where she is biased and didn't do a good report!' The boss admitted that he could not fault the reports. But the doubts lingered, and professional jealousy played a big role. If they had seen Lucie work, seen her meticulousness, her impartiality, her strong independent mind, they would have been knocked out by her professionalism as I was.

She was determined to go back to Canada to be with Léandre, who had returned the year before. It had been eight years that she had been away from her family and friends and she needed a bit of time in her own country which she loves dearly. I understood and respected that, and I agreed to go with her. We spent days listlessly packing boxes for Canada.

Out of choice my political life had come to an abrupt end. I knew that had I stayed it would have been difficult fitting into the new political culture, but more importantly I would have lost my family. That was a sacrifice too great for me to make. But still, my mind was unsettled and the mourning had descended.

* * *

The election was over and I had taken a plunge into the unknown. I had promised to join Lucie to go to live in Canada 'for a while' in 1992, and we were now in 1999! Right now though, I had no job and no income and had recently vacated my government house. It was a bleak period. I felt as if I had cut an umbilical cord to my decades of feverish activity pursuing a goal that fed my soul.

I had a discussion with Kgalema Motlanthe, the Secretary General of the ANC. He is a deep and thoughtful intellectual. I had always found him to be a person of integrity in the time that I worked with him in COSATU. He is quietly spoken and respectful and always seeks to unify the divergent strains of the organisation. I raised with him the decision that I had made, the discussions I had had with the future President and how we should manage the communications.

As agreed, a few days after the election, the ANC released a statement:

> *Discussions have been held between Comrade Jay Naidoo and Comrade Thabo Mbeki on his future role and an announcement will be made shortly in this regard. But we are happy to mention that Naidoo will remain involved in the process of transformation. The ANC is grateful for the sacrifices made by Naidoo and is appreciative of the contribution he has made in the struggle for democratic transformation in the country, ranging from his role as a leader in the labour movement; the formulation of the Reconstruction and Development Programme; as Minister for Posts, Telecommunications and Broadcasting; and during the entire process of establishing the new democratic government.*[17]

The statement noted that my decision to leave public life was 'due to personal and family reasons'.

I faced the media. There were many calls and the insinuation was that I had been sidelined. I put up a brave front but was reeling inside as I confronted the reality. I was really on the sidelines. Politics is unforgiving.

The inauguration of the new President was set for 16 June, on my daughter's birthday. Lucie travelled with me for her last report of the decade – her coverage of the 'Mandela decade' as a freelance journalist for Radio-Canada. I was in limbo and greeted people absently. Many were also unsure of what to say to me. I said to Lucie: 'Let's go back home immediately. I really don't feel in the mood to see people any more.' We travelled back to Johannesburg in silence.

She was also nervous. As she recounts in her biography, *Conflict of the Heart*:

I did my last report weighing every word and every comma, because I knew that these seventy seconds were my last. That hurt. After terminating the communications with the Radio-Canada newsroom, I collapsed. I didn't know whether to laugh or to cry; to celebrate or to go into mourning.[18]

Lucie left for Canada with Kami and Shanti. I stayed with Omar. It was comforting to have his company. He was present, non-judgemental, and we sat night after night watching television and eating silently. He had built a new home and in it he had made provision for a flat.

'Jay,' he said, 'you are my soul brother. You will always share this home with me. This is your space and you will always have it.' We hugged as brothers and I gratefully thanked my ancestors for the blessing of this unique friendship.

Nearly two weeks later I was invited to attend the opening of parliament by the newly inaugurated President. In his address he paused and, looking upwards to the gallery, he said:

In the telecommunications sector, there will be further developments with the issuing of new licences. This will have a further positive impact on the expansion and modernisation of our telecommunications infrastructure, the affordability of services to consumers and investment in the economy.

I am happy to inform the Honorable Members that former Minister, Jay Naidoo, will continue to work in this sector to assist in its further development domestically and to promote the African Connection, which is a critical element of the African Renaissance.

For many comrades who had been shocked by my decision, it was a welcome relief that I would remain engaged and they gave this announcement huge applause.

At that point though, I was making plans to go to Canada to see my wife and children. It was a welcome relief when I finally arrived in Gatineau and held them in my arms and felt safe in their love.

Lucie had searched the Internet and had found a house to rent for a year. It belonged to a professional family who was spending a year in France on sabbatical. The house was perfect. It had rooms for the kids and was fully furnished. The school was within walking distance. The area was beautiful, surrounded by forests and lakes that could be easily accessed. There were no burglar bars and no high walls; we rarely locked the doors and the suburban peace where kids rode bicycles in the street was comforting.

We did a bit of travelling around that summer. We hired a car and drove up with the children to northern Québec to watch the whales. I really wanted to do this. I had been asked in an interview when I had resigned what I wanted to do. 'I want to go and watch the whales in Tadoussac in northern Québec' was my answer. I loved the heaving boats that sailed so close to these magnificent creatures looking majestic in their freedom, and I ached for the freedom of simply following my own destiny. It was a healing experience.

Back home in Gatineau, I settled into domestic activities. It was summertime. I enjoyed mowing the lawn in a neighbourhood where there were no walls and all the gardens were open to public view. Without fences, there is grass in between the different houses. It is not a big gap – about three metres. One day I mowed the entire lawn – including that of my neighbour.

We planned to go away again for a couple of weeks to visit Lucie's mother. Louise now lived in Notre-Dame-des-Bois, a village in the Eastern Townships of Québec. She had come back several years earlier from the Arctic Circle and had settled down after retiring from teaching. She had bought a lovely 150-year-old house.

Notre-Dame-des-Bois, at the foot of Mont Mégantic, where there is an astronomical observatory, poised in the darkness of a mountain in a sparsely populated area, is an incredible place. I draw great strength from it when I am there – the rolling fields and forests and water and mountains. I feel invigorated by the energy of that place. It awakens my spiritual senses. I also have a very good relationship with Louise, whom we lovingly call Loulou, so it is always a pleasure going there.

When we returned home, our lawn was overgrown – my neighbour had mowed only his half of the lawn. It was clear that while our property in Québec had no walls made of brick and concrete, it did have invisible walls.

And that was the small trigger that started to get me down.

The incident illustrated the two ways of life. Life in Canada was peaceful and secure and my life in South Africa was unpredictable and often dangerous – it was a challenge even knowing where to park my car.

Johannesburg, the city I love, is a frontier town. It is a cosmopolitan melting cauldron, bursting at its seams, filled with constantly changing energy and the influx of millions of people who bring their cuisine, culture, language, music, art and craft, all searching for that fairy-tale pot of gold. It is truly an African city in the pangs of birth. There are times when the competition for scarce resources breaks out into violent conflict as happened in the early prospecting towns, but Johannesburg also has a generosity, warmth and an excitement that courses through my veins. It is the place that inspires dreams, some of which achieve reality and others that shatter into a thousand fragments.

But in Canada the freedom I found to walk in the streets free of fear – to have my kids walk to school unaccompanied – was priceless. It made me think deeply about our South African situation – our freedom for which so many have sacrificed so much was being strangled in its infancy by a wave of crime.

I could feel the signs of depression approaching. I had no sense of how I was going to earn an income or support my family. I was unemployed for the first time since my teenage years. I could not get a job in Canada. What was I going to do there? Be a gardener? Lucie had started working – writing a book – but no income would come out of that for a long while.

As I wrestled with my contradictory feelings on how to move forward and discussed my options with Lucie, I decided that I had to return to South Africa to see what was possible.

I met with President Mbeki as we had arranged. I recall sitting outside his office at Tuynhuys reflecting on the many times I had walked these corridors. As usual, the staff were frantically scurrying about to put out the interminable fires that flared across the country and the world. This political world is surreal. As long as it feeds on the speed of adrenalin, it takes few prisoners.

I was ushered into the presidential office and Mbeki shook my hand warmly, enquiring about the family. We chatted briefly about a few things and then he said: 'Hey, chief, you know Ivy Matsepe-Casaburri, the new Minister of Communications, feels you are too senior to be the Chair of Telkom.'

'Fine,' I said. Although this had been previously mooted as a possiblility, I had been half-expecting this response. I thanked him for his time and my parting words were: 'That's no problem. I'll find something else to do. I have a few ideas I have been thinking about.'

We shook hands and I took my leave. I would not see him one-on-one again.

Right now I was looking forward to my lunch date with Jayendra.

PART SEVEN

A New Beginning

As founders of the J&J Group, we feel strongly that business must not ignore the many social ills afflicting our country. We were part of a generation that made a difference in our struggle for freedom. Today, poverty and growing inequality persists. Therefore we want to continue to make a difference by using our skills, networks and resources to address these enormous challenges.

— Jayendra Naidoo, introducing the
J&J Group Development Trust in 2007

In the presence of a member of the party, the people are silent, behave like a flock of sheep and publish panegyrics in praise of the government of the leader. But in the street when evening comes, away from the village, in the cafés or by the river, the bitter unceasing anger makes itself heard.

— Franz Fanon, *The Wretched of the Earth*

To rich people in big houses, HIV may seem like a terrible disease to be avoided at all costs. But when you live on the edge every day, an illness that's still five to ten years away means very little. Telling me to protect myself is like water off a duck's back if I don't value my life.

— Tshekiso Molohlanyi (20), Khuma
township, North West

38

Jayendra and I met for lunch. As long-standing friends we saw each other regularly, but this lunch was for a specific purpose – to share ideas on the way forward for both of us.

Jayendra had been the Executive Director of NEDLAC, the socio-economic council seen as the platform for building the social contract between government and various social actors (labour, business and civil society), and ensuring accountability to a shared vision that went beyond traditional narrow corporatism.

By the end of 1998, after a period of acrimonious negotiations, poisoned by disagreements over GEAR and the main labour laws, including the Basic Conditions of Employment Act (BCOEA), NEDLAC had become a battleground on the broader political stage instead of a forum for rigorous public debate.

So, what next for Jayendra? Having mediated the main labour market legislation and successfully averted national strike action, he now faced the resistance of certain Ministers who felt that NEDLAC was an obstacle to government 'leadership'. After four intense and exhausting years he had already decided to step down while NEDLAC was on a relative high.

We agreed to lunch in Craighall Park at one of our favourite restaurants, Osteria Tre Nonni. Jayendra had already decided to join the Board of Worldwide Africa Investment Holdings,[1] a black empowerment company set up by Phuthuma Nhleko, Khaya Ngqula, Wiseman Nkuhlu and Max Maisela.

We were discussing our lives as old friends. And then, as we sat there, the owner of the restaurant came up to us and chuckled: 'Hey you, Jay and Jay, if you ever set up a business I want to buy shares in it.'

We looked at each other. Why hadn't we ever considered that? We had done so many things together. We'd been student activists, community organisers; we'd both gone into government. Why not form a company together?

I had been offered a range of institutional jobs. Jim Wolfensohn, President of the World Bank in Washington, had offered me a post when, in late 1999, I attended a conference hosted by the World Bank dealing with closing the digital divide. I stood up during question time and asked what Wolfensohn thought were the reasons for Africa not being able to mobilise investments to close the digital divide.

It was a very simple question but I wanted him to answer it. Speaking to the hundreds of people in the audience, Wolfensohn responded: 'That question was asked by Jay Naidoo. He is the ex-Minister of Communications from South Africa, and I would encourage him to answer that question by coming to work with us here in the World Bank!'

I had never been invited to a job interview in such a public way.

After the conference Wolfensohn spoke to me: 'Please come and see me tomorrow morning, but in the meantime talk to my Vice President, Nemat Shafik.'[2] Shafik indicated that the job involved the telecommunications programmes of the World Bank and explained the process.

The next morning, I politely declined the job offer and spoke to Jim Wolfensohn about the project I had in mind. As a result of my work on the African Connection policy framework, it was clear to me that building scalability was a key driver, and this meant that countries had to cooperate on the policy and regulatory fronts and harmonise their actions on the use of the spectrum. The World Bank could bridge this gap by working with African countries to achieve this goal and it had the investment capital to drive this strategy and leverage other multilateral agencies and the private sector.

'Absolutely!' Jim said. And he called Peter Woicke, who was the Managing Director and Executive Vice President of the International Finance Corporation.[3] The same day I met with Woicke, who took my suggestions very seriously.

In that meeting there were a number of people from Asia and Africa. They could do big transactions but what I was suggesting did not fit into the rule book and needed small resources. As I listened intently I understood the institutional challenges the World Bank faced. As I had walked into the foyer I noted the advertising branding the Bank as an innovative knowledge bank, but like all big institutions it was still tied to its past and struggled to translate its noble intentions into a practical programme of transformation and delivery. This was a lesson I learnt well in government.

The World Bank attracted the best brains in the world, with its generous pensions and tax-free salary packages – many ended up integrated into a system that put their kids in private schools, gave them access to medical insurance and allowed them a lifestyle that many would not have in their countries of origin.

While most of those I met were genuine activists who wanted to do more, they were trapped in a system in which the mandarins of the Washington Consensus ensured that there was a blind adherence to the new religion. That doctrine, from the 1980s, at the zenith of its global power, preached a mantra of privatise, liberalise and deregulate labour markets to encourage price competitiveness, cut fiscal deficits and decimate the state, but would later criticise these governments' institutional capacities.

The World Bank had imposed structural adjustment policies that restructured the economies of many developing nations and plunged tens of millions of men, women and children into poverty in Africa, Asia and Latin America by demanding huge cutbacks in social expenditure on health, education and agricultural support to the poor. As a result, the institution did not rate highly in the eyes of development activists. But it still has a critical role to play in the international development architecture if it can be harnessed to act as an equal partner with national and regional development partners in the developing world. This is how it worked with the wealthy developed nations in the reconstruction of Europe post-Second World War in the 1950s, and if it applied the lessons learnt there it could prove to be a valuable partner for the developing world now.

Anyway, I felt that it made more sense for me to focus on what I could do in South Africa. Lucie thought I was crazy to turn down an opportunity for a job that paid well and was an hour's flight from Gatineau. She shook her head in dismay but knew that I would not change my mind. And then, as always, she supported me in my decision.

There were other institutional job offers. But the pull of Africa was too strong. I had to return although I had no idea what I would be returning to.

So there we were, Jayendra and I, with choices. Jayendra, who had been offered a job to run a leading state corporation, was one of the key people I relied on to drive negotiations while in COSATU. Built like a rugby fly half, he oozes charm and confidence and his razor-sharp intellect had pierced the hardest armour in negotiations.

What should we do? Should we take a job in some corporation with a comfortable salary every month? Our strengths were in building public institutions capable of delivery; negotiating multifaceted agreements, usually between adversarial protagonists; and making sure they were adhered to.

We decided to embark on our next adventure together and build something memorable from scratch – the J&J Group. The organisation had a brand even before it was born.

* * *

It was scary thinking about setting up a business. Most of our lives had been spent on the other side of the negotiating table. Yet a major challenge of the new democracy was also the deracialisation of the economy. Given the apartheid distortions, particularly in the underdeveloped skills of the black majority five years into our democracy, the economy remained firmly entrenched in white hands.

This was an interesting challenge. Could we build an operating company that employed people rather than facilitated a share transfer that left a few enriched but made little impact on the production processes or business strategies? We decided that we should be very forthright in pursuing commercial success – right now I had to put bread on the table for my family.

We threw ourselves into our new project, starting by sprucing up the garage and outbuilding to Jayendra's home. Our objectives were to do good, have fun and make some money. This was the humble beginning of the J&J dream. We literally drew our vision on a whiteboard. We were going to build globally competitive businesses by identifying niche layers of needs that could be addressed successfully on a commercial basis and in which we would establish value-adding partnerships with companies that had strong technical and financial resources. We workshopped our ideas and agreed that we should focus on the information technology and financial sectors. We deliberately avoided investments in the telecommunications sector to forestall allegations of conflicts of interest. It was a principled decision.

We had a name; we had decided that the shareholding would be evenly split between us. All that was left to do was for us to register the company and to agree on our positions. 'What do you want to be?' Jayendra enquired.

We agreed that we would alternate the position of Chief Executive and Chairperson every year. However, we never rotated. I was the first Chairperson and Jayendra was the first Chief Executive as we entered into negotiations with potential investors. When the first year came to an end we decided to keep the status quo to be consistent.

We went from bank to bank to raise start-up capital. The key question was not what we had done in our lives – the fact that we had built successful unions, supervised major departments and institutions, and negotiated complex multi-billion-rand agreements didn't matter.

'What is your personal credit history? Do you have any prior business experience?' These were the questions asked by the banks' managers. It was clear that the system was not designed to help new entrepreneurs.

We consulted Michael Katz, one of Johannesburg's eminent lawyers, about our business plan. Both Jayendra and I had worked with him in the past and he was hugely helpful. In fact, he was thrilled at the idea, and as he was on Nedbank's Board of Directors he helped to facilitate a discussion with them. On the basis of a commercial decision, Nedbank then agreed to grant us an overdraft facility.

We had strong skills as builders of organisations but lacked the technical expertise as engineers, financial modellers and investors. We worked well with large institutions that had management expertise, products and services and an appetite for moving into new markets. We started with the information technology area which boasted high growth opportunities. We turned to the model that had made India a global IT giant and started discussions with the Tata Group, structuring a joint venture with them to replicate the Indian model in South Africa.

Inside South Africa, prompted by our new relationship with Nedbank, we explored a model that would use their technology platform to create a 'smart card' application to enable workers in the unions to access the credit market by aggregating their spending power in the same way we had achieved in collective bargaining. In this way the price of credit, services and goods would be discounted and workers would escape the clutches of moneylenders with their exorbitant interest rates.

It was a difficult business model but over the years as union organisers we had often encountered these *mashonisas* (loan sharks) outside the factory gates forcing workers to part with their pay cheques, usually under the threat of violence. But the business idea was ahead of its time and we did not have sufficient finances to sustain the challenges of gaining the confidence of the holders of capital and traction within the union movement.

Then the unthinkable happened – the IT bubble burst in 2001. With that came a global collapse of electronic commerce initiatives. Unlike our partners, we did not have deep pockets and the losses dealt us a blow.

Back to the drawing board. Our conclusion was that we should diversify to other sectors.

But with the Nedbank overdraft running low and interest payments compounding, we needed some working capital and we began to look for an institution that would invest in J&J. Our proposition was that we had a set of embryonic business ventures with significant partners and exciting prospects for the future. Most importantly we were a company of the new South Africa.

Eventually, the Old Mutual Group, the largest financial institution in the country, invested in J&J. In a series of interactions we developed a good relationship with Roddy Sparks, the head of the South African business division. His view was simply that Old Mutual already owned a large chunk of the old South African economy and as part of a sound business philosophy the company was keen to invest in the blue-sky value that the J&J Group and both Jayendra and I, as individuals, represented in the future.

With working capital and a second chance, we learnt very quickly how to identify opportunities. We also changed our key team, bringing in people with different commercial and business expertise to ours. We embarked on building a diversified operating company with a strong executive team.

Key individuals were Chris Jardine, an experienced executive at a large state-owned transport company, who was keen to join a small company with the right people where his talents could be applied in practice; and Duarte da Silva, another highly skilled entrepreneur who came to us with a plan to build a new financial services player. Chris became a shareholder in the J&J Group and Duarte became a partner and a shareholder in a new entity we set up, J&J Financial Services.

With Duarte at the helm we approached Credit Suisse, an investment company that was exiting South Africa, and agreed to acquire its operations. Years of tough work followed and in due course we merged our operating company, First South Financial Services, with the investment banking operations of Macquarie, an Australian bank that was a major global player in infrastructure with an interest in growth in Africa.

39

We elected to avoid the big, headline-seeking black empowerment deals and to concentrate on building a team with management capacity and businesses with lots of growth potential. We were also interested in medium-sized companies that had reached a certain critical mass, had good promise but were struggling to scale up. Growing such businesses would create value for all involved. Our strategy was a hands-on, value-adding partnership with a strong brand of entrepreneurialism.

However, we were about to discover a dark side of doing business.

Within our business model, we struck up a range of different business relationships with companies both in South Africa and internationally. We understood that the political terrain placed us at a disadvantage. In spite of the fact that both of us had dedicated the better part of our lives to the freedom struggle, whispers of our 'Indian-ness' began to surface.

At first we thought that these were simply the murmurings of competitive individuals who felt that we could be disqualified by raising the issue, but then a narrow Africanist mood began to rear its head. Never in all my years as a leader in the student, community and union movement had the fact of my Indian ancestry been used against me. But here in the democracy we had all fought so hard for, it became a material issue.

* * *

The Black Economic Empowerment (BEE) model was driven by 'established white capital', which was determined to stay in the driving seat of the economy and had already set up a comfortable co-existence between the old and new elites. The white captains of the establishment sought to build a bridgehead to the newly politically connected and the BEE policy quickly became a means by which black politicians could be recruited on to the boards of these companies to facilitate access to state procurement and public tenders. There would be no radical restructuring of these companies and in many cases the status quo remained unchanged.

As Jayendra reflects:

Some individuals and some black businesses have developed very close and non-transparent relationships with the public sector. We on the other hand were an independent business, growing incrementally, outside of the path of accumulation that involved public assets.[4]

It would take the ANC government eight years (from 1994 to 2002) to develop legislation on BEE to broaden the basis of participation in transactions and establish other indicators such as training, community responsibility and gender equity. But by this time the die had been cast.

Looking at the evolution of the economic transformation, I realised in retrospect that we had made a mistake at COSATU in not pushing more decisively for an economic CODESA in the run-up to 1994. Beginning in the late 1980s, much work had been done in COSATU through the Industrial Strategy Project and Economic Trends Group related to the restructuring necessary to transform the economy, improve competitiveness and drive the creation of jobs.

What had emerged out of this empirical research was that with the exception of certain companies, the economy was generally inefficient, heavily concentrated in conglomerates which in key sectors acted as cartels inflating prices, producing spectacular profits on the basis of huge tariffs and profit margins and colluding to keep new players out. There was recognition that with the reversal of sanctions South Africa would integrate into a competitive world economy. In this process certain sectors would suffer job losses but a restructuring process would support new sectors where job creation would grow.

We had studied economic models in the Scandinavian countries, the Netherlands and Australia in which a social compact between the major social partners including business was determined by political agreements between the social democratic parties and the labour movement. We had examined the

East Asian 'Tigers' (South Korea and Taiwan) to understand the role of the state in promoting development and the 'Southern Cone' economies (Brazil, Argentina, Chile) to realise the dangers of 'macroeconomic populism' and fiscal spending driving out of control. We realised that the engine for this growth path would be the social cohesion and political stability driven by the Alliance of the ANC, COSATU and the SACP.

COSATU fought for but failed to get the National Economic Forum (NEF) to become the forum for negotiation on a focused agenda of the country's future economic policy based on a reconstruction pact. But the general political climate was not conducive, especially after the end of the Cold War when the ideology of free-market disciples was rising aggressively. Also in the ANC ranks we were divided and many felt that economic policy was the prerogative of a new democratic government. Immediately after 1994, the NEF was subsumed into NEDLAC, the newly established statutory body, and COSATU's energies were focused on the negotiations on the new labour policy.

At the same time a number of South African conglomerates saw the opportunity to divest from South Africa. They argued strongly that international listings and shifting their headquarters to Western capitals, especially London, would enable their companies to access capital more cheaply internationally to fuel global growth and to deploy excess capital from South African business. The government, under considerable local and international pressure, buckled but laid down conditions. We would not have the political muscle in many instances to ensure compliance. There was a belief in some quarters of capital that they had the ear of the political elite. Valuable financial and institutional capital left our borders, and unlike other multinational companies who are champions of their countries of origin, the same could not be said of many of the South African companies that left.

I remember sharing a quiet reminder with a senior executive of a large life insurance company. 'The only certainty in politics is the shelf life of politicians. Everyone will tell you they have a black book of telephone numbers of important people. Run the business on the basis of sound partnerships with government to address the pressing developmental challenges and not on lobbying and making business decisions on the basis of relationships with eminent personalities.' My words fell on deaf ears.

BEE, in this format, brought with it the attendant weaknesses of patronage, cronyism and corruption, as factions vied for political positions that would put them in a preferential position to be chosen as the BEE partners in the rash of empowerment transactions that swept South Africa.

While we certainly needed to deracialise the economy and to build up a substantial black middle class, the emphasis shifted to wealth distribution via ownership of shares in existing white corporations and away from the key objectives of building new enterprises, creating jobs, improving competitiveness and tackling social inequity. It did raise the costs of delivering goods and services in South Africa, which many considered to be justified as a BEE premium. While many BEE companies did adopt a social development role there should have been some regulatory obligation on the beneficiaries of state procurement to contribute more specifically to community development.

What also emerged was a significant predatory elite who specialises in fronting and takes commissions and wins tenders to build roads and other infrastructure in mainly poor communities where it consistently fails to deliver anything. At the other end of the spectrum are some multinationals that blatantly use political connections to win state tenders. What we need is a South African and international blacklist that ensures that these companies are prosecuted in both the domestic and international arena. There has to be a consequence for anti-social, unethical business behaviour.

In the long term it did mean that structural unemployment in South Africa remained a stubborn and intractable problem. This would cause a serious social crisis for us in the future as millions of young people increasingly became alienated from an economic system that they legitimately felt excluded them.

* * *

In the midst of all of this, I was approached to fill the position of the Chair of the Development Bank of Southern Africa (DBSA). In 2000, while the Chair of Telkom had originally been earmarked for me, the position of Chairperson of the DBSA was intended for Mac Maharaj. Like me, Mac had stepped out of government as the Minister of Transport in 1999. But he was in a difficult position; for a whole range of reasons, linked to time spent in exile, Mac had a hostile relationship with Mbeki.[5]

I was certainly not part of Mbeki's inner team and never had been, but was somewhat less of a threat than Mac was seen to be. Besides, I had firmly declared my intentions not to return to government or even to continue in the National Executive Committee (NEC) of the ANC after 2002.

Trevor Manuel had floated Mac's name to be the Chairperson of the DBSA, but I was later told that this was allegedly vetoed by the President. At the time,

I was not aware of this, so when Trevor asked me to become Chairperson in 2000, I recollected that the DBSA had been an important platform for our interaction with Derek Keys in the discussions around the NEF and leading up to the negotiated political settlement.

I was animated by the prospect. Ironically, the DBSA had been initiated by P.W. Botha in the 1980s to be a slush fund managed through the Department of Foreign Affairs to finance development projects in the Bantustans to give them some semblance of viability. It had mixed success but had built up a level of project management and policy expertise.

In 1994 we were faced with the choice of closing down the institution or transforming it. In line with our developmental vision the cabinet opted for the latter, giving the DBSA responsibility for municipal infrastructure, which encompassed meeting the basic needs of the poor for water, electricity, roads, sanitation and refuse removal and extending its mandate to the Southern African Development Community (SADC) region. It would work alongside four other development finance institutions dealing with economic infrastructure, housing, small enterprise development and land and agriculture. This development finance system would act proactively as a key catalyst to close the financing gap between what the state and private sector were doing in order to deliver basic infrastructure services in the townships.

I saw the DBSA as having the potential to achieve some of the strategic objectives that the RDP could not – it had the capacity, it had the balance sheet, it could raise its own income. It had a relationship with the most powerful ministry in government, and I had a solid relationship with the Minister of Finance, Trevor Manuel. It was also not a site of political contestation.

The CEO was Ian Goldin. Together with Wiseman Nkuhlu, the Chairperson, Ian had done an excellent job to stabilise the Bank and to institutionalise the changes that we had put in place from 1994 within the development framework of the new democratic government.

Following Ian's move to the World Bank in 2001 and the internal restructuring that took place, I felt that the time had arrived for the DBSA to play a stronger role in addressing the challenges that we were facing. Trevor Manuel and I head-hunted and eventually appointed Mandla Gantsho as the new CEO. He was the dynamic Finance Executive in the DBSA who had been seconded to the International Finance Corporation (IFC) on a one-year programme.

In the process of the transition and stabilising the team around Mandla when he got back, we agreed to re-examine the whole mandate of the DBSA.

The board argued for a 'quantum leap' and a different way of measuring achievement. We were a development bank that had to remain financially sustainable but whose indicators were not measured only in terms of how much money it lent. The Bank had to be evaluated against a range of other development impact criteria, from the creation of jobs and the training of youth and women from local communities to measuring the outcomes of such investment, as well as against criteria such as the number of homes connected to electricity, sanitation and water.

The emphasis was crystallised into a triple role for the DBSA – that of partner, adviser and financier – with our staff imbued with development activism. Our plan for the future required us to interact with local communities, to strengthen technical assistance to local government to do feasibility studies, design projects and acquire capacity to deliver on them.

In our political transition this had been the weakest link. In 1994 we had decided to discard much of the existing structures but neglected the challenge of building institutional capacity. Most mayors and councillors elected lacked experience as many of the most skilled comrades had migrated to positions in the national and provincial levels of government.

We had found that in many local authorities, particularly the rural or district ones, there was very little capacity to build systems – to be able to deliver the required engineering expertise – and too few project managers, financial experts and managers.

I recognised that while South Africa was financially constrained as a developing country, our bigger challenge was transforming money into bricks and mortar in a way that improved the lives of ordinary people.

As the politics settled, another reality hit us. The election periods paralysed service delivery as political factions battled each other to gain a foothold for the positions of councillors and mayors. Often the turnover was so dramatic that new councillors were in the majority and had to first learn the complex matters of managing local authorities. In many cases the first action was to replace the key managers and deploy their 'own' people.

In my mind this was the single biggest factor undermining service delivery. Patronage blurred the lines of separation between our intention to create a professional civil service and an accountable political leadership. Party-political deployment, especially at local government level, had the effect of creating loyalty to the political leader or faction and not to the efficient functioning of our public institutions.

As the ANC has often reiterated, there were people who joined the party not to advance its lofty ideals but to pursue careerist and commercial opportunities through the public tendering process. In a context where the economy is not producing opportunities, this would be a natural evolution anywhere in the world. The poor, young, unemployed, with few opportunities to escape the poverty of the townships and squatter camps, watch the emergence of a politically connected elite and believe that the party and the state are the means of escaping a fate that offers them little hope. Alternatively they turn to crime, believing they have the right to property that those more privileged have. The rise in brutal crime knows no colour. It represents a division between those who have and those who do not have anything to lose.

Back at the DBSA we had to think creatively how we would reinforce the government's programme of delivery. Partnerships with the private sector and a new compact with our shareholder, the national government, were key. Our primary focus was the financing of water, sanitation, electrification and roads in poorer, disadvantaged areas – where the private sector would not go.

But the biggest source of investment in this period was driven by the private sector. We had to focus on the public-private partnerships that would leverage the finance, technology and management expertise into successful implementation of projects. The Maputo Corridor was an example of an economic project with a lot of developmental spin-offs; linking the port of Maputo to the industrial heartland of Gauteng created a corridor that stimulated local economic development all along the way. This was a regional integration project along a profitable transport route and the private sector could invest for a commercial return. A key innovation was enabling the Mozambican government to deliver on its commitments through a blended financial model that was calculated against the whole highway from Johannesburg to Maputo.

Another innovation led to public-private partnerships (PPP) on health. The first example of this in the southern African region was in Lesotho. According to Admassu Tadesse, the head of our international division:

The government had resolved to renew the only tertiary hospital, the 100-year-old Queen Elizabeth in the capital Maseru. The cost of sending patients to Bloemfontein and other South African hospitals was escalating out of control and the Lesotho government put out a Request for Proposals for a PPP, advised by the International Finance Corporation, the private sector division of the World Bank. This was won by one of the largest hospital groups in South Africa in consortium with medical groups and staff at the hospital. The DBSA provided long-term debt funding of close to R800 million; the government of Lesotho put in R400 million as their equity investment and set a fixed tariff for delivery for a menu of specified procedures. The transaction also placed an obligation on the private consortium to contribute R40 million in equity and to rebuild the referral coordination from a primary health care clinic level, thereby ensuring a comprehensive renewal of the health system's delivery value chain.[6]

In the past, the DBSA had been committed to a principle of 'additionality', which meant that it would not compete with the private sector. One of the first things I did as the Chairperson of the DBSA was to scrap that rule. We would not subordinate our business strategy to the whims and veto of the private sector. As in the Lesotho model we would be a catalyst and anchor for the building of public-private partnerships in infrastructure that delivered a return on investment to citizens, government and the private sector, while driving sustainable development.

With the challenge of delivery at the forefront of our development agenda, the board resolved in 2004 to set up a Development Fund to deal with building human capacity and systems in many of our municipalities. I felt that our institution had to be measured, not as a separate entity only, but against the infrastructure problems in our country.

The Minister of Provincial and Local Government, Sydney Mufamadi, who had acted as my deputy in COSATU, had launched Project Consolidate, an attempt to shore up the capacity of local authorities in partnership with the state corporations and the private sector. An analysis had shown that close to 136 municipalities faced serious service-delivery and capacity-building challenges.

It was clear that we were at breaking point. Service-delivery protests in 2004/2005 flared across the country – many based on legitimate grievances from concerned township residents. Many robust discussions with the Minister of Finance, Trevor Manuel, took place, and the question was how to move the DBSA beyond what he termed – unfairly, I believe – an image of 'glorified hedge fund' and project financier to drive sustainable delivery in a decisive way. But it carried a grain of truth, in that our major focus had not been on the poorest of the poor or on servicing the most dysfunctional municipalities. I realised we had to intervene more decisively as 'solution providers' to solve the critical issues of institutional and market failure.

The consequence was the launch of the Siyenze Manje Project in 2006. In this bold and groundbreaking initiative we recruited a number of retired engineers, project managers and financial experts, many of them previously white civil servants, and linked them to young black professionals who came from the local areas, and deployed these teams of people. They were not consultants with short-term perspectives and slick PowerPoint presentations. These were people who sat with local government and helped over a multi-year period to transfer skills, develop systems and ensure that these capital projects were delivered and municipal infrastructure grants at a national level were used.

When the DBSA was criticised for employing retired whites in this initiative my response was: 'I don't think for one moment that poor people in our collapsing and dysfunctional municipalities are concerned with the colour of the skin of those who bring water, electricity, roads and basic services to their homes. In fact, the real black empowerment we need to focus on is the creation of opportunities for the poorest of the poor. I am of the view that many of the individuals clamouring stridently on this issue are from the middle classes claiming their part of the political real estate. In my view the poor are too busy struggling to survive.'

This period also coincided with the launch of a new policy programme, the Accelerated and Shared Growth Initiative for South Africa (AsgiSA), which placed infrastructure at the core of our growth path. This reversed a period of underinvestment in infrastructure under our strict fiscal programme in which bureaucrats cut expenditures in areas not visible to the public, leading to serious challenges in maintenance and extension of infrastructure related to water, sanitation, energy and transport.

When Mandla Gantsho's term as CEO ended and he moved to the African Development Bank (ADB) as Vice President, we brought in Paul Baloyi, a seasoned business executive from Nedbank, whose childhood years were firmly rooted in the poverty and overcrowding of Alexandra township.

I never questioned Paul on his political affiliations. I felt that was irrelevant. He understood the challenge of poverty, as he had grown up in the teeming chaos of Alex and he had fought his way up the corporate ladder through his discipline, self-will and merit. He carried values of humility and understood the new direction that the board had set for the DBSA. Our strategy was to take greater risks, lower the cost of funding to the poorest municipalities and ensure that the Bank was financially sustainable.

My approach to my role as Chairperson was never to micro-manage operations of the Bank. The role of the board was to develop the vision and strategy and performance milestones and to execute our fiduciary responsibilities. I would have a fortnightly meeting with Paul to assess development outcomes based on a 'no surprises' policy. I was determined not to confuse the lines of accountability and set up contesting centres of power. I also realised that it would be impossible for me to understand the detail of the thousands of transactions the Bank did, and although an office had been historically set for the Chairperson of the Bank I rarely used it. My role was providing the aerial cover for the management team and blocking political interference from all sides. Our shareholder compact was what committed us to specific targets with government, and these would be reviewed on a quarterly basis, but I was resolutely opposed to operational decisions being made outside the management and board structures.

Paul's arrival coincided with another very important appointment, that of Gwede Mantashe, who was an activist from my COSATU days. I had great respect for his organising capabilities. He was from a rural background in the former Transkei. As a mineworker in Witbank he rose to be Chairperson of the Highveld Region of COSATU as a strategic leader in turbulent times of heavy state repression. When Kgalema Motlanthe ascended to Secretary General of the ANC, Gwede became the next General Secretary of the National Union of Mineworkers (NUM).

In 2006 he stepped down as General Secretary of the NUM and, following lengthy discussions, agreed that he would take the position as Group Executive for Strategic Operations at the DBSA. 'I want to learn about development finance. I want to bury myself in the work of the Bank, learn the ropes from my peers and spend the next few years here,' he said to me. Gwede's appointment, as head of Strategic Projects, was meant to send a strong signal that the board's vision of 'development activism' was not a mere slogan and that political obstacles at a local government level would be dealt with firmly. Fortunately Paul and Gwede worked well together.

The priority was to define our intervention in addressing delivery challenges, which on a number of occasions meant taking on the bureaucracy in our municipalities. Inefficiency often hid unethical behaviour and corruption and there was always the insecurity of bureaucrats in any organisation, public or private, who feared being exposed as poor leaders. We had to tread very carefully through this minefield of politics. With decades of union and political experience, Gwede could get things done.

The reality I had learnt from the RDP was that development implementation is complex and long term. What is manifested as the lack of basic services, housing, joblessness, violence and increased ill health and disease can be traced back to the failure of education and health systems, and the lack of access to credit or collateral by the poor because many do not have the right to land title or permanent jobs. What we had to understand was what inputs we made in money, technical skills and policy and development facilitation could get the right measureable development outcomes.

Most importantly, the Development Fund became an organisation alongside the Bank with its own board but plugged into its operations arm. In discussions with Minister of Finance Trevor Manuel and the Treasury team, we embarked on an ambitious programme to scale up the Development Fund's operations and deploy teams working within those municipalities that lacked capacity. Soon there were over 500 professionals working inside of government on delivering thousands of projects; supporting city and town managers in addressing systemic weaknesses in management, billing systems, town planning and training; and unlocking billions of rand sitting in the municipal infrastructure grants at a national level.

In the middle of this fundamental transformation exercise, Gwede was nominated for the position of Secretary General of the ANC in the furious internal battles for the election of national office bearers of the ANC at its forthcoming congress in Polokwane in December 2007.

We had several discussions about this and the implications for the DBSA. Gwede, reluctant at first, eventually agreed to stand for office – he was a key candidate for the Alliance partners. He was elected Secretary General of the ANC, alongside President Zuma.

By 2008 our policy, developmental planning and regulatory capacity had grown, our international business formed a separate division and our activities in the region exploded with a focus on driving regional integration.

As I retire as Chairperson of the DBSA, after nearly ten years, it is with great memories, and the knowledge that the institution has grown from humble beginnings (R200 million from government's initial commitment of R5 billion callable capital) to become a close to R45 billion development finance institution that thrives on innovation and has pushed the envelope beyond that of traditional development banks. It is an organisation we can all be proud of.

40

In 2002 my son, Kami, returned to South Africa to live with me. Lucie had spent a year in South Africa after living three years in Québec but decided to go back for two years to see Léandre through college, and Shanti chose to stay with her. We had a family on two continents, seeing each other for about ten days every two months.

Kami's decision at the age of ten to come to live with me was a seminal one. My life was turned upside down. I had to adjust to having someone to take care of: prepare breakfasts, buy clothes and deliver to school on time. I had been living at Omar's for a few years and I did not even have to think about shopping for groceries.

Now I had moved into Omar's old house and the buck stopped with me. I hired a housekeeper, Rosie Tsebe, who had worked for a close friend of mine, Rick Menell, for many years. Rosie was able to cook and drive and had a great magnetic presence with a booming voice and resounding laugh. She was to become the anchor in the home.

Kami quickly settled into his routine. He is very focused on what he wants to do with his life and is quickly irritated by inane conversation. I made my first mistake soon after Lucie and Shanti had returned to Canada.

Arriving home early one Friday afternoon, I proudly exclaimed, 'Hey Kami, I have cancelled my meetings for the day. Let's go out to tenpin bowling, watch a movie and catch dinner somewhere.' He looked at me and said quietly: 'Papa, next time you want to make arrangements for us talk to me. I am busy now watching my favourite TV programmes and still have to finish my homework.'

It was an important lesson for me to ponder as I sheepishly trailed to my room and turned on the television. Kids today are different. They have more things to do and more information available than we could ever imagine. Technology and the Internet have brought the world within their grasp. I reflected on how each generation has progressed materially.

My father had never flown on an aeroplane; I had only done so in my mid-twenties and here my children were global citizens crossing the continents when they were a few weeks old. I have often imagined a conversation with my father: 'Dad, I am married to a French-speaking woman from Québec, my kids speak French as their mother tongue and were a few weeks old when they were doing transatlantic flights. But they move in and out of cultures, religions and languages seamlessly. They are global citizens.'

My father had never left the former province of Natal and he would have struggled with the concept of an intercontinental relationship with a foreigner with Irish, French and Mohawk Indian blood. But I am sure that he would have embraced Lucie and my kids. He had, in fact, introduced me to the wider world through his insistence on listening to the BBC.

Kami and I spent two years living alone at this end of the planet although we would meet up with Lucie, Shanti and Léandre as often as we could. The two sacred breaks were summer vacation in Québec during July and August and then over Christmas and the New Year. This arrangement came with a heavy emotional burden, especially for Lucie.

It was impossible for me to leave my work in South Africa and relocate to Québec even for a short while. I wasn't ready to become a full-time gardener just yet. Lucie had become a successful writer criss-crossing Québec selling thousands of books on her experiences in Africa. Halls and libraries were always full to capacity when she gave a presentation. She achieved best-seller status with her first book *Mon Afrique*, a personal biography of her decade in Africa in the 1990s covering the Mandela era, from his liberation to the end of his public life.

Lucie is passionate about painting a positive picture of South Africa in Québec. At the same time, she is forthright on the issues that she believes in, such as crime, corruption and the rights of women. I marvel at the way in which ordinary people embrace her positive energy.

We looked forward to being reunited. We had lived apart for five of the past six years and wanted to re-nurture our relationship. We realised that there would be a period of readjustment. We had lived separate lives and were used to the long absences. But we still loved each other.

In December 2004 I was approaching 50, with all the attendant angst of a mid-life crisis. Life seemed suddenly overwhelming. I yearned for the intimacy of marriage but our lives felt so different. My life was in Africa and Lucie had her roots in Québec. It was a bridge too far to cross in our geographic dislocation. It was essentially a make or break point for us.

On the first night of her return, we had a heart-rending, furious row. It was raw emotion. As the days wore on our anger subsided, but the hurt remained. We decided that we should go to joint counselling. Whether we stayed together or separated we would still need professional help because of the impact it would have on our children.

As we celebrated my birthday with our friends from Canada and South Africa I realised that my life would be empty without Lucie and the kids. We loved each other deeply and it would be soul-destroying to break up now. We put our issues aside to focus on the positive things that had united us. We resolved to work tirelessly to rebuild our relationship. Lucie would return in summer when the school term ended in Canada. The months passed by. We spoke often and emailed each other and communicated online every day. We stayed in touch with each other – feeling the joy and the sadness, the tears of happiness and sorrow, the travails of each day.

In 2005 I went to Canada and helped Léandre to pack up and settle him in a flat that he was sharing with some friends. I have a fantastic relationship with Léandre. To me he is my son and he treats me as his second father. He has a really easy approach to life and I often think he takes more after me than his mother. As we carried his bed out we were both excited by the idea of him having his own place. He was now eighteen and starting university.

It was natural that he would want to break free. We laughed at my own experiences of moving out of my parents' house and then we saw Lucie standing on the balcony bawling her eyes out.

In surprise we turned to her. 'Maman! Why are you crying?' we both exclaimed.

She responded angrily: 'You men. You will never understand what goes through a mother's heart. He is my son and now he is leaving home with his bed. He won't be sleeping under my roof any more.' We got the message.

In July 2005 we spent a month in a little run down chalet on the shore of Lac Mégantic, in the Eastern Townships of Québec, a small town where Lucie's mother had been born. It was idyllic. The kids loved the freedom of riding their bikes to town to fetch food or visit friends. We weren't concerned as long as they wore their helmets. The stress of worrying about crime had vanished and removed a cloud of despair I felt about our life in Johannesburg. I felt mentally exhausted over the safety of my kids. I had to be the chauffeur and the security guard, making sure they had their cellphones on them, immediately imagining the worst if they did not respond to our calls. Criminals were assassinating the freedom we had fought so hard for.

Here in Québec, the province of a million lakes, we celebrated that freedom we most desperately sought – the right to a safe environment. I marvelled at how Canada, with almost the same natural resources as South Africa, had built a dominant middle class. Amongst our friends there, many of them professionals, there was always comfort but not excessive luxury. In fact, in Montréal it was rare to see a large BMW or Mercedes-Benz. Lucie and her Canadian friends who visit us in South Africa are always surprised to see so many luxury vehicles on South African roads and are struck by the stark inequalities.

Lucie was terrified by crime and violence. It weighed heavily on her, aggravating the anxiety and depression she already suffered from. Although she loved South Africa I recognised the tranquillity of her life in Québec. She longed for her family and friends and wanted the kids to experience their other culture.

Every day we discussed how to make the adjustment. But she was committed in coming to spend a good five years in South Africa again. Before leaving, she said: 'You know that Trempette is coming with us.' Trempette was her cat, a mass of black fur that she had rescued from a farm near Gilles Le Bigot's village. 'Well,' I said, 'I can buy you a black cat when we get to Johannesburg.' That was a mistake I regretted as soon as the words sprang from my mouth. Naturally, Trempette made the trip to Johannesburg.

I realised subsequently how valuable cats are to people's psychological states and grew to love Trempette as an animal with a definitive personality. In South Africa I had never grown up with cats. It was always dogs who lived outside and ate the scraps from our table. Here I was transporting across the world a cat that not only ate special food and had tasty desserts but which also slept in our bed.

These were the details of our life in Québec, and as we delved into each one we got to know each other even more intimately. It was not about the passion we shared for the freedoms we both believed in. It was the daily conversations about cuisine and combining our cultures and discovering new things about each other. We swam and built campfires in the evenings, played cards and badminton with the kids. It was simple living and it built a solid foundation for our trip back to South Africa.

41

In the meantime the political scenario in South Africa was becoming increasingly convoluted. One of the biggest blots on our history has to be our handling of the HIV/AIDS epidemic. In the immediate aftermath of my leaving government in 1999 a raging debate had flared on the government's policy. It forced Mandela into making a public statement asking government to unite in the face of a 'common enemy'. Government leaders were incensed and it was soon afterwards that the apparatchiks were howling for Mandela's blood.

I was still on the ANC NEC, which remained my only link to the politics of the country. Etched in my mind is that eventful ANC meeting of the NEC which Madiba, now the former President, had attended in March 2002. He spoke painfully on the issue of HIV/AIDS:

> I have phoned my President [Mbeki] several times and left messages. I have been told by the cabinet secretary and staff that the President would return my calls. They never came. I am able to speak to Presidents across the world but I am unable to speak to my President.

Madiba went on to outline his concerns about the strategy to combat HIV/AIDS and appealed for a common front. He had recently met with the AIDS activist Zackie Achmat, seriously ill after refusing to take antiretrovirals (ARVs) in order to push for the demand that government provide treatment to all South Africans suffering from AIDS. He touched Madiba profoundly when he said to him: 'How often were you offered freedom and you refused it?'

While Madiba spoke I could see the faces of comrades caught in the dilemma of the appeals of our founding father and the contrarian position of our President. My heart ached as I saw Mbeki's half-closed eyes, head and chin raised, staring into space. Madiba finished his address, moved slowly to his seat and sat upright. This was a wounded man. He had been deeply hurt.

And then the cacophony of dissident voices tore into the former President. I could not believe that the attacks could be that crude, basically attacking Madiba for undermining ANC President Mbeki. It was a sad day and I resolved that at the next ANC national conference in Stellenbosch, in December 2002, I would step down from the NEC. I was exhausted by the narrow politics of the time.

What troubled me even more were the reactions of some comrades I had worked closely with in the past in grassroots movements. I was told by one, 'Jay, you do not understand. This is a conspiracy of the pharmaceutical industry which wants to force us to spend money on ARVs so that they can make profits.' I was shocked.

*   *   *

For years I have been involved in the loveLife Trust, an NGO committed to fighting the HIV/AIDS epidemic – and trying to do so in a less-than-optimal policy and funding environment. I had been approached in 2004 by the Henry Kaiser Foundation, a United States philanthropic organisation that had invested heavily in the fight against HIV. I recommended that it contact Cheryl Carolus, a politically savvy, committed activist whom I had worked with in the 1980s when she was a leader of the UDF, and who later became the High Commissioner in London. She was a skilled communicator with an understanding of building organisations.

Given all my own commitments, I agreed to serve as Cheryl's deputy. Although I was not hugely impressed with loveLife's media messages, I felt compelled to do something about a pandemic that was killing our people and a misguided government that was aggravating the situation.

HIV was first flagged in the mid-1980s as a significant risk in the unions and the progressive health sector.[7] The migrant worker system had eroded the social and family fabric in the southern African region. Dormitory, single-sex hostels bred an environment in which social disintegration was certain. Unregulated prostitution festered and the state and the bosses turned a blind eye to the situation.

The NUM raised this issue in COSATU, which began to look at long-term solutions, including creating family housing and decriminalising prostitution. At the time of Mandela's release, our incidence of HIV/AIDS was the same as that of other emerging countries, such as Brazil. The higher-risk segments of the population were in the mines; and the long-distance drivers plying the transport corridors in southern Africa combined the different strains of HIV and increased its potency.

In 1991, a formal conference convened by the ANC Health Department and hosted in Maputo alerted us to the significant risk we faced in relation to the spread of HIV/AIDS. Emerging out of that conference was a commitment to mobilise action and to set up the National Aids Coordinating Committee of South Africa (NACOSA), headed by Dr Nkosazana Dlamini-Zuma. Clearly the dying apartheid regime had little interest in the issue, and the ANC and the internal democratic forces had to take a leading role.

Once in power, the new Minister of Health, Nkosazana Dlamini-Zuma, wasted little time in mobilising her department. Her first campaign was to drive an anti-smoking campaign. Faced with a cabinet in which two Deputy Presidents were smokers, as were half the other members, it was an uphill battle. Although I supported the campaign I felt that this was not a fight easily won. But she persisted.

The campaign was far-reaching – not only banning the link between smoking and advertising and sport, but also extending the ban to all public places. And the first place to start was the cabinet room. Soon all smokers were pushed out of the common room where we had our teas to outside the building. It was amazing to see the group of powerful men huddled in the freezing cold of winter, guiltily puffing away. It was to become our most successful public campaign on health.

We all had high hopes for the battle against the scourge of HIV/AIDS. The infection was beginning its deadly embrace across all communities and we had to act strongly if we were to contain it. However, the Department of Health commissioned a controversial play, *Sarafina*, dramatising the AIDS challenge, and government became embroiled in a communications nightmare that left many of our activists outraged at the wasted expenditure. The Director General of Health, Dr Olive Shisana, was one of the casualties of the saga.

Following *Sarafina*, we embarked on a slippery downhill slide when a group of technical experts led by Olga Visser, a technician at the H.F. Verwoerd

Hospital, was brought into cabinet to parade a miracle cure called Virodene, which eventually turned out to be toxic. The stage was set for a clash with the medical and scientific professions.

At the AIDS Conference in Durban in 2000, with the epidemic sweeping South Africa and over 4 million people infected, the more than 10 000 delegates from around the world held their breath hoping that what had been speculated – that the President of South Africa had questionable views on HIV – was not true. Mbeki proceeded to say: 'It seems to me that we could not blame everything on a single virus.' He also questioned the medical treatment asking: 'Does HIV cause AIDS? Is AZT an effective treatment in preventing mother-to-child transmission of HIV?' There was horror in the audience and this quickly spilled out into society.

By contrast, at the close of the same conference, former President Mandela said:

> *AIDS is clearly a disaster, effectively wiping out the development gains of the past decades and sabotaging the future.*
>
> *Now . . . the poor who on our continent will again carry a disproportionate burden of this scourge – would, if anyone cared to ask their opinions, wish that the dispute about the primacy of politics or science be put on the back burner and that we proceed to address the needs and concerns of those suffering and dying.*[8]

The following year, Archbishop Desmond Tutu, another leader of the struggle, added his voice with the same urgency: 'It is important that we recognise that we are facing a major crisis and that we want to invest as many resources as we did when we fought against apartheid. This is not a state of emergency but it is a national emergency.'[9]

I welcomed these statements by our two most respected national icons but they were drowned out by actions such as Mbeki's appointment of an AIDS Council – packed with well-known AIDS denialists. This was a declaration of war on the best globally known ANC activists in the medical field, such as Professor Jerry Coovadia, Professor Salim Karim, Professor Malegapuru Makgoba and countless others.

Frustrated with the arrogance of government, the people turned to the one weapon they knew – mass action. Formed in 1997, the Treatment Action

Campaign (TAC) has fought a ferocious battle to defend the rights of those living with HIV. Over the years, our feisty ANC activists, led by Zackie Achmat as well as the eminent judge Edward Cameron, defied the government and resorted to building a mass-based formation.

The social crisis linked to HIV/AIDS is huge and incalculable. My first encounter with Minister of Health Manto Tshabalala-Msimang was with David Harrison, the CEO of loveLife in 2005. We sat and twiddled our thumbs for over two hours waiting for her, only to be informed by a departing Deputy Minister Nozizwe Madlala-Routledge that the delay was a consequence of an urgent meeting between the provincial members of the executive council (MECs) and the Minister with Dr David Resnick, one of the denialists appointed by Mbeki on to his international advisory group. When she did finish we had the opportunity to have a very unsatisfactory meeting while she had lunch. I was livid.

Sometime later, our next interaction, at the launch of the loveLife offices in June 2005, was equally bizarre. In her speech Tshabalala-Msimang said:

> [T]here is no cure for HIV, there is nothing that kills the virus at the moment. I think all that we can do is to boost the immune system, to ensure that the immune system is able to defend us against the virus, so that we can live with the virus as we live with other bacteria in our body and we do not die because they are in our body.
>
> And I am hoping that loveLife will seriously join us in this campaign of Vuka South Africa, Move for Health. Other elements of the lifestyle campaign are of course as you know the promotion of good nutrition, I have spoken about this already. May I add, don't forget garlic, don't forget lemon, don't forget olive oil, don't forget beetroot, don't forget ama dumbe, don't forget spinach, these are very important components. Yes they are indeed and if you have the opportunity to get hold of African potato, please use it too, it helps.[10]

We were astounded. The epidemic was killing our people and here was the national Minister of Health advocating not for complementarities of good nutrition but a bizarre alternative to ARVs. Sometime later, on a visit to family in 2007, the disheartening impacts of HIV were brought home on a deeply personal level. I was moved to write about it as a guest columnist:

A recent visit to my family in Durban once again brought home to me the harsh reality of the HIV/AIDS pandemic.

A six-year-old is being cared for by the family and the housekeeper, as his mum died of AIDS and he is HIV-positive.

My sister's retired housekeeper, now in her 60s, is taking care of four orphan grandchildren because both their parents died of AIDS. Being confronted by the effects of HIV/AIDS only in an extended family context is a comfort few of us have.

With about 800 people dying daily, imagine the ripple effect it has on society.

Forget the statistics. It is just not possible to quantify in concrete terms what impact the constant grief and trauma are having on our society. But that does not mean that we should deny its existence or pretend that we can continue being vibrant and productive against such odds.[11]

My children were traumatised by the fact that this little child would probably not live beyond his teenage years. They could not understand my explanations of how we had condemned this child to such a life. Why, given my fights in the past for freedom, they asked, was I not fighting for young kids like him?

I felt indicted by my silence about the abuse that our people were going through in their country of birth.

In an interview in New York in 2003, while attending the UN General Assembly, Thabo Mbeki said: 'Personally, I don't know anybody who has died of AIDS.' And when asked whether he knew anyone with HIV, he added quietly: 'I really, honestly, don't.'[12] This was said when all medical and scientific evidence pointed to an epidemic that affected over 4 million South Africans at that time and made our country the epicentre of the global pandemic, and when it was widely circulated that one of Mbeki's communications officers had died of an AIDS-related illness.

Not only had we become the epicentre of HIV but this coincided with a TB epidemic, and the rising social cost of malnutrition meant that these three epidemics, according to our respected Academy of Science of South Africa, interacted with people's immune systems in various ways, and with fatal consequences.[13]

Within ten years, starting from a baseline of infection equivalent to our peers in countries like Brazil, our statistics had rocketed. By 2006, scientific estimates were that close to 5 million people had been infected; that's one in every six adults. Life expectancy had fallen to 49, a drop of thirteen years as a result of the HIV epidemic; and infectious and parasitic diseases had become the leading underlying cause of death in South Africa.[14]

Mortality increased at an alarming rate, especially amongst mothers and children. We rank amongst the pariahs of the world with our failures in health delivery leading to over 260 mothers and children under five dying each day due to causes that are largely preventable: complications during pregnancy; new born and childhood illnesses; HIV/AIDS; and malnutrition.[15]

The health system, faced with this overwhelming burden, could scarcely cope, and according to experts close to 80 per cent of new cases being treated were related to HIV/AIDS. Management systems began to collapse and not even the heroic efforts of individual health practitioners and activists were sufficient to deal with the deluge. Our grand Millennium Development Goals (MDGs) were flung out of the window and our statistics were more in line with a country in the throes of a brutal civil war. Something had to change. Political anger was mounting in the country.

42

Kofi Annan, as the Secretary General of the United Nations addressing a high-level meeting of African heads of state and key policy makers to discuss innovative approaches to meeting the millennium development goals (MDGs) in Ethiopia, said: 'Hunger is a complex crisis. To solve it we must address the interconnected challenges of agriculture, health care, adverse and unfair market conditions, weak infrastructure and environmental degradation.'[16]

In 2002, the Global Alliance for Improved Nutrition (GAIN) was launched at the UN General Assembly Special Session on Children, as a public-private partnership to tackle the malnutrition facing more than 2 billion people in the world, around a third of humanity.

The midwife of GAIN was Sally Stansfield, a senior officer at the Gates Foundation. Responding to an email from Melinda and Bill Gates for new initiatives that had the potential to improve health and save lives, she had sent in a concept note that there was conclusive evidence that undernutrition, particularly in micro-nutrients, was a significant cause of infant mortality, lack of cognitive development and lower productivity in countries concerned. A few hours later came a response from Bill Gates affirming the need for some action on this front in line with the Foundation's mandate of saving lives and its philosophy that 'Every life has equal value'.

This quickly morphed into the launch of GAIN in 2002, as it conformed to the Foundation's emphasis on public health and its impact on mothers and children and proposed a public-private partnership to address the crisis. The key work of GAIN on mass fortification, the first area of focus for the alliance, was based on the outstanding programme spearheaded by the United Nations Children's Fund (UNICEF) on salt iodisation, which reached 70 per cent of the world's population and contributed to a tremendous reduction in and prevention of goitre and brain damage.

The organisation was structured so that it was to have the World Bank acting as its banker and fiscal agent, the United Nations Development Programme (UNDP) its host administrator and the United Nations Office for Project Services (UNOPS) the outsourced human resources and services department. GAIN was intended to be flexible and with a more rapid multilateral response than that of the intergovernmental bureaucracy of the United Nations system, which had a particular antipathy to working with the private sector.

In 2003 I was approached by then Deputy Executive Director of UNICEF, Kul Gautem, to consider taking up the Chair of GAIN. I was initially hesitant, knowing through my involvement in the United Nations Advisory Committee on Information Communications Technology in 2000, convened by Annan's office, how the out-of-the-box ideas that we had synthesised were drowned in the weighty debates and endless resolutions at the United Nations General Assembly.

However, the scale of the challenges on a global level in the twenty-first century was formidable and required a new approach to the cumbersome political diplomacy that was the basis of the United Nations formation after the Second World War. Kofi Annan was keen to harness the partnership with civil society and the private sector towards a shared vision of sustainable human development.

I watched how Annan's humanist commitment to sustainable human development was crushed by the deadweight of the political bureaucracies. I had shared his anguish at the missed opportunities to build a better world and the unrelenting surge to deal with conflicts through military and economic aggression. The world needed global governance and the United Nations was the only credible system that fulfilled the various criteria for this, albeit insufficiently.

Kul Gautem was a native of Nepal; calm and measured, he made an appeal to me: 'We need someone like you from the developing world, especially Africa, who has the experience of being in civil society, government and business.' After some consideration and discussion I agreed that my name be put forward to the enabling group of GAIN.

* * *

Science had broken the development barrier and proved that nutrition forms the basis for and is the cornerstone of human survival and the quality of health in overall development. In sub-Saharan Africa alone, the statistic was that 148 of every 1 000 children would die before they reached the age of 5 compared to 6 of every 1 000 children in industrialised countries, and 38 per cent of these children in Africa would be stunted.[17] Maternal and child undernutrition 'contributes to 3.5 million deaths each year and is responsible for about 11 per cent of the global disease burden'.[18] There was an urgent need to respond to this international crisis.

Given the closure of the development space in South Africa and the increasing arrogance of the administration, I was excited by the challenge of a global campaign against 'Hunger and Malnutrition'. My work in GAIN brought me into direct contact and discussion with the global health community. Simultaneously I was fascinated by the way in which President Lula was unfolding his campaign on hunger in Brazil, arguing that the state bureaucracy should justify all its investment plans in relation to the priority of putting food on the table three times a day for every family. When he became President in 2002 Lula did not hesitate to cut defence and other fruitless expenditure in order to bolster the fight against poverty.

Soon after, he expanded the poverty grant – Bolsa Família – which today

> *reaches 12 million families, more than 46 million people, a major portion of the country's low-income population. The model emerged in Brazil more than a decade ago and has been refined since then. Poor families with children receive an average of R$70.00 (about US$35) in direct transfers. In return, they commit to keeping their children in school and taking them for regular health checks. And so Bolsa Família has two important results: helping to reduce current poverty, and getting families to invest in their children, thus breaking the cycle of intergenerational transmission and reducing future poverty.*[19]

This must rank as one of the biggest fiscal stimulus packages for the poor in the world.

President Lula then instituted a results-based management system set up in the President's office accountable to him to monitor progress and issue public reports on the Ministers and departments of government. I had met him on a few occasions since leaving government and I was infected with his passion and enthusiasm.

In my position as Chair of GAIN I was keen to look at the global architecture for addressing the challenge of malnutrition. Development had to be taken into the communities and the streets and out of the hands of professional diplomats, career bureaucrats and the thriving development industry and poverty elite who regularly parachute into (especially) Africa armed with a missionary zeal to save us from ourselves. Development is not linear and solutions are not just solved like a technical problem on a production line. In the local ecosystem with many conflicting interests we needed to build genuine ownership and a broad coalition that would lead to a balance of forces necessary to bring the required changes to social behaviour. On the global level it was crucial that we build a movement that was driven by and spoke to the needs of ordinary people and which is owned by local communities.

At my first meeting of the GAIN board in Geneva I was shocked by the fact that the board was run by a dozen outside consultants and that many, especially from the multilateral agencies, saw GAIN as both a partner and a competitor. In the run-up to the launch of GAIN many had expressed the view that additional resources should be channelled through them rather than a new organisation being established. As I listened to the debates I was taken aback at how little independent oversight the board itself actually had over strategy and programmes of the organisation.

After my first meeting the Executive Director suggested that I use a facilitator to help me chair the next GAIN board. I felt compelled to rectify the perception that I was just another compliant African activist dependent on the largesse of some Northern NGO.

I responded: 'Thank you, Mr Director, but given my history, I do think I have sufficient experience to chair a meeting. In fact, in the future I want to be consulted on the agenda and no document will be submitted to the board until I have perused it. Moreover, I do not want to see any more consultants in our board meetings unless I have agreed to their presence.'

That certainly did not endear me to a bureaucracy that felt that with their United Nations contracts, their primary loyalty lay with the institutions from which they had come. It was not too long before the relations between a board that insisted on delivery targets as a benchmark and a management team whose backgrounds were primarily in the public sector, and unused to the system of outcome-driven performance, came to a head.

The bulk of the mass fortification projects were bogged down; there was no clear picture of our finances and no clear procedures for managing GAIN's expenses and the administrative costs that had burgeoned with the number of consultants and service providers we had contracted.

I felt dragged into another meaningless international bureaucracy with a high degree of arrogance from management and I had an extensive discussion with Sally Stansfield and Katherine Kreis, two dynamic and passionate colleagues from the Gates Foundation, in which I offered to resign. I spoke openly about my frustrations at enforcing my fiduciary responsibility and not being someone's 'rubber stamp'. In the discussion we converged in our analysis and worked together on a turnaround strategy.

We had to ensure greater transparency in the management of the finances, shift to a results-based performance management framework that would focus on outcomes, and strengthen the delivery capacity. Clearly we needed a succession plan. Sally and I discussed this with the Executive Director and he agreed to step down at the 2004 board meeting in Johannesburg. However, he refuted this agreement and an explosive meeting resulted in a split board with the majority agreeing to suspend the Executive Director.

An interim acting Executive Director, Marc van Ameringen, who I had worked with as part of the Canadian International Development Research Centre (IDRC) in the early 1990s, was brought in with a brief to present a comprehensive report on the state of health of GAIN, including a detailed financial audit, in January 2005, to an extraordinary board meeting. This meeting demonstrated the terminal crisis we faced. A settlement was reached and the Executive Director left. The board agreed to a radical plan to restructure the organisation into a Swiss foundation with its own rules and procedures and accountable to its board.

Existing staffers were asked to reapply for the new positions in GAIN. The board reasserted its authority over the staff and repatriated the funds from the World Bank to its own control. Contracts with all country project advisers were terminated, a Programme of Work and Budget to be approved annually was introduced and stringent administrative and financial systems were implemented. Importantly, new programme streams included Building Partnerships and Performance Monitoring and Evaluation.

In a short period of time, Marc van Ameringen was confirmed in his appointment and an entirely new, motivated team was put into place. I had worked closely with Marc during our political transition when he ran the IDRC office in Johannesburg. He had worked tirelessly with the mass organisations in this transition period and used the IDRC's convening power to provide valuable input and outreach to the global intellectual resources we wanted to tap into. It was a marked difference to the arrogance we experienced in other global institutions that flooded South Africa at the time with a mission to shape our thinking and political and economic choices.

By 2005 I felt confident that GAIN was on track to tackle its target of reaching a billion people. The large-scale fortification programmes began to roll out. New innovative partnerships were actively pursued to harness the technological, management and research capacity of the private sector into meeting the needs of those at the base of the pyramid.

In the last five years, the team, led by Marc van Ameringen, has cleaned out the past legacy and has firmly driven our delivery into reaching our objectives. Our programmes in South Africa and China have reached a stage where we are able to see the practical impact in the reduction of micro-nutrient deficiencies with over 40 per cent reduction of folic acid deficiencies in pregnancy, and a similar result in China in the reduction of the prevalence of anaemia in women and children. These programmes are already reaching over 273 million people, and with the existing programmes in 26 countries reaching fruition over the next few years, the 1 billion milestone should be reached.

As the mass fortification rolled out, a new area of work opened up in terms of infant and young child nutrition. The *Lancet* report released in 2006 reported at least 3.5 million deaths of children that could be attributed to maternal and child undernutrition. The stake was planted in the ground. Should we take up this challenge?

It was controversial, given the role that some multinationals had played in the breastfeeding debacle – where women in developing countries had been discouraged from breastfeeding in favour of formula in bottles. This had influenced declines in breastfeeding rates and had dreadful consequences in poor countries where the water that was used for the milk formula was often contaminated. Eventually it led to the adoption of the Code on the Marketing of Breastmilk Substitutes by the World Health Organization (WHO) World Assembly. Today UNICEF estimates that a non-breastfed child living in disease-ridden and unhygienic conditions is between 6 and 25 times more likely to die of diarrhoea, and 4 times more likely to die of pneumonia, than a breastfed child.[20]

While it was indeed correct to reinforce a public campaign that endorsed six months of exclusive breastfeeding, we need to address the socio-economic and cultural reasons and the issue of women's rights that are obstacles to decreasing these rates. At the same time we need complementary foods or weaning foods produced by the private sector or through public-private partnerships that cater for children from 6 to 24 months and for working mothers and those infected with HIV, where there is a danger of mother-to-child transmission of the virus, and that are affordable and accessible. Undernutrition in those crucial months, from conception to two years, if not addressed, would have a permanent negative impact, leading to death, stunting, reduced cognitive development, anaemia and other micro-nutrient deficiencies.

What is clear to me now is that global hunger and malnutrition are key indicators of the state of health in the world. By all accounts, the situation is deteriorating in the current global recession and the number of hungry in the world has reached over 1 billion people. The bulk of the poor we are targeting live in Africa south of the Sahara and in the Indian subcontinent.

The GAIN experience was important in shaping my thinking on global solutions for the majority of the 2 billion people we are trying to target, who live at the bottom of the economic pyramid, and can mainly be reached through leveraging market channels. We have built a global alliance with over 600 companies in the world, ranging from global multinationals to smaller national companies in the developing world. It is key that we utilise the market-based models of these companies with their tremendous organisational, logistical and distribution capability and their technological and management expertise. We know that by incentivising the private sector and constructing public-private partnerships that include all key stakeholders, we can sustainably deliver healthier, nutritious and affordable foods to the bottom of the pyramid.

An example was the support we gave to a partnership between a French multinational working with a non-profit social enterprise, the Grameen Bank in Bangladesh.[21] In this case Professor Mohammad Yunus had raised the possibility with Franck Riboud, the Chief Executive of Danone (who had served on the board of GAIN), of setting up a social enterprise that took the milk from dairy cooperatives, mainly run by women and which were financed by the Grameen Bank, and produced a fortified yoghurt product that could be sold in the schools by village women at an affordable price.

It was on a trip to visit the factory, a drive of more than a day from Bangladesh by bus, that I came face to face with the intractable problems of development. Bangladesh is probably one of the poorest countries in the world.

In the monsoon season heavy damage is done to the country's infrastructure and the land is inundated with floods.

Yet in the villages I met women who took pride in the fact that the Grameen Bank had lent them money without collateral. For many of these women it was the first time anyone had lent them money. They now had human dignity. Their lives had value.

I have known Mohammad Yunus for over a decade and have always been fascinated by his story. He recounted to me:

I was a Professor teaching economics at the university. Every time I left the university I would encounter absolute poverty in the surrounding villages. One day I asked the women of the village why they did not grow some crops and they replied that they did not have the money to buy seed. On enquiring how much they needed I was surprised that the group of 42 families only needed US$27, which I lent to them.

A year later a delegation returned to me with the full amount. It planted an idea of building a network that would promote micro-credit especially to rural women and requiring no collateral except that they organise themselves into groups that will exert peer pressure on social behaviour. When the formal banks felt that there was too much risk in lending the rural women money and my personal guarantees were not worth much, I went to the Reserve Bank of Bangladesh and got permission to set up the Grameen Bank. Today we have over 8 million borrowers who own the Bank and our loans total over US$100 million a month.

Yunus and the Grameen Bank were awarded the Nobel Peace Prize in 2006 and Bangladesh is on track to meet a number of its MDGs.[22] It is a tribute to non-state actors such as the Grameen Bank and BRAC (Bangladesh Relief Assistance Committee),[23] which employ tens of thousands of people and have loaned billions of dollars to the world's poor. Reaching millions of people across the world, especially women, BRAC and Grameen Bank have built an international solidarity movement in micro-credit that has spread across Africa and Asia.

Another outstanding private sector leader who I convinced to join the board of GAIN was Dr Anji Reddy, the founder of the New York-listed company Dr Reddy's Laboratories. Starting from humble roots in Hyderabad,

Andhra Pradesh, India, Anji, who became an intimate friend, had built a global pharmaceutical company with huge investments in both generic and discovery-led medicines.

I remember an earlier conversation with this elder in which he said: 'Jay, a successful business is one that gives a good return to shareholders who risk their capital when they invest in your company; but a great business will seek to do this in a way that benefits the customers, the communities and the society in which we serve. A business person who does not invest in solving inequality and poverty is very short-sighted.'

I accompanied him on site visits to the social projects that Dr Reddy's Labs were involved in and was amazed at what I found. He had mobilised fellow Chief Executives of major companies to set up the Naandi Foundation to ensure that schoolchildren received a nutritious, hot midday meal. While this was a policy on government books, there had been a mixed bag of usually negative results. The intuitive Chief Minister Chandrababu Naidu of the Andhra Pradesh State had convened a meeting facilitated by Dr Reddy, and Naandi was born as a public-private partnership.[24]

I had met the Chief Minister on my first trip to India as the Minister for Reconstruction and Development. He astounded me with a question I considered impertinent: 'Mr Naidoo, why do you spell your name wrong and do you speak Telugu?'

To which I replied, somewhat offended, that because I was fourth-generation South African, I did not speak Telugu, and that my surname was probably spelt as Naidoo, rather than Naidu, as a result of a bureaucratic mistake made by the British colonial administration.

I went with Naidu's team to see the huge real-estate investments he was making to build a high-tech city to rival Bangalore. I was sceptical, given the towering buildings that were mostly empty, as he waxed on lyrically about his engagements with major global companies to attract them to Hyderabad and his commitment to use IT to deliver services to the citizens of Andhra Pradesh.

Almost a decade later, in 2007, on a return visit to Hyderabad, I saw the realisation of his vision with a host of buildings housing software companies and international call centres as far as the eye could see. Naidu was out of power then and I was with a delegation of the DBSA studying the development experiences of India. We went to visit him. He was as ebullient as ever, determined to claw his way back to power.

We visited the Naandi kitchens, which had centralised the preparation of food to high standards, with ongoing monitoring, and which drew on hundreds of small enterprises to deliver hot food to over half a million children in the city. We also saw how through a concentrated programme, Dr Reddy provided street children with the theoretical and technical training to become call centre operators in a 90-day period.

These were living examples of sustainable development and the work of extraordinary leaders from the business sector in complete contrast to the swashbuckling global executives jetting into crowds of adoring zealots and disciples, celebrating individualism and feeding the greed of a global plundering elite that stands at the centre of the world economy.

*   *   *

My exchanges with these business pioneers have made me determined to build a cadreship of entrepreneurs who use their remarkable abilities to tackle poverty and harness innovation, skill and scientific and managerial experience. I believe that a private sector committed to long-term sustainability has to incorporate development into its core business agenda. A business that is profitable in a sea of poverty will at some point be overwhelmed by a tidal wave of a social crisis of unmet expectations that results in extremism, violence and civil strife. An old proverb from my childhood reminds me that 'if you do not share your wealth with your neighbour, then one day you will share his poverty'.

43

In October 2007 Jayendra, Chris Jardine and I had a discussion on succession planning at J&J. The business had established itself and I felt a compelling urge to go back to a single-minded focus on sustainable development. We had broadened the shareholding in J&J the previous year, bringing in a range of mass-based organisations from trade unions to NGOs, and had set up the J&J Group Development Trust to drive a social development strategy.

I was now keen to operationalise the Trust and this fitted into our succession planning. I would focus on building the Trust; Chris would become the Chief Executive of the J&J Group; and Jayendra would take over as Executive Chairperson. We broke this news carefully so as not to upset our market, business partners and the management team. We convened an evening to unveil our new business strategy.

'The greatest obstacle to most people's freedom is dire poverty and inequality in our society. We all understand that contributing to our country's development is vital for our business success. Social development is therefore a core part of the J&J Group of companies,' I said to an enthusiastic audience.

The J&J Group Development Trust would support me in my work globally and in South Africa to catalyse discussions aimed at finding solutions to our urgent challenges. We had to change the paradigm. All sectors had a contribution to make and I was exhausted by the ideologues across the political spectrum. People could not eat ideology. They demanded practical and concrete steps to deal with their aspirations.

One of the people who understands this all too well is Emma Mashinini, who sits on our Board of Trustees. Emma captures the spirit of our past. Her passion and stature had earned her the title of 'Mother of the trade union movement'. My memories of her span nearly three decades and I still vividly recall our first meeting: I entered Khotso House, the headquarters of the South African Council of Churches (SACC), and saw this short, robust woman addressing a crowd of workers. She personified the image of leadership through her magnetic personality, her eyes dancing with the joy of life and her indomitable spirit.

Emma was radical and principled. I was captivated. After the meeting Jayendra introduced me to his 'boss' – Emma Mashinini, the General Secretary of the Commercial, Catering and Allied Workers Union of South Africa (CCAWUSA). She hugged me and said: 'Oh, my two sons! Very good that you have both joined the union movement. We have much to do.' We have been 'her boys' ever since. She still is the matriarch of our social network, commanding enormous energy even in her late seventies.

Speaking straight from the heart, as has always been the case, she has little hesitation in shooting down arrogance and the loss of the values for which she fought so hard. Emma is a disciplinarian as a leader and demands the same of others. With her honesty and integrity she captures the hearts of even the most hard-nosed business people.

It is people like Emma, Albertina Sisulu, my mother and the thousands of working-class mothers I have encountered who have been my bedrock, infusing me with their energy when I was flagging. And it is to these truest South African patriots that I owe a debt of gratitude for what I became.

* * *

I was keen for the J&J Group Development Trust to shift its emphasis from a set of disparate but valuable projects to a strategy that would aim to create new business models for successful delivery that could be scaled up and replicated in partnership with the communities we were involved in – together with government and the private sector.

Our focus would be on looking at strategy, implementation and integrated community development in the health and education sectors. My experience of the project that our joint venture company Macquarie First South was involved with was instructive.

For years we had ploughed significant resources and time into supporting Inkwenkwezi Primary School in Diepkloof, Soweto. This was a school that had fallen into disrepair and was a regular hang-out for gangsters and drunken gamblers. At the same time it was trying to educate children mostly from the squatter areas made up of migrants from the former Transkei who were mainly Xhosa-speaking. They came from homes that were largely dysfunctional, with few having electricity and water, and where most of the parents were unemployed and at the bottom of the social ladder.

Our first step was to meet and support the newly appointed Principal, Maropa 'Skipper' Lekgalake. He was not Xhosa-speaking and his appointment was initially resisted by the parents but he soon proved them wrong by his hard work, discipline and commitment to the children. He impressed our team with his determination to instil discipline amongst his teachers, insisting they were at school on time, that their lessons were properly prepared and that they were in the classrooms teaching. Working with him, we focused our efforts on fixing up the physical infrastructure, repairing the leaking ceilings, setting up a library, organising a proper staffroom and transforming an old disused toilet block into a kitchen.

He arranged the provision of a hot meal for the children by recruiting a team of mothers to cook, which dramatically improved school attendance and the concentration of the children in their learning. Sports were introduced and in time the school became a buzz of activity. The community noted the positive changes and became more involved. At the same time, teacher commitment improved. Skipper would often say: 'Jay, running a school is a complicated business. I need to set the example and be a role model. These children are my responsibility and the buck stops with me. I do not need some bureaucrat in government or union telling me how to run my school.'

With great fanfare the provincial government introduced a computer lab. But for three years the Principal, supported personally by me and by our team, tried to get the computers switched on and connected to the Internet. It never happened. Team after team visited the school and failed to deliver. Eventually, three years later, we were informed that the unused computers had become obsolete. No one was fired for the failure to get this lab up and running. In short, there was no consequence for such a fruitless expenditure, not to mention the untold damage to a generation of learners from squatter camps who passed this museum of modern technology daily as they trod their way to their classrooms. We had failed them.

This – as in hundreds of other cases across our country – was an example of rule by remote control: what Skipper describes as 'the endless stream of memos that demand information' irrelevant to the challenges he faces in the trenches where he has to be the Principal, the teacher, the parent, the social worker looking for kids that disappear or fail to come to school. The system is not designed to make committed teachers and Principals succeed.

On another occasion he remarked: 'You know, Jay, most of these kids are condemned to a cycle of abuse and poverty. One thing that no one can take away from them is education. I want them to learn English. Every day I want them to sit in the library and to read. I know that the experts talk about mother tongue instruction but for these kids the one skill they will need to get any job is to be able to communicate in English.'

How could I fault his logic? I realised that we needed a real debate about the crisis in our education system. The national education budget has increased from R69 billion in 2005 to R105 billion for the 2007/08 fiscal year. Today it stands at R165 billion, the largest item of expenditure on our national budget. Despite sharp increases in education spending since apartheid ended, South African children consistently score at or near rock bottom in the UNESCO-run international achievement tests in mathematics, science, literacy and numeracy – even against far poorer African countries such as Kenya or Botswana.

For me this is critical. NGOs can never replace the role of the state. They can build models that have to be scaled up by the state. They can provide immediate assistance that may not be available from the state. More especially, they must focus on organising and mobilising people to demand not only political rights but their social and economic rights. Civil society is essential to our democracy; we need a strong civil society to demand accountability of teachers, nurses, councillors and the highest levels of government.

The parents had placed their trust and hopes in Skipper creating a culture of learning for their children. But there were some education union leaders who felt that they had co-responsibility in managing the school. I supported him in asserting his authority and discipline.

I recall reading, in 2008, allegations that a senior South African Democratic Teachers Union (SADTU) leader in Gauteng had threatened children from Alexandra's KwaBhekilanga Secondary School with 'extreme violence' if any of them came to school during a teacher strike, which was against the Gauteng Department of Education's attempts to hold teachers accountable for shirking work.[25]

Having been the convenor of the unity talks between different teacher organisations that led to the formation of SADTU in 1992, I was horrified by the apparent silence from senior union leadership in this regard.[26] I thought back to the founding principles of the inaugural congress of SADTU, with Mandela expressing the great hope that this powerful new organisation would be at the forefront of building a culture of learning in our schools and reversing the legacy of neglect that was ranked as the one of the worst excesses of apartheid.

Here were senior leaders promising the opposite. While the majority of teachers are dedicated professionals eager to give our children a real opportunity to achieve their dreams, I wondered whether in organising COSATU as a 'blue-collar' federation, we were not responsible for blurring the line between professional and worker, which was a fierce debate at the time. I remember my childhood when becoming a teacher or a nurse was seen as a preferred profession and such individuals were highly respected as community leaders.

Today our education system continues to be dragged down by the legacy of apartheid and the negligence of a minority and the fact that many teachers lack the content knowledge in the subjects they are teaching. Perhaps more telling is the finding that many Grade Six teachers failed the tests set for their learners.[27]

In August 2009 President Jacob Zuma put his finger on the pulse of the nation when he said to an *imbizo* (gathering) of school Principals: 'Teachers in former whites-only schools teach in class for an average 6.5 hours a day, while teachers in disadvantaged communities (that is, black townships) teach for around 3.5 hours a day. The result is that the outcomes are unequal.'

He added: 'We must ask ourselves to what extent teachers in many historically disadvantaged schools unwittingly perpetuate the wishes of Hendrik Verwoerd, if they decide to teach for about three hours a day.'[28]

And then he continued: 'Everybody knows that there is a high percentage of unqualified teachers in the classrooms. If they aren't given a chance to study, people mustn't be surprised about the poor matriculation results. This isn't rocket science. We just need to get the basic things right.'

Seven hours a day of education is a 'non-negotiable issue' for the ANC. 'Fridays and paydays are ordinary school working days,' Zuma said to loud applause. He also expected learners to 'be in class, on time, learning, respectful of their teachers and each other, and [to] do their homework'. If only we could succeed in turning around the education system, I believe this would represent the major victory in our progress in addressing inequality and poverty in our country.

44

Now that my family had all settled in South Africa we started to rebuild our lives. The children returned to the French school and were very happy. Then, in September 2007, Lucie went into hospital for a hysterectomy. We were assured that it would be a standard procedure. I accompanied her to the hospital on the day. As I left her at the doors of the theatre she said to her doctor: 'I hope you slept well last night. I want to see my husband again soon.' We laughed and I retired to the ward that she would be brought back to.

The hours ticked by. I wondered why it was taking so long. Then Lucie was wheeled through, accompanied by the doctor. She looked at me and I could see the tension in her eyes. 'There has been a complication,' she said. Lucie's bladder had been punctured. I felt myself reeling.

A little while later my head cleared and Lucie, still drowsy, asked: 'What happened? Have you fixed the problem?' We were assured that the two punctures had been repaired. Lucie was connected to a catheter and had to have it for a week.

A week later we went back for a check-up and the catheter was removed. But the leak persisted and Lucie had to wear adult napkins. The doctor assured us that she had done hundreds of these operations. We placed our lives in her hands. A second operation was proposed and it failed. Lucie even had to go to Canada in nappies to launch her third book. It was a nightmare, she said.

We spent Christmas 2007 in the hospital. Lucie was heading towards clinical depression again. I could feel it and I could understand why. Wearing nappies and a catheter with a urine bottle is a humiliating experience. She refused to go out in public. Our lives were constrained by this botched medical experience.

With the dawn of a new year a heavy cloud hung over our heads. We prepared for the third operation. Once again, we were assured of its success.

The third operation failed. And so did the fourth one.

We were desperate and started to search for doctors across the world. Lucie and I travelled to India. We agreed that she should spend some time in an ashram while we researched the advances in India that had been made in the field of vesico-vaginal fistulas (VVF). It was a good trip. Lucie reconnected with our old friend Vijay at the spiritual centre of the Aurobindo Ashram in Pondicherry in the south of India. She spent time with their doctors, all practising the ancient rituals of addressing the body, mind and spirit in a holistic way. She recovered some of her confidence and began to feel more positive.

At the same time I made some enquiries about which hospitals in India specialised in repairing VVFs. We honed it down to a specialised hospital in Chennai, the port that my great-grandmother had left from over 100 years ago.

Lucie cried over her fear of the future and I hugged her as she fell asleep. However there was a flickering of hope at the end of the tunnel.

We discussed the operation with the kids and they agreed with our decision. We all had been affected by the consequences of the botched operations. Kami especially was very enraged, asking frequently, 'Why don't we sue these doctors, Papa?' I could empathise with his feeling of helplessness.

We started to make preparations for the return trip to India. Two weeks before leaving I received a call from the head of Gynaecology at the University of the Witwatersrand. He had also examined Lucie and although he had done many operations like this he felt that he did not have the necessary experience and specialisation to perform the repair job after so many operations. Lucie and I loved his openness and we trusted him. He had mentioned that there was a single doctor, a gynaecologist, practising in Bloemfontein who was reputed to be the country's best specialist in repairing VVFs.

This was a call to say he had the information and he gave me the details of the doctor and said he had already briefed him. Lucie and I were stunned. We were in two minds.

'Bloemfontein!' I said. 'Lucie, you know not long ago I was not allowed to even stay there without a permit.'

We agreed that we had nothing to lose. The great advantage was of course that Bloemfontein was only 400 kilometres from home whereas India was thousands of kilometres away. Lucie flew there for a series of tests the next day. We spoke on the phone that night and she sounded happy. She had met who she believed was the doctor who could save her from her ongoing nightmare.

'Lucie,' he said, 'I will only agree to help you if you agree to stay in hospital for five weeks. There are very serious complications that have taken place. It's a delicate operation and I need you to accept that the recovery is long and difficult.'

A week later I drove Lucie to the Bloemfontein Medi-Clinic. The doctor came in and welcomed Lucie and shook my hand warmly. He had come to meet with me and also to give Lucie peace of mind as she went into the operation. I prayed for the procedure to work.

I walked along with Lucie to the operating theatre. I saw the tears in her eyes and felt them rising in mine too. She was drowsy with the pre-med sedative. I held her hand tightly as she was taken by the green-gowned theatre nurses. 'She will be fine,' they said reassuringly. 'He is a brilliant doctor.'

The hours ticked by. I paced restlessly up and down the corridors, wondering why things were taking so long, and why time seemed to move by so slowly. Four hours later I could not bear the anxiety any longer and went to camp outside the theatre. The operation was still in progress and the staff insisted I return to the ward. They would call me as soon as it was over. I waited another harrowing two hours and then received a call: 'Your wife is in the intensive care unit. You can come now.'

I entered the highly sanitised environment. It was cold. I felt a shiver run up my spine. I saw Lucie. She looked so vulnerable. She was also connected to various monitors and drips. I was desperate to hear what had happened. 'It's been a long operation,' the ward sister said. 'There was much damaged tissue. It is inexplicable how much wrong was done. But the doctor says it went well.'

I held Lucie's hand and prayed. She was still heavily sedated but awoke and asked groggily, 'What happened? How long has it been?'

'It went well,' I answered, 'but you need to sleep.'

'Put some logs in the fire. I am freezing cold,' she replied, slipping in and out of consciousness. We piled more blankets on her. The nurse administered morphine for the excruciating pain and she fell back into a deep sleep.

The next morning the doctor arrived. Lucie was more lucid. We discussed with him the details of the operation. 'The recovery is the most important phase. You will have to get into a routine. There is physiotherapy, certain exercises and then the medical treatment. You need to keep your mind clear. Try to keep occupied,' he commented wisely.

As I travelled back to Johannesburg I thought about what he had said. We had to make the hospital bed a second home to help Lucie's psychological health. That was as important for the healing process as the surgical part. I organised DVDs, books, magazines and games and installed her computer and Internet to keep her in touch with the world.

For the next six weeks I followed a routine. Leaving the kids with Rosie on the Friday evening, I travelled down to Bloemfontein to spend weekends with my wife. She had formed a whole social circle with the staff, both the Afrikaans and the black nurses. They were kind, compassionate and professional. I was really impressed with the quality of health care. Lucie was recovering well but had suffered permanent damage to her bladder function. She still needed to use the bathroom sometimes several times a night – a condition she will have to live with for the rest of her life.

Six weeks later I brought her back home. Our children, family and friends were so relieved. We could now celebrate. We discussed again the sensitive subject of legal action against the doctors who had botched the first operations. For Lucie, I realised, it was about putting the sorry chapter behind her. For a year she had lived in nappies and in hospitals. Her confidence had evaporated, her professional life had had to be abandoned and, most importantly, she felt she had not played her role as a mother.

I consulted with some of the best malpractice attorneys in Johannesburg. The long consultations resulted in nothing. South African malpractice laws are weak. The medical profession protects its own. The delays are huge, the costs astronomical and the remedies available to aggrieved patients are vague. We were forced to abandon our legal remedy. But Lucie still had to bury her memories of the past year. She wrote a heart-rending account of her experience and posted them to the two doctors involved in the first operations.

I promised myself that I would campaign for a Patients' Charter so that ordinary people are aware of their rights with respect to health care. This entire saga was an expensive and traumatising experience but it brought us closer together. I realised that my family was priceless. If anything had happened to Lucie it would have shattered me.

* * *

In October 2007 Lucie and I had been together for seventeen years. We decided that we would like to do something different to celebrate our relationship. I was invited to an International Telecommunications Union (ITU) Africa Connect conference in Kigali, Rwanda. The Secretary General of the ITU, Hamadoun Toure, is a close personal friend and the first African to hold this position.

I had spoken at the launch of his election campaign, much to the disgust of the bureaucracy in the South African Department of Communications who were lukewarm in supporting his candidacy. 'How could you ask Jay Naidoo to speak at your election launch?' they demanded. 'He is not involved in government any more.'

To which Hamadoun replied: 'I trust and believe in Jay. I do not need permission from any government or person to decide who my friends are. He addressed the meeting at my personal invitation and that does not need anyone's permission.'

When Hamadoun convened the meeting in Kigali, it was to fulfil an election promise that the ITU would act proactively to promote the closing of the digital divide in Africa. My support for that vision was shared and passionate, but it coincided with our wedding anniversary.

Lucie, forever the journalist, grabbed the opportunity to visit Rwanda, a country devastated by the genocide that had seen the extermination of close to a million people. Occurring in 1994, the same year as our democracy had been born, we were too absorbed in our own challenges to understand the magnitude of events in Rwanda. The world slept through the genocide that saw some of the most horrific slaughter of innocent men, women and children. Both Lucie and I were keen to understand how a country recovers from such a huge gaping wound that tore apart peaceful and co-existing communities.

We stayed at the Hôtel des Mille Collines, the same hotel that the film *Hotel Rwanda* used to capture on celluloid the horrors of what happened. Lucie also did the pre-research for a more detailed journalistic trip to Rwanda while I attended the conference.

We took the time to realise one of the adventures on our 'bucket list' – visiting the gorillas in the mountains of Rwanda. Our trip to the mountains started in darkness. The roads were winding and dangerous and potholes were frequent. Our driver knew his business and I encouraged Lucie to doze off to avoid the trauma of our crazy drive through the countryside.

The mists shrouded this land of a thousand rolling hills and valleys. We passed fields and fields of crops, and people hard at work tilling the earth early in the morning. As we came to the towns we saw the farmers walking with large bundles on their heads or riding bicycles heavily laden with goods. There seemed to be a marketplace in every town. Most of the trade was bartering.

We arrived at the base camp of the Safari Lodge. There were only a limited number of guests who were permitted to travel. It was expensive, I thought, for a day visit at US$500 per person. When we arrived at the edge of the forests and saw a group of armed rangers I understood why the costs involved were high. The mountain gorillas are under threat of extinction and under pressure from creeping populations encroaching on their territories. As the government was unable to support the efforts, it fell to tourists and wildlife advocacy groups to raise the money necessary to protect these graceful animals and to educate neighbouring communities on their value for the whole of humanity.

We started a long walk to the sanctuary of the gorilla family. Along the way we learnt about the vegetation and the staple foods of these beautiful creatures – leaves, stems, flowers and their favourite, young bamboo shoots. We were warned that the animals were wild and that sudden movements could trigger a hostile reaction. We heard them before we saw them. Suddenly, breaking through the underbrush, two screaming young juveniles burst out, almost touching my sleeve. We halted, sat and watched the furry animals ignoring us as they tumbled in the brush. They looked so intelligent and human. The mother lurked in the background, keeping a watchful eye on her infants but shielded from our sight by the thick underbrush. I could not believe that anyone would want to make a trophy from such an exquisite example of our diversity.

As we crouched and watched this for almost five minutes we heard the deep growl of an adult. It was the father, sensitised to foreigners in his abode, crashing through the bamboo forest with a roar and thump of his hairy chest. They were terrifying sounds and we squirmed as they grew closer. The ranger stood in front of us and, trying out a series of gorilla grunts, he answered back. Then we saw the adult in all his magnificence. He was towering, a white mane across his back. This was the alpha male, the silverback weighing in at over 250 kilograms. He recognised the ranger, slowed down and headed towards the young bamboo shoots. He squatted heavily next to them and continued eating, pretending to ignore us.

We stayed for at least three hours and marvelled as more members of the family joined the male. They went about their business as if we were not there.

It was a priceless experience that we would never forget. We had vanished off the face of the earth to spend an unforgettable time in the kingdom of these magical creatures.

We returned to Kigali late that night and snuggled into bed with a bottle of champagne. It had been the perfect anniversary celebration.

The next day I threw myself into the conference. It was opened by President Kagame and I was later to spend time with him and David Himbara, my friend who worked as head of Strategy in his office. We chatted about our respective experiences in building a democracy after a traumatic experience. As the President reminded me in our meeting, 'Everyday we have to work on reconciliation. We have to make it part of our daily tasks to talk about the past and to build the bridge to the future. There is no other way.' This was a President I felt was in touch with the pulse of the people.

He cut a controversial figure in some international circles – a warrant for his arrest had been issued in France because of his involvement in leading the rebel army against the ruling Hutu junta. France had played an ambiguous role in Rwanda. But every person I chatted with, from the taxi driver to the cleaners in the hotel to the waiters in the restaurant, felt that he was a unifying influence as Rwanda left its past behind and was building a new future.

One of the most striking things we noticed was the absence of litter. David explained: 'The last Saturday of every month is dedicated to everyone – from the President downwards – going into communities to pick up litter.' That was what was making Rwanda a comparative success. There was virtually no crime. There was virtually no litter. There was virtually no corruption.

The President also insisted that every meeting any public official called dealt first with the challenge of HIV/AIDS. As a result of Rwanda's efforts AIDS-related infections had decreased from an all-time high of 16 per cent to below 3 per cent. The problem was confronted head-on. Every person who needed to be was on treatment; test results were compiled in real time using cellphones. I thought back to the chaos in our campaign. We could learn so much from those who had the least resources. That had always been our strength in our fight for freedom. Now political arrogance was strangling the life out of our people.

Later that night I took Lucie out to a romantic dinner at the top of the Hôtel des Mille Collines. It was a beautiful evening and we looked forward to a delicious meal with a good bottle of wine. As we finished our starters

Hamadoun Toure walked in. He was accompanied by an old friend, Tarek Kemel, the Egyptian Minister of Communications.

'You and Madame must join us,' he insisted, speaking in French. He turned to Lucie and with his disarming charm enquired about her trip, saying, 'You know Jay has promised to bring you to my homeland, Mali. I heard that you want to visit Timbuktu.'

This was another stop on our list of places to visit, the fabled centre of scholars and commerce in the mystical trading kingdom of the Mandingo Askia dynasty (1493–1591).

We could not refuse his invitation. We joined the table and soon afterwards several Ambassadors and Ministers arrived. We were having a wonderful time until we started discussing the progress that Rwanda had made after the horrors of the genocide. The Minister of Communications from Sudan was seated almost directly opposite Lucie.

Darfur had always burned a hole in our conscience. It was a human catastrophe that saw innocent women and children caught in the crossfire of a brutal civil war between the predominantly Muslim North and the Christian South. Wars are almost always about the insanity of power-hungry leaders or the scramble for resources. In this case it was the 'black gold' of oil hidden under the shifting sands of the Sudanese desert.

The Minister made some remark about the problems in Sudan, not mentioning the war, to which Lucie replied: 'So what do you say about Darfur; about the 300 000 or so people who died?'

The air was chilled by the ensuing silence. This was a meeting of diplomats. These questions were never asked in such a blunt way.

I was tempted to respond in two ways. One was to kick Lucie under the table and try to get her to drop the subject, and the other was to sit back and watch this unfolding, knowing Lucie had already worked out every scenario. She is a piercing journalist who leaves no stone unturned, especially when confronting political bullies.

The Minister blustered: 'There is no civil war. It is just exaggerated by the media; there are less than 9 000 people who have died.'

That was a red flag to an angry bull and Lucie butted in: 'So how many have to die before it is seen as a problem by the Sudanese government?'

The table hushed. You could have cut the air with a blunt knife it was so thick with tension.

But that's the woman I married. Diplomacy should never hide the truth about the abuse of power. I love Lucie's simple honesty and integrity so much.

45

It was in December 2007 at Polokwane that the course of South Africa's future changed. The ANC Congress, held every five years to report back to the membership and elect a new team for the party, proved on this occasion to be a turning point in the country's political history.

The delegates were clearly divided into two camps, one noisier than the other. They heckled the Chairperson, Mosiuoa 'Terror' Lekota, a UDF activist and Minister of Defence, giving the soccer rolling hand signal, indicating 'time to change the team'.

They walked around the grounds and in the marquee in large groups singing and dancing to a large repertoire of songs. '*Aw'dedele abanye, aw'dedela uMsholozi*' ('Give way to others, give way for uMsholozi' [Jacob Zuma's clan name]). Their T-shirts blazed: '100% Jacob Zuma'.

Solitary fingers faced upwards. What did that mean? 'One time!' Thabo Mbeki was standing for a third term for ANC president – the president wanted to be elected once more. 'Zimbabwe!' they called out, because that was Robert Mugabe's line too. Large groups of these delegates came from the same areas. Informal networks created bonds of local solidarity. For the first time there were numbers of women from rural areas. As they struggled to survive in the informal economy, Mbeki's project of gender equity amongst the elite was not seen as addressing their basic needs.

These were the ordinary delegates who arrived in buses and taxis; they were served their food in tents and received a staple diet of rice or pap with some meat or chicken. Those in power, by contrast, typically arrived in 4 x 4s (the Porsche Cayenne and Range Rover were favourites), and went to lunch in the air-conditioned network lounge where they were offered fabulous wines.

The result of the election came as a depressing shock to them. Some literally broke down in tears. How could this come about? Not since 1952, when Dr James Moroka lost the Congress vote in favour of Chief Albert John Mvumbi Luthuli, was a sitting ANC President voted out of office – and now, for the first time in history, a sitting ANC President of South Africa.

And yet, to those who were attuned to it, this moment had been a long time coming.

A warning sign was the fact that between 2002 and 2007 the membership of the ANC increased dramatically, from 416 846 to 621 237. But even more significant was the remarkable shift in the socio-economic profile of ANC members. By 2007, of the ANC members in Gauteng, 42 per cent were unemployed; 30 per cent lived in informal settlements; 44 per cent did not have water in their dwellings; 47 per cent had less than a matric; and 25 per cent of households had less than R1 000 monthly disposable income.[29]

What was of special interest was that at Polokwane, one out of four of the delegates came from the Eastern Cape – and the membership of the Eastern Cape had doubled between 2005 and 2007.

A study of Polokwane compared this rapid growth to the habit of the single-cell amoeba. Amoebas reproduce themselves by splitting. In the context of the ANC, sharp divisions were emerging within branches. The only way dissatisfied members could recapture leadership was to split away and create a new branch – all one needed was 100 members at R12 each. And so the ANC grew.

Two different things were happening inside the ANC. On the one hand, middle-class and professional ANC members were moving out of the branches as they were deployed to national and provincial legislatures, the executive or public service, or joined the private sector.[30]

An ANC Gauteng membership survey in July 2006 found that the result of the flight from the branches was 'a growing resentment in some quarters against what is seen as a new, educated elite that is using ANC members and office-bearer status as a stepping stone to employment elsewhere'.[31] And, on the other hand, to fill the decline of membership at branch level, a new generation of activists moved in, creating a grassroots mass base inside the ANC. Thousands of the new members were workers – and COSATU members.

Pushed into a corner, marginalised by an all-powerful state and scorned by the sitting President, COSATU responded with what it knew best. Zwelinzima Vavi, the charismatic working-class leader who had worked his way through the ranks after being dismissed in the 1987 mineworkers' strike at the Klerksdorp mine, led COSATU. 'Back to the factories, shops, mines and our communities,' he urged. 'Let us build the branches of the ANC to reflect the interests of the working class and the poor.'

I had met Vavi in the mid-1980s and was impressed by his passion and rousing militancy. He was from a large family; born in Hanover in the Northern Cape, he grew up close to Queenstown in the township of Sada created to house farm workers evicted from white-owned farms and also as a place to which the regime could banish troublesome activists. He had been active in COSAS, the students' body organising schoolchildren, and had several run-ins with the security police. In 1983, having matriculated, he had the choice of going into exile. Knowing he had elderly parents who he needed to support, he chose a job in the Vaal Reefs No.8 shaft. Within weeks he was elected to the NUM as a shaft steward.

I respected Vavi. His whole life represented a fight for the human dignity that apartheid had stripped from generations before him. When we were setting up the COSATU regional structures I recruited him as the Regional Secretary of the Western Transvaal region and then later brought him to the COSATU headquarters as a National Organising Secretary. He proved to be an invaluable asset and was a natural selection as the Deputy General Secretary to Sam Shilowa when I left in 1993 to lead the twenty COSATU leaders into parliament.

It is legendary that Mbeki never once in his tenure as President met Vavi one on one, the leader of the largest organisation in our nation's history, an organisation that had a significant impact on the socio-economic development of our country and was a member of the Tripartite Alliance!

As early as 2003, COSATU complained about this attitude:

All too often, COSATU's letters do not even get the courtesy of a response, and we are routinely told that 'government must govern; there is no dual power, there is no co-determination, and COSATU must not treat the Alliance as a bargaining chamber'.[32]

In fact, it is important to remember the prophetic words of Nelson Mandela as he stepped down voluntarily to hand over the reins of the presidency to Thabo Mbeki at the 50th national conference of the ANC at Mafikeng in 1997:

*Let me also assure you that even as an ordinary foot soldier of the Party,
I reserve the right to criticise you when I observe you making mistakes.
Do not surround yourself with 'yes men', for they will do you and the
nation incalculable harm. Listen to your critics, for only by so doing will
you become aware of the disaffection that ails your people and be able to
address them.*

On the day of the elections at Polokwane, the 'Phoenix' of disillusionment
about the hegemony of elites came home to roost with the fiery defeat of the
Thabo Mbeki legacy.

Polokwane was the battleground between an overconfident elite and a
discontented mass base. Jacob Zuma, a wily grassroots leader with a strong
appeal to the overwhelming majority of poor in the country, captured that spirit.
He was the antithesis of what was seen as arrogant leadership in a government
out of touch with the people. Backed by the legions of workers, Zuma was not
the obvious choice, given that there was controversy surrounding him and that
he did not have clear leftist credentials.

Polokwane lifted the lid off the pressure cooker. The media headlines painted a picture of anxiety, fear and lawlessness. Jacob Zuma was described as a
flawed leader with a stained record and with messy personal finances. His views
on polygamy and the role of tradition and culture sparked further controversy.
As an individual and a leader he has openly admitted his limitations, but the
working class and the people trusted him more than the incumbent at the
time who was derided for being aloof.[33] They yearned for someone who would
understand their desperate pleas for help as the ravages of poverty, hunger and
inequality bit deeply.

* * *

By early 2009 GAIN was operating in over 26 countries in the developing
world across the different continents. I had been invited to many international
conferences and I took advantage of this to raise the profile of the impending
human disaster of hunger and malnutrition. I addressed the Parliamentary
Committee in the House of Commons, European Union representatives and
donors across the world:

*Malnutrition accounts for 11 per cent of the global burden of disease. Each
year it kills 3.5 million children under five years old and impairs hundreds*

of thousands of growing minds. Countries may lose up to 2 to 3 per cent
of their Gross Domestic Product (GDP) as a result of vitamin and mineral
deficiencies.[34]

Speaking at the launch of the *Lancet* report[35] on undernutrition in Washington DC in January 2008, a cold fact hit me: 80 per cent of our problem of malnutrition could be put into twenty countries in South Asia and sub-Saharan Africa where half the population lives on less than the internationally accepted poverty line of US$1.25 per day. I knew from my discussions with leading scientists in the world that iron, iodine and zinc deficiencies could lead to a 10 per cent reduction in the life earnings of an individual. As I travelled home I wondered what more I could do in my own country.

I turned to the health activists I had worked with in the past. I was keen to understand how we were measuring up to the MDGs as I had been invited to address the Trusteeship Council Chamber of the United Nations on Poverty and Hunger in April 2008.[36]

The information I sought was not readily available. I turned to an old friend, Jack Koolen, born in Holland, who had spent much of his life in South Africa and is married to a South African. He was head of an international consultancy firm, Monitor, and led its operations in the Middle East, Africa and Asia.

Working with Jack I consulted a range of leaders in the TAC, loveLife and COSATU and the many outstanding health activists who I had worked with in the 1980s. With a small team, I put together a diagnostic that shocked me. Not only were we out of sync with the rest of the world, we were going backwards in terms of nearly all health indicators. This was both a leadership and a social crisis.

I took my presentation to the Secretary General of the ANC, Gwede Mantashe, early in 2008. Gwede listened very carefully and then asked one of the senior leaders from the Health Department to comment on the diagnostic I had done. The facts spoke for themselves. I was then asked to brief the Chairperson of the ANC subcommittee on health and education, Dr Zweli Mkhize.

He was a senior confidant of Jacob Zuma and a medical doctor, at one stage the MEC of Health in KwaZulu-Natal, one of the worst-affected provinces.

Having clashed with the contrary views of the then Health Minister, Zweli had moved to a new portfolio dealing with Finance. As a sober-minded professional and respected leader, he requested that I give a presentation to the next formal meeting of the ANC subcommittee. In the presence of the Director General of Health I presented the facts and was then asked to co-chair a consultative roadmap process using the DBSA as the convenor.

By that time the DBSA had started to significantly strengthen its policy engagement teams, and the Health Roadmap process was taken forward by the new Group Executive, Ravi Naidoo, who had joined the Bank after many years of experience in the policy think tank of COSATU and in government. For the first time in a decade, dozens of activists and experts active in shaping the health struggle in our country were drawn into a dialogue that also included the private sector. The questions we had to answer were very simple:

How many people were dying?

What were they dying of?

How many of these deaths were avoidable?

In a benchmarking exercise we were found to fall far short of our peers in the world, including Brazil, Chile, Mexico, China and many countries in Africa. The clearest factors were an incoherent political leadership, a breakdown of management systems and the absence of a results-based culture in the system. Many of the professionals on the ground, reeling under the burden of long hours, understaffing and decaying infrastructure, felt that the bureaucratic leadership was insensitive, not knowledgeable in the field, and operating by remote control with its insistent demands for information.

Important experiments involving hospital management, professionals and unions to develop new business models for workplace reorganisation (for example, the case study of what was declared in 1997 to be the largest hospital in the world, the Chris Hani Baragwanath Hospital) had been stymied by the bureaucracy.[37]

The Health Roadmap process aimed to provide a diagnostic of the problems we faced, identify the gaps and prepare a way forward that would capture the key thrusts that a new administration would have to focus on to reverse the deadly tide. As part of this new approach at the DBSA, the Bank was commissioned by the Education Ministry to complete a similar process in basic education.

Change was in the air. With Mbeki recalled from his tenure as President, a number of Ministers also departed and a new Minister of Health, Barbara Hogan, was appointed.

A feisty and principled activist for years, and marginalised because of her independent opinions in the powerful parliamentary committee on Finance, Hogan was about to retire when she was thrown into the lion's den. Fortunately for her and those of us convening the roadmap process, she embraced the process and assumed political leadership. The momentum propelled the decisions we had to make.

The roadmap process concluded in November 2009 with a broad consensus and a ten-point plan of action. It was an extraordinarily frank and honest engagement that faced head-on the failures of HIV/AIDS policies and the shortcomings of our health care management and institutions. This ten-point plan would later be translated into the Department of Health's Strategic Plan, guiding a number of important shifts in how the country would tackle its health challenges. The pseudoscience was finally buried.

* * *

As I reflect on the last fifteen years I am conscious of the successes we have achieved in our political transition. No sane person, no matter how discontented, wants to return to the dark period of apartheid and discard the rights we have won under the new Constitution. Millions of people now have been given access to water, electricity, houses, sports fields, telephones, sanitation and roads. The quality of life has improved overall for our people.

At the same time we struggle to make our schools run properly; our people struggle for decent health care; safety and security are very real concerns for our communities. Those with disposable income have privatised many of the services democracy promised to deliver with the dramatic growth in private health care, private security and private education.

Much of this is a consequence of the poor performance of the public institutions of the state. The current administration has focused the country's attention on the outcomes that would drive improvement of the quality of life of our population. It is critical that these don't just remain commitments on paper. There have to be consequences. People, no matter how senior they are in political life, must be removed if they cannot meet the performance they have individually committed to. Strengthening accountability will go a long way to rebuilding the trust of our people.

While there are many campaigns aimed at improving service delivery and clamping down on corruption, the creation of a professional civil service is a prerequisite for our success on these fronts. Civil servants must be encouraged to develop a path linked to a successful career in the government service.

I believe party-political deployment has created a discontinuity in many state institutions where political loyalty often ranks above competency and senior civil servants can find their efforts compromised by political office bearers who are senior to them in party structures. This is not an issue unique to South Africa but a characteristic across the developed and developing world. In countries where there are degrees of political appointment there is a much greater transparency involved and these are subjected to public scrutiny.

It also means that the Competition Commission must intensify its sterling work in aggressively tackling price collusion and cartels that are suffocating growth and artificially raising prices of basic goods and services in our country. This means defending the integrity of these institutions against political interference as we put unscrupulous business and social behaviour under the microscope.

Violent crime and corruption are today cited as major disincentives to domestic and foreign investment and a big driver of emigration that deprives us of the much-needed skills for growth. It astonishes me that some of our leaders dismiss this as the 'chicken run' while safe in the custody of VIP protection and a 'blue light' brigade. Every skilled South African who leaves our country seriously undermines our capacity to build our economy and renew our society.

While the legislative and administration systems have to be strengthened to deal with this, it is imperative that we also return to the subject first raised by Nelson Mandela – the 'RDP of the soul'. We have emerged from a brutal period of social exclusion and yet we have not addressed the psychological damage we have all suffered. The rapaciousness of an elite, the madness of vicious xenophobic attacks, the crudeness of racism that arises out of a criminal incident, and the brutality of homicides bring to the fore the deep underlying tensions and schisms in our society that we have papered over.

In post-war Germany, emerging out of the horror of the Holocaust, serious investment was made in developing a common set of human values and civic pride in schools, churches, communities and families.

We have created a remarkable social security net with 13 million grants reaching as many families. We are seeing the reduction of poverty. But malnutrition remains high and we need to look at the quality of expenditure at a household level. In many other countries, such as Brazil, Mexico, Chile, China and India, conditionalities are introduced that require a change of social behaviour of recipients. This may include attendance of children at school, compulsory immunisation or compulsory visits to antenatal clinics for pregnant mothers who are incentivised with transport and food vouchers.

Importantly, education must be reformed, school governance improved and headmasters given the authority to enforce discipline. Inspections and compulsory tests at regular intervals as has been proposed should be used to measure the literacy and numeracy of students. We cannot afford to wait twelve years to find that our children struggle to read, write and acquire skills in mathematics and science. A massive programme to improve subject knowledge of teachers should be undertaken and skilled teachers from South Africa and the world, irrespective of race, should be aggressively recruited. We should invest heavily in school libraries and build the school as a centre of learning in the community.

We will have to pay particular attention to the youth of our country. My involvement in loveLife showed that the post-1994 generation is lacking a strong sense of purpose, identity and belonging and still seeking a new identity. Youth unemployment is alarmingly high and this represents a ticking time bomb in our society. They feel alienated by our discourse on key issues such as HIV, drug abuse or moral regeneration campaigns that tend to emphasise the waywardness of youth versus the commitment to the struggle of their parents.

A key challenge is going to be the choices we make in the growth path and what its impact will be on job creation. The structure of work gives people a sense of dignity. In the early days of our democracy we had discussed harnessing the countrywide infrastructure of the South African National Defence Force to create a national youth corps. It's time for us to return to the basics. We need to harness the creativity and innovation of the private and public sectors to give greater meaning to the lives of young people.

This does mean making tough choices going forward. The poor live far from work opportunities and this means that we need to build a safe, reliable and subsidised public transport system that connects our cities to the townships.

We need to finalise a youth employment scheme that builds a ladder to the formal sector and puts disposable income in the pockets of young people and gives them organisational and work experience.

Finally I think we need to proceed down the track of negotiating a compact that addresses the key economic and social challenges of our country. The economic restructuring costs of the transition which did result in major job losses in certain sectors were borne largely by the union movement and the poor. At the same time there is a vast reservoir of people in our society who have never had the opportunity to work. The major demand echoing amongst the poor is the demand for their voices to be heard. The negotiations will be tough and will involve compromises on all sides within the context of the fiscal and capacity constraints we face as a country.

This is not about some turf battle between powerful individuals or an experiment in empire building. It has to be about fixing up what is broken and rebuilding the public institutions of our country. We will ignore this imperative at our peril as the number of permanently jobless South Africans grows and we find ourselves unable to sustain a social grant system that today allows people to at least survive.

As we continue to learn from the lessons of the past we need to return to the spirit of volunteerism that characterised our freedom struggle. There is an army of talented South Africans, across the race spectrum, inside and outside of South Africa (many of whom I have already encountered), who want to see our magnificent country succeed. They are often prepared to volunteer for work without remuneration or title. We should embrace this partnership with open arms and a warm heart.

* * *

I am optimistic about the future of South Africa, especially after encountering the conflict and poverty in other countries around the world. As a priority we need to tackle the deep sense of disillusionment and gloom that suffocates us. There are many whites who believe they have given too much and a majority of black people who feel they have not gained much from democracy. This is a lethal mixture that requires wise and courageous leadership. Certainly we need to quieten the demagogues that fan division and strengthen the dialogue on the most controversial issues that divide us.

We face two paths: a low road to social exclusion and violent conflict in which a new elite simply replaces an old one; or a high road if we return to the traditions and values that characterised our past. Ultimately we need leaders who serve the nation, take an uncompromising stand on performance and possess a steely determination to deal with the corruption that is an epidemic and that will consume our democracy if we fail to act.

Recently I have had the wonderful opportunity to engage with scientists at the centre of palaeontological research into human evolution. As we endeavour to understand the origins of the human species we are now more convinced than ever before that southern Africa is the cradle of humanity. Since the 1924 discovery of the skull of the Taung Child – a 2.5 million-year-old human ancestor – southern Africa, and more particularly South Africa's Cradle of Humankind surrounding Sterkfontein, has become the single richest area where fossilised remains of some of the earliest hominids are found.

As I visit the capitals of the world, I marvel at how they have marketed their heritage of the last few thousand years and I wonder why we don't feel a bursting national pride at the fact that our heritage spans millions of years.

Africa is our ancestral home. The Tree of Life, which overarches the Earth and links people from Paris to Mumbai, from New York to Johannesburg and from São Paulo to Beijing, has its roots firmly embedded in African soil. Millions of years ago our ancestors embarked on a remarkable journey that started in Africa and took our human lineage to the rest of the world.

Let us start the voyage of discovery to build a South African identity rich in its cultural diversity and tolerant of our differences. That is what millions of people fought for, dreamt of, hoped for, when we voted in our miraculous political transformation and placed the mantle of leadership on the shoulders of our beloved President Nelson Mandela on 27 April 1994.

Conclusion

Overcoming poverty is not a gesture of charity. It is an act of justice. It is the protection of a fundamental human right, the right to dignity and a decent life. While poverty persists, there is no true freedom.

— Nelson Mandela

Let us not wallow in the valley of despair, I say to you today, my friends.

And so even though we face the difficulties of today and tomorrow, I still have a dream. It is a dream deeply rooted in the American dream.

I have a dream that one day this nation will rise up and live out the true meaning of its creed: 'We hold these truths to be self-evident, that all men are created equal.'

— Martin Luther King, Jr

If you want to go fast, walk alone. If you want to go far, walk together.

— Old African proverb

I am embracing my new journey with frequent, sometimes physically exhausting, intercontinental travel in order to spend more time with my family and to pursue my passion for development in Africa and the rest of the developing world. After all, we are the first generation that has the capacity, resources and technology to eliminate the growing hunger, poverty and inequality in the world.

I continue to experience the generosity of poor communities, their profound indigenous knowledge and their patience. It transports me back to a time in my union days when we shared a vision of social justice and we knew the society we aspired to would be based on the absence of malice, self-enrichment and political arrogance.

Unless we act now, the face of the future for an overwhelming majority of our people is an HIV-positive, starving child confronting the ravages of a civil war in some part of our global village. What we need today is a new global movement that can deliver on the dreams of our people, where hunger, poverty and discrimination on the basis of race, gender and religion is a feature of the past. Political trust has been broken and the world's institutions are undermined because of the failure of our leaders.

The voice of the people must be heard again. That is our new struggle. We need to confront power with truth.

* * *

Some have asked why I did not return to the unions after working in government. My response has always been: 'A new leadership had been elected. I had confidence that the working class would elect leaders of integrity. COSATU had evolved, circumstances had changed and there was not much of a role I could continue to play there.' It was always clear, too, that if the leaders ever wanted to talk to me or seek advice, they could reach me at any time or place.

Towards the end of September 2009 I attended the 10th Congress of COSATU. With Ronald Mofokeng, the second National Treasurer in my time, and Chris Dlamini, the first Vice President, we reminisced on the past and the humble path we had started to carve close to 30 years ago. The rousing toyi-toyi, the breadth and depth of the discussions, the analysis of the documents warmed our hearts and made us proud. This institution with its 3 000 delegates representing close to 2 million workers was very much alive and playing the role intended at its formation.

I felt proud of the institution, although there are areas that I believe COSATU should put under the microscope, including the role of its affiliates in improving the quality of delivery in health, education and the broader public sector.

The key ingredient will always be leadership. Will the leadership in both the public and private sectors lead us forward in a new spirit of service and the absence of arrogance as we chart a way forward that is inclusive, consultative and participatory?

* * *

Lucie returned to Montréal in July 2009 for two years. Kami had finished high school and wanted to study at one of the top science colleges there. It is an intermediary college with a two-year programme that prepares students for university or for entering the formal economy. He had spent the major part of his life in South Africa and now wanted to spend some time in his other country and culture and to connect with his family in Québec, where his brother and his grandparents live.

We went to visit Madiba and Graça Machel to say goodbye and to have a cup of tea with the man who has been such a big part of our lives. He was lucid and still emanated the magnetic energy that draws billions of people to him although his hearing was more challenged and he walked with greater difficulty.

'What do you want to become?' he asked Kami, who to our great surprise replied: 'I want to become like my parents.'

After chatting for a while Madiba ordered everyone, including Graça, out of the room and motioned to me to take a seat closer to him. What does he want alone with me? I wondered.

'Now Jay,' he said, 'you are putting on too much weight around your waist. It is not healthy. You need to do some exercise. Well, as I said to Oprah Winfrey not long ago, you need to buy yourself a big ball and to lie on it with your stomach over and circle the room several times every morning. That will help keep your weight down,' he advised me seriously.

As we left the house, Lucie and the kids pried open the conversation. We laughed the whole way home and even today the memory of this conversation brings tears to my eyes. This is what makes Madiba such a unique and special person – he truly cares.

We invited Rosie Tsebe to Canada for a holiday and to be at Léandre's wedding. She was excited and had made many friends who had visited us in South Africa and who were keen to welcome her in Québec. We set up the house in Montréal and she and I were struck by one particular incident. We had hired a firm to do a thorough clean of the house. As they went systematically through the house and arrived in the kitchen, they got down on their knees and scrubbed the floors meticulously, using a sharp blade. Rosie and I watched in wonder – they were all adult white men and took such pride in their work. It was not something we had ever seen in South Africa.

I am at peace with myself now.

I have a deep and profound relationship with Lucie and our great kids. Léandre married Élise Anne Basque, a petite and brilliant mathematician, in the summer of 2009 in Canada. It was a beautiful wedding that ushered in a new phase in my life. I am growing older and hopefully wiser. I have learnt many things and have even greater lessons yet to learn. I look forward to the new experiences every day brings. I need to spend more time with my children.

I was struck by the prophetic words of Barack Obama on the occasion of Father's Day:

> *I came to understand that the hole a man leaves when he abandons his responsibility to his children is one that no government can fill. We can do everything possible to provide good jobs and good schools and safe streets for our kids, but it will never be enough to fully make up the difference. That is why we need fathers to step up, to realize that their job does not end at conception; that what makes you a man is not the ability to have a child but the courage to raise one.*[1]

Right now I must prepare for my next trek to Montréal. I know I will experience the racial profiling that is inevitable at Western airports. It is remarkable how these 'random' checks always yield an overwhelming majority of people who do not conform to a European Caucasian identity: 'Why are you travelling here? Where do you live? What work do you do? Why does your wife live in Canada?'

I have vowed to stay calm as my senses are yet again bombarded by the prejudice I will surely face. I will continue dreaming and fighting for a world in which my children will be measured not by the colour of their skin but by their intellect and the values of their character; and I will hope for a time when the world's people will belong to the human race rather than to some individual nationality.

I wonder when science and spirituality will be the foundations of society and a colour-conscious world will realise that of the tens of thousands of genes in the human genome only a handful determine the colour of one's skin.

I know that it will not be in my lifetime. But as sure as the sun rises and sets every day, that dream will one day be a reality and the world will experience a golden age when racism is a distant memory and leaders in all sectors of our society are honest and see themselves as servants of the greater humanity in us all.

In the meantime, I will continue to add my small contribution to the cause of sustainable human development. I do so buttressed by the anchor of powerful love and my relationship with Lucie and my children and strengthened by the values wired into my DNA by Angamma and Bakkium.

Abbreviations

ACTU	Australian Council of Trade Unions
AFL-CIO	American Federation of Labor-Congress of Industrial Organizations
AFSCME	American Federation of State, County and Municipal Employees
ANC	African National Congress
ASSOCOM	Association of Chambers of Commerce
AWB	Afrikaner Weerstandsbeweging
BCOEA	Basic Conditions of Employment Act
BEE	Black Economic Empowerment
BLATU	Black Transport Union
BPC	Black Peoples Convention
BRAC	Bangladesh Relief Assistance Committee
CAAA	Comprehensive Anti-Apartheid Act
CAB	Complaints Adjudication Board
CAHAC	Cape Areas Housing Action Committee
CBM	Consultative Business Movement
CCAWUSA	Commercial, Catering and Allied Workers Union of South Africa
CEC	Central Executive Committee (COSATU)
CGIL	Confederazione Generale Italiana del Lavoro (Italian General Confederation of Labor)

CLC	Canadian Labour Congress
CODESA	Convention for a Democratic South Africa
COSAS	Congress of South African Students
COSATU	Congress of South African Trade Unions
CTH	Cheadle, Thomson and Haysom (legal firm)
CTUC	Commonwealth Trade Union Council
CUSA	Council of Unions of South Africa
CUT	Central Única dos Trabalhadores (Brazil)
DBSA	Development Bank of Southern Africa
DG	Director General
EPG	Eminent Persons Group
ETC	Economic Transformation Committee
FCI	Federated Chamber of Industries
FCWU	Food and Canning Workers Union
FOSATU	Federation of South African Trade Unions
FRELIMO	Front for the Liberation of Mozambique
GAIN	Global Alliance for Improved Nutrition
GAWU	General and Allied Workers Union
GDP	Gross Domestic Product
GEAR	Growth, Employment and Redistribution
GNU	Government of National Unity
GWU	General Workers Union
IAJ	Institute for the Advancement of Journalism
ICFTU	International Confederation of Trade Unions
IDRC	International Development Research Centre
IFP	Inkatha Freedom Party
ILO	International Labour Organization
IMF	International Monetary Fund
IT	Information Technology
ITU	International Telecommunications Union

LMG	Labour Monitoring Group
MAWU	Metal and Allied Workers Union
MDC	Movement for Democratic Change
MDG	Millennium Development Goal
MDM	Mass Democratic Movement
MK	Umkhonto we Sizwe
MP	Member of Parliament
MPLA	Popular Movement for the Liberation of Angola
NACOSA	National Aids Coordinating Committee of South Africa
NACTU	National Council of Trade Unions
NEC	National Executive Committee
NEDLAC	National Economic Development and Labour Council
NEF	National Economic Forum
NEHAWU	National Education, Health and Allied Workers Union
NGO	Non-Governmental Organisation
NIC	Natal Indian Congress
NLC	Nigerian Labour Congress
NUM	National Union of Mineworkers
NUMSA	National Union of Metal Workers of South Africa
NUSAS	National Union of South African Students
OATUU	Organisation of African Trade Union Unity
PAC	Pan Africanist Congress
PEBCO	Port Elizabeth Black Civic Organisation
PPWAWU	Paper, Pulp, Wood and Allied Workers Union
RDP	Reconstruction and Development Programme
SAAWU	South African Allied Workers Union
SABC	South African Broadcasting Corporation
SACC	South African Council of Churches
SACCAWU	South African Commercial, Catering and Allied Workers Union

SACCOLA	South African Consultative Committee on Labour Affairs
SACP	South African Communist Party
SACTU	South African Congress of Trade Unions
SACTWU	Southern African Clothing and Textile Workers Union
SADC	Southern African Development Community
SADF	South African Defence Force
SADTU	South African Democratic Teachers Union
SAMWU	South African Municipal Workers Union
SANROC	South African Non-Racial Olympic Committee
SAPS	South African Police Service
SARHWU	South African Railways and Harbour Workers Union
SASO	South African Students Organisation
SATS	South African Transport Service
SAYCO	South African Youth Congress
SEIFSA	Steel and Engineering Industries Federation of South Africa
SFAWU	Sweet, Food and Allied Workers Union
SRC	Student Representative Council
SWAPO	South West African People's Organisation
TAC	Treatment Action Campaign
TRC	Truth and Reconciliation Commission
TUC	Trades Union Congress (British)
TUCSA	Trade Union Council of South Africa
UDF	United Democratic Front
UDW	University of Durban-Westville
UN	United Nations
UNDP	United Nations Development Programme
UNICEF	United Nations Children's Fund
UNISA	University of South Africa
UNITA	National Union for the Total Independence of Angola
UNOPS	United Nations Office for Project Services
UTP	Urban Training Project
UWUSA	United Workers Union of South Africa

WCC	World Council of Churches
WFTU	World Federation of Trade Unions
WTO	World Trade Organization
YCW	Young Christian Workers

Notes

Part One

1. Madiba is the clan name of Mandela, and it is a sign of affection and respect for his family and others to address him thus. Many prisoners on Robben Island came to be known by their clan names – Walter Sisulu, for example, was Xamela, and Govan Mbeki was Zisi.
2. Mandela, N. 1994. *Long Walk to Freedom: The Autobiography of Nelson Mandela*. Johannesburg: Macdonald Purnell, p.553.
3. Telephonic interview with Vanessa Watson, 25 March 2010.
4. It was only later, with the publication of Mandela's autobiography, that we realised how much the cost to his family had haunted him for 27 years and nagged at his conscience – at times, as with the death of his eldest son, almost breaking his heart.
5. The Harare Declaration was a document shepherded by Oliver Tambo before he had his massive stroke in August 1989, and was the outcome of extensive consultations with ANC structures, heads of the Frontline States in southern Africa, the Mass Democratic Movement and prison representatives on Robben Island.

Part Two

1. I am indebted to my oldest sister, Dimes, who has done a great deal of research for her siblings and the following generations so that they might know their roots.
2. Government of India. 2000. 'Report of the High Level Committee on the Indian Diaspora'. See www.indiandiaspora.nic.in/diasporapdf/chapter7.pdf (accessed on 9 October 2009).

3. The ship's records suggest Angamma met Narainasami Pillay, a Telegu-speaking 32-year-old man from Nellore in the state of Andhra Pradesh, either in the compound while passengers waited for the boat to fill up, or on the ship itself. Their colonial ID numbers identified them as having disembarked from *Coldstream 1 (EA)* together.

4. Government of India. 2000. 'The Indian Diaspora'. See www.indiandiaspora.nic.in/ (accessed on 9 October 2009).

5. 'Coolie' is a derogatory term used to refer to manual labourers. In the South African context, 'coolie' is a slur specifically directed at Indians. 'Coolie mentality' thus refers to an apparent internalised oppression by members of that community assimilated into subservient positions.

6. The Group Areas Act (No.41 of 1950) entrenched the apartheid government's policy of 'separate development'. Forced removals were commonplace as people were uprooted from their homes because of the arbitrary demarcation of residential areas belonging to a specific race group. See South African History Online, www.sahistory.org.za (accessed on 14 May 2009).

7. Land legally owned by black people, from which they were later forcibly removed.

8. Traditional stiff porridge made of maize meal.

9. On 21 March 1960, at least 69 men, women and children were shot dead in the township of Sharpeville, some 70 kilometres south of Johannesburg, by jittery police during a peaceful demonstration against passes.

10. The Population Registration Act (No.30 of 1950) facilitated racial discrimination based on arbitrary distinctions. It provided for a national register of each person's racial classification, which in turn determined a person's place of residence, type of education, jobs, wages and freedom of movement.

11. Blacks were divided by the pass system, which was imposed on the 'Bantu', the majority of the population, who were further divided into ethnic categories and assigned to 'homelands'.

12. Steve Biko. 2004. 'Letter to SRC Presidents'. *I Write What I Like*. Johannesburg: Picador Africa, p.17.

13. The Wages Commission was started by a group of white students at the University of Natal who lobbied for changes to the standard of minimum wages. Their research into the poverty datum line became 'a yardstick for setting minimum wage levels'. See www.sahistory.org.za/pages/governance-projects/labour-history/73-strikes.htm (accessed on 11 May 2009).

14. Although hundreds of Durban dock workers who downed tools in 1969 were dismissed, this period was characterised by increased industrial action amongst African workers, who were restricted by draconian legislation such as the pass laws and a migrant labour system. It was also the period of the establishment of the Wages Commission.

15. Muhammad Ali, 1966, in resisting the American Army draft into the Vietnam War.

16. 'Amandla' ('Power'); 'Ngawethu' ('Is Ours').

17. Slogan coined by Steve Biko for the South African Students Organisation (SASO), which resonates with the call of the ANC Youth League in 1944.

18. These are some of the statements made by Steve Biko in his presidential address to SASO, December 1969. See Chapter 2 in Biko, I Write What I Like.

19. Steve Biko, SASO leadership training programme, December 1971.

20. Marabastad had once been a multiracial working-class neighbourhood, which Es'kia Mphahlele famously describes in Down Second Avenue (Johannesburg: Picador Africa, 2004). During the apartheid era Africans were removed and resettled in townships designated for Africans only.

21. Groote Schuur is a world-renowned research hospital where the first human heart transplant was performed in 1967 by Professor Chris Barnard. See www.gsh.co.za (accessed on 6 April 2010).

22. Chris Madibeng Mokoditoa, Sipho Buthelezi, Saths Cooper and several other members, including the trade unionist Drake Koka, Strini Moodley and Mathew Diseko.

23. South African Institute of Race Relations (SAIRR), Race Relations Survey, Vol.26, 1972, p.390.

24. In 1971, the departments of Indian Affairs and of Coloured Relations had stated that student bodies under their respective control would not be permitted to affiliate to SASO since Indians and coloureds had nothing in common with African students.

25. Interview with Gessler Nkondo, senior lecturer at the University of the North (Turfloop) in SAIRR, Race Relations Survey, Vol.28, 1974, p.373.

26. On 25 April 1974, members of the Armed Forces Movement seized control of Lisbon. President Caetano, who had headed the authoritarian regime since 1968, resigned. During the early part of the year, FRELIMO (Front for the Liberation of Mozambique) was increasingly active in the field, led by its

President Samora Machel. In June, negotiations began and it was agreed that Mozambique would become completely independent on 25 June 1975. On 16 September, third-ranking FRELIMO leader Joaquim Chissano was appointed Prime Minister of the transitional government in Mozambique.

27. In Turfloop, 450 to 500 students ignored the warning to disperse and police charged with batons and fired tear gas cartridges. Cars belonging to members of the university staff were stoned and four members of staff injured. Three student leaders, Gilbert Sedibe, P. Nefolovhodwe and Cyril Ramaphosa, were detained under the Terrorism Act.

28. The 'politics of boycott' have their roots in the All-African Convention (AAC) in 1936. Outside the Transkei, where it sought to promote the cause of peasant resistance to state land rehabilitation schemes, it functioned mainly at an intellectual level. Through the affiliated Non-European Unity Movement and the Society of Young Africa, it heaped abuse on organisations it saw as collaborationist, advocating boycott of their activities (see Lodge, T. 1983. *Black Politics in South Africa since 1945*. Johannesburg: Ravan Press). The Unity Movement was resurrected as the New Unity Movement in 1985.

29. SAIRR, *Race Relations Survey*, Vol.28, 1974, p.377.

30. *The Star*, 24 June, quoted in SAIRR, *Race Relations Survey*, Vol.30, 1976, p.131.

31. *The Star*, 24 June, quoted in SAIRR, *Race Relations Survey*, Vol.30, 1976, p.131.

32. Five years later, in 1952, Nelson Mandela was appointed by the Joint Planning Committee as 'volunteer in chief' and Ismael Cachalia (of Indian descent) as his deputy. This was the team that would lead three stages of disobedience in the Defiance Campaign. For more information, see www.sahistory.org.za/ pages/governance-projects/organisations/saic/saic.htm (accessed on 25 May 2009).

33. These days, our relationship has mellowed. Buthelezi calls me 'homeboy' and embraces me when he sees me.

34. Brigadier Piet Goosen, head of the Eastern Cape Security Branch at the time, is no longer alive. Amnesty for the murder of Steve Biko was refused by the TRC on 16 February 1999. See www.justice.gov.za/trc/PR/1999/p990216a.htm (accessed on 29 April 2009).

35. Umkhonto we Sizwe, meaning 'Spear of the Nation', was the military wing of the ANC and SACP alliance. It is commonly referred to as MK.

Part Three

1. Job reservation refers to the laws in the various sectors that reserved skilled and some semi-skilled jobs for whites only, at much higher salaries.

2. See Baskin, J. 1991. *Striking Back: A History of COSATU*. Johannesburg: Ravan Press, Chapter 1.

3. 'Bunny chows' are a unique local working-class delicacy – a half loaf of bread, hollowed out and filled with the steaming hot curry of your choice.

4. The ANC led an alliance of liberation movements, which included the South African Indian Congress, the South African Congress of Trade Unions (SACTU), the Coloured People's Congress and the tiny white Congress of Democrats. These formed the basis of the Congress network which still had its adherents although they operated underground.

5. Interview with A.C. Naicker, 2008.

6. Ndlovu means 'elephant' in isiZulu.

7. Interview with A.C. Naicker, 2008.

8. 'Allies in the Community', *The Shop Steward*. See www.cosatu.org.za/shop/ss0406-10.html (accessed on 12 August 2008).

9. Cited in Nieftagodien, N. 2004. 'The Township Uprising: September–November 1984' in *Turning Points in History*, 5. Johannesburg: Department of Education, Institute for Justice and Reconciliation and STE Publishers.

10. Chief Luthuli was President General of the ANC from 1952 until his mysterious death in 1967. He accepted the Nobel Peace Prize in December 1961.

11. In South Africa shebeens are unlicensed taverns usually run by women in their homes.

12. TRC Report Vol.3, Chapter 6, para 192. See http://www.polity.org.za/polity/govdocs/commissions/1998/trc/volume3.htm (accessed on 17 May 2009).

13. Lodge, *Black Politics*, pp.28, 39.

14. Baskin, *Striking Back*, p.34.

15. Baskin, *Striking Back*, p.35.

16. Baskin, *Striking Back*, p.36.

17. This was a system of limited representation in parliament that included coloured and Indian South Africans while the African majority was excluded. This divisive attempt at political 'reform' was met with fierce resistance by the anti-Tricameral Parliament campaign, which ensured a very low coloured and Indian voter turn-out. See www.sahistory.org.za/pages/library-resources/official%20docs/tricameral-parliament.htm (accessed on 11 May 2009).

18. Maree, J. 1984. *The Independent Trade Unions 1974–1984: Ten Years of the South African Labour Bulletin.* Johannesburg: Ravan Press, pp.216–17.
19. Maree, *The Independent Trade Unions*, p.263.
20. The LMG was located in the Sociology of Work Unit at the University of the Witwatersrand and run by lecturers who were also participating in the FOSATU national education programme.
21. Jean Middleton, *Sechaba*, 2 February 1984. See http://www.anc.org.za/show.php?doc=ancdocs/pubs/umrabulo/umrabulo19/forces.htm (accessed on 6 April 2010).
22. Maree, *The Independent Trade Unions*, p.274.
23. Maree, *The Independent Trade Unions*, p.278.
24. Maree, *The Independent Trade Unions*, p.275.
25. Baskin, *Striking Back*, p.45.

Part Four

1. Cited in Baskin, *Striking Back*. See also 'A Giant has Risen', *The Shop Steward*. See www.cosatu.org.za/shop/ss0406-2html (accessed on 8 October 2008).
2. Baskin, *Striking Back*, pp.59–60.
3. The pass laws were a brutal system introduced to control and trace the movements of black people outside the Bantustans. Black people were only permitted to stay in the cities of white South Africa to serve the economy and the whims of the racist minority. This justified the existence of black people as temporary sojourners in white South Africa and that their political aspirations were to be exercised in the barren Bantustans, which constituted less than 13 per cent of the country's land mass. The penalty for being caught without a pass was incarceration.
4. See http://newritings.wordpress.com/2009/02/11/cabral-tell-no-lies-claim-no-easy-victories/ (accessed on 28 March 2010).
5. A state under the control of authorities, which include curfews and strict policing. Successive States of Emergency were declared during the 1980s as a form of repressive control and a means to clamp down on activists.
6. See Chapter 20 for more on the changing relationship between COSATU and Inkatha.
7. Communiqué of the meeting between the Congress of South African Trade Unions, the South African Congress of Trade Unions and the African National Congress, 5–6 March 1986. See www.anc.org.za/ancdocs/history/congress/sactu/docs/pr860307.html (accessed on 5 July 2008).

8. Interview with James Motlatsi by Lesley Lawson, 2001.

9. It was later revealed that a government 'slush fund' had paid for the launch of UWUSA.

10. 'Jay Naidoo on the State of Emergency' in *South African Labour Bulletin* (*SALB*), August 1986, Vol.11(7), p.6.

11. Baskin, *Striking Back*, p.141.

12. 'Jay Naidoo on the State of Emergency' in *SALB*, August 1986, Vol.11(7), p.2.

13. 'Jay Naidoo on the State of Emergency' in *SALB*, August 1986, Vol.11(7), p.6.

14. Baskin, *Striking Back*, p.169.

15. Markham, C. 1987. 'Lessons' of the OK Strike' in *SALB*, Vol.12(3), p.17.

16. Baskin, *Striking Back*, p.174.

17. Baskin, *Striking Back*, p.174.

18. Necklacing was a brutal form of violence inflicted on perceived police informants or apartheid spies or agents. It involved placing a rubber tyre around the neck of the perceived or alleged spy or agent, followed by a flammable material, before setting it alight. The practice often took place in front of others and reflected communities taking the law into their own hands.

19. SARHWU became a dominant union in the South African Transport Service but it would take several more bloody strikes in the weeks before Mandela's release in February 1990 before SARHWU was finally recognised as the representative union.

20. SAPA. 'De Kock Tells TRC How he Blew up Khotso and COSATU Houses', 29 July 1998. See www.doj.gov.za/trc/media/1998/9807/s980729e.html (accessed on 2 August 2009).

21. See 'Simon Ngubane Still on Strike', April 1987. Big Fish Productions: Director, Melanie Chait.

22. Lenin, V.I. 1999 [1920]. *'Left Wing' Communism: An Infantile Disorder*. Chippendale, NSW: Resistance Books.

23. 'The Significance of COSATU'. Talk given by Jay Naidoo, General Secretary of COSATU, at the University of Natal, Pietermaritzburg, 19 March 1986. See *SALB*, April–May 1986, Vol.11(5), pp.33–39.

24. M.P. Naicker, 'African Mineworkers Strike of 1946'. See www.anc.org.za/ancdocs/history/misc/miners.html (accessed on 28 March 2010).

25. See www.anc.org.za/ancdocs/history/misc/miners.html#(6) (accessed on 28 March 2010).

26. For more detail on the experiences of black miners see Callinicos, L. 1981. *Gold and Workers*. Johannesburg: Ravan Press; and the scholarly works of Allen, V.L. 2003. *The History of Black Mineworkers of South Africa* Volumes

1–3. London: The Moor Press and Merlin Press; and Moodie, D. 1994. *Going for Gold*. Berkeley and Los Angeles: University of California Press.

27.   For an in-depth assessment and overview of the NUM strike, see Butler, A. 2007. *Cyril Ramaphosa*. Johannesburg: Jacana.

28.   Butler, *Cyril Ramaphosa*, pp.195–96.

29.   Piero Gleijeses, 'Cuito Cuanavale revisited'. See www.mg.co.za/article/2007-07-11-cuito-cuanavale-revisited (accessed on 28 March 2010).

30.   Stein, P. 'Although Apartheid is Gone'. A Maverick Production for SABC: Director, Melanie Chait.

31.   Marie, S. 1987. 'Sarmcol Killings', *SALB*, January–February, Vol.12(2): pp.3–4.

32.   Maré, G. 1988. 'Inkatha: "By the Grace of the Nationalist Government?"', *SALB*, February, Vol.13(2), pp.63–73.

33.   Interview with UDF activists. 1988. 'The Community was Forced to Defend Itself', *SALB*, January, Vol.13(2), pp.34–37.

34.   See Kentridge, M. 1990. *Unofficial War: Inside the Conflict in Pietermaritzburg*. Cape Town: David Philip, Chapter 27.

35.   This was not the end of the story. Thulani Ngcobo was gunned down in front of a fast-food outlet in January 1990 – rough justice in a climate where there was no popular faith in the system of law and order in the apartheid state.

36.   Letter from Jay Naidoo to Oscar Dhlomo, 14 August 1989, cited in Baskin, *Striking Back*, p.341.

37.   Mao, *On Guerrilla Warfare*, chapter 1. See www.eastofhateandfear.com/archives/tse_tung.html (accessed on 20 February 2010).

38.   See www.encyclopedia.jrank.org/articles/pages/5958/Anti-Apartheid-Movement. html (accessed on 23 September 2009).

39.   Von Holdt, K. 1988. 'The Battle Against the Bill', *SALB*, February, Vol.13(2), pp.5–11.

40.   Baskin, *Striking Back*, p.262.

41.   Many of the veteran workers recalled how the ANC's three-day stay-away campaign in 1961 had been called off on the second day.

42.   Fine, A. and Webster, E. 1989. 'Transcending Traditions: Trade Unions and Political Unity' in Moss, G. and Obery, I., eds. *South African Review 5*. Johannesburg: Ravan Press, p.270.

43.   Baskin, *Striking Back*, p.290.

44.   Botha, B. 1988. 'You Can't Operate in an Unrest Situation', *SALB*, Vol.13(3), p.26.

45.   Baskin, *Striking Back*, p.268.

46.   Botha, 'You Can't Operate in an Unrest Situation', p.26.

47. Webster, E. and Sikwebu, D. 2010. 'Tripartism and Economic Reforms in South Africa and Zimbabwe' in Fraile, L., ed. *Blunting Neoliberalism: Social Dialogue in Transitional Societies.* Basingstoke, Hampshire: Palgrave Macmillan.

48. Interview with Stephen Gelb, 19 March 2009.

Part Five

1. A military-type armed vehicle, with bulletproof windows, prevalent in townships across apartheid South Africa since the 1970s. One of the distinguishing features was the open roof, which allowed state police to patrol from 'above' – an advantageous position to kill from.

2. Mandela speech at Kings Park rally. See www.anc.org.za/ancdocs/history/ mandela/1990/sp900225-1.html (accessed on 28 March 2010).

3. See www.anc.org.za/ancdocs/history/minutes.html (accessed on 28 May 2008).

4. The Freedom Charter was officially ratified by the ANC in the following year after Chief Luthuli insisted that it be circulated to all the branches in the country to be discussed and adopted.

5. The Laboria Minute was an agreement between three social partners – the trade unions (COSATU and NACTU), government and employers (SACCOLA) – and recognised basic worker rights, including the right to organise and bargain collectively.

6. Webster and Sikwebu, 'Tripartism and Economic Reforms' in Fraile, ed., *Blunting Neoliberalism.*

7. See Shubin, V. 1999. *ANC: A View from Moscow.* Cape Town: Mayibuye Books.

8. Interview with Alec Erwin by Lesley Lawson, April 1999.

9. Slovo, J. 1990. 'Has Socialism Failed?' See www.sacp.org.za/docs/history/failed. html (accessed on 18 May 2009).

10. Slovo, 'Has Socialism Failed?'

11. Pagé, L. 2003. *Conflict of the Heart.* Cape Town: David Philip, p.10.

12. Pagé, *Conflict of the Heart*, p.15.

13. For more on Lucie's dilemma, see Pagé, *Conflict of the Heart.*

14. The NEF agreement, 29 October 1992. See www.nedlac.org.za/about-us/ background/national-economic-forum.aspx (accessed on 28 March 2010).

15. Mandela, N. 20 December 1991. Address to CODESA. See www.anc.org.za/ ancdocs/history/transition/codesa/anc.html (accessed on 20 July 2009).

16. See Pagé, *Conflict of the* Heart, p.89.

17. In apartheid South Africa, especially as resistance escalated in the 1980s, the security police had acquired enormous powers, to the extent that they

persuaded the politicians at the top of the necessity of bypassing the courts and eliminating opponents through death squads.

18.   This was a highly secret ANC operation, masterminded by Mac Maharaj and Joe Slovo, approved by ANC President Oliver Tambo in the late 1980s, to prepare the masses for a 'People's War' should the apartheid state prove to be intransigent or treacherous during the negotiations.

19.   Mandela, N. 13 April 1993. Televised address to the nation on the assassination of Chris Hani. See www.anc.org.za/ancdocs/history/mandela/1993/sp930413.html (accessed on 20 May 2009).

Part Six

1.   Nelson Mandela, 2 May 1994 (Carlton Centre).

2.   Speech by Nelson Mandela announcing the ANC election victory, Carlton Hotel, 2 May 1994. See www.anc.org.za/show.php?doc=/ancdocs/speeches/1994/sp940502.html (accessed on 21 August 2009).

3.   State of the Nation Address by the President of South Africa, Nelson Mandela, Houses of Parliament, Cape Town, 24 May 1994. See www.anc.org.za/ancdocs/history/mandela/1994/sp940524.html (accessed on 20 February 2010).

4.   Nelson Mandela, State of the Nation Address, 24 May 1994. See www.anc.org.za/ancdocs/history/mandela/1994/sp940524.html (accessed on 21 August 2009).

5.   Conversation with Derek Keys recounted in an interview with Bernie Fanaroff by Jay Naidoo, 5 April 2009.

6.   Nelson Mandela, Budget Debate Opening Address, '100 Days Speech', 18 August 1994, Cape Town. See www.anc.org.za/ancdocs/history/mandela/1994/sp940818.html (accessed on 28 May 2008).

7.   President Nelson Mandela, Inaugural Address to a Joint Sitting of Parliament, 24 May 1994.

8.   This demonstrated the findings of what scholars Seidman and Seidman termed 'the law of reproduction of institutions'. It taught them, they observed, 'that unless the lawmakers deliberately changed the institutions that shaped them, economies would likely continue to grind out resource allocation patterns that perpetuated poverty and oppression. Almost no third world practitioners addressed in detail the issue of how to plan the institutional changes required to implement for more desirable patterns of [the use of] resources' (Seidman, A. and Seidman, R.B. 1991. *State and Law in the Development Process: Problem Solving and Institutional Change in the Third World*. New York: Macmillan, p.205).

9. See Stats SA, www.statssa.gov.za/census01/census96/HTML/press/Part003. html (accessed on 25 August 2009).

10. IDRC. 1999. 'Working for Water: Removing Alien Plants in South Africa'. See www.idrc.ca/en/ev-5156-201-1-DO_TOPIC.html (accessed on 25 February 2010).

11. The Brahma Kumaris World Spiritual University. See www.bkwsu.org/index_ html (accessed on 8 August 2009).

12. Gelb, S. 'The Politics of Macroeconomic Reform'. Paper presented on the Politics of Economic Reform hosted by DBSA and Southern Africa and Development Policy Research Unit, University of Cape Town, January 1998.

13. Amner, R. 1998. 'Getting Radio Active' in De Beer, A.S., ed., *Mass Media towards the Millennium*. Pretoria: Van Schaik Publishers, p.151.

14. ILO report. 2009. 'Global Employment Trends for Women'. See www.new-ag.info/08/04/focuson/focuson6.php (accessed on 8 April 2010). In some countries, legislation makes it impossible for women to inherit land when their husbands die. They can also often not pass the land on to their daughters (see, for example, Judy Oglethorpe, 'AIDS, Women, Land, and Natural Resources in Africa: Current Challenges', *Gender & Development*, Vol.16, March 2008, pp.85–100).

15. Summary and Main Points of Sri Aurobindo's Teachings by Roy Posner. See www.kheper.net/topics/Aurobindo/main_points.html (accessed on 29 January 2010).

16. Pagé, *Conflict of the* Heart, pp.356–57.

17. SAPA. 1999. 'Jay Naidoo Quits Parliament', 10 June.

18. Pagé, *Conflict of the Heart*, p.365.

Part Seven

1. See www.waih.co.za (accessed on 21 February 2009).

2. Shafik is now Permanent Secretary in the UK Department for International Development. See www.dfid.gov.uk/aboutdfid/bio-minouche.asp (accessed on 11 March 2009).

3. See www.ifc.org/ifcext/about.nsf/Content/Peter_Woicke (accessed on 11 March 2009).

4. Interview with Jayendra Naidoo, 2008.

5. See O'Malley, P. 2007. *Shades of Difference: Mac Maharaj and the Struggle for South Africa*. Johannesburg: Penguin Books.

6. Interview with Admassu Tadesse, Group Executive: International Division, DBSA, March 2010.

7. See Lurie, P. 1987. 'AIDS and Labour Policy' in *SALB* Vol.12(8), 8 October.

8. Nelson Mandela, 2000. Closing address at the 13th International AIDS Conference, 13 July, Durban, South Africa. See www.anc.org.za/ancdocs/ history/mandela/2000/nm0714.html (accessed on 13 March 2009).

9. Cited in Gumede, W. 2008. *Thabo Mbeki and the Battle for the Soul of the ANC*. London: Zed Books, p.149.

10. Transcript of speech made by Minister of Health, Manto Tshabalala-Msimang, at the launch of loveLife, June 2005.

11. Naidoo, J. 2007. 'Walk the Talk' in *Financial Mail*, 23 November, p.18.

12. See Murphy, V. 2003. 'Mbeki Stirs up AIDS Controversy'. BBC News Online, 26 September. See news.bbc.co.uk/2/hi/africa/3143850.stm (accessed on 18 December 2009).

13. The Academy of Science of South Africa (ASSAF) has also argued that improved nutrition alone cannot replace HIV or TB drugs. ASSAF. 2007. 'HIV/ AIDS – TB & Nutrition'. See www.assaf.org.za/images/3060%20ASSAf%20 HIV%20TB%20and%20Nutrition%20condensed.pdf (accessed on 14 April 2009).

14. Previously, diseases of the circulatory system were our leading underlying causes of death. See Statistics South Africa. 2005. 'Mortality and Causes of Death in South Africa: 1999–2005'.

15. Department of Health, Medical Research Council, Save the Children, UNICEF and University of Pretoria, *Every Death Counts Report*.

16. Secretary General Kofi Annan's opening remarks at a high-level event on 'Innovative approaches to meeting the hunger millennium development goal in Africa', 5 July 2004, Addis Ababa, Ethiopia.

17. UNICEF. 2008. *State of the World's Children*. See www.unicef.org/sowc (accessed on 10 April 2010).

18. Black, R.E., Allen, L.H., Bhutta, Z.A., et al. 2008. 'Maternal and Child Undernutrition: Global and Regional Exposures and Health Consequences'. *Lancet*, 371, pp.243–60.

19. See web.worldbank.org/WBSITE/EXTERNAL/COUNTRIES/LACEXT/BRA ZILEXTN/0,,contentMDK:21447054~pagePK:141137~piPK:141127~theSiteP K:322341,00.html (accessed on 4 March 2010).

20. See www.unicef.org/malaysia/Breastfeeding_Challenges_and_Rights.pdf (accessed on 4 March 2010).

21. See Yunus, M. with Weber, K. 2007. *Creating a World Without Poverty: Social Business and the Future of Capitalism*. New York: Public Affairs.

22. The Millennium Development Goals (MDGs) are global targets set by the United Nations to address the various aspects of extreme poverty by 2015. The eight goals are: (1) eradicate extreme hunger and poverty; (2) achieve universal primary education; (3) promote gender equality and empower women; (4) reduce child mortality; (5) improve maternal health; (6) combat HIV/AIDS, malaria and other diseases; (7) ensure environmental sustainability; and (8) develop a global partnership for development. See www.unmillenniumproject.org (accessed on 18 October 2009).

23. BRAC was founded in 1972 by Fazle Hasan Abed in the wake of the destruction caused by the Bangladesh war of independence. See www.brac.net/index.php?nid=2 (accessed on 18 October 2009).

24. Naandi (Sanskrit for 'new beginning') is an Indian organisation promoting child rights, safe drinking water and sustainable livelihoods. See www.naandi.org (accessed on 18 October 2009).

25. In 2009, when the South African Council of Educators (SACE) announced plans to name and shame abusive teachers, instead of supporting this attempt to rid our schools of pervasive child abuse, Mr Ronald Nyathi issued a derisive response arguing that exposing names of serial sex offender teachers would ruin their careers. See also Blaine, S. 2009. 'Schools "not Stable until Zuma is President"' in *Business Day*, 23 January. See www.businessday.co.za/articles/topstories.aspx?ID=BD4A923998 (accessed on 23 October 2009).

26. See allafrica.com/stories/200806090594.html (accessed on 23 October 2009).

27. See www.pmg.org.za/report/20100203-briefing-department-basic-education-matric-results-and-challenges-ass (accessed on 4 March 2010).

28. Address by the President of the Republic of South Africa, Jacob Zuma, on the occasion of the President's national interaction with school principals, 7 August 2009, Durban International Convention Centre. See www.thepresidency.gov.za/show.asp?type=sp&include=president/sp/2009/sp0807111.htm&ID=1971 (accessed on 18 October 2009).

29. Webster, E. and Callinicos, L. 2008. '"Elephant in the Room": A Sociology of Polokwane'. Unpublished paper.

30. Matshiqi, A. 2005. 'In Movement' in Edigheji, O. (ed.), *Trajectories for South Africa*, Special edition on Policy: Issues and Actors, Vol.18. Johannesburg: Centre for Policy Studies, p.46.

31. ANC membership, Gauteng report, July 2007.

32. Cited in Webster, E. and Buhlungu, S. 2004. 'Between Marginalisation and Revitalisation? The State and Trade Unionism in South Africa' in *Review of African Political Economy*, No.100, pp. 39–56. See www.swopinstitute.org.za/files/RoapeEWSB.pdf (accessed on 4 March 2010).

33. Salopek, P. 21 September 2008. 'South Africa's Mbeki aloof to the end' in *Chicago Tribune*. See articles.sun-sentinel.com/2008-09-21/ news/0809200103_1_thabo-mbeki-jacob-zuma-young-democracy (accessed on 6 April 2010). See also iafrica.com. 22 September 2008. 'From aloof to resigned'. See http://news.iafrica.com/features/1166240.html (accessed on 6 April 2010).

34. Vitamin and Mineral Deficiency Report – China. See www.unicef.org/ videoaudio /PDFs/darchina.pdf (accessed on 29 June 2009).

35. Naidoo, J. 2008. 'The US Launch of The Lancet's Series on Maternal and Child Undernutrition', 16 January. See edited transcript www.wilsoncenter.org/ events/docs/LancetNaidooTranscript.pdf (accessed on 29 June 2009).

36. United Nations General Assembly Thematic Debate on the Millennium Development Goals. April 2008. Jay Naidoo (Panelist 1), 'Recognising the Achievements, Addressing the Challenges and Getting Back on Track to Achieve the MDGs by 2015'.

37. NALEDI. 2005. 'An Investigation into the Management of Public Hospitals in South Africa: Stressed Institutions, Disempowered Management', December. Report commissioned by DPSA. See www.naledi.org.za/pubs/2006/DPSA_ research_report_2006.pdf (accessed on 15 June 2009).

38. Recent reports on the work of geneticist Keith Cheng of the Pennsylvania State College of Medicine suggest that 'variations in skin color may arise from a single gene among the tens of thousands that determine human appearance'. See www.hmc.psu.edu/pathology/residency/experimental/cheng.htm (accessed on 10 May 2010).

Conclusion

1. Obama, Barack. 2009. 'We need Fathers to Step Up' in *Parade*, 21 June. See www.parade.com/news/2009/06/barack-obama-we-need-fathers-to-step-up. html (accessed on 27 October 2009).

Index

JN stands for Jay Naidoo.